TABLE OF CONTENTS

WORLD WAR II

After their defeat at the end of World War I (1914–1918), the German people's spirit was crushed. The country hungered for new leadership. In 1934 one man led the Nazi party to take over the German government. That man was Adolf Hitler.

Hitler's desire for power led him to declare war on Germany's neighboring countries. By the end of 1940, Germany had defeated France, Poland, Norway, the Netherlands, and Denmark. Germany then partnered with Italy and Japan to form the Axis powers. Their combined goal was to rule much of the world.

Meanwhile, Great Britain and the Soviet Union (USSR) joined forces with other countries. They created the Allied powers to battle the Axis. The United States stayed out of the fight at first. But Japan's attack on the U.S. naval base at Pearl Harbor in Hawaii on December 7, 1941, pushed the United States into the war.

World War II (1939–1945) lasted six years. By May 1945, Hitler's rule had collapsed and Germany surrendered to the Allies. In August the United States dropped two atomic bombs on Japan. This final act led to the surrender of Japan and the end of the war.

The Axis powers were broken, but the Allied victory was costly. The exact number of lives lost in the war, both soldier and civilian, will never be known. Historians estimate a body count between 50 to 70 million.

The leaders of the Allied forces are now household names: Franklin Delano Roosevelt, Joseph Stalin, Dwight D. Eisenhower, Winston Churchill, George S. Patton. But the war was fought and won by the courage of ordinary men and women. They were the true heroes of World War II. These are some of their stories.

KEY DATES OF WORLD WAR II

SEPTEMBER 1939: Hitler's forces invade Poland, starting World War II. Britain and France respond by declaring war on Germany.

JULY 1940: Germany begins bombing England.

JUNE 1941: Germany invades the Soviet Union.

DECEMBER 1941: Japan bombs the U.S. naval base at Pearl Harbor, Hawaii. The United States declares war on Japan.

JUNE 1942: Allied forces defeat Japan in the Battle of Midway.

SEPTEMBER 1943: Italy surrenders.

JUNE 6, 1944: Allied troops launch the massive D-day invasion of France.

MARCH 1945: Allied troops capture the island of Iwo Jima.

MAY 1945: Germany surrenders to the Allies.

AUGUST 1945: Atomic bombs code-named "Little Boy" and "Fat Man" dropped on the Japanese cities of Hiroshima and Nagasaki.

SEPTEMBER 1945: Japan surrenders, officially ending World War II.

ALLIED AND AXIS BOUNDARIES, 1939

SOVIET UNION
CHINA
JAPAN
PHILIPPINES
Pacific Ocean
Allied Controlled
Axis Controlled
Neutral
FINLAND
SOVIET UNION
SWEDEN
NORWAY
Atlantic Ocean
ESTONIA
LATVIA
North Sea
DENMARK
LITHUANIA
IRELAND
GREAT BRITAIN
NETHERLANDS
PRUSSIA
POLAND
BELGIUM
GERMANY
SLOVAKIA
N
W
E
S
SWITZERLAND
FRANCE
HUNGARY
ROMANIA
Black Sea
PORTUGAL
ITALY
YUGOSLAVIA
BULGARIA
SPAIN
TURKEY
GREECE
SYRIA

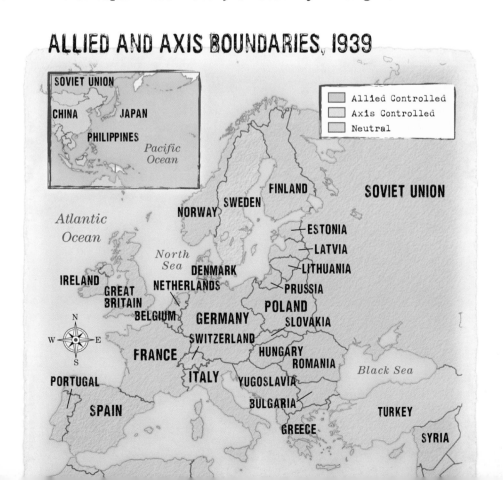

CH. 2

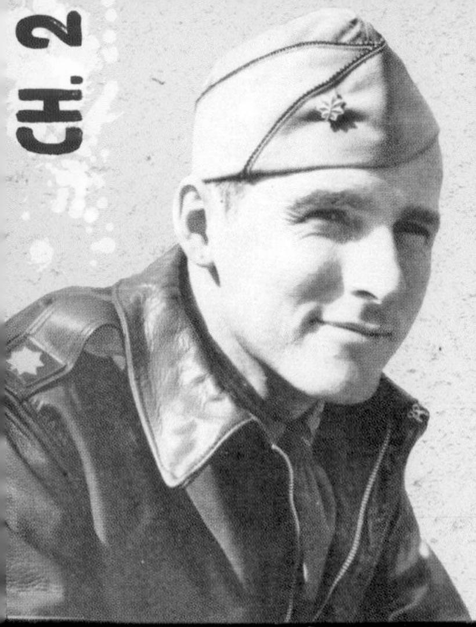

William Edwin Dyess: The Bataan Death March

Captain William Edwin "Ed" Dyess was a 25-year-old from Albany, Texas. While defending the Philippines, he fought bravely for four long months. On April 9, 1942, American and Filipino soldiers were forced to surrender to the Japanese. Dyess became one of more than 70,000 men forced into the Bataan Death March.

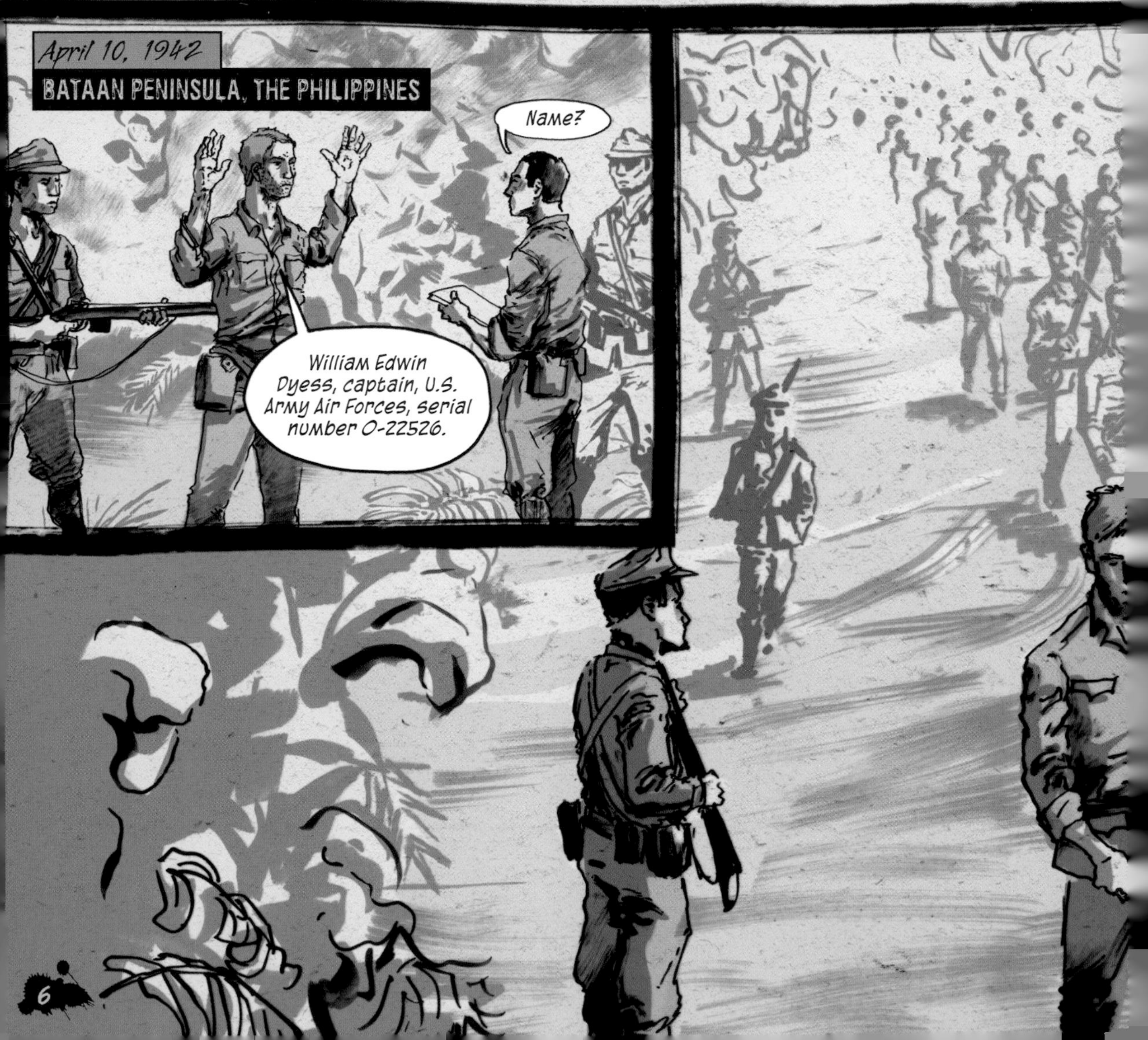
April 10, 1942
BATAAN PENINSULA, THE PHILIPPINES
Name?
William Edwin Dyess, captain, U.S. Army Air Forces, serial number O-22526.

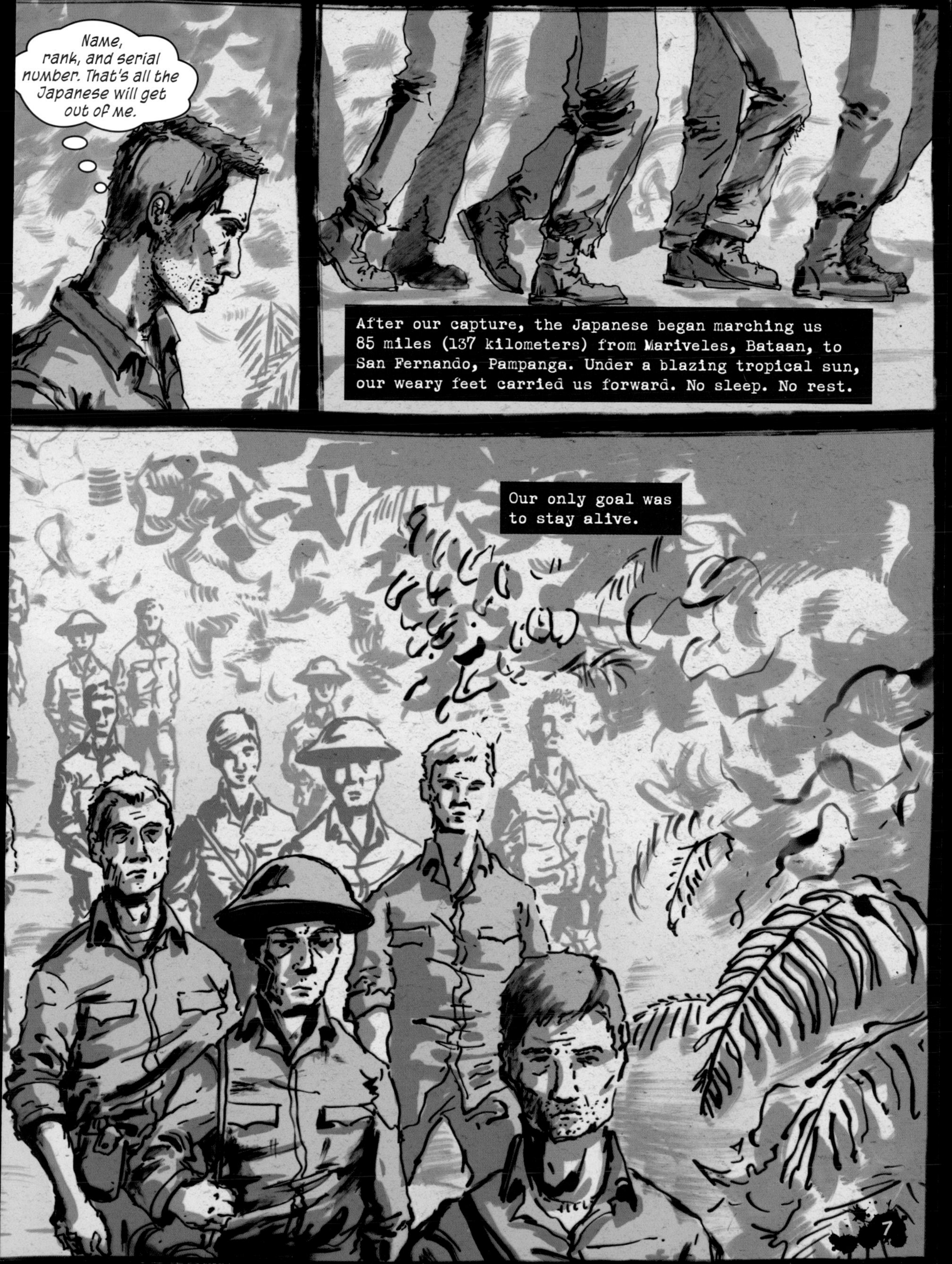
Name, rank, and serial number. That's all the Japanese will get out of me.
After our capture, the Japanese began marching us 85 miles (137 kilometers) from Mariveles, Bataan, to San Fernando, Pampanga. Under a blazing tropical sun, our weary feet carried us forward. No sleep. No rest.
Our only goal was to stay alive.

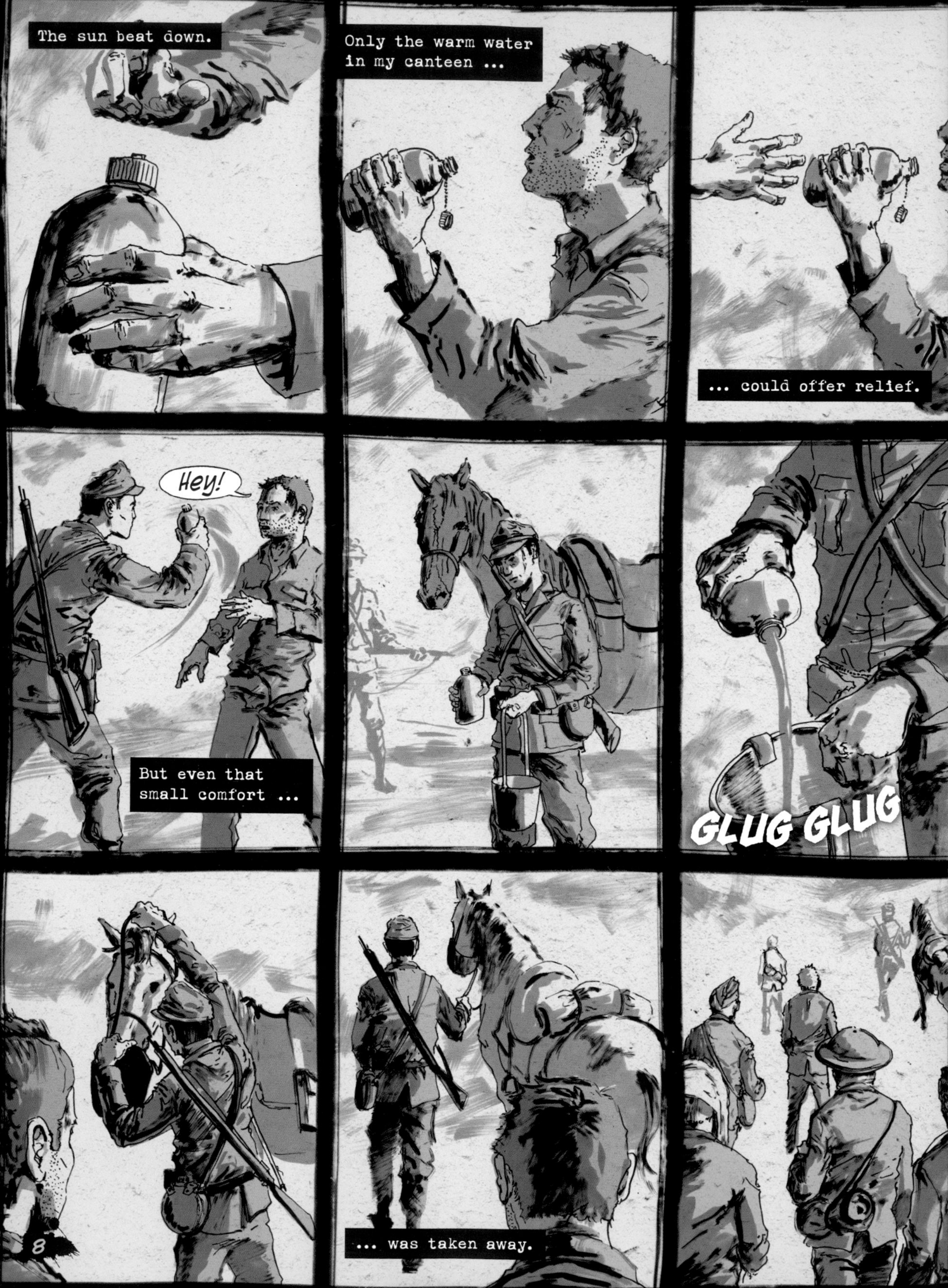

The sun beat down.
Only the warm water in my canteen ...
... could offer relief.
Hey!
But even that small comfort ...
GLUG GLUG
... was taken away.

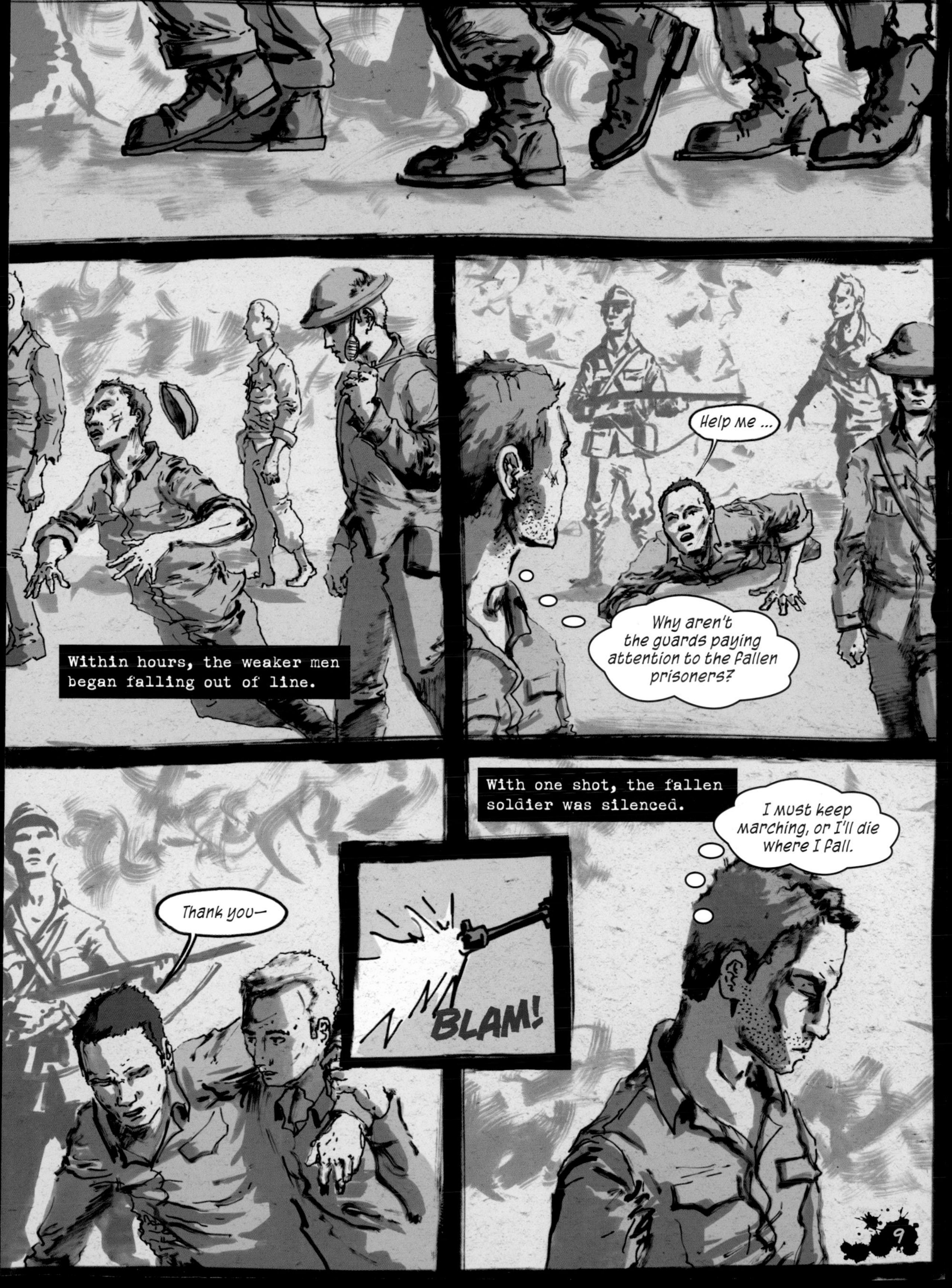

Within hours, the weaker men began falling out of line.
Help me ...
Why aren't the guards paying attention to the fallen prisoners?
Thank you—
BLAM!
With one shot, the fallen soldier was silenced.
I must keep marching, or I'll die where I fall.

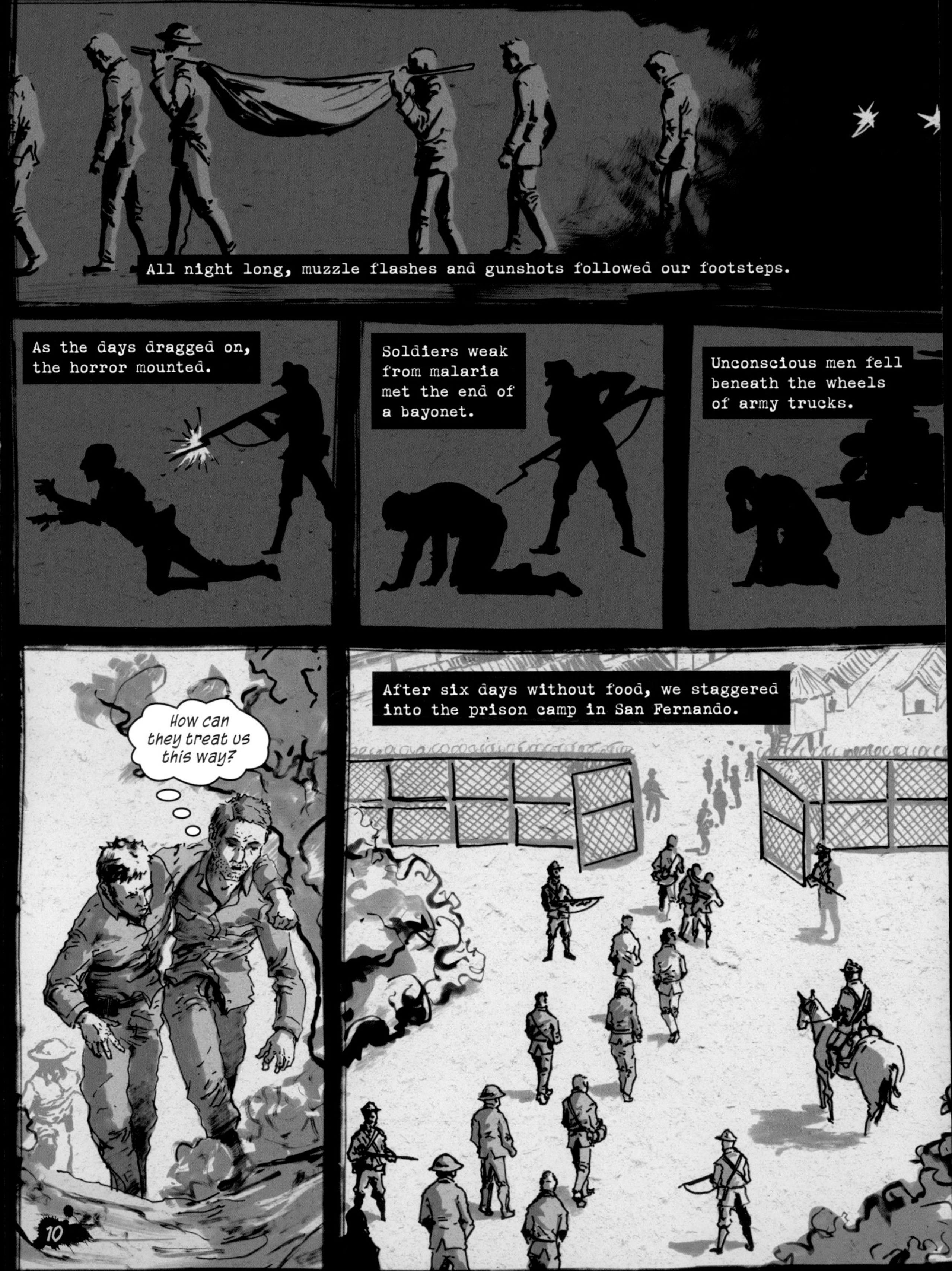
All night long, muzzle flashes and gunshots followed our footsteps.
As the days dragged on, the horror mounted.
Soldiers weak from malaria met the end of a bayonet.
Unconscious men fell beneath the wheels of army trucks.
How can they treat us this way?
After six days without food, we staggered into the prison camp in San Fernando.

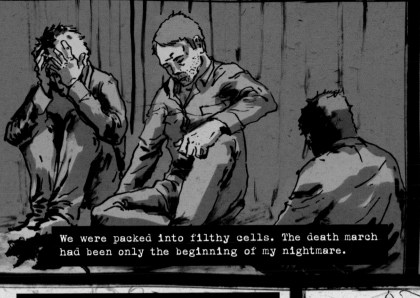

We were packed into filthy cells. The death march had been only the beginning of my nightmare.

But the Japanese had not broken my spirit.

I've got to escape.

Almost one year later, I did just that.

Come on! Now is our chance!

While on unguarded work duty, I disappeared into the jungle with nine other Americans and two Filipino soldiers.

Dyess spent weeks on the run before eventually returning to the United States. Upon his return, he rose to the rank of lieutenant colonel.

On December 22, 1943, a training mission turned deadly. Rather than crash his burning plane into a populated area, he guided it to a vacant lot. He died a hero in the process.

11

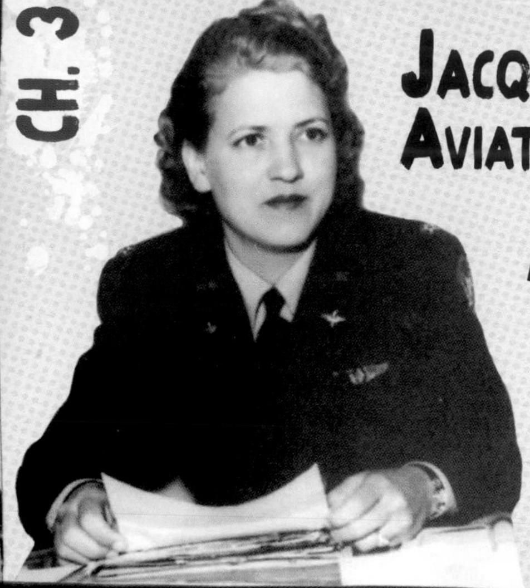

Jacqueline Cochran: Aviation Pioneer

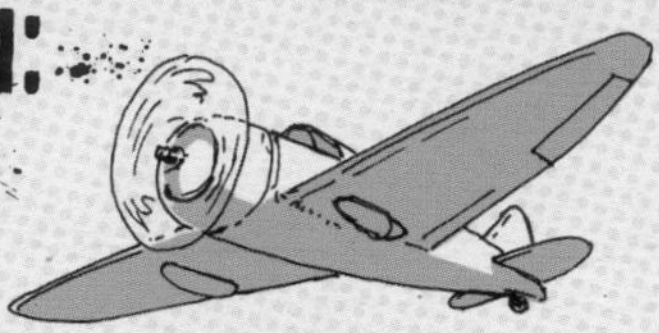

In the 1930s Jacqueline Cochran's fame as an aviator grew as she set one world record after another. By 1938 she was the best female pilot in the country. When the world plunged into global conflict, Cochran knew women could play an important role in the skies.

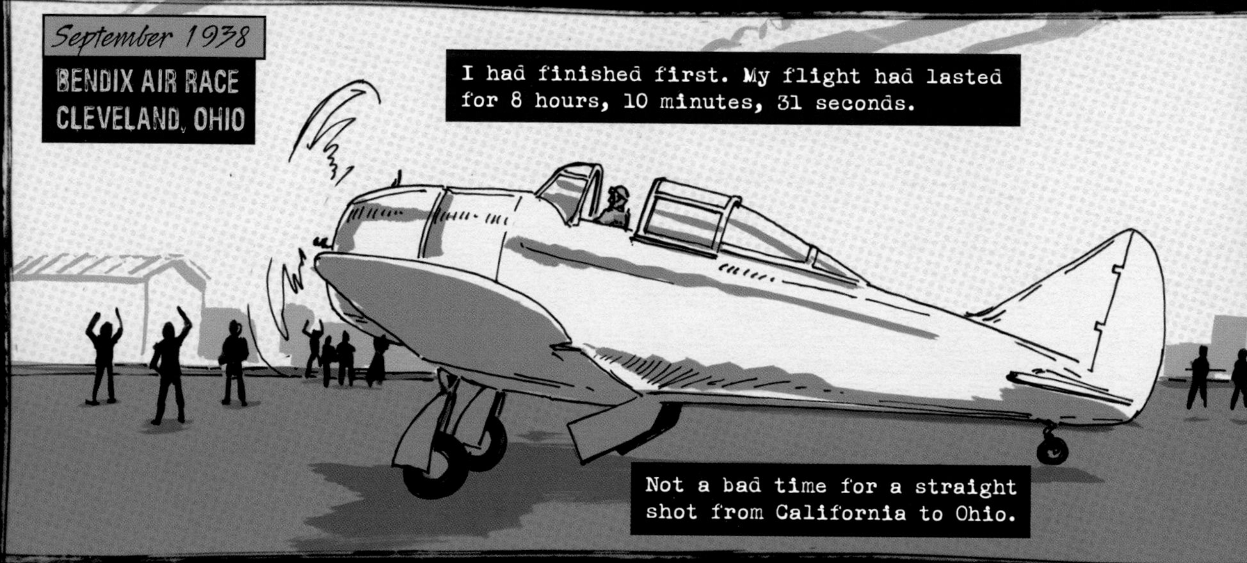
September 1938
BENDIX AIR RACE
CLEVELAND, OHIO
I had finished first. My flight had lasted for 8 hours, 10 minutes, 31 seconds.
Not a bad time for a straight shot from California to Ohio.

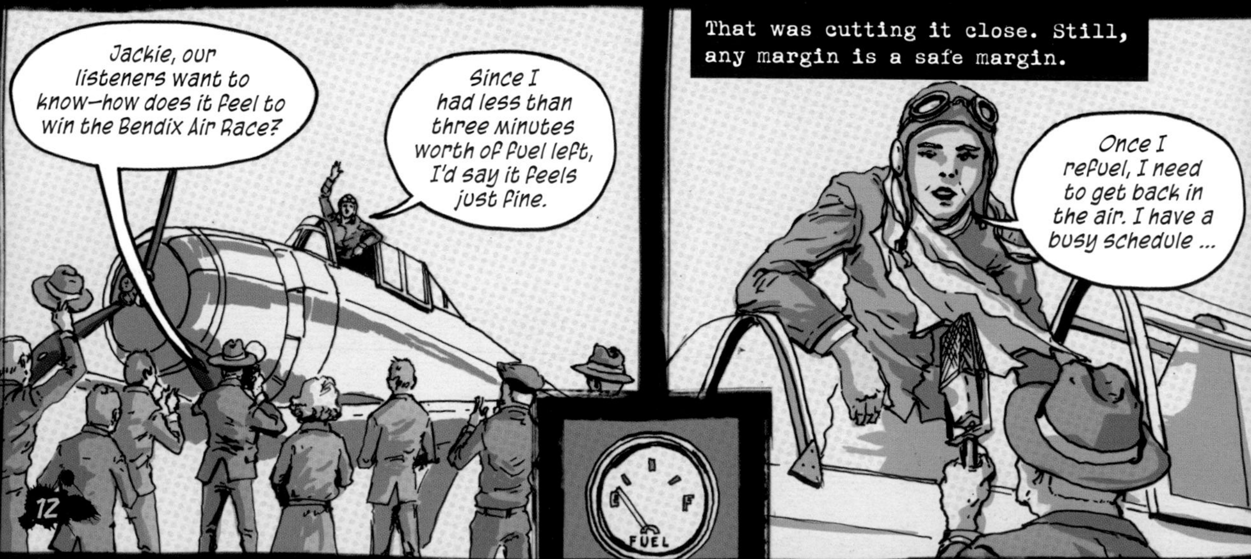
Jackie, our listeners want to know—how does it feel to win the Bendix Air Race?
Since I had less than three minutes worth of fuel left, I'd say it feels just fine.
FUEL
E
F
That was cutting it close. Still, any margin is a safe margin.
Once I refuel, I need to get back in the air. I have a busy schedule ...

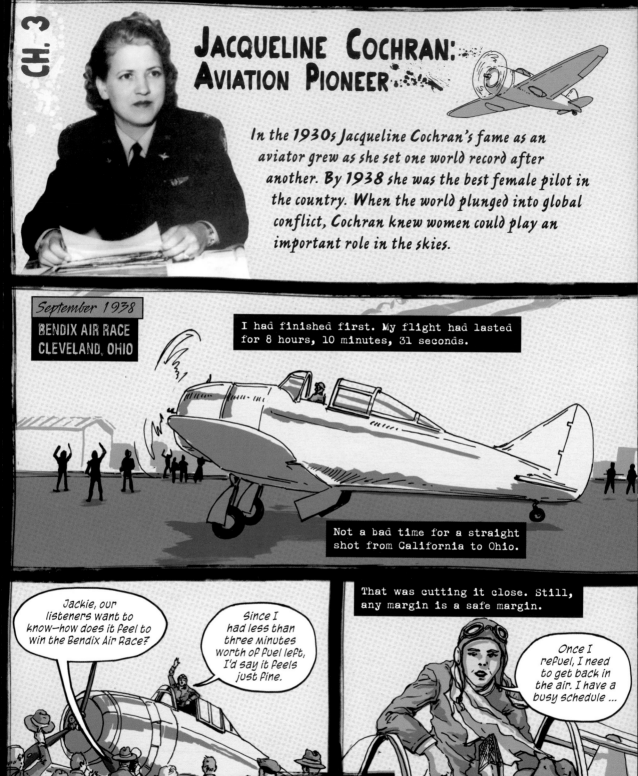

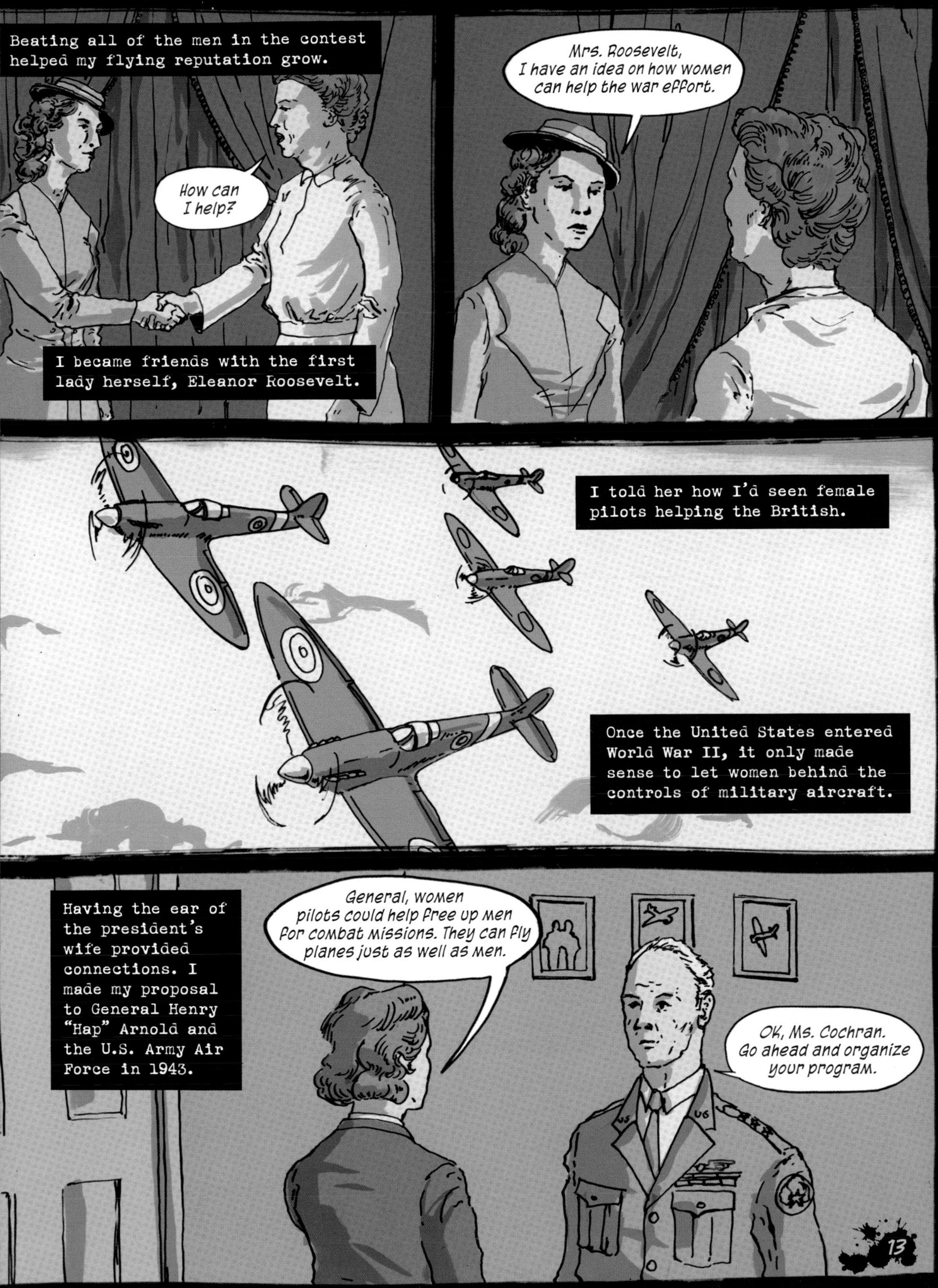
Beating all of the men in the contest helped my flying reputation grow.
How can I help?
I became friends with the first lady herself, Eleanor Roosevelt.
Mrs. Roosevelt, I have an idea on how women can help the war effort.
I told her how I'd seen female pilots helping the British.
Once the United States entered World War II, it only made sense to let women behind the controls of military aircraft.
Having the ear of the president's wife provided connections. I made my proposal to General Henry "Hap" Arnold and the U.S. Army Air Force in 1943.
General, women pilots could help free up men for combat missions. They can fly planes just as well as men.
OK, Ms. Cochran. Go ahead and organize your program.

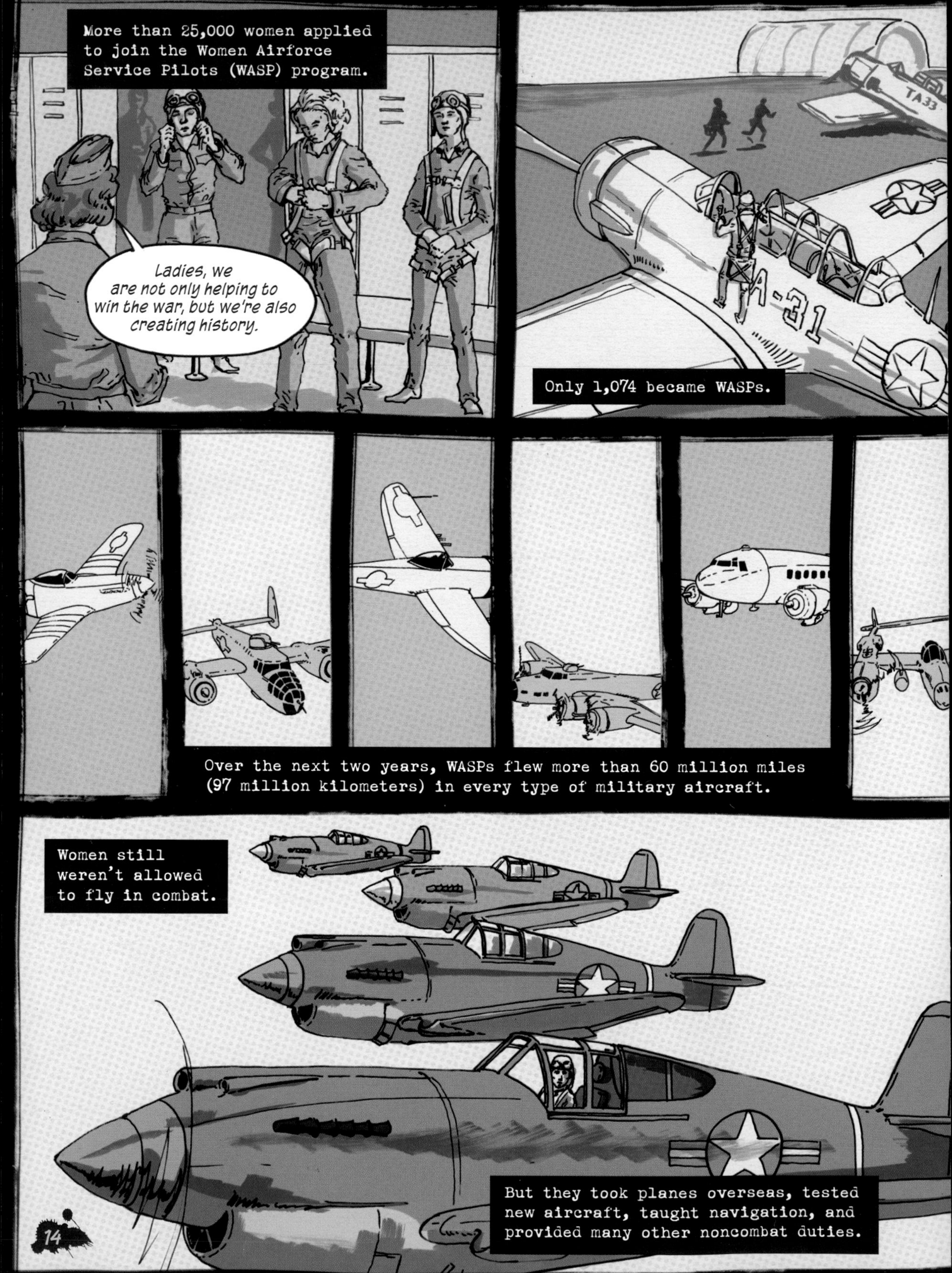
More than 25,000 women applied to join the Women Airforce Service Pilots (WASP) program.
Ladies, we are not only helping to win the war, but we're also creating history.
TA33
A-31
Only 1,074 became WASPs.
Over the next two years, WASPs flew more than 60 million miles (97 million kilometers) in every type of military aircraft.
Women still weren't allowed to fly in combat.
But they took planes overseas, tested new aircraft, taught navigation, and provided many other noncombat duties.

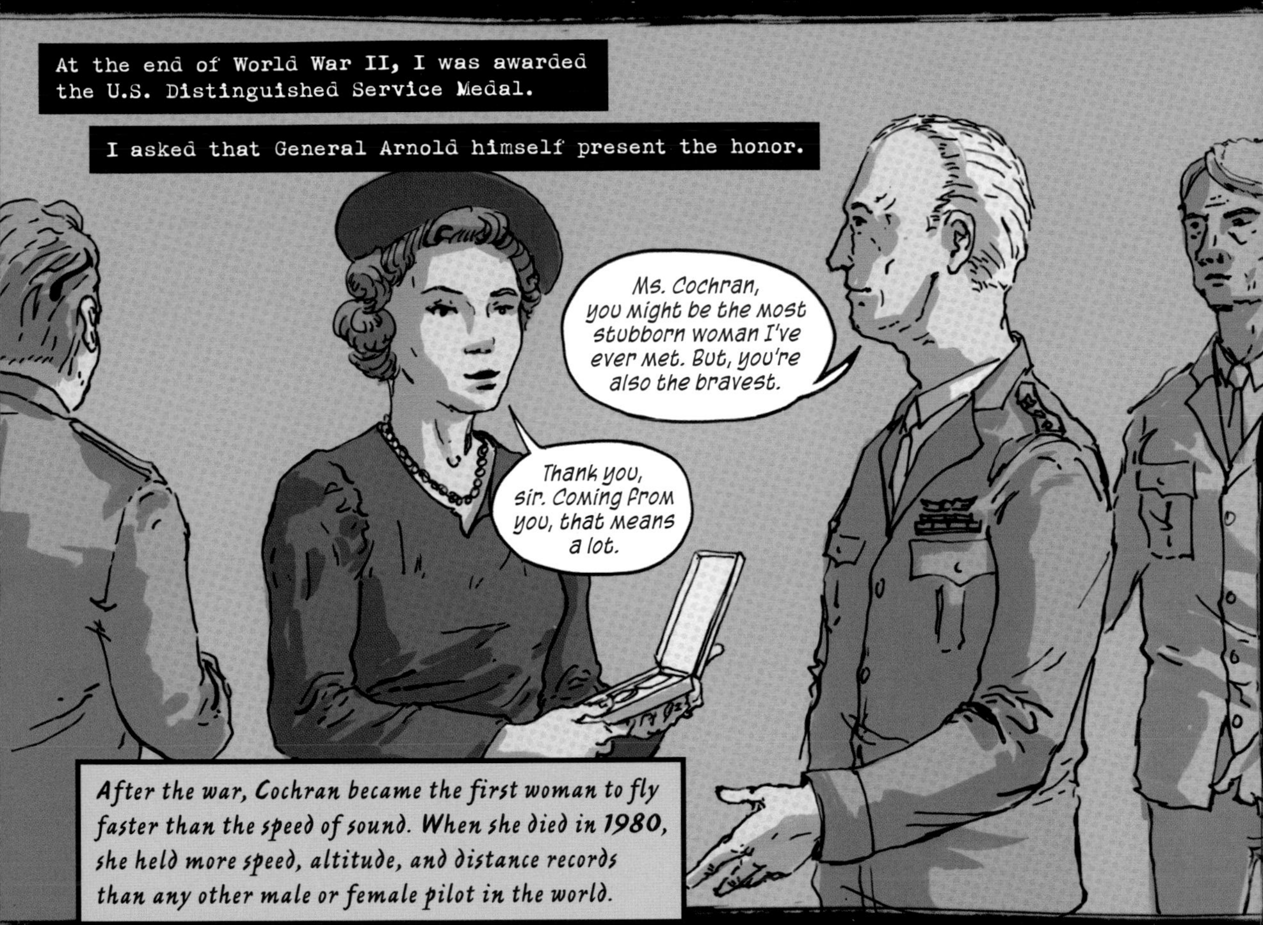
At the end of World War II, I was awarded the U.S. Distinguished Service Medal.
I asked that General Arnold himself present the honor.
Ms. Cochran, you might be the most stubborn woman I've ever met. But, you're also the bravest.
Thank you, sir. Coming from you, that means a lot.
After the war, Cochran became the first woman to fly faster than the speed of sound. When she died in 1980, she held more speed, altitude, and distance records than any other male or female pilot in the world.

JACKIE'S STAMP

On March 9, 1996, the Post Office issued a 50-cent stamp commemorating Jacqueline Cochran. The stamp honored her many accomplishments, before, during, and after World War II. The stamp shows a painting of Cochran after winning the 1938 Bendix Air Race.

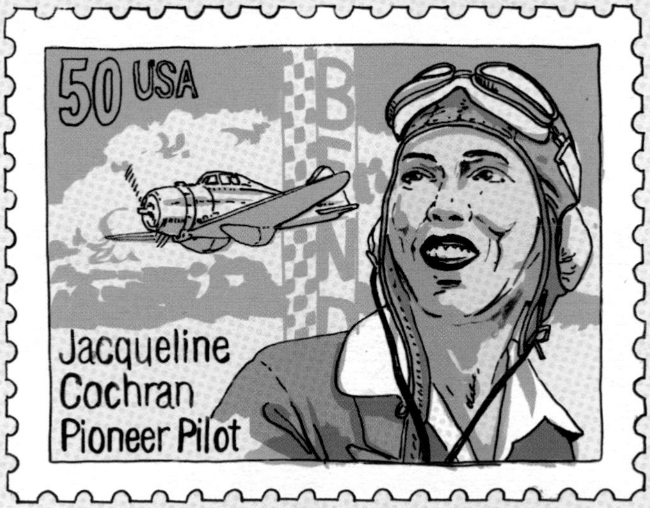
50 USA
Jacqueline
Cochran
Pioneer Pilot

CH. 4

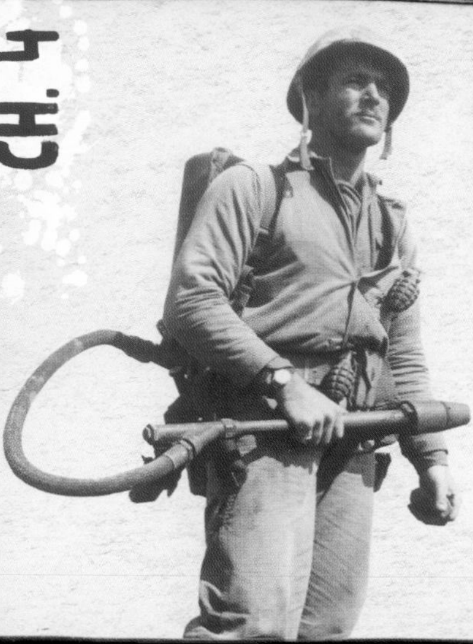

Charles W. Lindberg: Flag Over Iwo Jima

North Dakota native Charles W. Lindberg was a flamethrower operator for the 3rd Platoon, Easy Company, 28th Regiment. Lindberg's platoon fought at the base of Mount Suribachi on the Japanese controlled Pacific island of Iwo Jima. On February 23, 1945, he took part in the first American flag-raising on Iwo Jima.

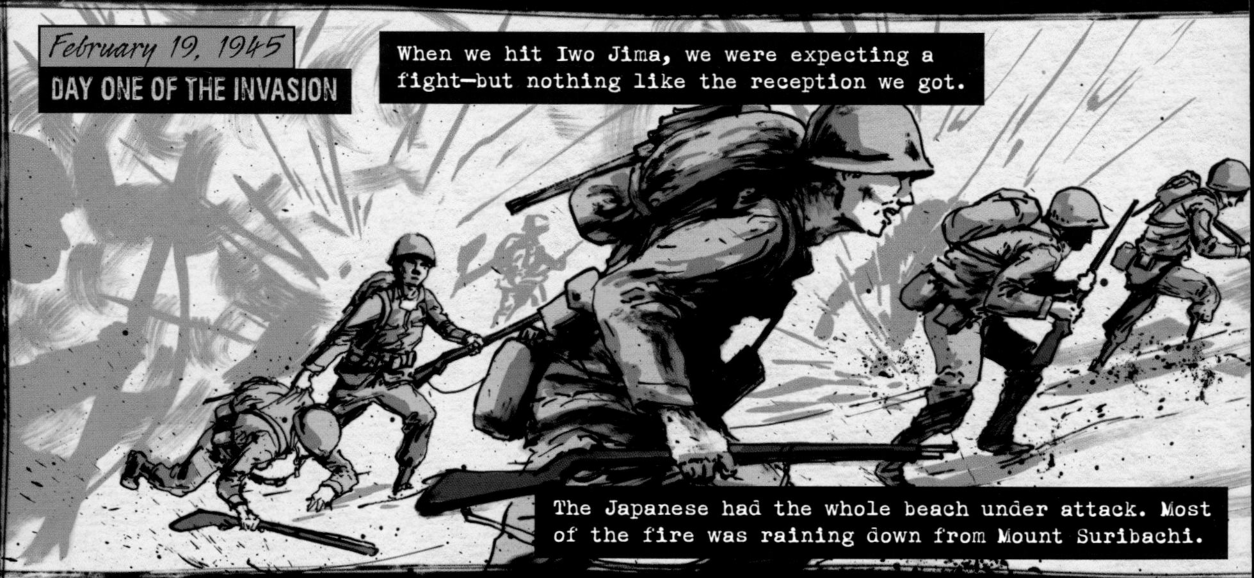
February 19, 1945
DAY ONE OF THE INVASION
When we hit Iwo Jima, we were expecting a fight—but nothing like the reception we got.
The Japanese had the whole beach under attack. Most of the fire was raining down from Mount Suribachi.

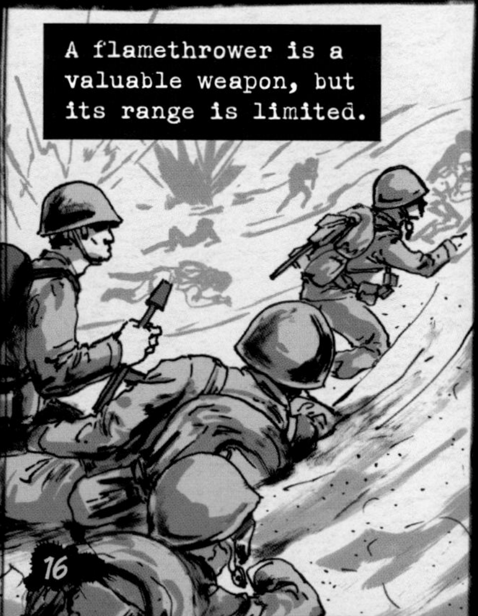
A flamethrower is a valuable weapon, but its range is limited.

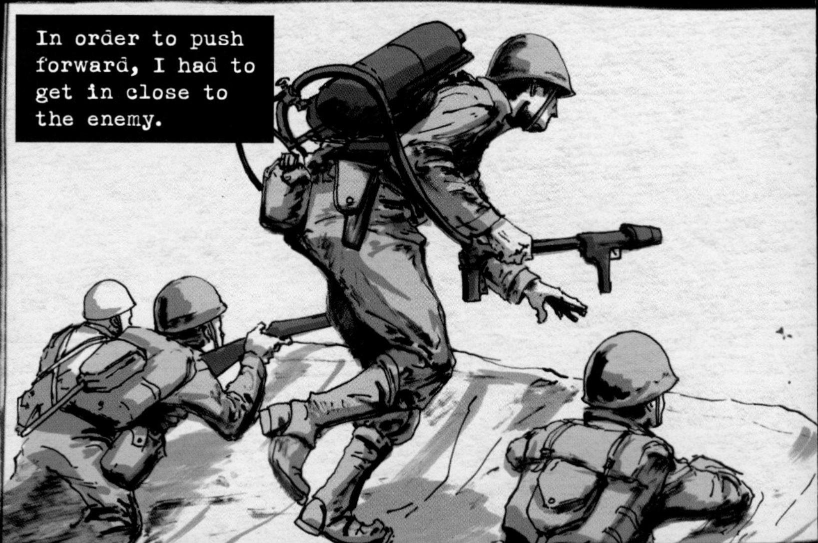
In order to push forward, I had to get in close to the enemy.

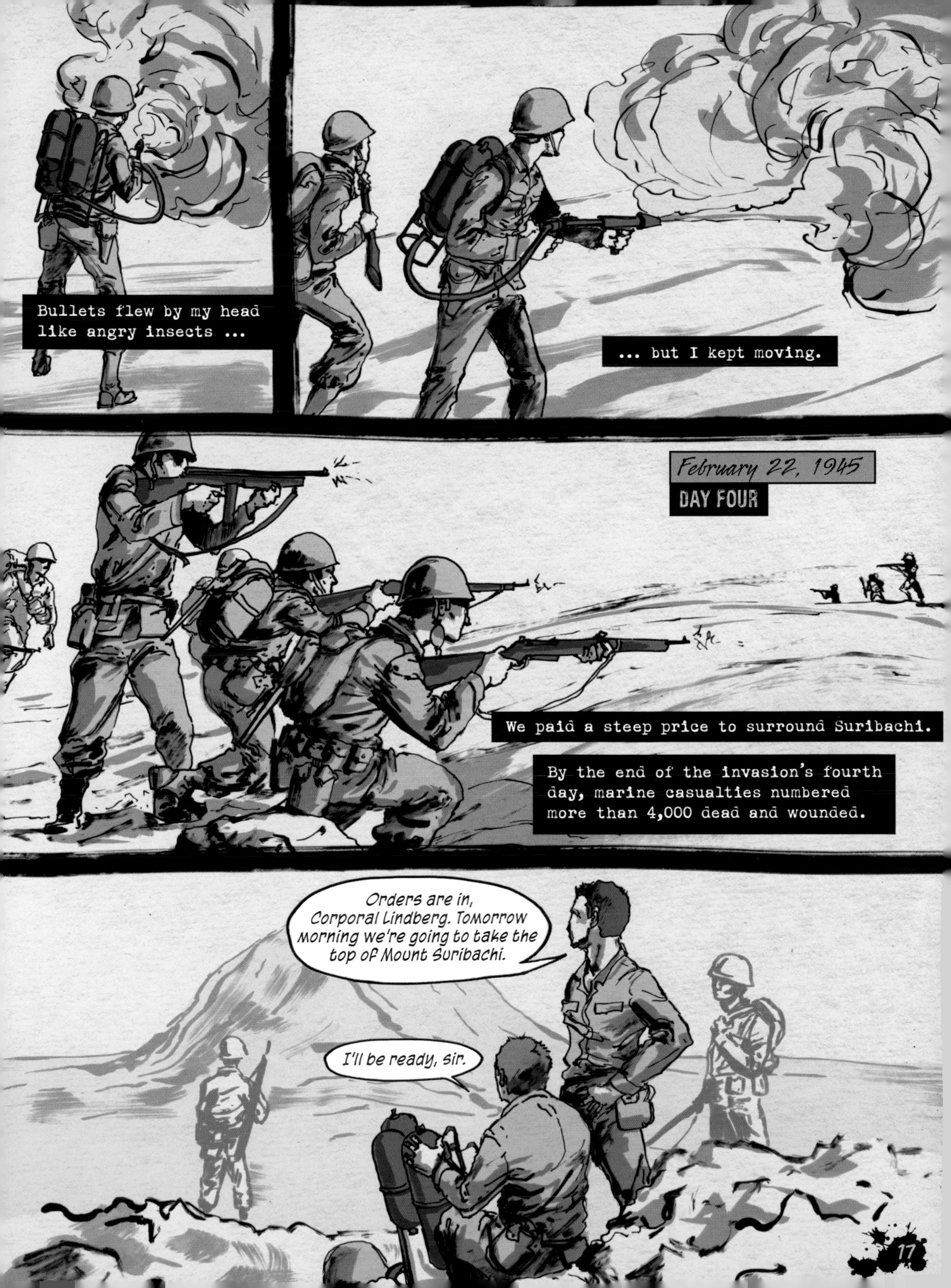
Bullets flew by my head like angry insects ...
... but I kept moving.
February 22, 1945
DAY FOUR
We paid a steep price to surround Suribachi.
By the end of the invasion's fourth day, marine casualties numbered more than 4,000 dead and wounded.
Orders are in, Corporal Lindberg. Tomorrow morning we're going to take the top of Mount Suribachi.
I'll be ready, sir.

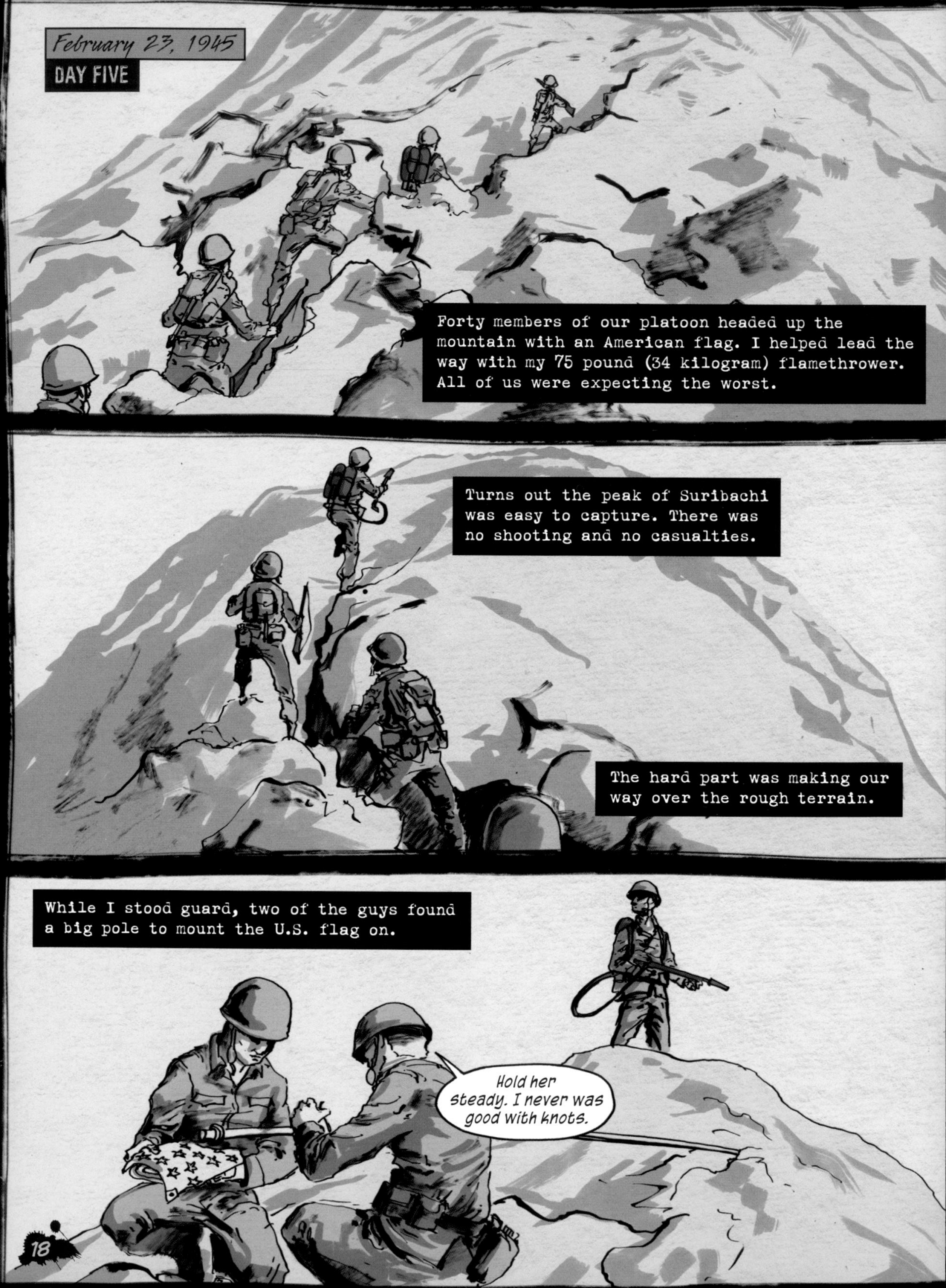
February 23, 1945
DAY FIVE
Forty members of our platoon headed up the mountain with an American flag. I helped lead the way with my 75 pound (34 kilogram) flamethrower. All of us were expecting the worst.
Turns out the peak of Suribachi was easy to capture. There was no shooting and no casualties.
The hard part was making our way over the rough terrain.
While I stood guard, two of the guys found a big pole to mount the U.S. flag on.
Hold her steady. I never was good with knots.

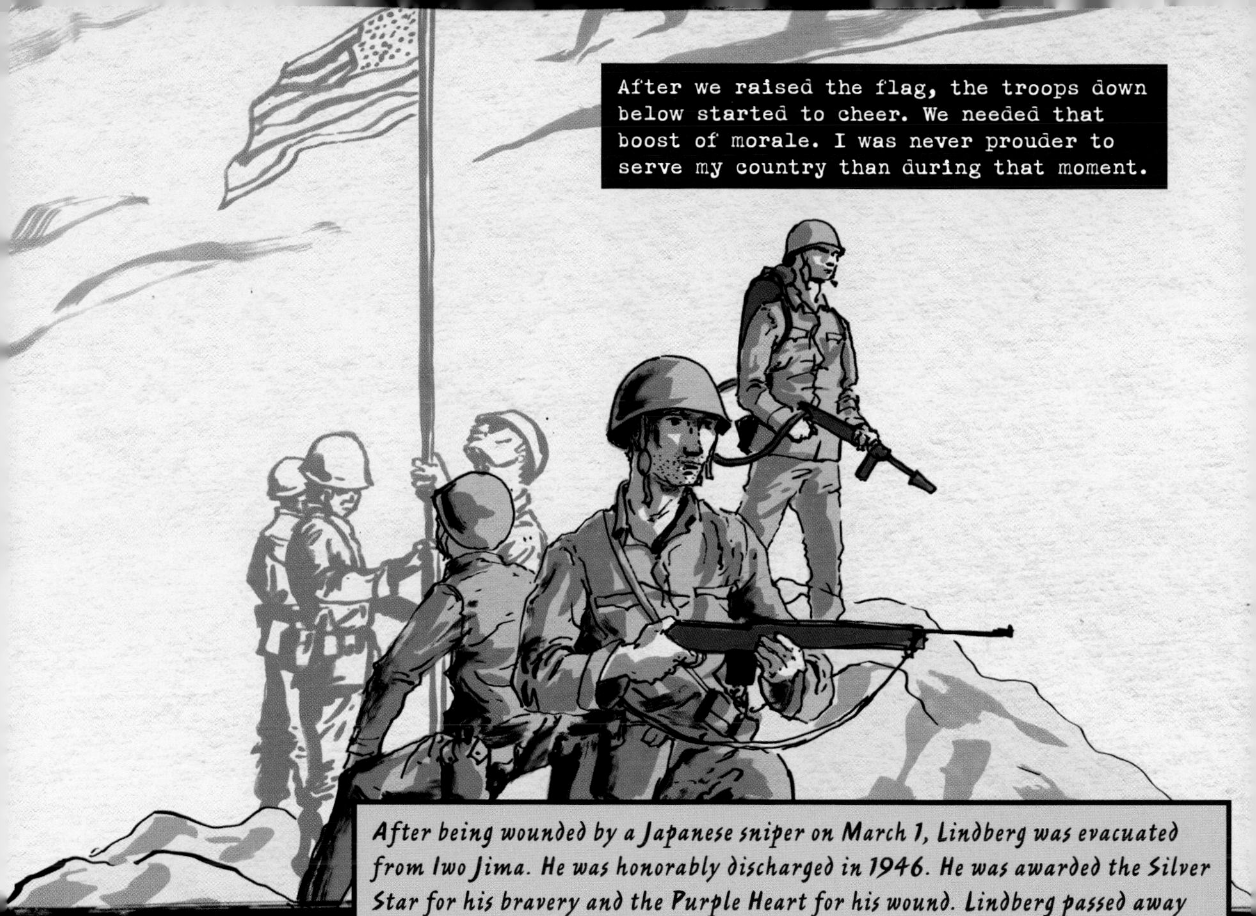
After we raised the flag, the troops down below started to cheer. We needed that boost of morale. I was never prouder to serve my country than during that moment.

After being wounded by a Japanese sniper on March 1, Lindberg was evacuated from Iwo Jima. He was honorably discharged in 1946. He was awarded the Silver Star for his bravery and the Purple Heart for his wound. Lindberg passed away on June 24, 2007, the last survivor of the first flag-raising on Iwo Jima.

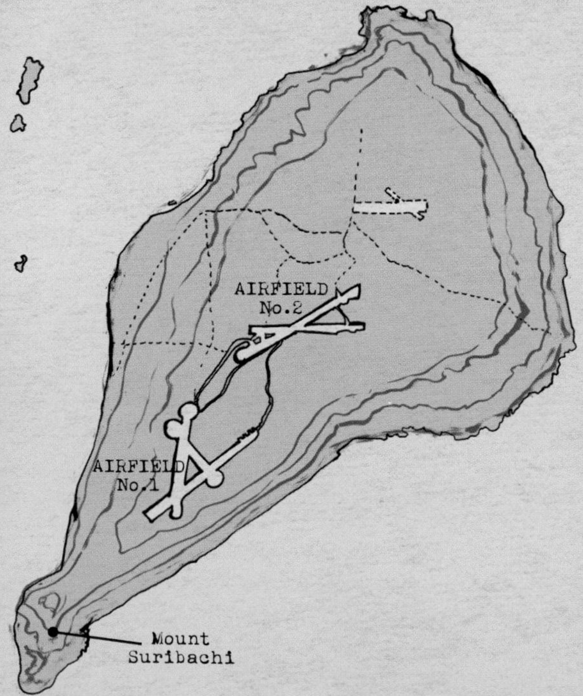
AIRFIELD No.2
AIRFIELD No.1
Mount Suribachi

THE IMPORTANCE OF IWO JIMA

The Japanese had two runways in place on Iwo Jima. A third landing strip to the north was incomplete. Controlling these runways on Iwo Jima provided emergency landing spots for damaged U.S. B-29s on their way home after bombing Japan. Ultimately, an estimated 20,000 Allied lives were saved by being able to land on Iwo Jima for repairs. But more than 25,000 men from both sides died in the battle for the island.

CH. 5

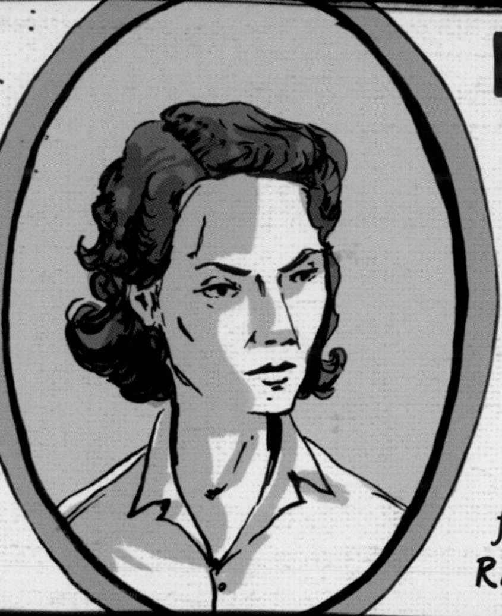

LUCIE AUBRAC: FRENCH FREEDOM FIGHTER

Lucie Aubrac was a history teacher, a mother, a wife, and a member of the French Resistance. Her husband, Raymond, was an engineer who also secretly worked against the German occupation of France. Aubrac and her husband often helped men on the run from the German secret police escape from France. These skills proved important when Raymond was captured by the Nazis.

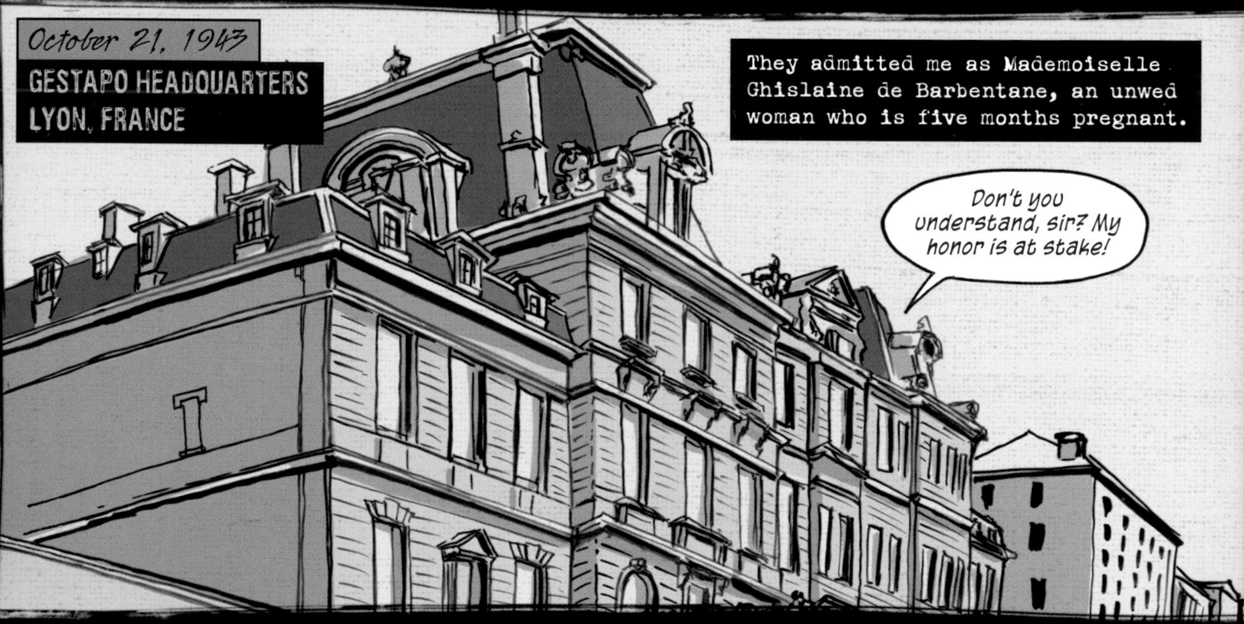

October 21, 1943
GESTAPO HEADQUARTERS
LYON, FRANCE
They admitted me as Mademoiselle Ghislaine de Barbentane, an unwed woman who is five months pregnant.
Don't you understand, sir? My honor is at stake!

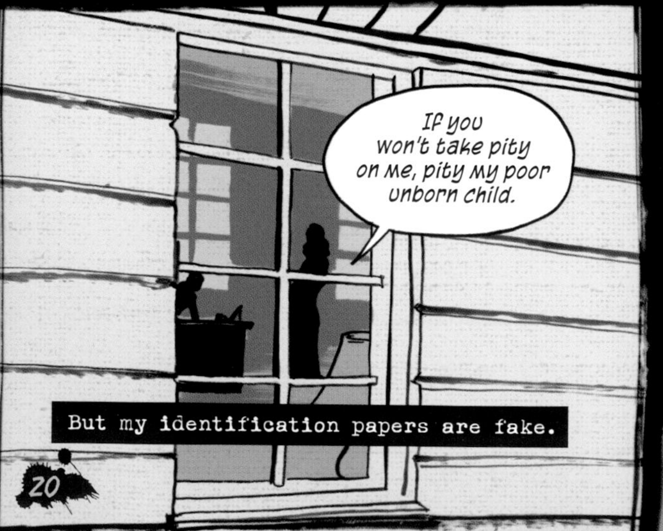

If you won't take pity on me, pity my poor unborn child.
But my identification papers are fake.

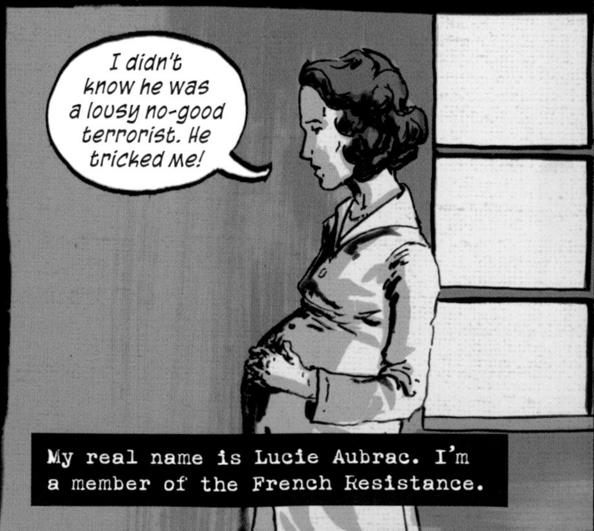

I didn't know he was a lousy no-good terrorist. He tricked me!
My real name is Lucie Aubrac. I'm a member of the French Resistance.

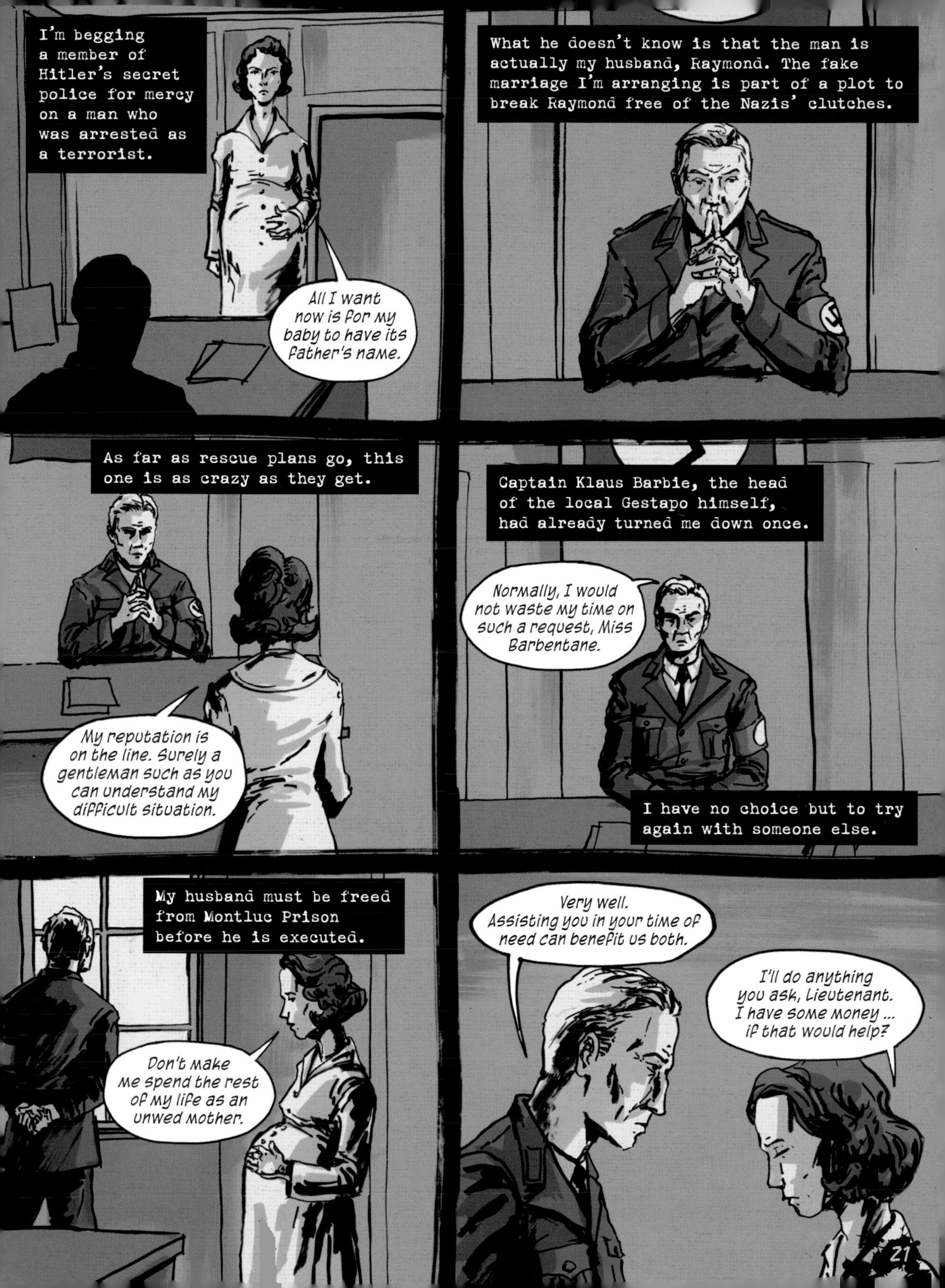

I'm begging a member of Hitler's secret police for mercy on a man who was arrested as a terrorist.
All I want now is for my baby to have its father's name.
What he doesn't know is that the man is actually my husband, Raymond. The fake marriage I'm arranging is part of a plot to break Raymond free of the Nazis' clutches.
As far as rescue plans go, this one is as crazy as they get.
My reputation is on the line. Surely a gentleman such as you can understand my difficult situation.
Captain Klaus Barbie, the head of the local Gestapo himself, had already turned me down once.
Normally, I would not waste my time on such a request, Miss Barbentane.
I have no choice but to try again with someone else.
My husband must be freed from Montluc Prison before he is executed.
Don't make me spend the rest of my life as an unwed mother.
Very well. Assisting you in your time of need can benefit us both.
I'll do anything you ask, Lieutenant. I have some money ... if that would help?

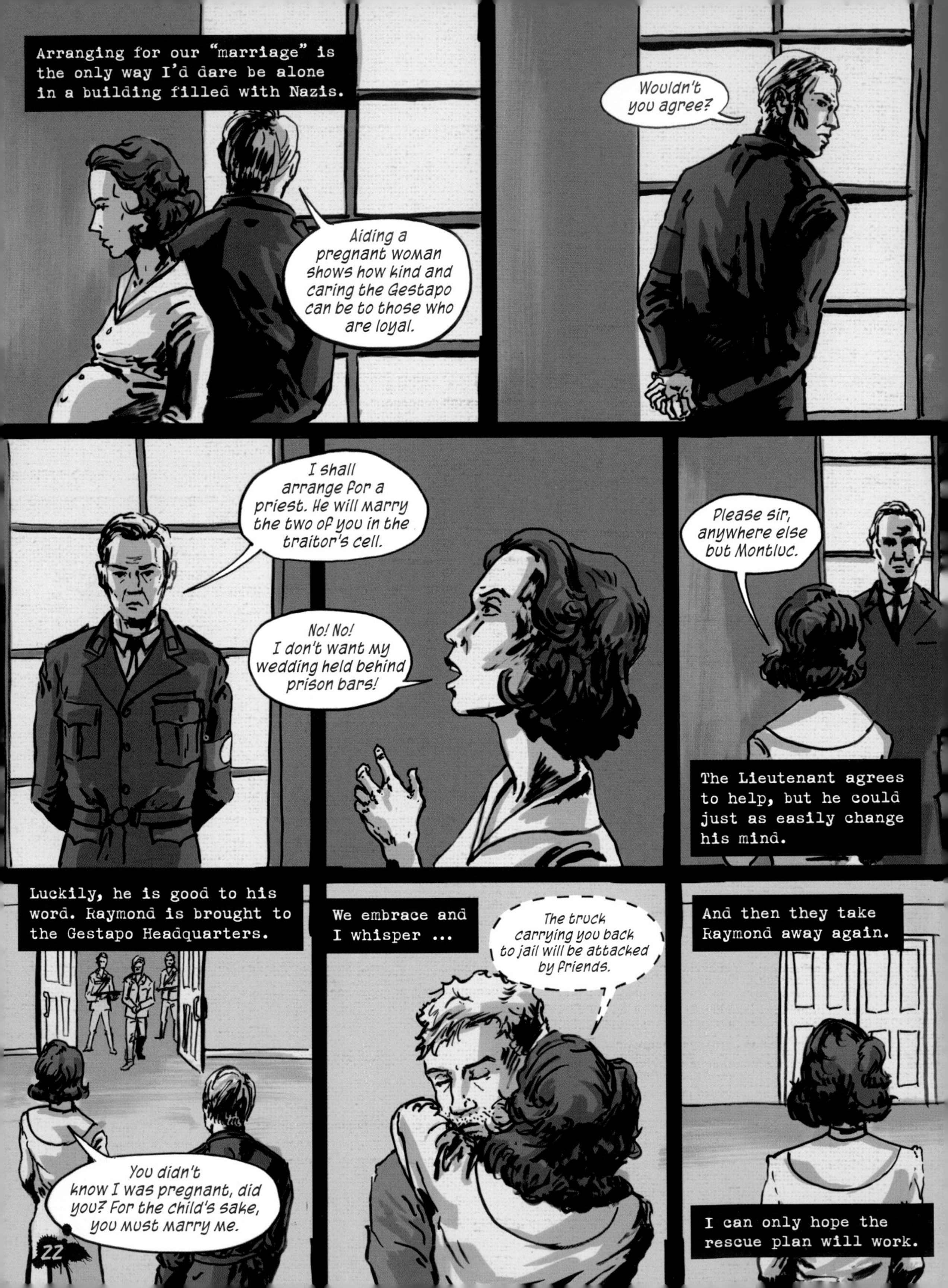

Arranging for our "marriage" is the only way I'd dare be alone in a building filled with Nazis.
Aiding a pregnant woman shows how kind and caring the Gestapo can be to those who are loyal.
Wouldn't you agree?
I shall arrange for a priest. He will marry the two of you in the traitor's cell.
No! No! I don't want my wedding held behind prison bars!
Please sir, anywhere else but Montluc.
The Lieutenant agrees to help, but he could just as easily change his mind.
Luckily, he is good to his word. Raymond is brought to the Gestapo Headquarters.
You didn't know I was pregnant, did you? For the child's sake, you must marry me.
We embrace and I whisper ...
The truck carrying you back to jail will be attacked by friends.
And then they take Raymond away again.
I can only hope the rescue plan will work.

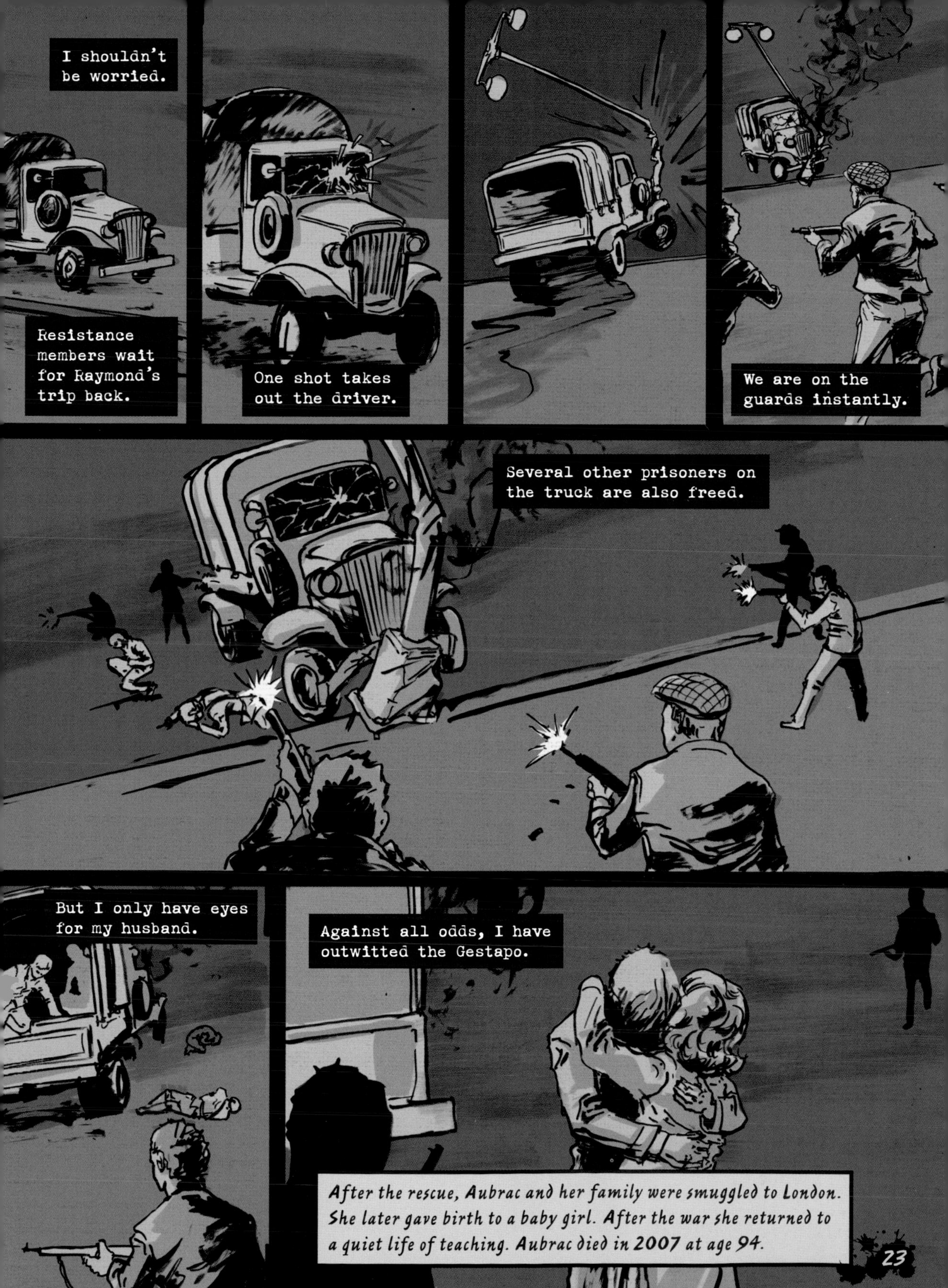

I shouldn't be worried.
Resistance members wait for Raymond's trip back.
One shot takes out the driver.
We are on the guards instantly.
Several other prisoners on the truck are also freed.
But I only have eyes for my husband.
Against all odds, I have outwitted the Gestapo.
After the rescue, Aubrac and her family were smuggled to London. She later gave birth to a baby girl. After the war she returned to a quiet life of teaching. Aubrac died in 2007 at age 94.

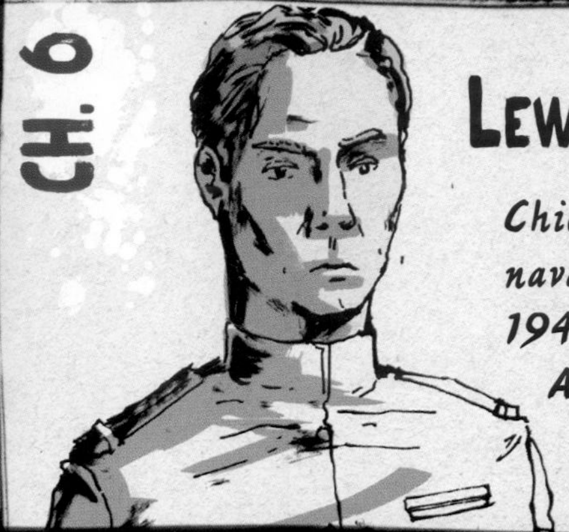
CH. 6

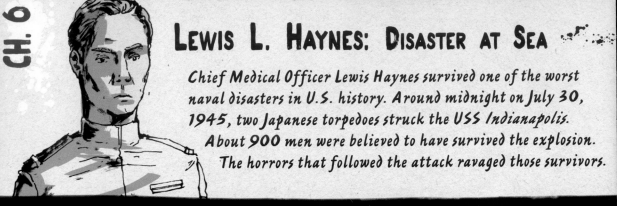

Lewis L. Haynes: Disaster at Sea

Chief Medical Officer Lewis Haynes survived one of the worst naval disasters in U.S. history. Around midnight on July 30, 1945, two Japanese torpedoes struck the USS Indianapolis. About 900 men were believed to have survived the explosion. The horrors that followed the attack ravaged those survivors.

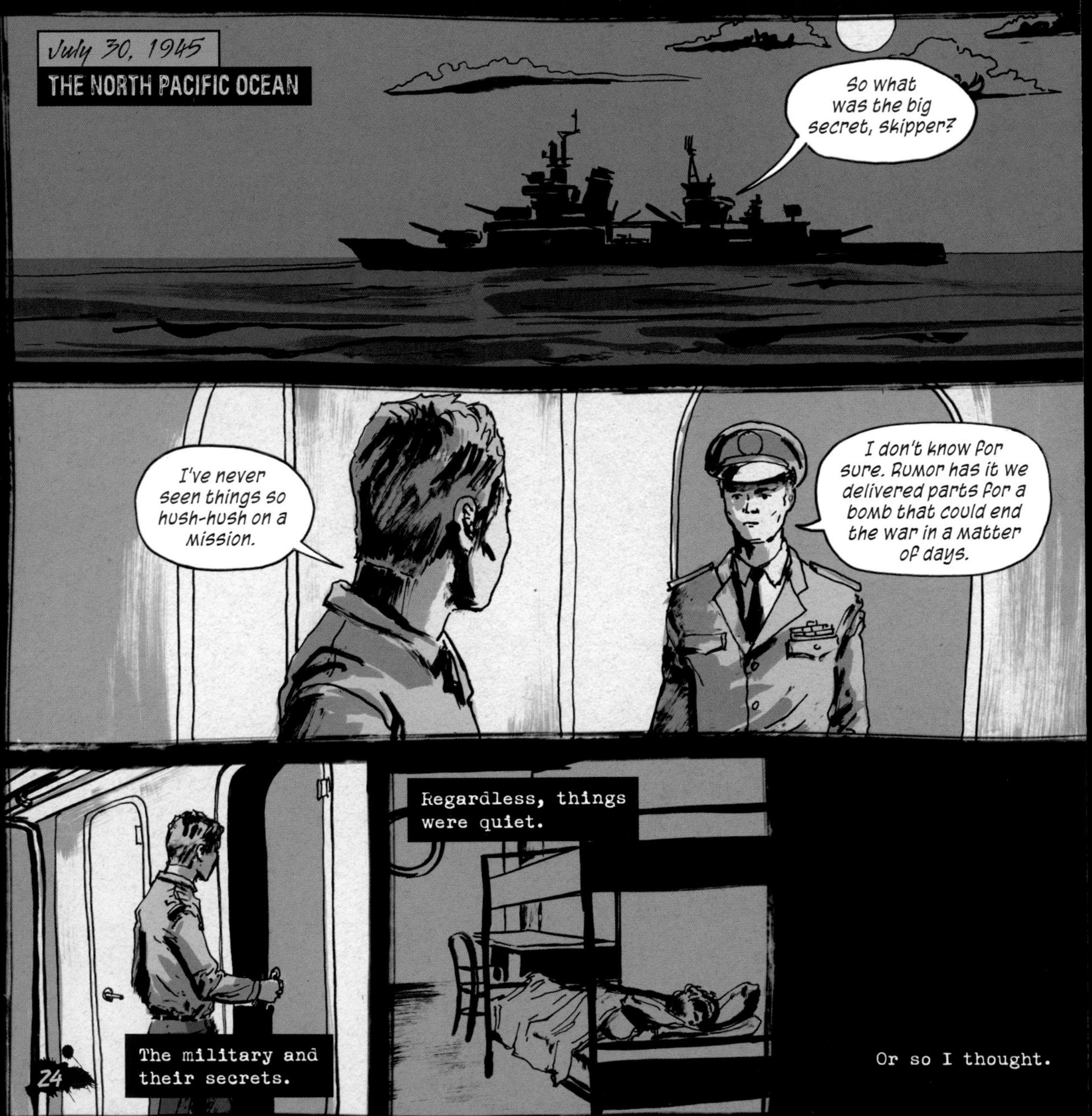
July 30, 1945
THE NORTH PACIFIC OCEAN
So what was the big secret, skipper?
I've never seen things so hush-hush on a mission.
I don't know for sure. Rumor has it we delivered parts for a bomb that could end the war in a matter of days.
The military and their secrets.
Regardless, things were quiet.
Or so I thought.

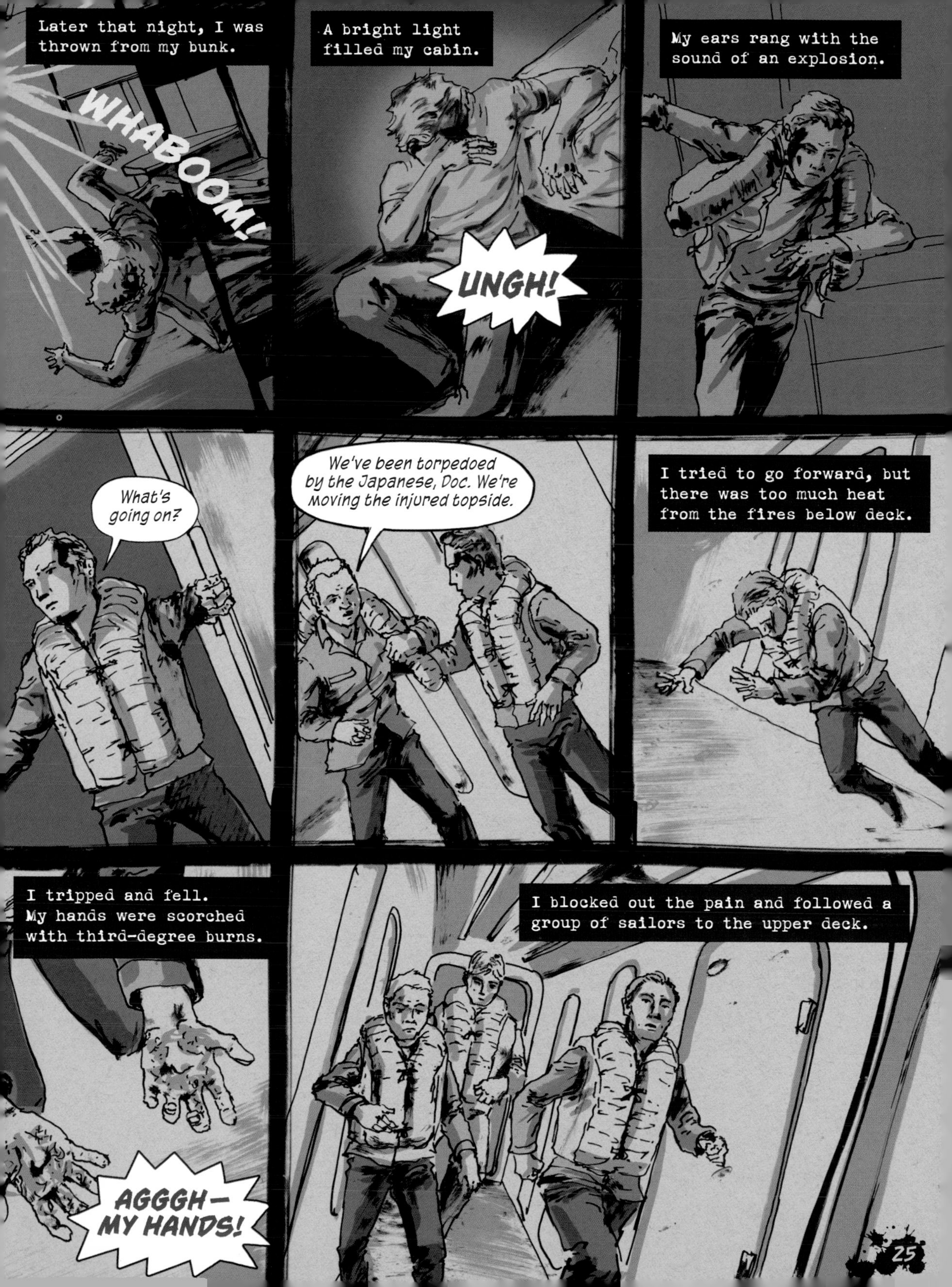

Later that night, I was thrown from my bunk.
WHABOOM!
A bright light filled my cabin.
UNGH!
My ears rang with the sound of an explosion.
What's going on?
We've been torpedoed by the Japanese, Doc. We're moving the injured topside.
I tried to go forward, but there was too much heat from the fires below deck.
I tripped and fell. My hands were scorched with third-degree burns.
AGGGH— MY HANDS!
I blocked out the pain and followed a group of sailors to the upper deck.

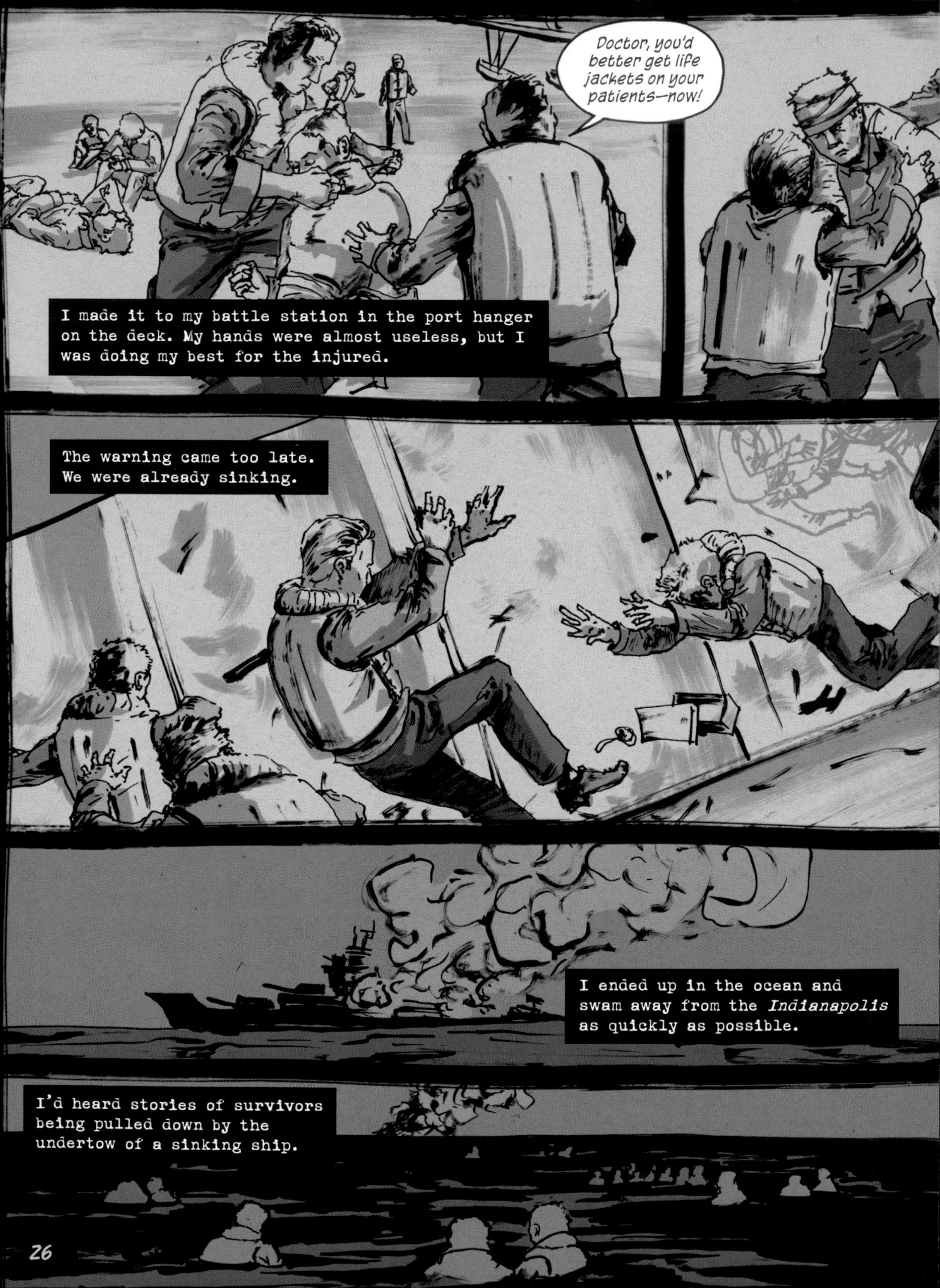
Doctor, you'd better get life jackets on your patients—now!
I made it to my battle station in the port hanger on the deck. My hands were almost useless, but I was doing my best for the injured.
The warning came too late. We were already sinking.
I ended up in the ocean and swam away from the *Indianapolis* as quickly as possible.
I'd heard stories of survivors being pulled down by the undertow of a sinking ship.

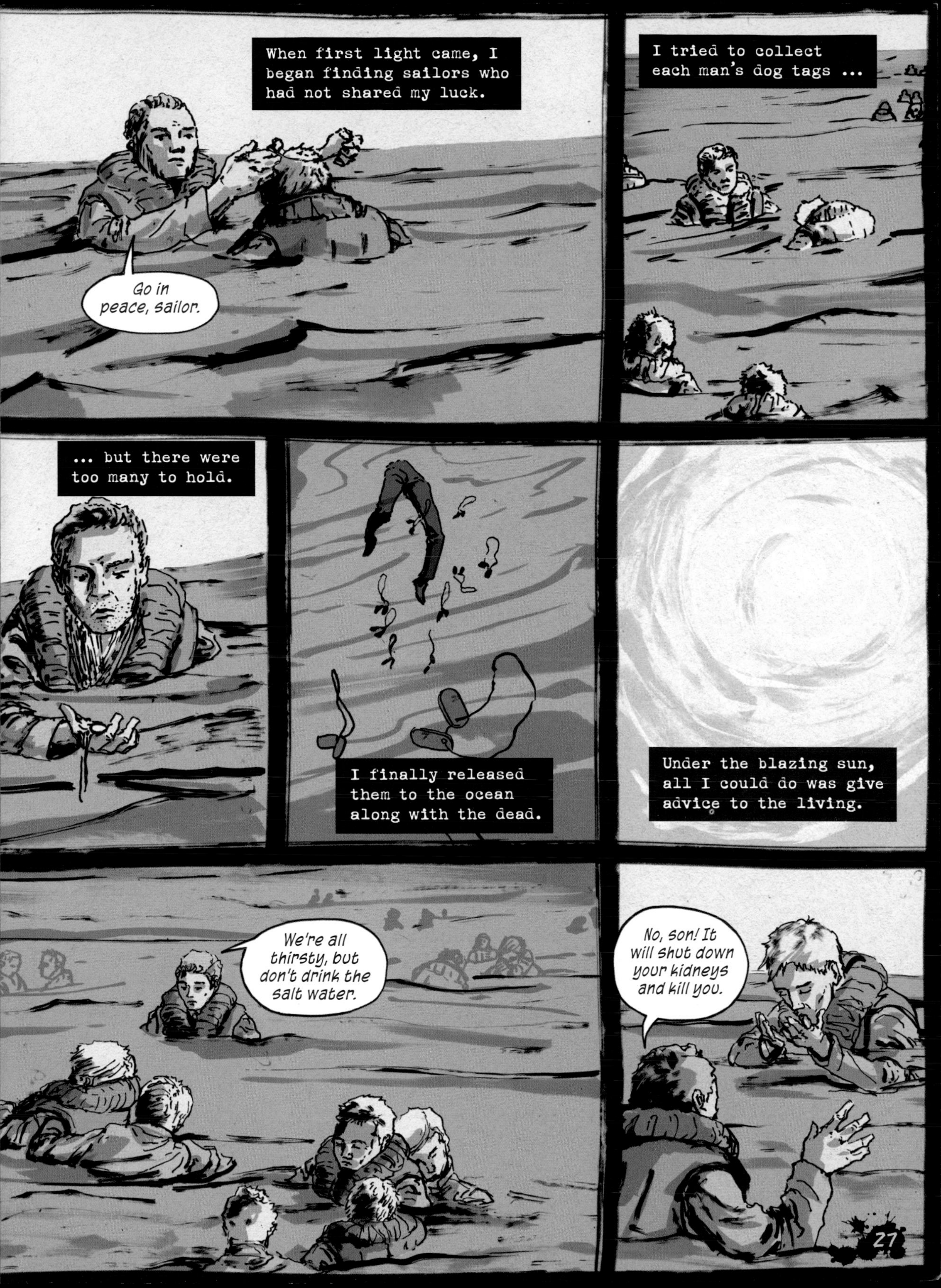
When first light came, I began finding sailors who had not shared my luck.
Go in peace, sailor.
I tried to collect each man's dog tags ...
... but there were too many to hold.
I finally released them to the ocean along with the dead.
Under the blazing sun, all I could do was give advice to the living.
We're all thirsty, but don't drink the salt water.
No, son! It will shut down your kidneys and kill you.

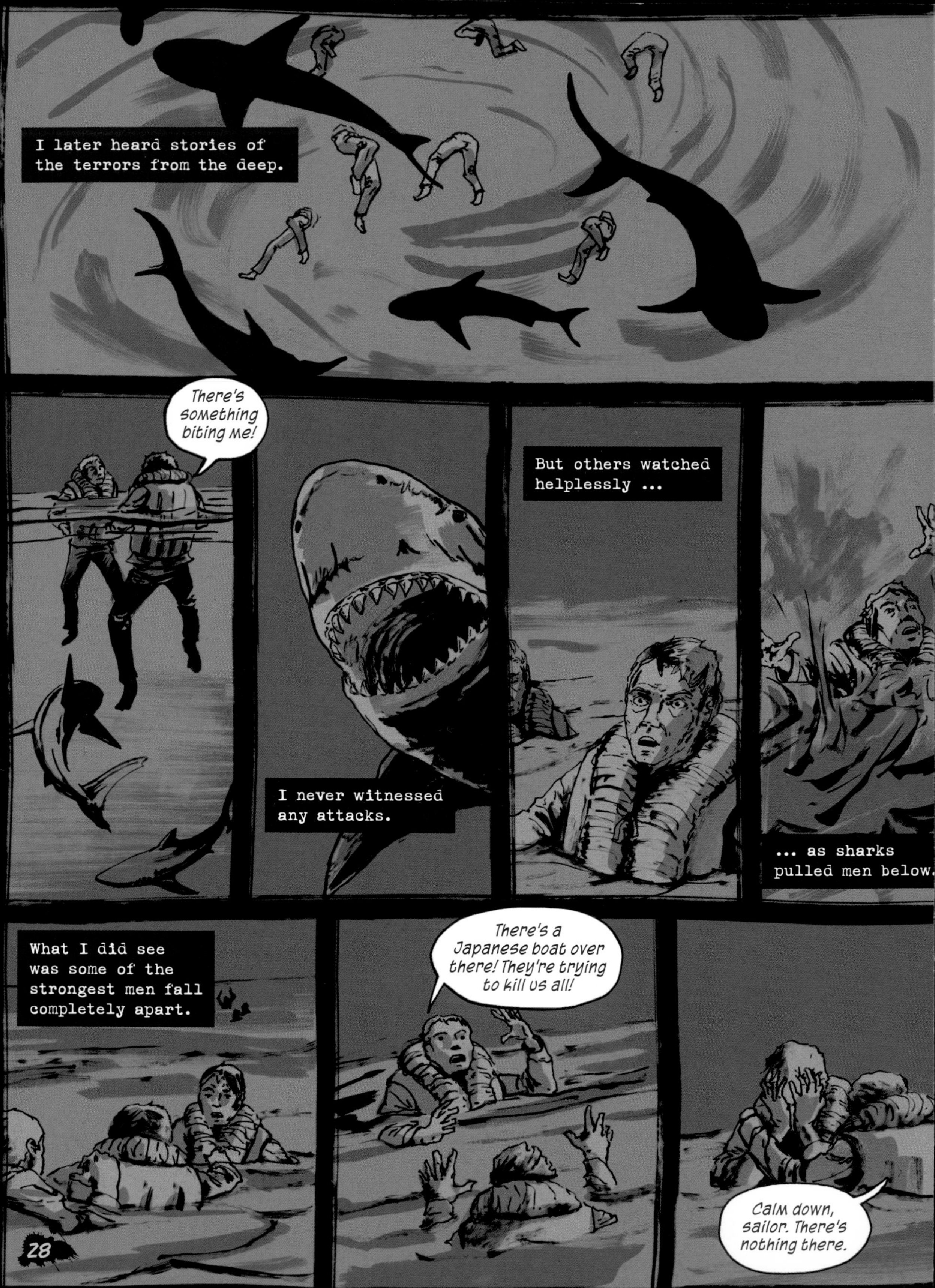
I later heard stories of the terrors from the deep.
There's something biting me!
I never witnessed any attacks.
But others watched helplessly ...
... as sharks pulled men below.
What I did see was some of the strongest men fall completely apart.
There's a Japanese boat over there! They're trying to kill us all!
Calm down, sailor. There's nothing there.

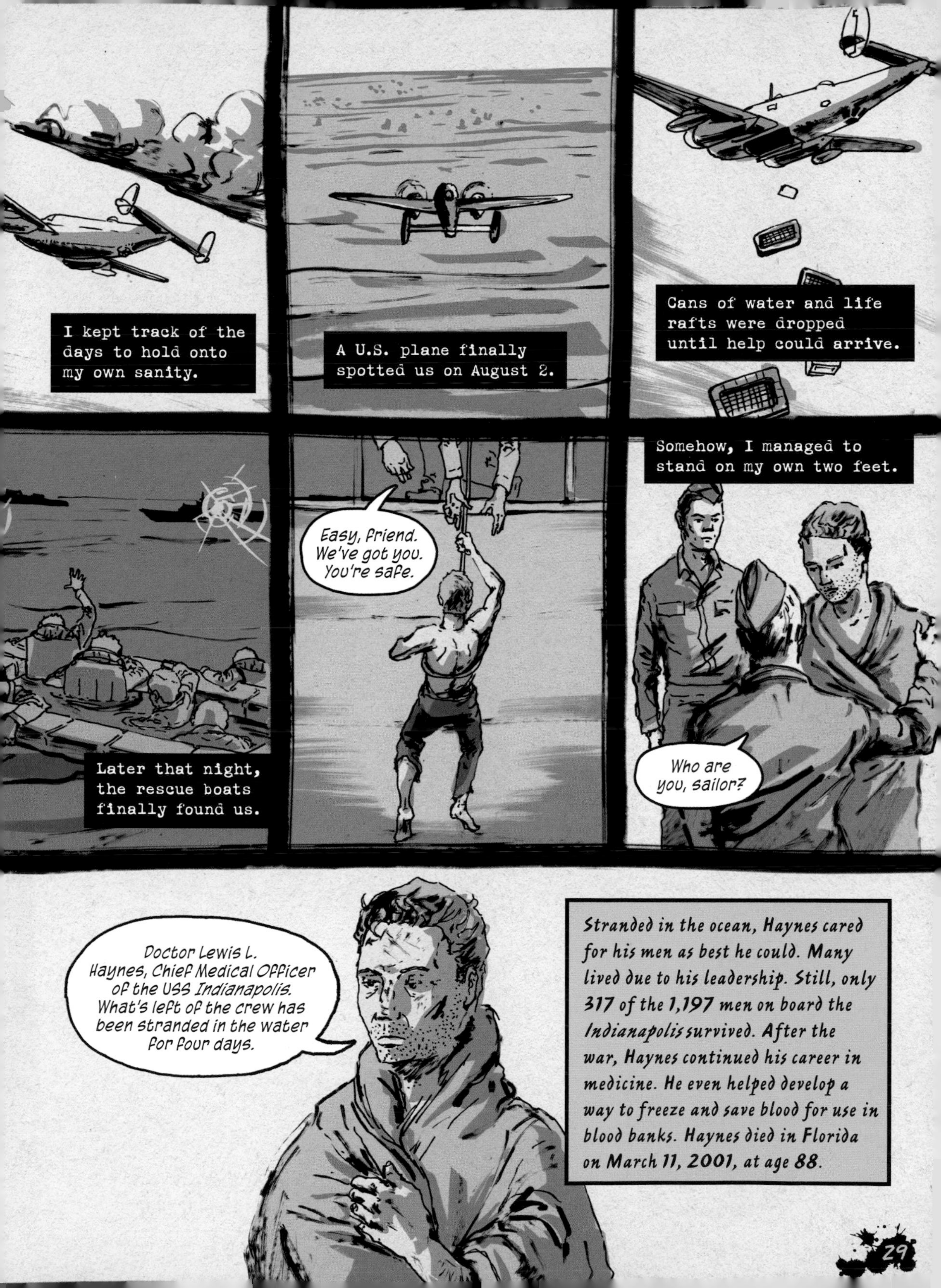
I kept track of the days to hold onto my own sanity.
A U.S. plane finally spotted us on August 2.
Cans of water and life rafts were dropped until help could arrive.
Later that night, the rescue boats finally found us.
Easy, friend. We've got you. You're safe.
Somehow, I managed to stand on my own two feet.
Who are you, sailor?
Doctor Lewis L. Haynes, Chief Medical Officer of the USS Indianapolis. What's left of the crew has been stranded in the water for four days.
Stranded in the ocean, Haynes cared for his men as best he could. Many lived due to his leadership. Still, only 317 of the 1,197 men on board the Indianapolis survived. After the war, Haynes continued his career in medicine. He even helped develop a way to freeze and save blood for use in blood banks. Haynes died in Florida on March 11, 2001, at age 88.

GLOSSARY

ALLIED POWERS (AL-lyd PAU-uhrs)—countries united against Germany, Italy, and Japan during World War II, including France, the United States, Canada, Great Britain, the Soviet Union, and others

AXIS POWERS (AK-siss POU-urs)—a group of countries including Germany, Italy, and Japan that fought together in World War II

BAYONET (BAY-uh-net)—a long metal blade attached to the end of a rifle

CASUALTY (KAZH-oo-uhl-tee)—someone who is injured, captured, killed, or missing in an accident, a disaster, or a war

GESTAPO (guh-STAH-poh)—the secret police of Nazi Germany

MALARIA (muh-LAIR-ee-ah)—a serious disease that people get from mosquito bites; malaria causes high fever, chills, and sometimes death

MORALE (muh-RAL)—a person or group's feelings or state of mind

NAVIGATION (NAV-uh-gay-shun)—using instruments and charts to find your way in an airplane or other vehicle

NAZI (NOT-see)—a member of the National Socialist Party led by Adolf Hitler that controlled Germany before and during World War II (1939-1945); the Nazi emblem was the swastika, an ancient religious symbol

PLATOON (pluh-TOON)—a small group of soldiers who work together

RANGE (RAYNJ)—the longest distance at which a weapon can still hit its target

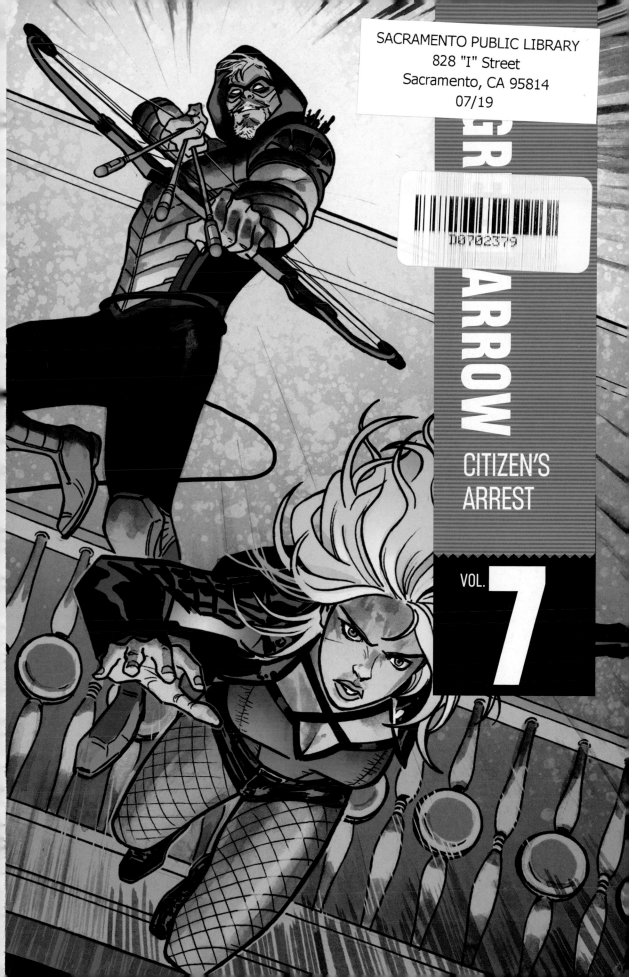

GREEN ARROW

CITIZEN'S ARREST

VOL. **7**

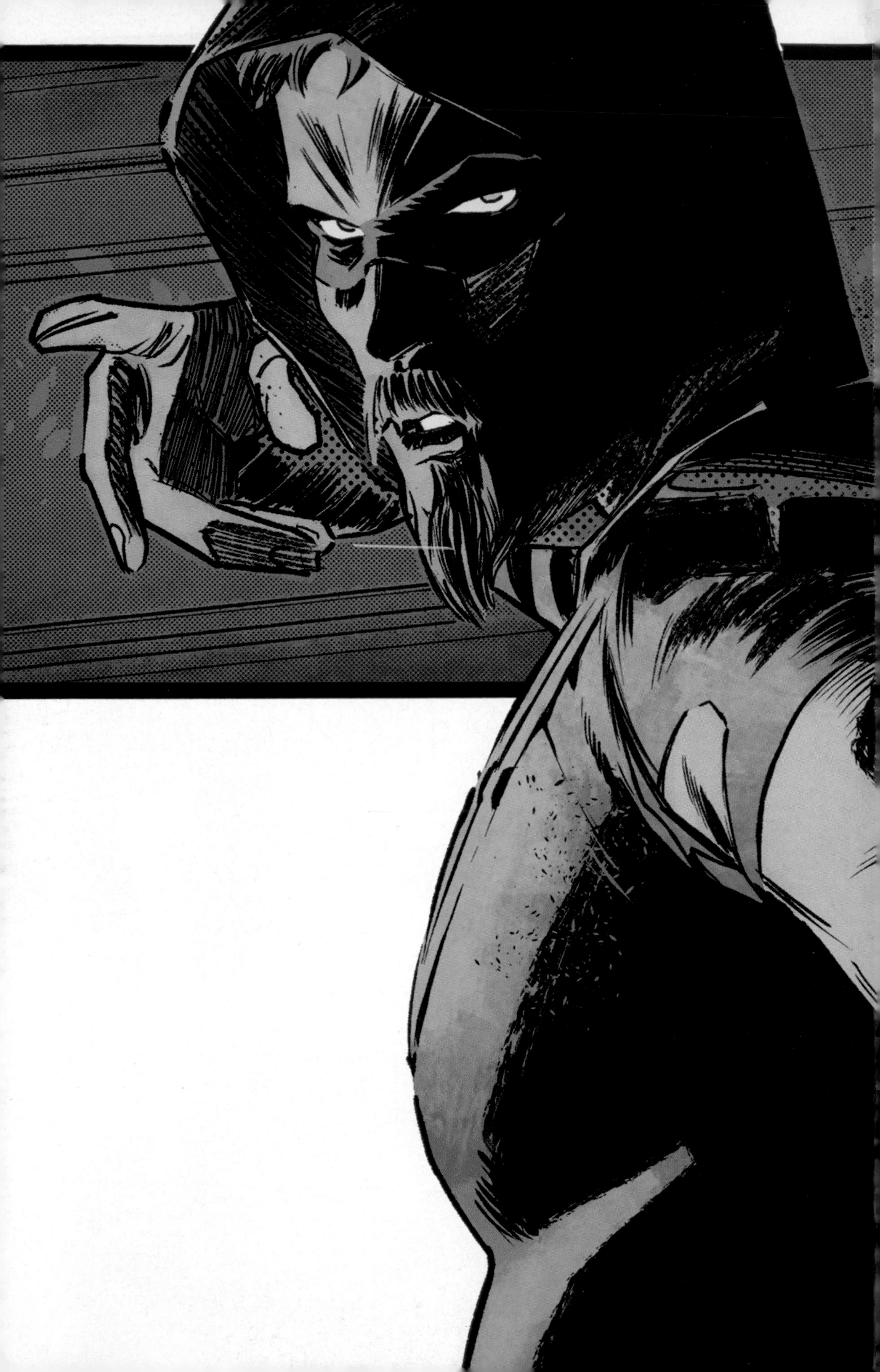

GREEN ARROW

CITIZEN'S ARREST

writers

JULIE BENSON
SHAWNA BENSON

artists

JAVIER FERNANDEZ
GERMAN PERALTA
CARMEN CARNERO

colorists

JOHN KALISZ
TRISH MULVIHILL

letterer

DERON BENNETT

collection cover artist

ALEX MALEEV

SUPERMAN created by JERRY SIEGEL and JOE SHUSTER
By special arrangement with the Jerry Siegel family

VOL.
7

KATIE KUBERT	Editor – Original Series
DAVE WIELGOSZ	Assistant Editor – Original Series
JEB WOODARD	Group Editor – Collected Editions
ERIKA ROTHBERG	Editor – Collected Edition
STEVE COOK	Design Director – Books
CURTIS KING JR.	Publication Design
ERIN VANOVER	Publication Production
BOB HARRAS	Senior VP – Editor-in-Chief, DC Comics
PAT McCALLUM	Executive Editor, DC Comics
DAN DiDIO	Publisher
JIM LEE	Publisher & Chief Creative Officer
BOBBIE CHASE	VP – New Publishing Initiatives & Talent Development
DON FALLETTI	VP – Manufacturing Operations & Workflow Management
LAWRENCE GANEM	VP – Talent Services
ALISON GILL	Senior VP – Manufacturing & Operations
HANK KANALZ	Senior VP – Publishing Strategy & Support Services
DAN MIRON	VP – Publishing Operations
NICK J. NAPOLITANO	VP – Manufacturing Administration & Design
NANCY SPEARS	VP – Sales
MICHELE R. WELLS	VP & Executive Editor, Young Reader

GREEN ARROW VOL. 7: CITIZEN'S ARREST

DC Comics, 2900 West Alameda Ave., Burbank, CA 91505
Printed by LSC Communications, Kendallville, IN, USA. 6/14/19. First Printing.
ISBN: 978-1-4012-8523-4

Library of Congress Cataloging-in-Publication Data is available.

PEFC Certified
This product is from sustainably managed forests and controlled sources
PEFC
PEFC/29-31-337
www.pefc.org

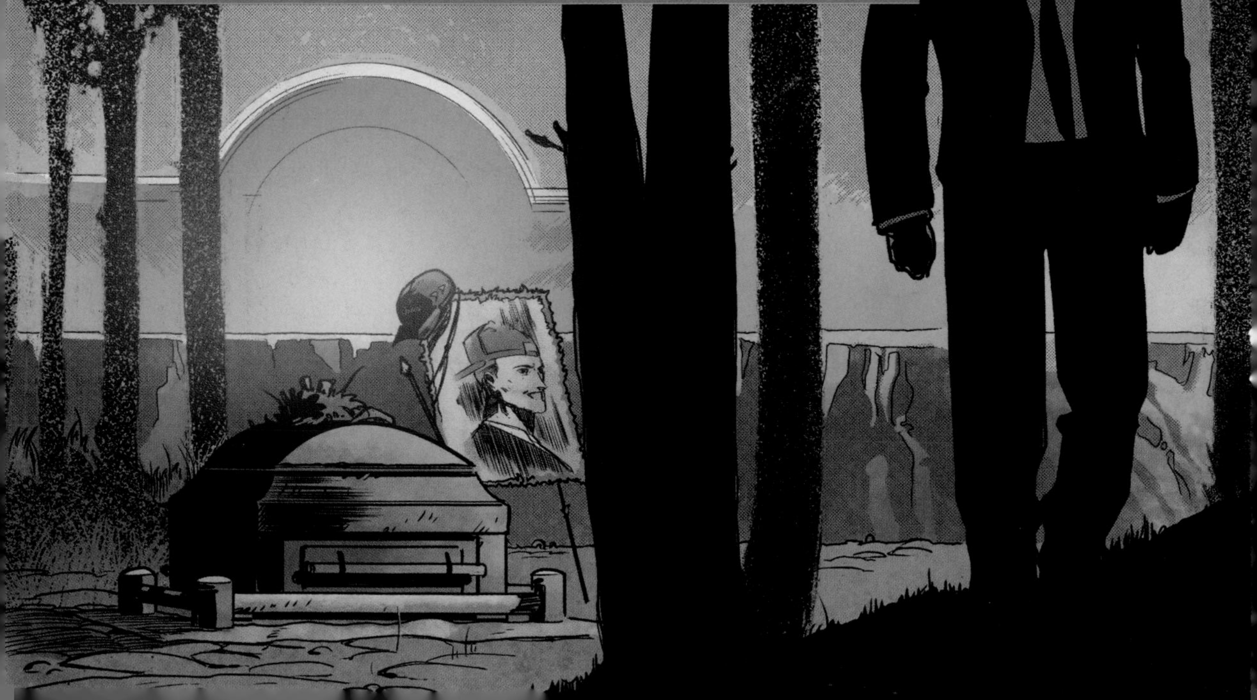

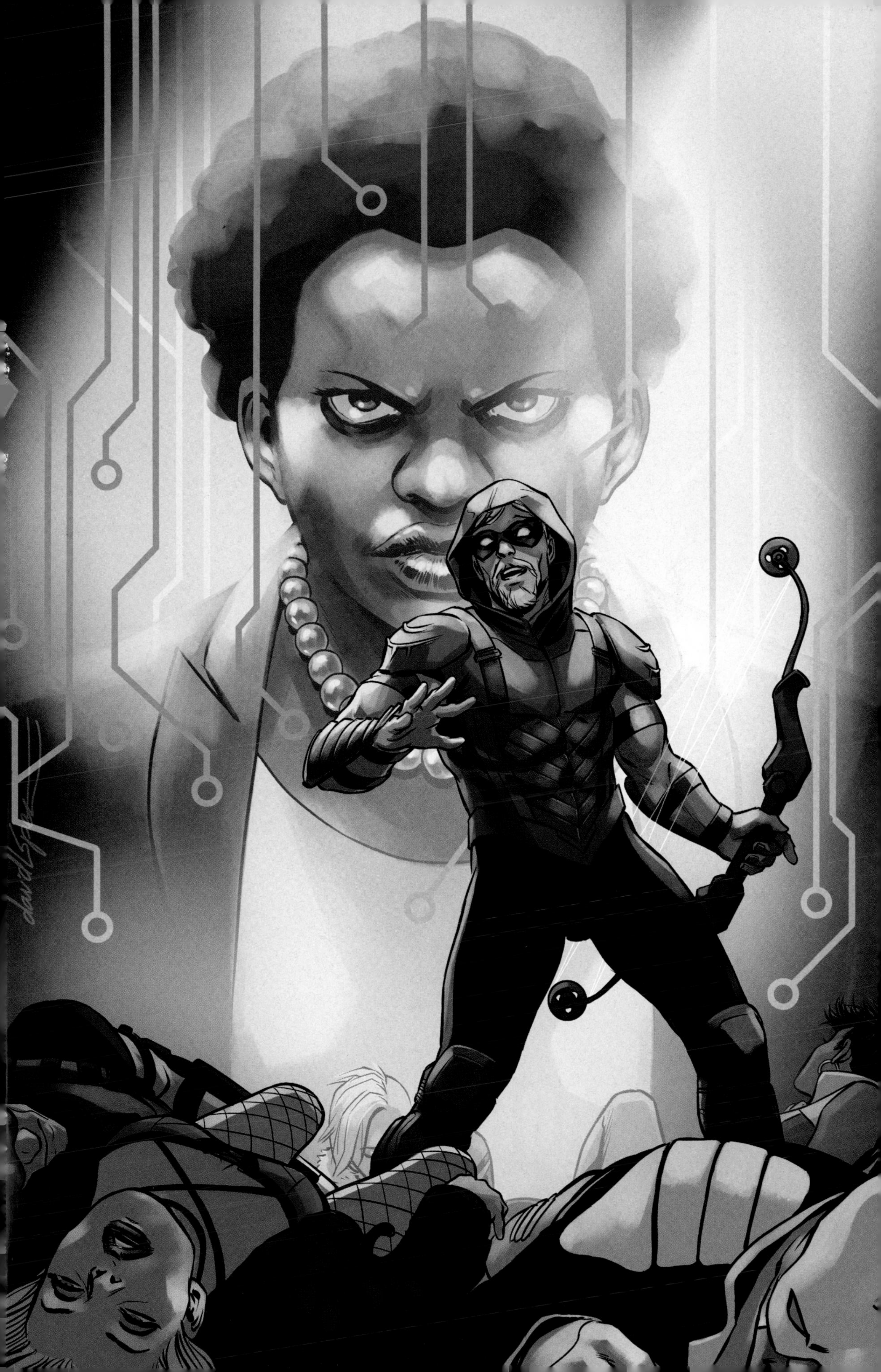

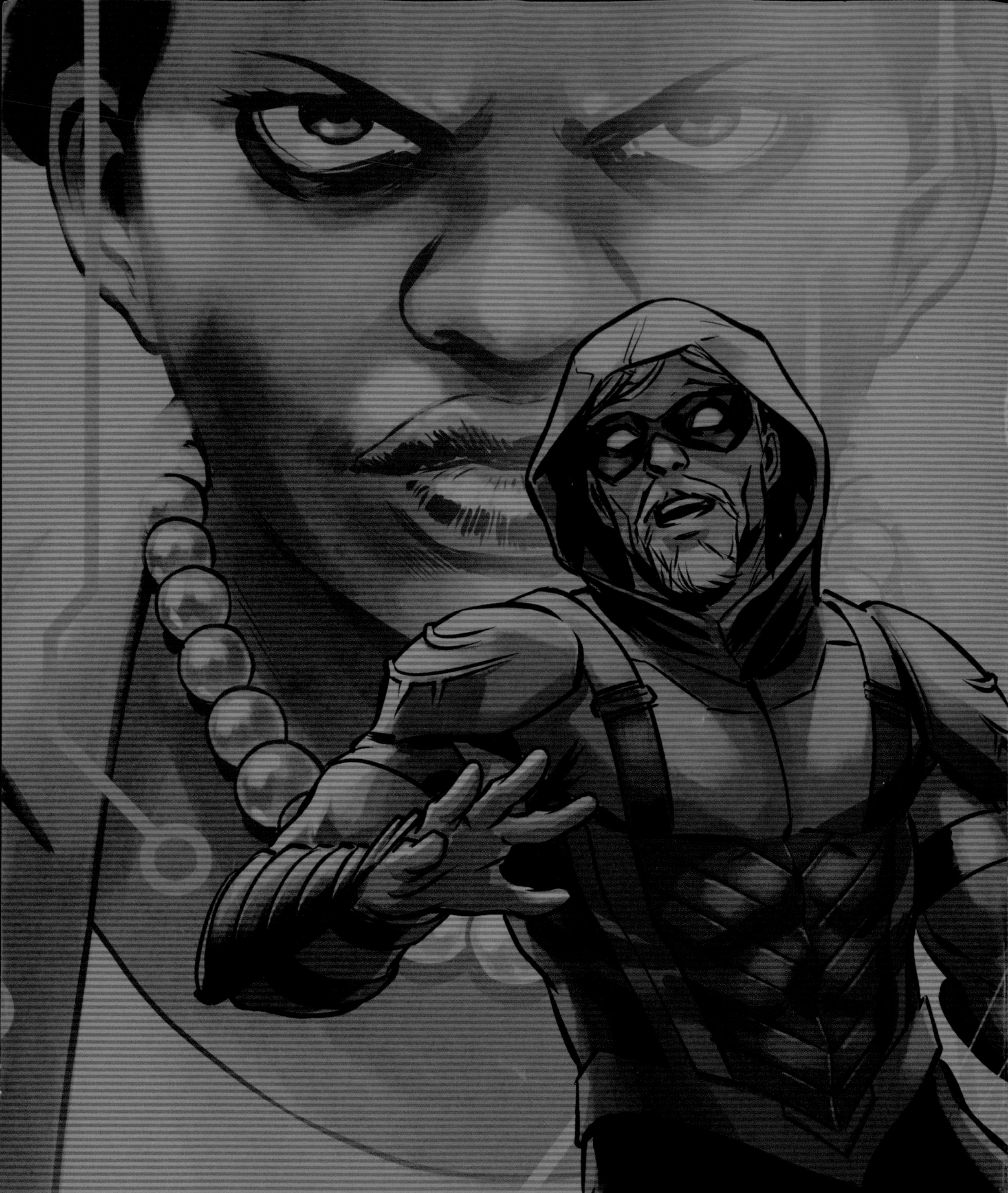

GREEN ARROW
ANNUAL #2

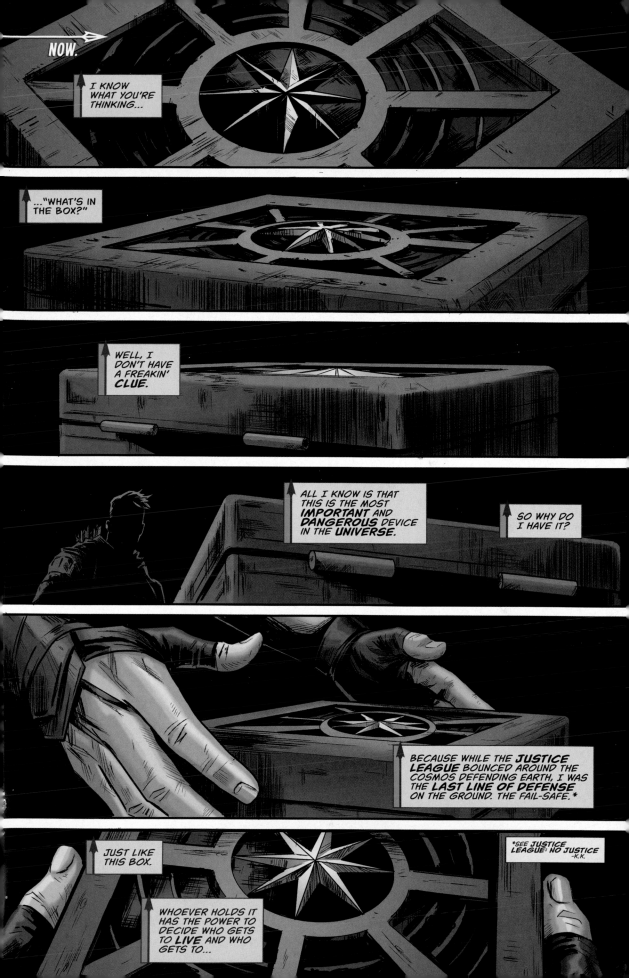

I KNOW WHAT YOU'RE THINKING...

..."WHAT'S IN THE BOX?"

WELL, I DON'T HAVE A FREAKIN' CLUE.

ALL I KNOW IS THAT THIS IS THE MOST IMPORTANT AND DANGEROUS DEVICE IN THE UNIVERSE.

SO WHY DO I HAVE IT?

BECAUSE WHILE THE JUSTICE LEAGUE BOUNCED AROUND THE COSMOS DEFENDING EARTH, I WAS THE LAST LINE OF DEFENSE ON THE GROUND. THE FAIL-SAFE. *

JUST LIKE THIS BOX.

*SEE JUSTICE LEAGUE: NO JUSTICE —K.K.

WHOEVER HOLDS IT HAS THE POWER TO DECIDE WHO GETS TO LIVE AND WHO GETS TO...

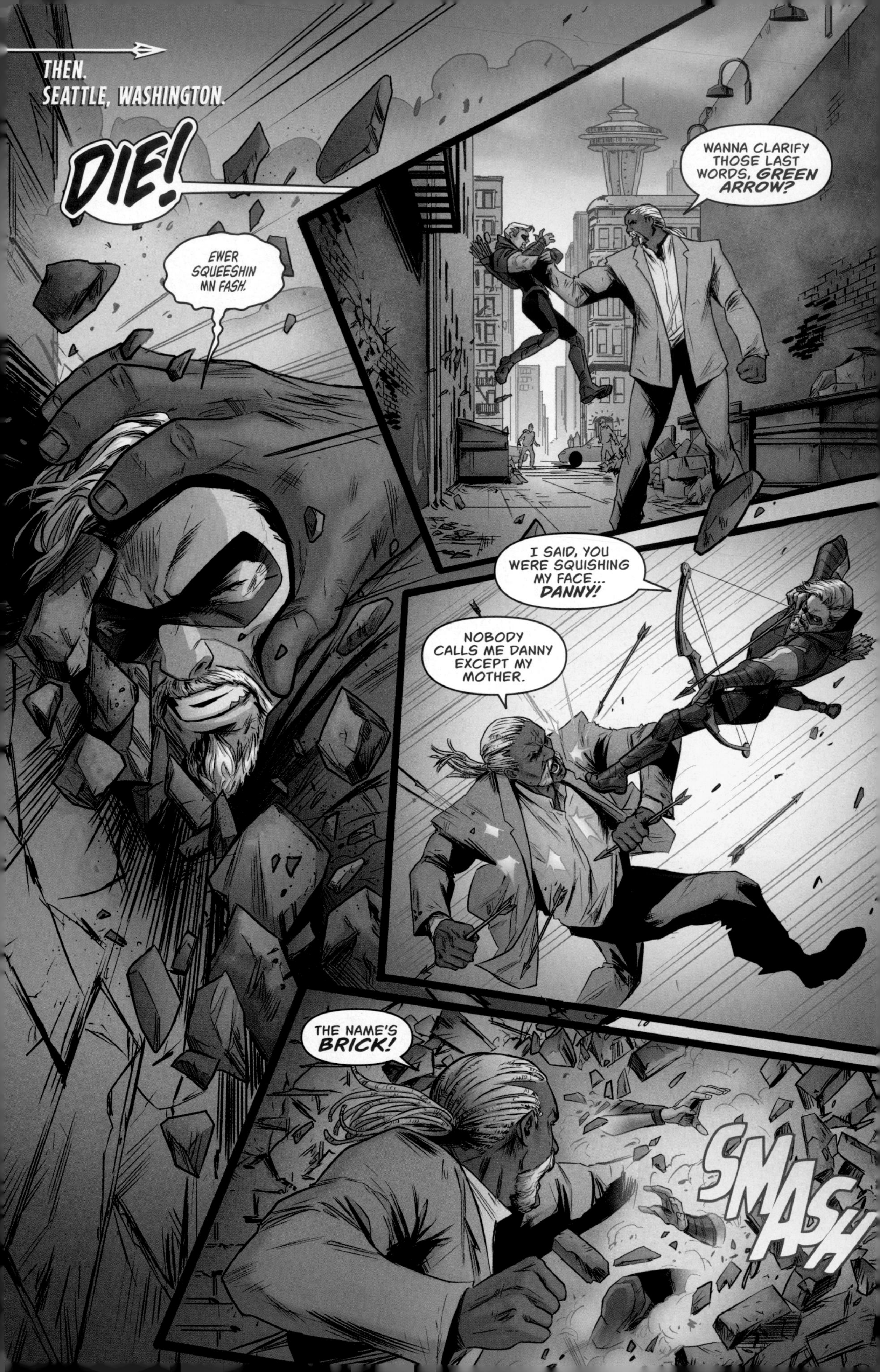
THEN.
SEATTLE, WASHINGTON.
DIE!
EWER SQUEESHIN MN FASH.
WANNA CLARIFY THOSE LAST WORDS, GREEN ARROW?
I SAID, YOU WERE SQUISHING MY FACE... DANNY!
NOBODY CALLS ME DANNY EXCEPT MY MOTHER.
THE NAME'S BRICK!
SMASH

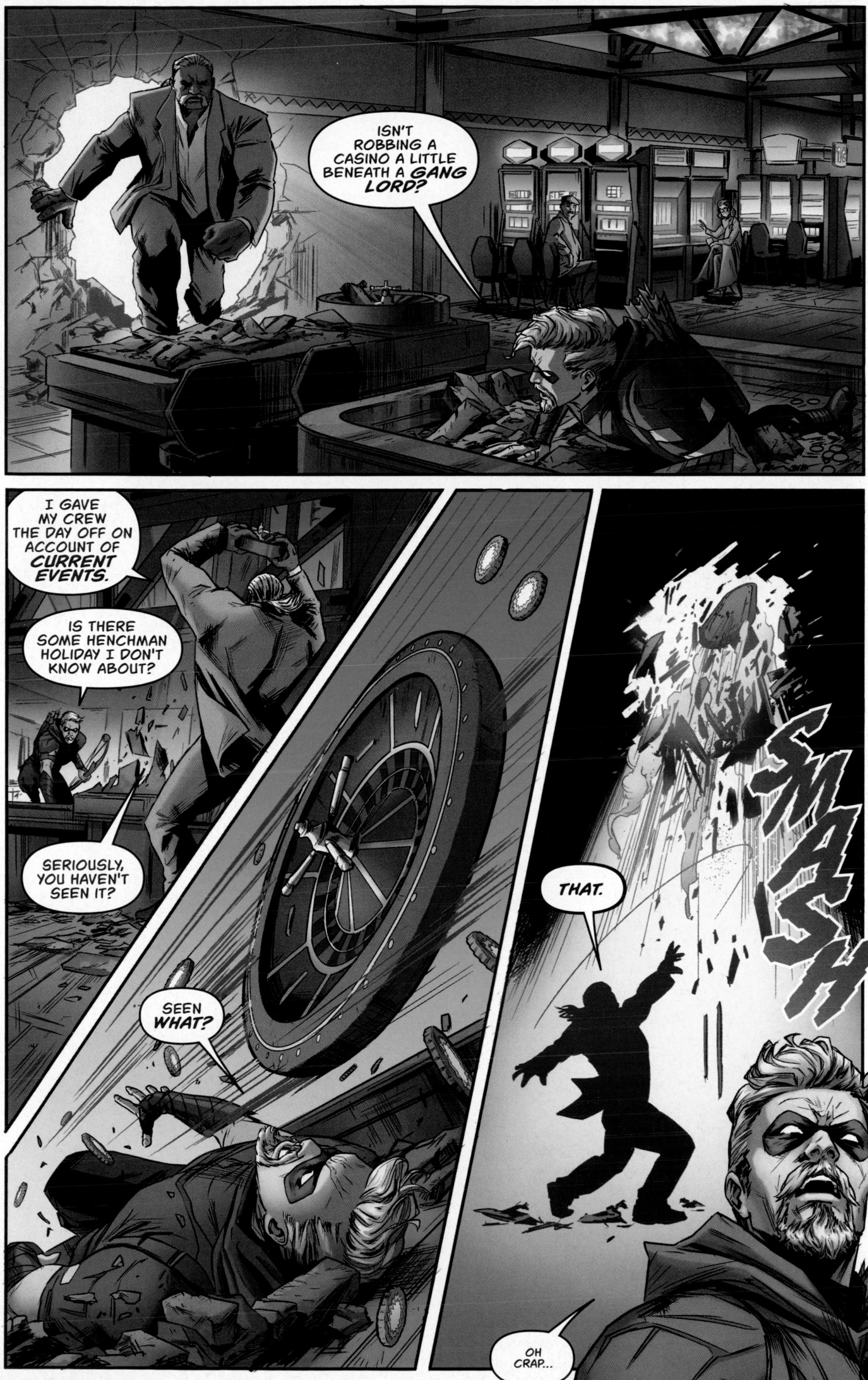
ISN'T ROBBING A CASINO A LITTLE BENEATH A GANG LORD?
I GAVE MY CREW THE DAY OFF ON ACCOUNT OF CURRENT EVENTS.
IS THERE SOME HENCHMAN HOLIDAY I DON'T KNOW ABOUT?
SERIOUSLY, YOU HAVEN'T SEEN IT?
SEEN WHAT?
THAT.
SMASH
OH CRAP...

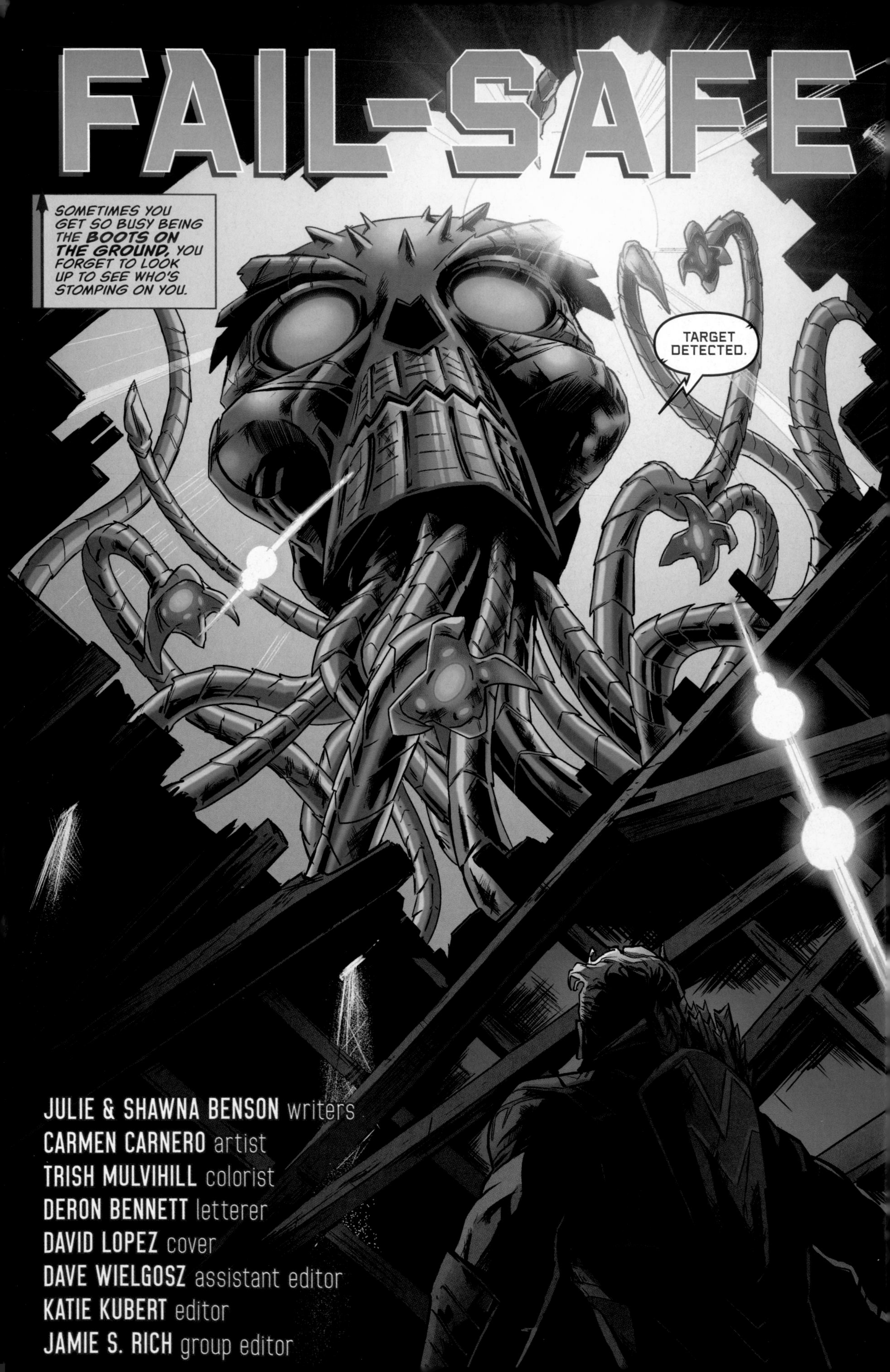
FAIL-SAFE
SOMETIMES YOU GET SO BUSY BEING THE BOOTS ON THE GROUND, YOU FORGET TO LOOK UP TO SEE WHO'S STOMPING ON YOU.
TARGET DETECTED.
JULIE & SHAWNA BENSON writers
CARMEN CARNERO artist
TRISH MULVIHILL colorist
DERON BENNETT letterer
DAVID LOPEZ cover
DAVE WIELGOSZ assistant editor
KATIE KUBERT editor
JAMIE S. RICH group editor

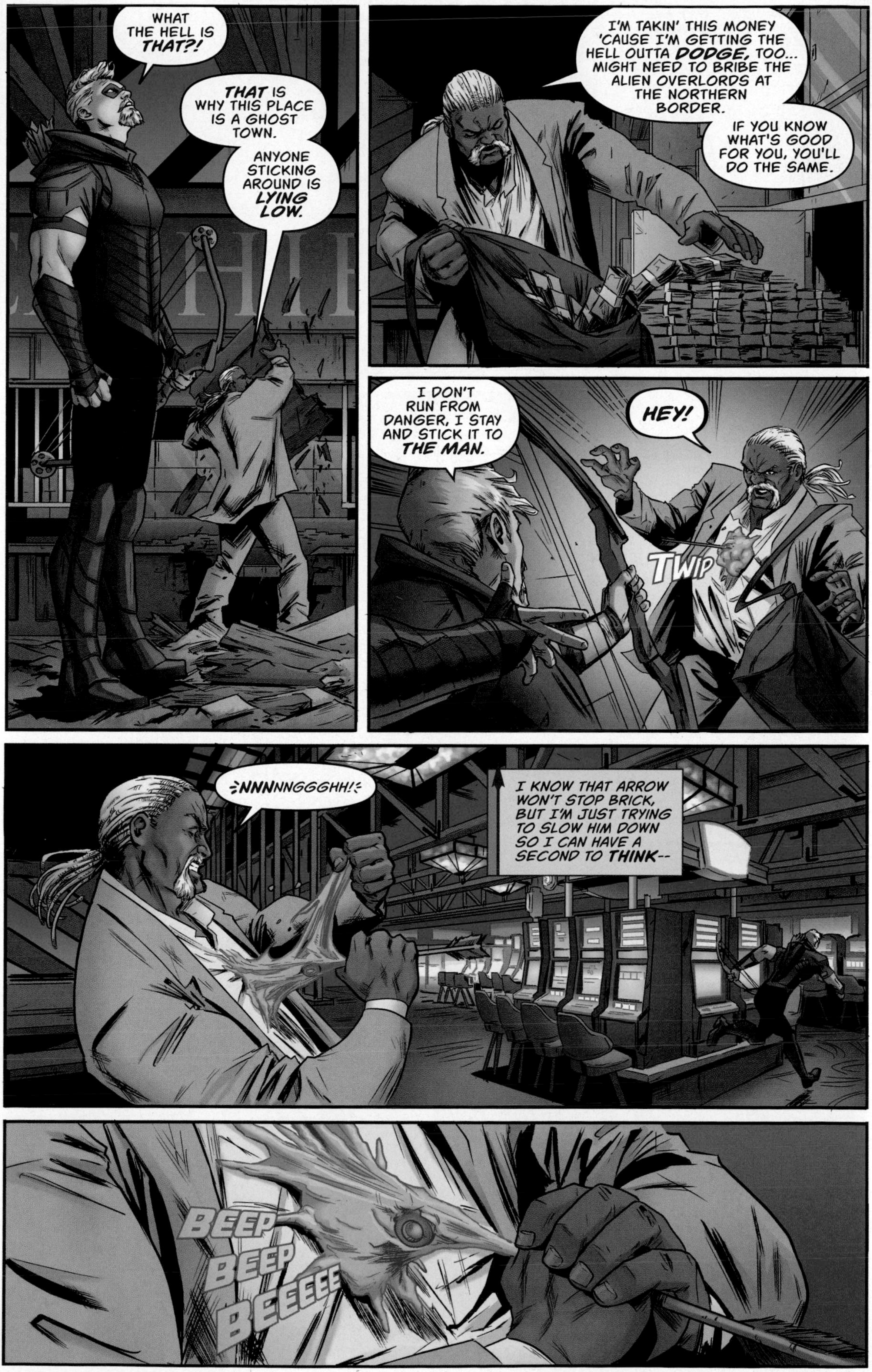
WHAT THE HELL IS THAT?!
THAT IS WHY THIS PLACE IS A GHOST TOWN.
ANYONE STICKING AROUND IS LYING LOW.
I'M TAKIN' THIS MONEY 'CAUSE I'M GETTING THE HELL OUTTA DODGE, TOO... MIGHT NEED TO BRIBE THE ALIEN OVERLORDS AT THE NORTHERN BORDER.
IF YOU KNOW WHAT'S GOOD FOR YOU, YOU'LL DO THE SAME.
I DON'T RUN FROM DANGER, I STAY AND STICK IT TO THE MAN.
HEY!
TWIP
NNNNNGGGHH!
I KNOW THAT ARROW WON'T STOP BRICK, BUT I'M JUST TRYING TO SLOW HIM DOWN SO I CAN HAVE A SECOND TO THINK--
BEEP
BEEP
BEEEEE

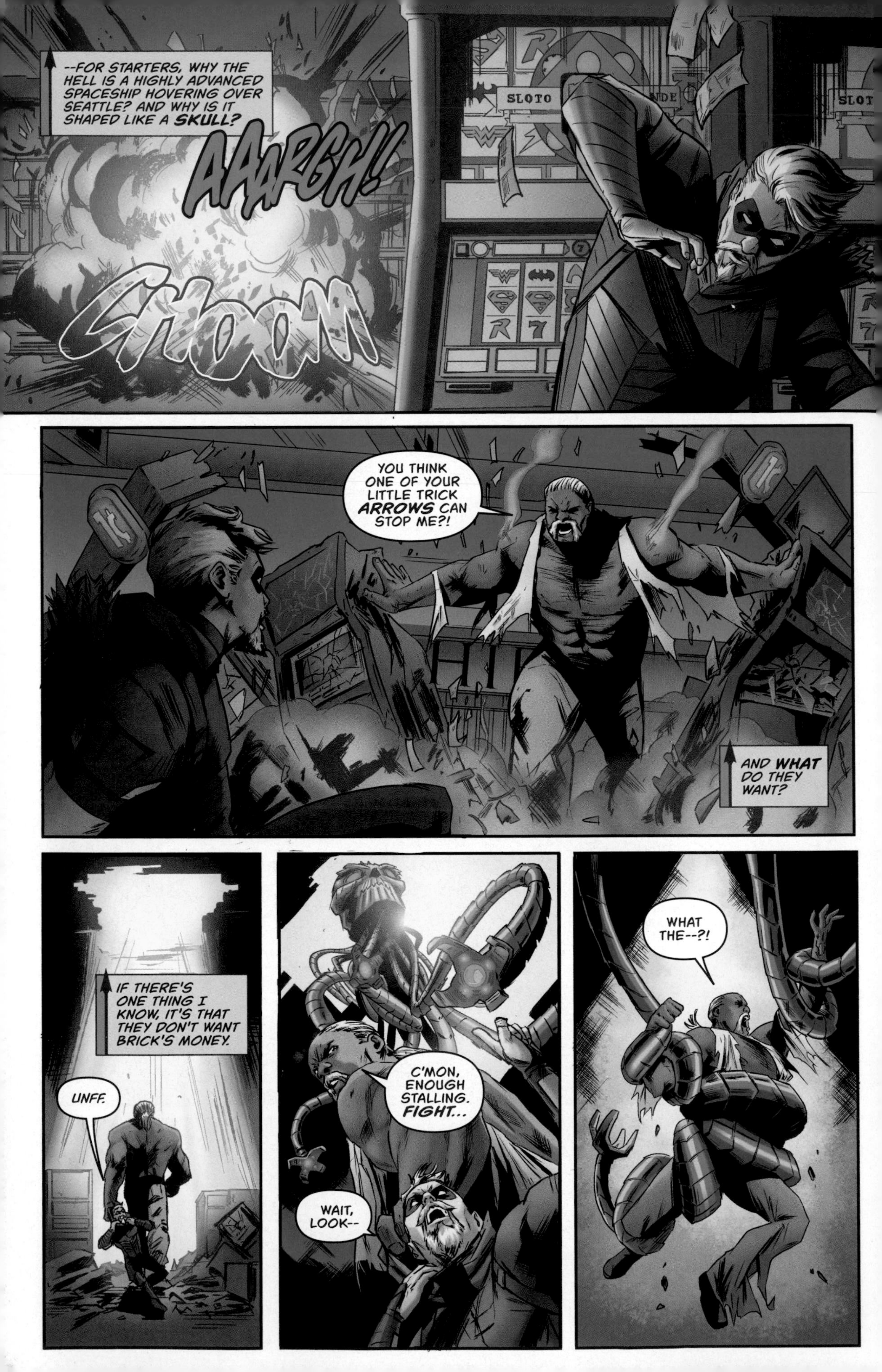
--FOR STARTERS, WHY THE HELL IS A HIGHLY ADVANCED SPACESHIP HOVERING OVER SEATTLE? AND WHY IS IT SHAPED LIKE A SKULL?
AAARGH!
CHOOM
SLOTO
SLOT
YOU THINK ONE OF YOUR LITTLE TRICK ARROWS CAN STOP ME?!
AND WHAT DO THEY WANT?
IF THERE'S ONE THING I KNOW, IT'S THAT THEY DON'T WANT BRICK'S MONEY.
UNFF.
C'MON, ENOUGH STALLING. FIGHT...
WAIT, LOOK--
WHAT THE--?!

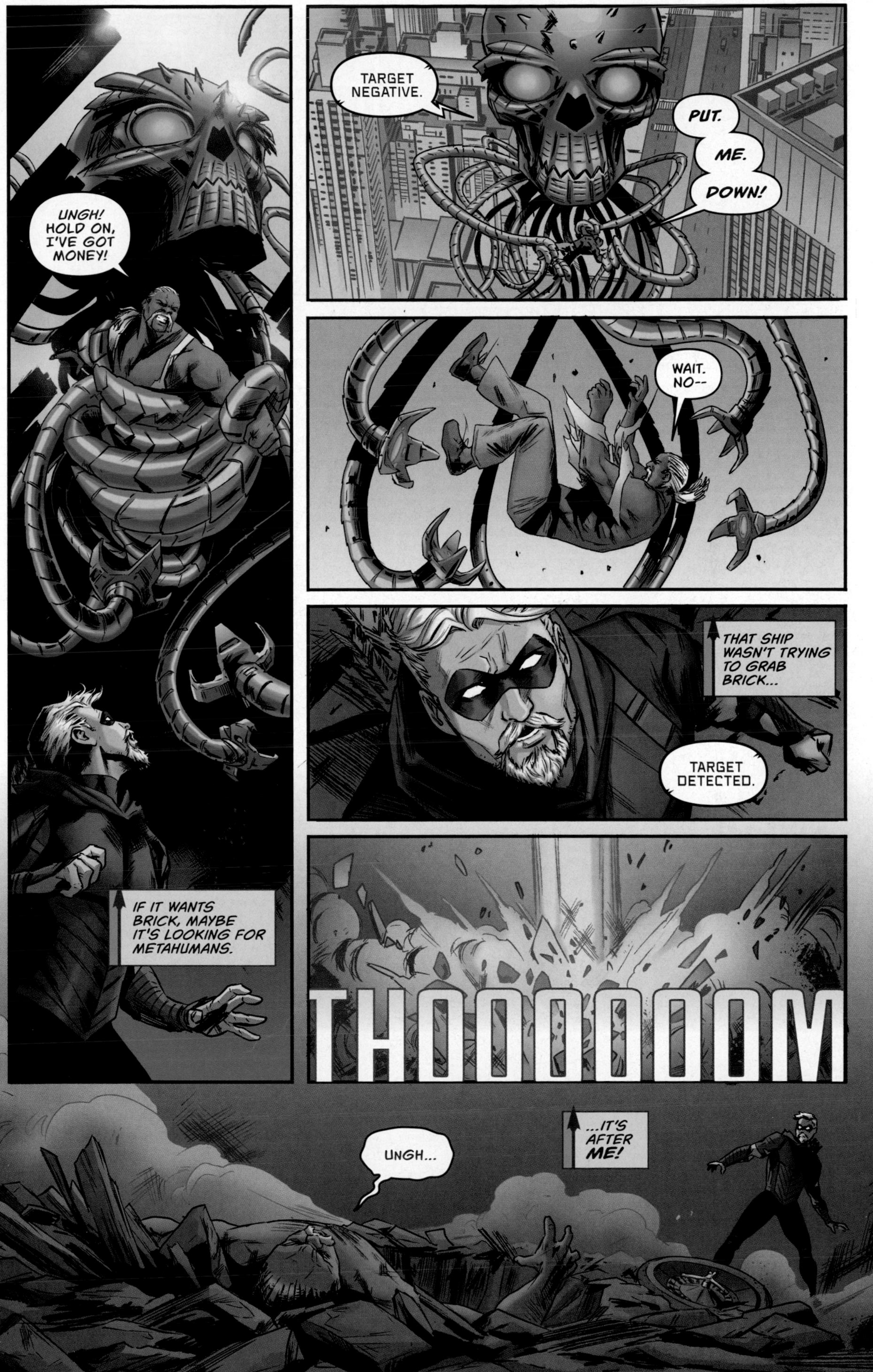
UNGH! HOLD ON, I'VE GOT MONEY!
IF IT WANTS BRICK, MAYBE IT'S LOOKING FOR METAHUMANS.
TARGET NEGATIVE.
PUT.
ME.
DOWN!
WAIT. NO--
THAT SHIP WASN'T TRYING TO GRAB BRICK...
TARGET DETECTED.
THOOOOOOM
UNGH...
...IT'S AFTER ME!

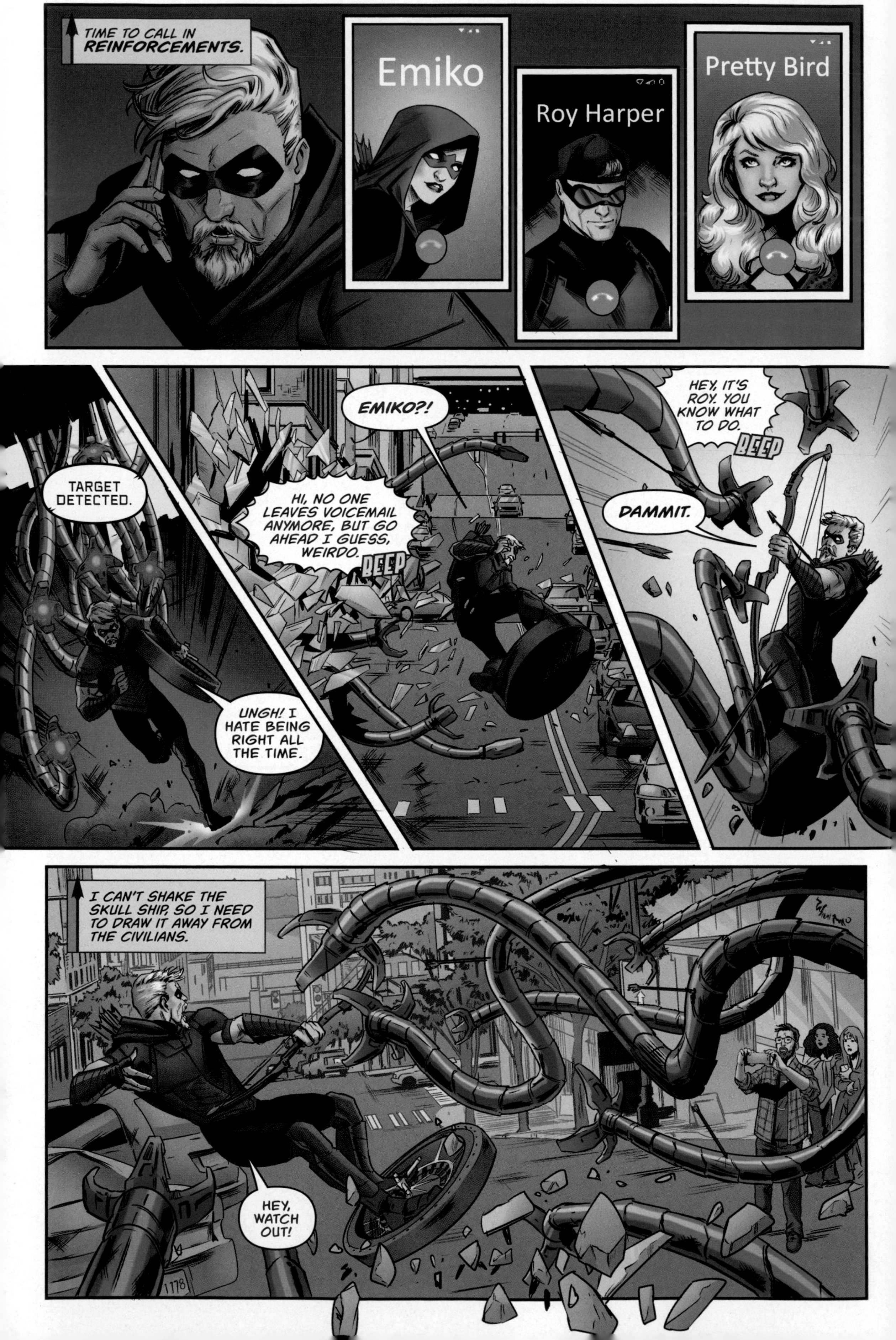
TIME TO CALL IN REINFORCEMENTS.
Emiko
Roy Harper
Pretty Bird
TARGET DETECTED.
UNGH! I HATE BEING RIGHT ALL THE TIME.
EMIKO?!
HI, NO ONE LEAVES VOICEMAIL ANYMORE, BUT GO AHEAD I GUESS, WEIRDO.
BEEP
HEY, IT'S ROY. YOU KNOW WHAT TO DO.
BEEP
DAMMIT.
I CAN'T SHAKE THE SKULL SHIP, SO I NEED TO DRAW IT AWAY FROM THE CIVILIANS.
HEY, WATCH OUT!

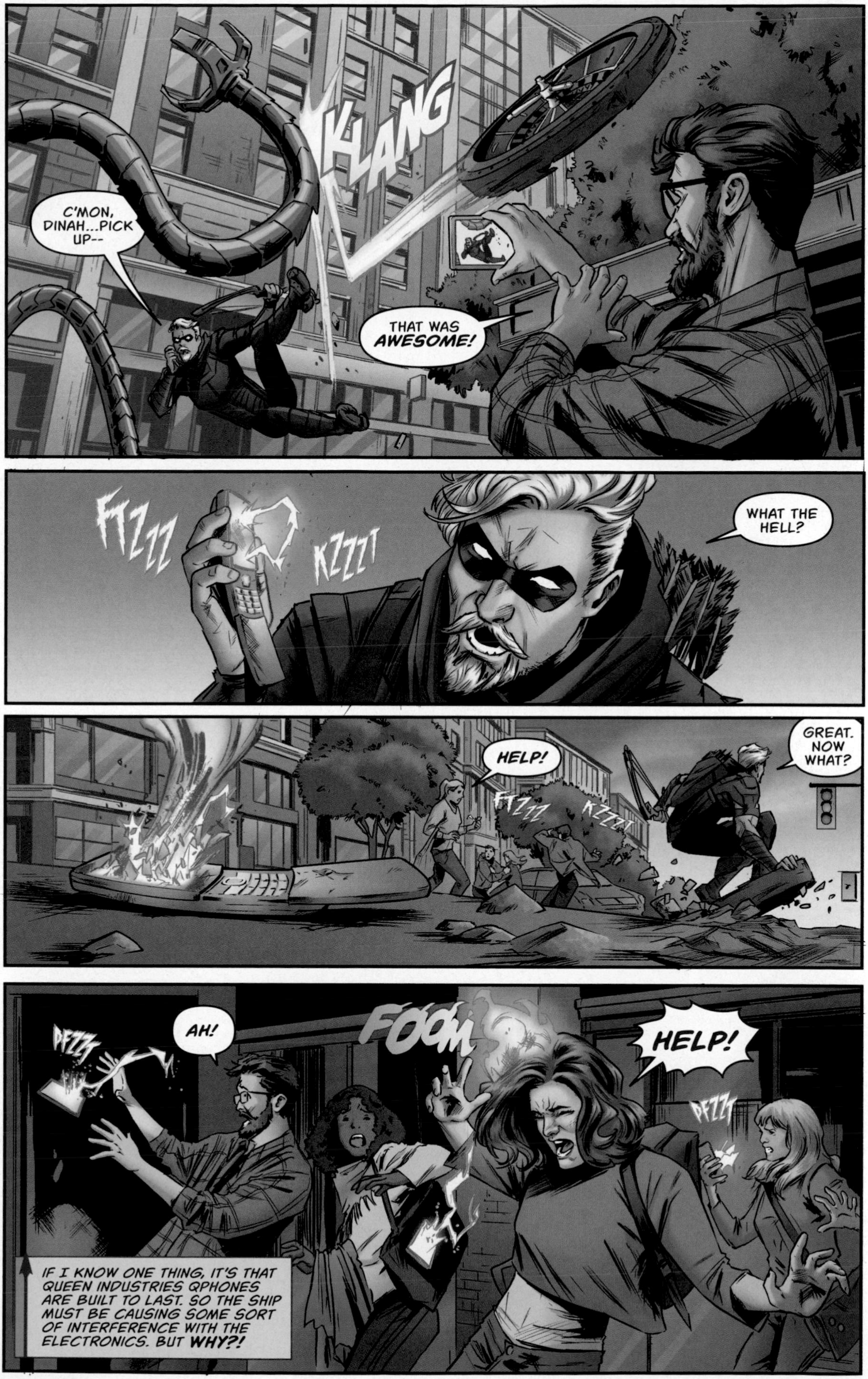
KLANG
C'MON, DINAH...PICK UP--
THAT WAS AWESOME!
FTZZZ
KZZZT
WHAT THE HELL?
HELP!
FTZZZ
KZZZT
GREAT. NOW WHAT?
AH!
PFZZT
FOOM
HELP!
PFZZT
IF I KNOW ONE THING, IT'S THAT QUEEN INDUSTRIES QPHONES ARE BUILT TO LAST. SO THE SHIP MUST BE CAUSING SOME SORT OF INTERFERENCE WITH THE ELECTRONICS. BUT WHY?!

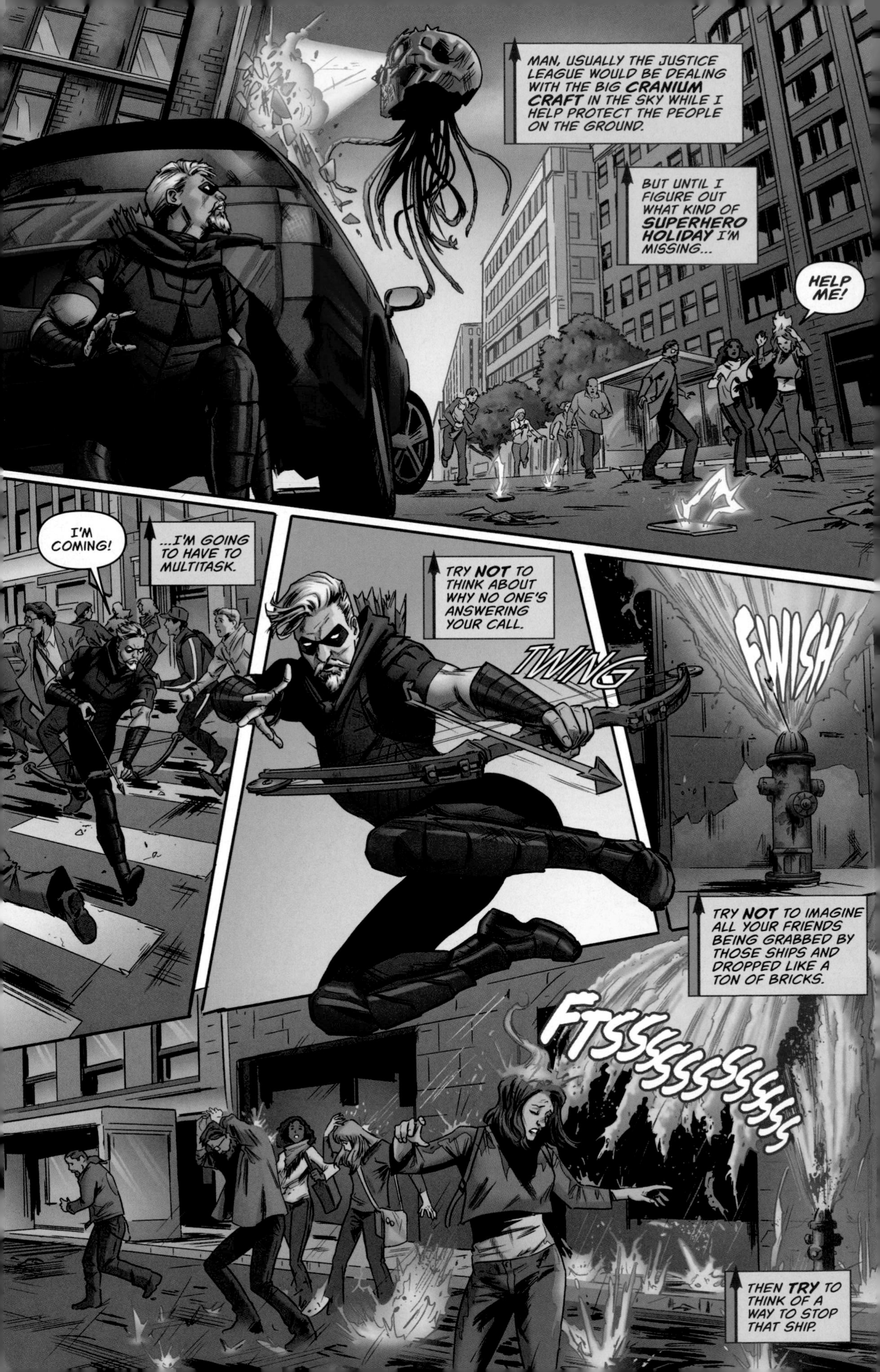
MAN, USUALLY THE JUSTICE LEAGUE WOULD BE DEALING WITH THE BIG CRANIUM CRAFT IN THE SKY WHILE I HELP PROTECT THE PEOPLE ON THE GROUND.
BUT UNTIL I FIGURE OUT WHAT KIND OF SUPERHERO HOLIDAY I'M MISSING...
HELP ME!
I'M COMING!
...I'M GOING TO HAVE TO MULTITASK.
TRY NOT TO THINK ABOUT WHY NO ONE'S ANSWERING YOUR CALL.
TWING
FWISH
TRY NOT TO IMAGINE ALL YOUR FRIENDS BEING GRABBED BY THOSE SHIPS AND DROPPED LIKE A TON OF BRICKS.
FTSSSSSSSSSSS
THEN TRY TO THINK OF A WAY TO STOP THAT SHIP.

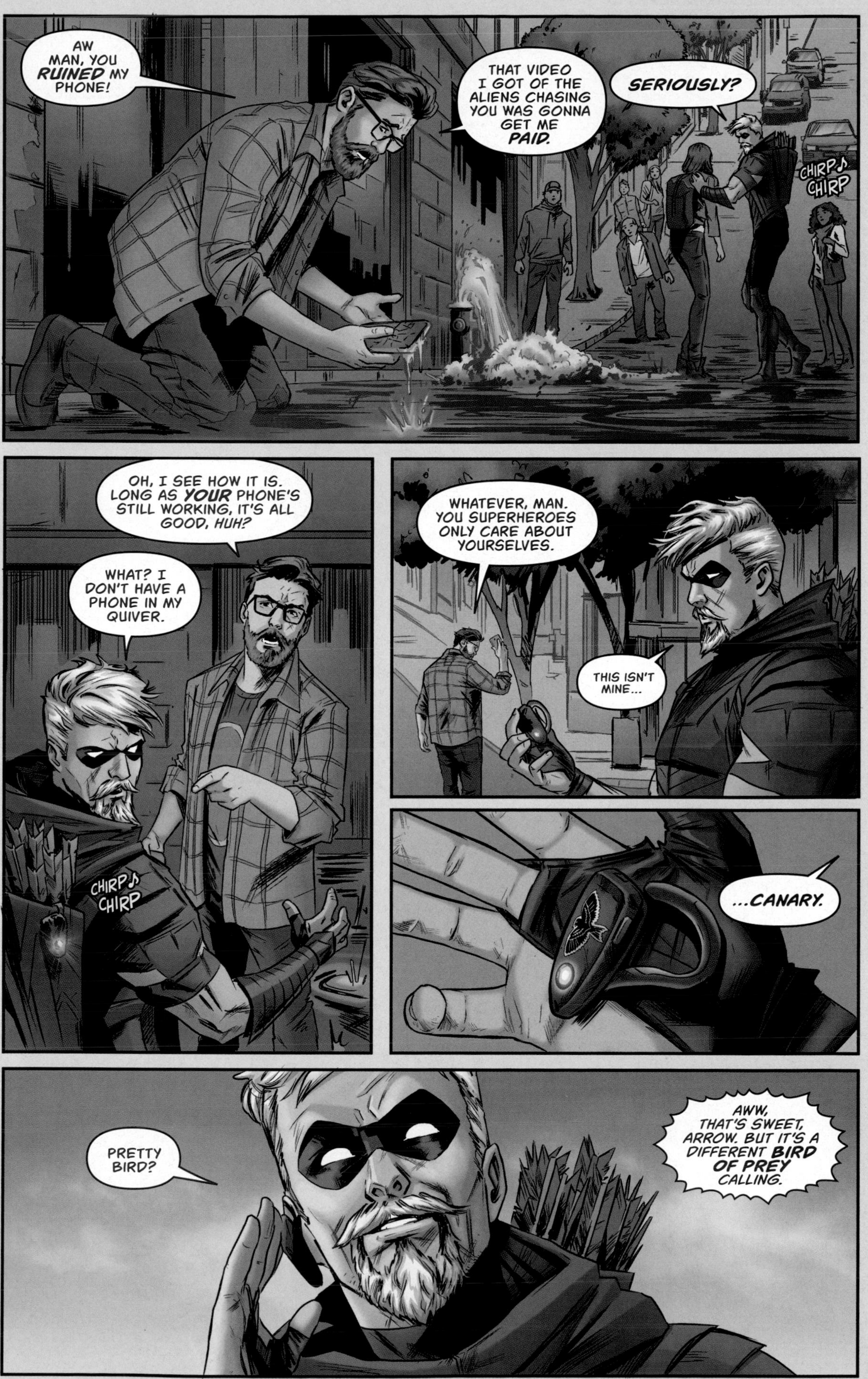
AW MAN, YOU RUINED MY PHONE!
THAT VIDEO I GOT OF THE ALIENS CHASING YOU WAS GONNA GET ME PAID.
SERIOUSLY?
CHIRP♪ CHIRP
OH, I SEE HOW IT IS. LONG AS YOUR PHONE'S STILL WORKING, IT'S ALL GOOD, HUH?
WHAT? I DON'T HAVE A PHONE IN MY QUIVER.
CHIRP♪ CHIRP
WHATEVER, MAN. YOU SUPERHEROES ONLY CARE ABOUT YOURSELVES.
THIS ISN'T MINE...
...CANARY.
PRETTY BIRD?
AWW, THAT'S SWEET, ARROW. BUT IT'S A DIFFERENT BIRD OF PREY CALLING.

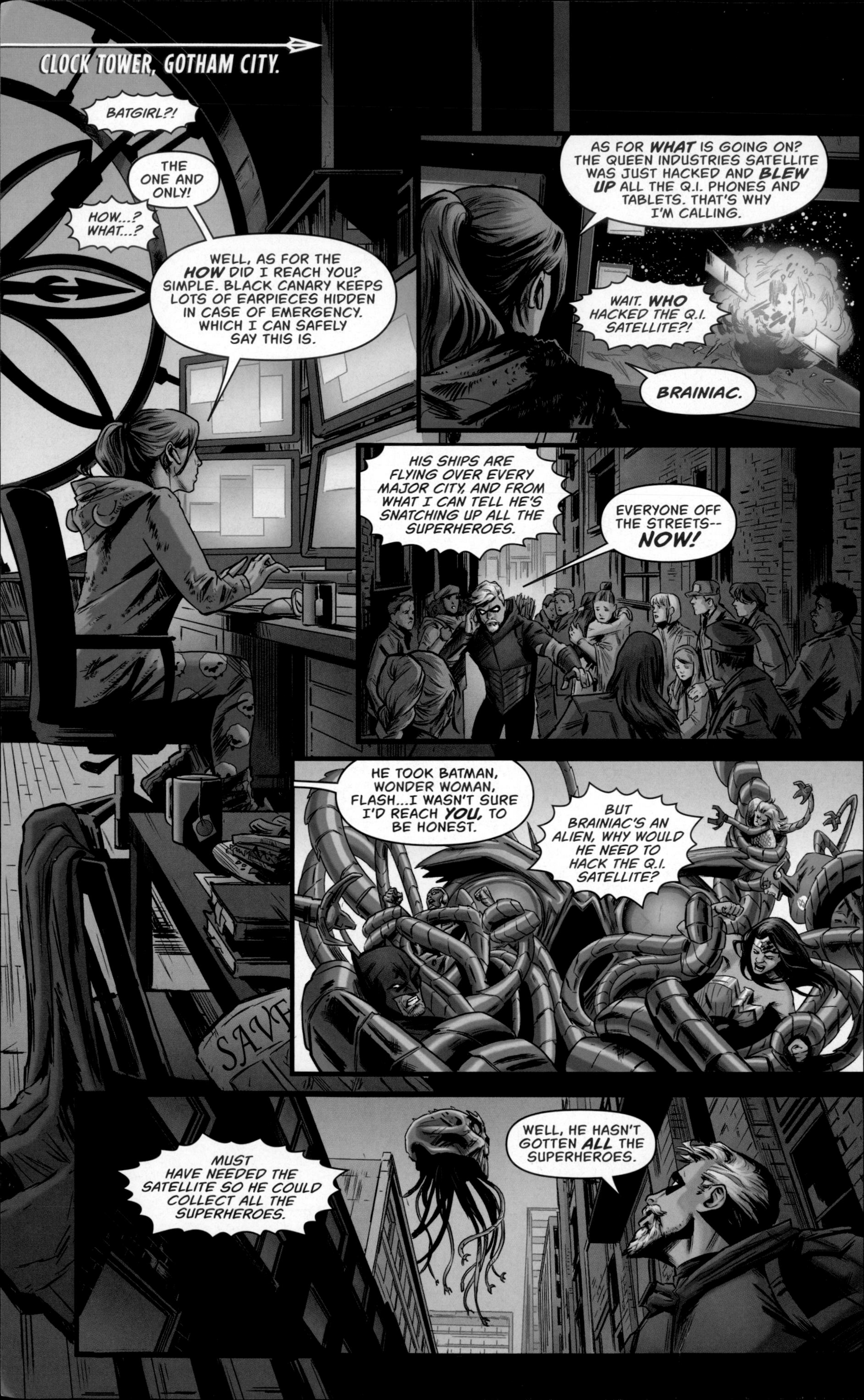
CLOCK TOWER, GOTHAM CITY.
BATGIRL?!
THE ONE AND ONLY!
HOW...? WHAT...?
WELL, AS FOR THE HOW DID I REACH YOU? SIMPLE. BLACK CANARY KEEPS LOTS OF EARPIECES HIDDEN IN CASE OF EMERGENCY. WHICH I CAN SAFELY SAY THIS IS.
AS FOR WHAT IS GOING ON? THE QUEEN INDUSTRIES SATELLITE WAS JUST HACKED AND BLEW UP ALL THE Q.I. PHONES AND TABLETS. THAT'S WHY I'M CALLING.
WAIT. WHO HACKED THE Q.I. SATELLITE?!
BRAINIAC.
HIS SHIPS ARE FLYING OVER EVERY MAJOR CITY, AND FROM WHAT I CAN TELL HE'S SNATCHING UP ALL THE SUPERHEROES.
EVERYONE OFF THE STREETS-- NOW!
HE TOOK BATMAN, WONDER WOMAN, FLASH...I WASN'T SURE I'D REACH YOU, TO BE HONEST.
BUT BRAINIAC'S AN ALIEN, WHY WOULD HE NEED TO HACK THE Q.I. SATELLITE?
MUST HAVE NEEDED THE SATELLITE SO HE COULD COLLECT ALL THE SUPERHEROES.
WELL, HE HASN'T GOTTEN ALL THE SUPERHEROES.

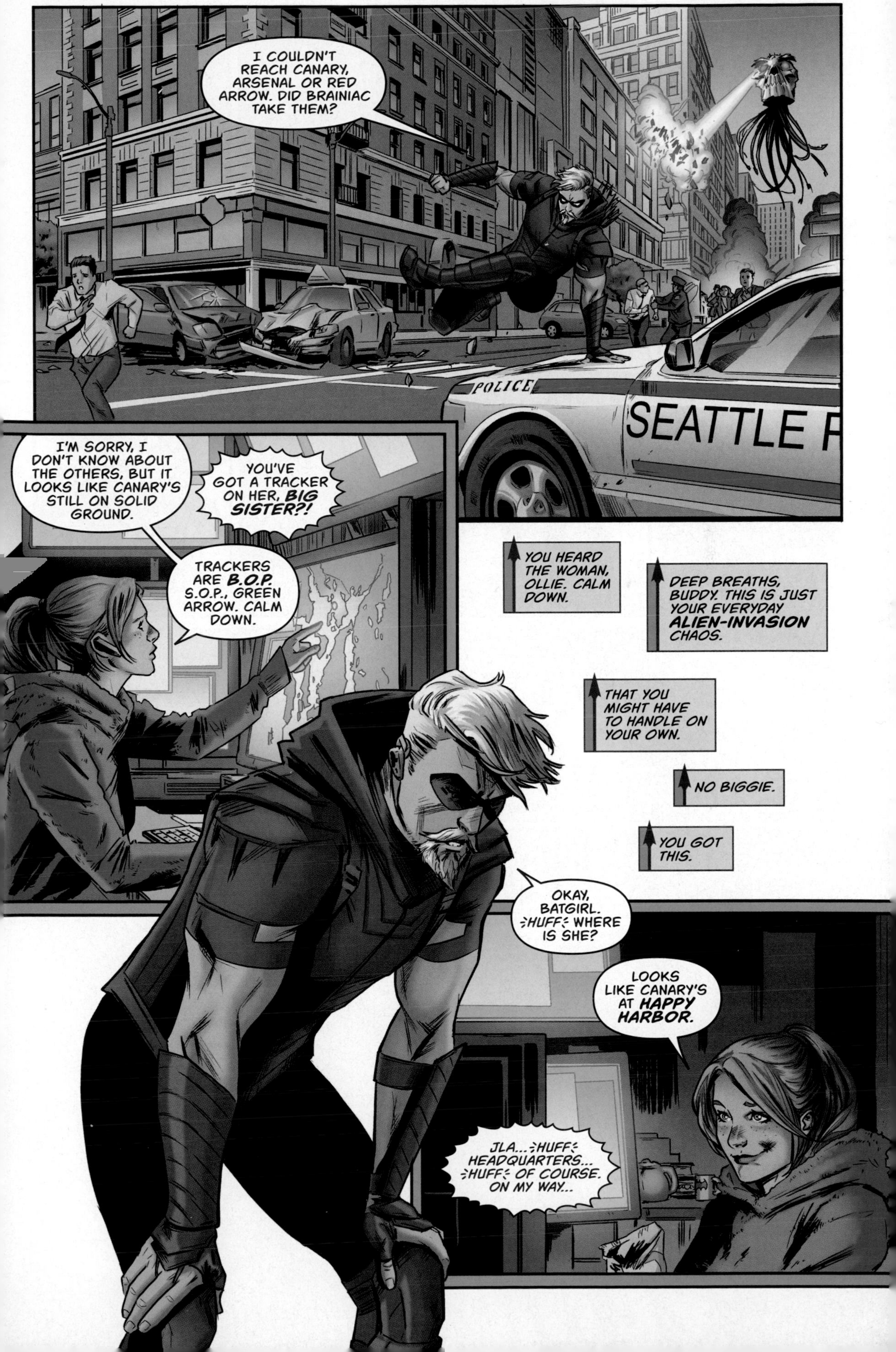

I COULDN'T REACH CANARY, ARSENAL OR RED ARROW. DID BRAINIAC TAKE THEM?
POLICE
SEATTLE P
I'M SORRY, I DON'T KNOW ABOUT THE OTHERS, BUT IT LOOKS LIKE CANARY'S STILL ON SOLID GROUND.
YOU'VE GOT A TRACKER ON HER, BIG SISTER?!
TRACKERS ARE B.O.P. S.O.P., GREEN ARROW. CALM DOWN.
YOU HEARD THE WOMAN, OLLIE. CALM DOWN.
DEEP BREATHS, BUDDY. THIS IS JUST YOUR EVERYDAY ALIEN-INVASION CHAOS.
THAT YOU MIGHT HAVE TO HANDLE ON YOUR OWN.
NO BIGGIE.
YOU GOT THIS.
OKAY, BATGIRL. HUFF WHERE IS SHE?
LOOKS LIKE CANARY'S AT HAPPY HARBOR.
JLA... HUFF HEADQUARTERS... HUFF OF COURSE. ON MY WAY...

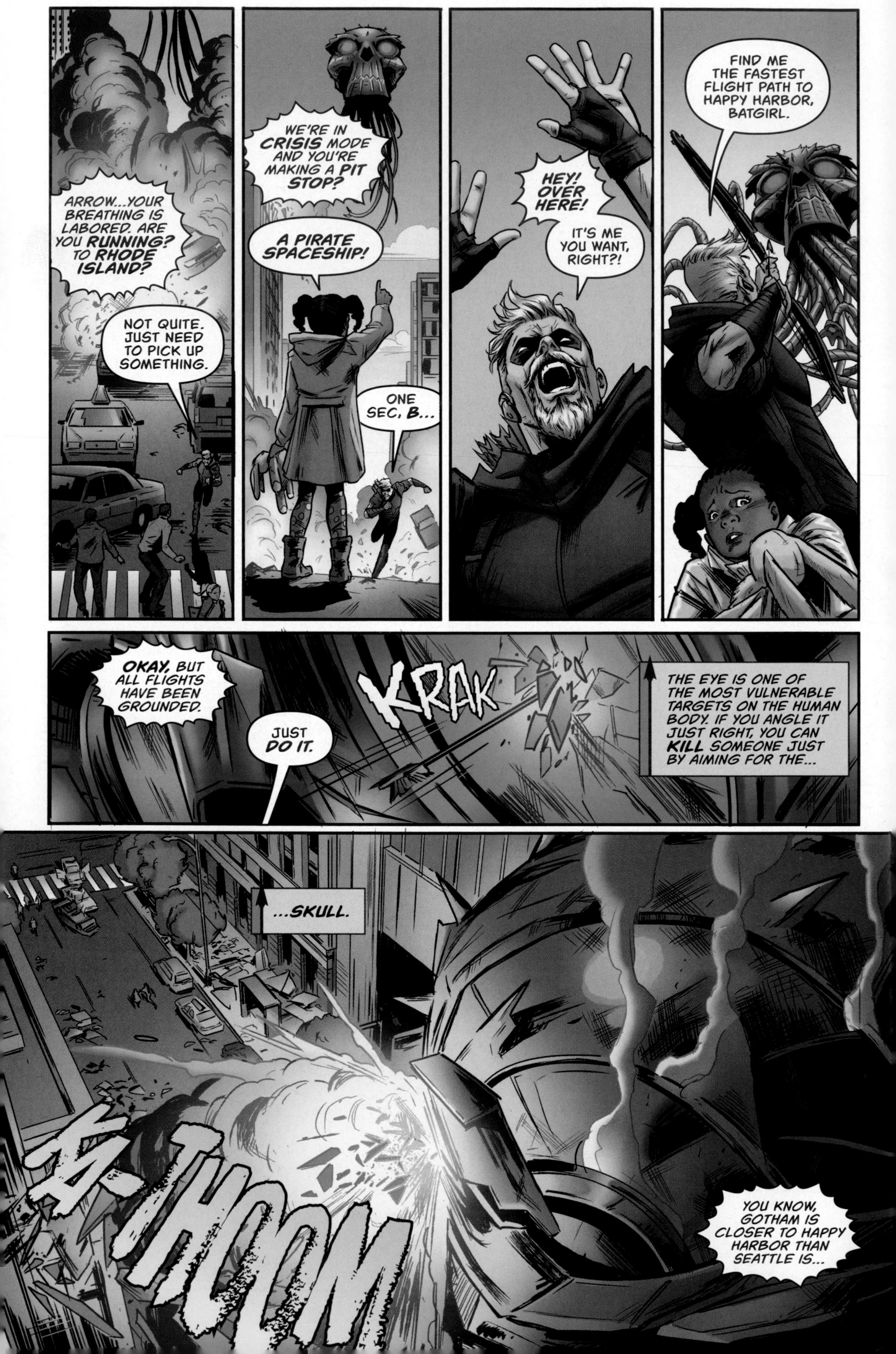
ARROW...YOUR BREATHING IS LABORED. ARE YOU RUNNING? TO RHODE ISLAND?
NOT QUITE. JUST NEED TO PICK UP SOMETHING.
WE'RE IN CRISIS MODE AND YOU'RE MAKING A PIT STOP?
A PIRATE SPACESHIP!
ONE SEC, B...
HEY! OVER HERE!
IT'S ME YOU WANT, RIGHT?!
FIND ME THE FASTEST FLIGHT PATH TO HAPPY HARBOR, BATGIRL.
OKAY, BUT ALL FLIGHTS HAVE BEEN GROUNDED.
JUST DO IT.
KRAK
THE EYE IS ONE OF THE MOST VULNERABLE TARGETS ON THE HUMAN BODY. IF YOU ANGLE IT JUST RIGHT, YOU CAN KILL SOMEONE JUST BY AIMING FOR THE...
...SKULL.
K-THOOM
YOU KNOW, GOTHAM IS CLOSER TO HAPPY HARBOR THAN SEATTLE IS...

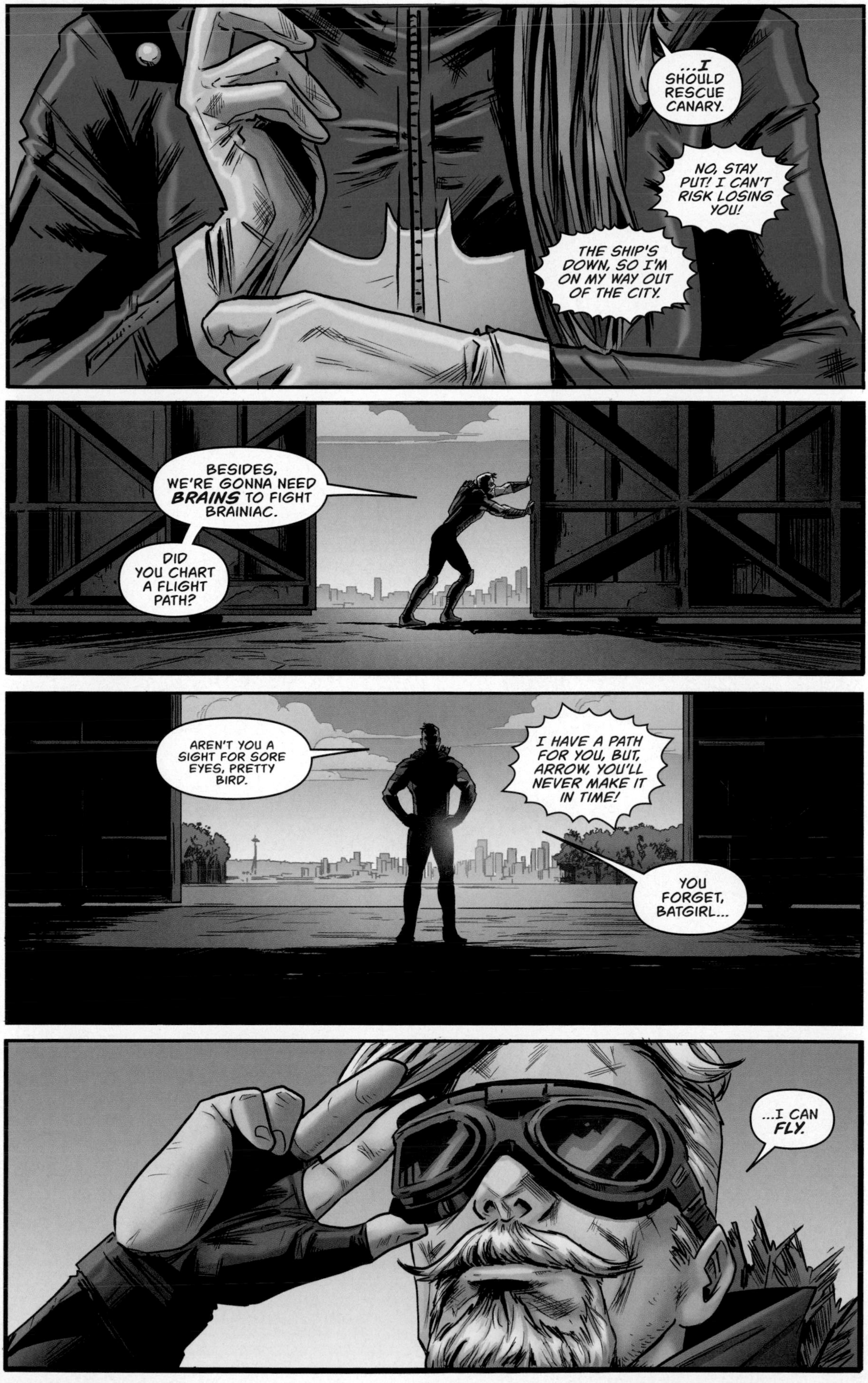
...I SHOULD RESCUE CANARY.
NO, STAY PUT! I CAN'T RISK LOSING YOU!
THE SHIP'S DOWN, SO I'M ON MY WAY OUT OF THE CITY.
BESIDES, WE'RE GONNA NEED BRAINS TO FIGHT BRAINIAC.
DID YOU CHART A FLIGHT PATH?
AREN'T YOU A SIGHT FOR SORE EYES, PRETTY BIRD.
I HAVE A PATH FOR YOU, BUT, ARROW, YOU'LL NEVER MAKE IT IN TIME!
YOU FORGET, BATGIRL...
...I CAN FLY.

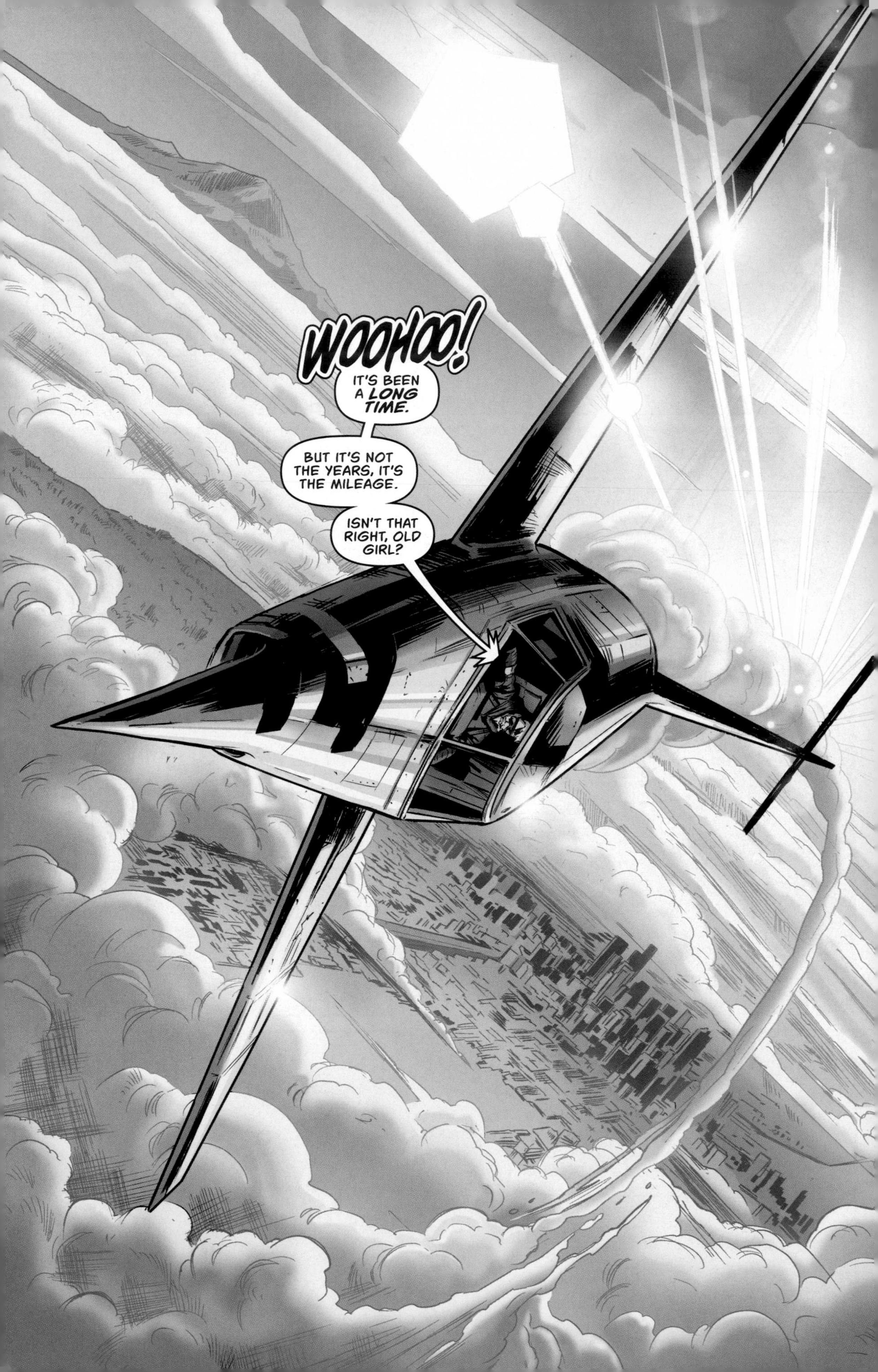
WOOHOO!
IT'S BEEN A LONG TIME.
BUT IT'S NOT THE YEARS, IT'S THE MILEAGE.
ISN'T THAT RIGHT, OLD GIRL?

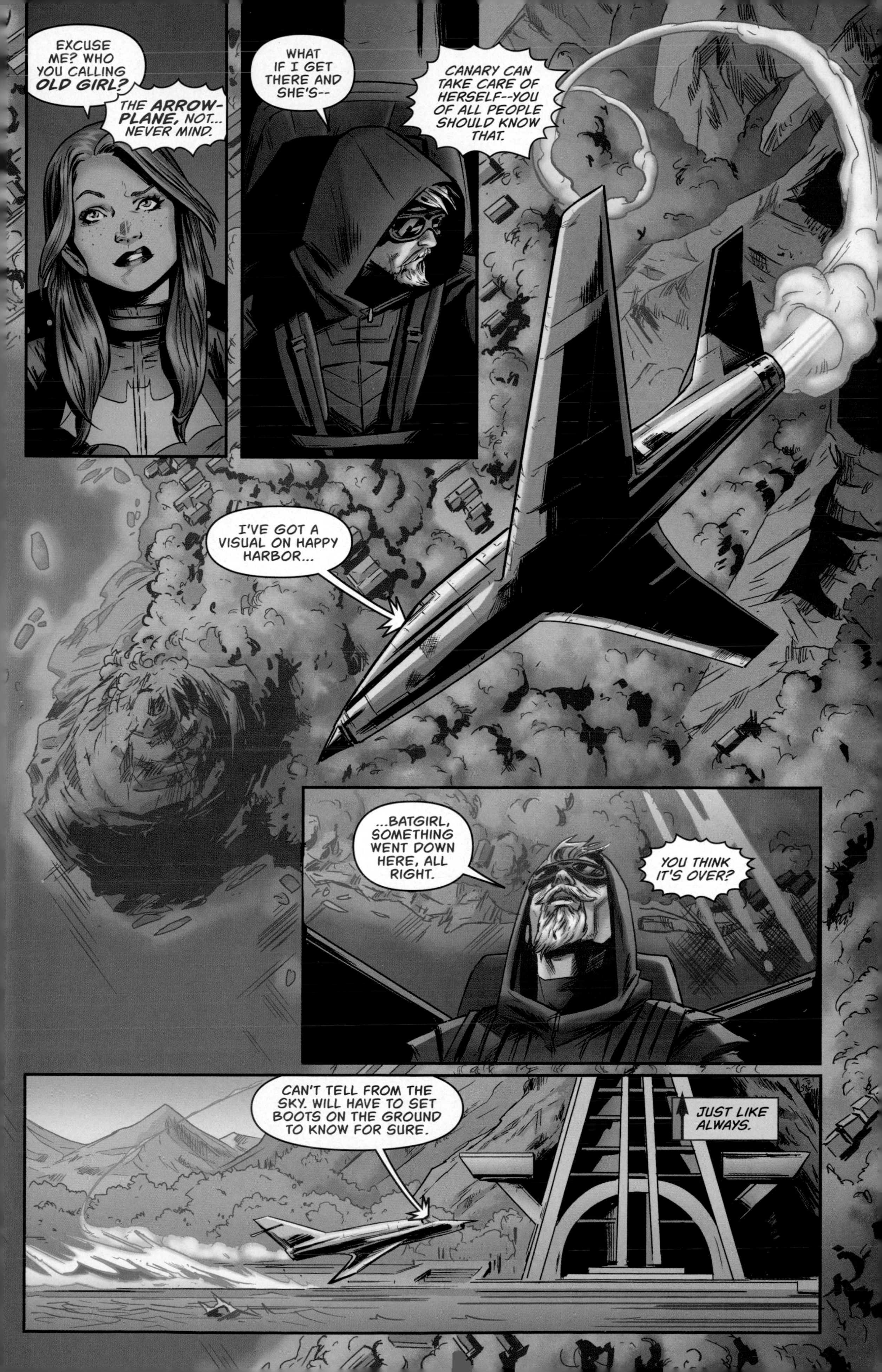
EXCUSE ME? WHO YOU CALLING OLD GIRL?
THE ARROW-PLANE, NOT... NEVER MIND.
WHAT IF I GET THERE AND SHE'S--
CANARY CAN TAKE CARE OF HERSELF--YOU OF ALL PEOPLE SHOULD KNOW THAT.
I'VE GOT A VISUAL ON HAPPY HARBOR...
...BATGIRL, SOMETHING WENT DOWN HERE, ALL RIGHT.
YOU THINK IT'S OVER?
CAN'T TELL FROM THE SKY. WILL HAVE TO SET BOOTS ON THE GROUND TO KNOW FOR SURE.
JUST LIKE ALWAYS.

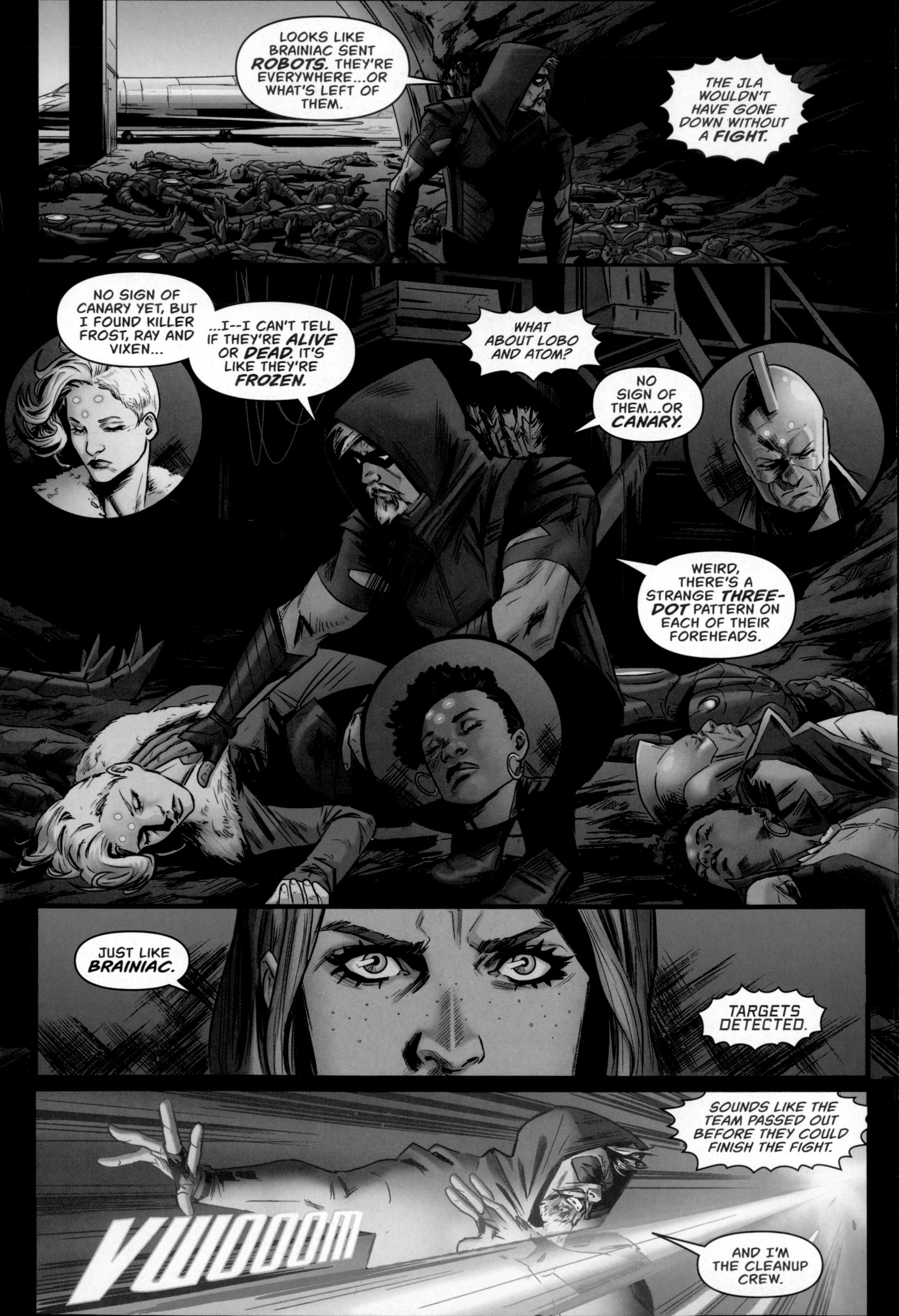

LOOKS LIKE BRAINIAC SENT ROBOTS. THEY'RE EVERYWHERE...OR WHAT'S LEFT OF THEM.
THE JLA WOULDN'T HAVE GONE DOWN WITHOUT A FIGHT.
NO SIGN OF CANARY YET, BUT I FOUND KILLER FROST, RAY AND VIXEN...
...I--I CAN'T TELL IF THEY'RE ALIVE OR DEAD. IT'S LIKE THEY'RE FROZEN.
WHAT ABOUT LOBO AND ATOM?
NO SIGN OF THEM...OR CANARY.
WEIRD, THERE'S A STRANGE THREE-DOT PATTERN ON EACH OF THEIR FOREHEADS.
JUST LIKE BRAINIAC.
TARGETS DETECTED.
SOUNDS LIKE THE TEAM PASSED OUT BEFORE THEY COULD FINISH THE FIGHT.
VWOOOOM
AND I'M THE CLEANUP CREW.

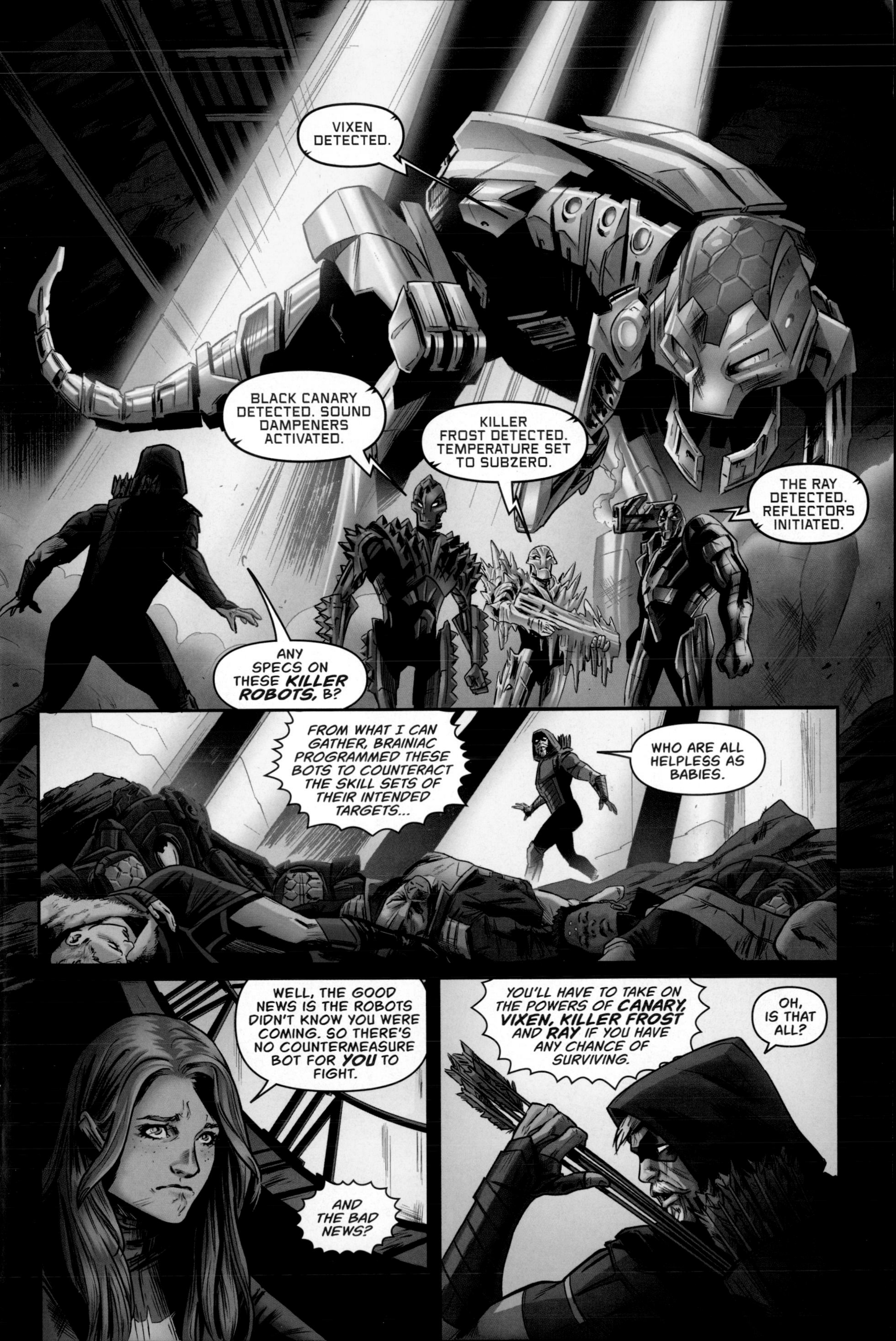
VIXEN DETECTED.
BLACK CANARY DETECTED. SOUND DAMPENERS ACTIVATED.
KILLER FROST DETECTED. TEMPERATURE SET TO SUBZERO.
THE RAY DETECTED. REFLECTORS INITIATED.
ANY SPECS ON THESE KILLER ROBOTS, B?
FROM WHAT I CAN GATHER, BRAINIAC PROGRAMMED THESE BOTS TO COUNTERACT THE SKILL SETS OF THEIR INTENDED TARGETS...
WHO ARE ALL HELPLESS AS BABIES.
WELL, THE GOOD NEWS IS THE ROBOTS DIDN'T KNOW YOU WERE COMING. SO THERE'S NO COUNTERMEASURE BOT FOR YOU TO FIGHT.
AND THE BAD NEWS?
YOU'LL HAVE TO TAKE ON THE POWERS OF CANARY, VIXEN, KILLER FROST AND RAY IF YOU HAVE ANY CHANCE OF SURVIVING.
OH, IS THAT ALL?

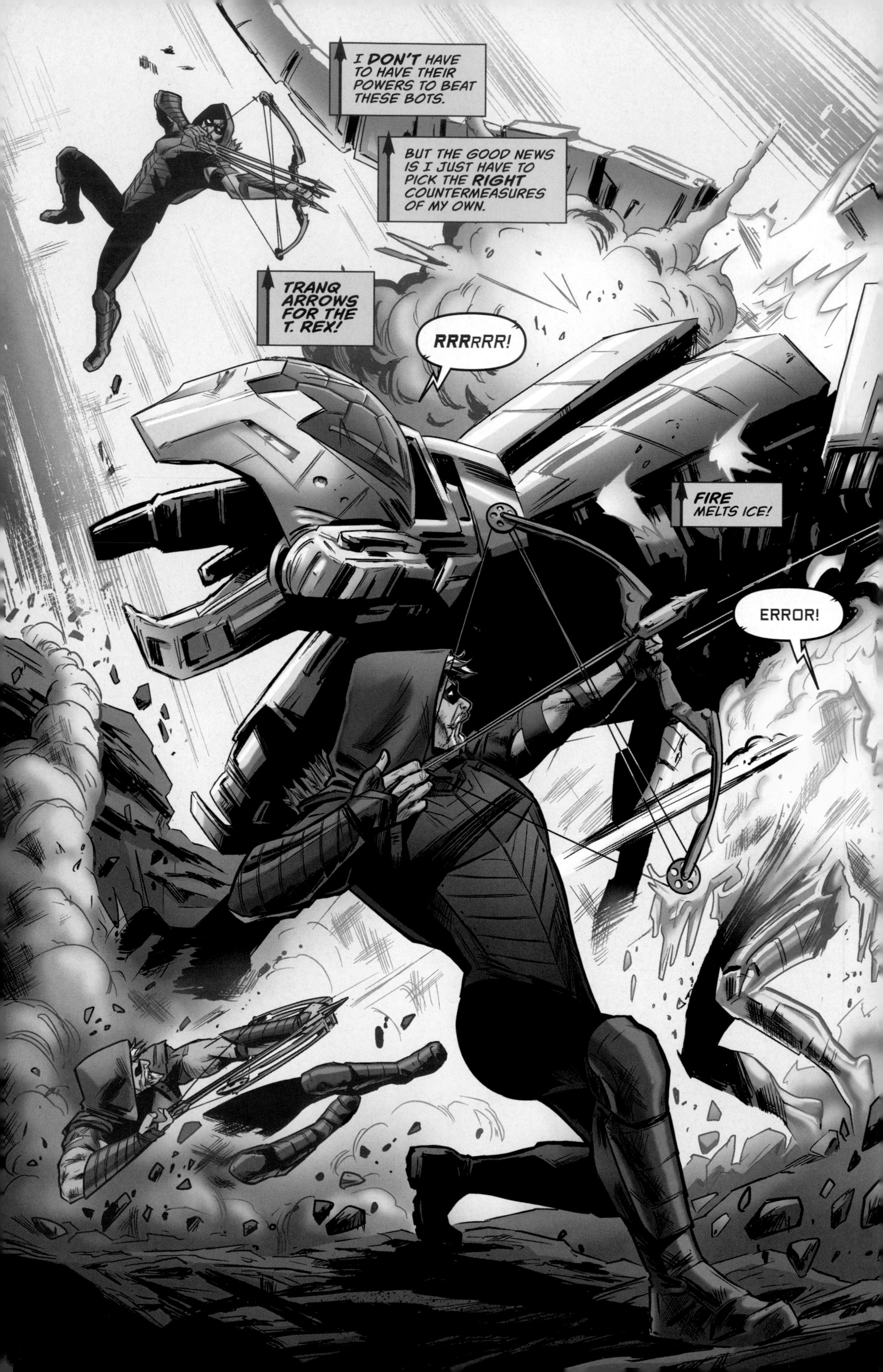
I DON'T HAVE TO HAVE THEIR POWERS TO BEAT THESE BOTS.
BUT THE GOOD NEWS IS I JUST HAVE TO PICK THE RIGHT COUNTERMEASURES OF MY OWN.
TRANQ ARROWS FOR THE T. REX!
RRRRRR!
FIRE MELTS ICE!
ERROR!

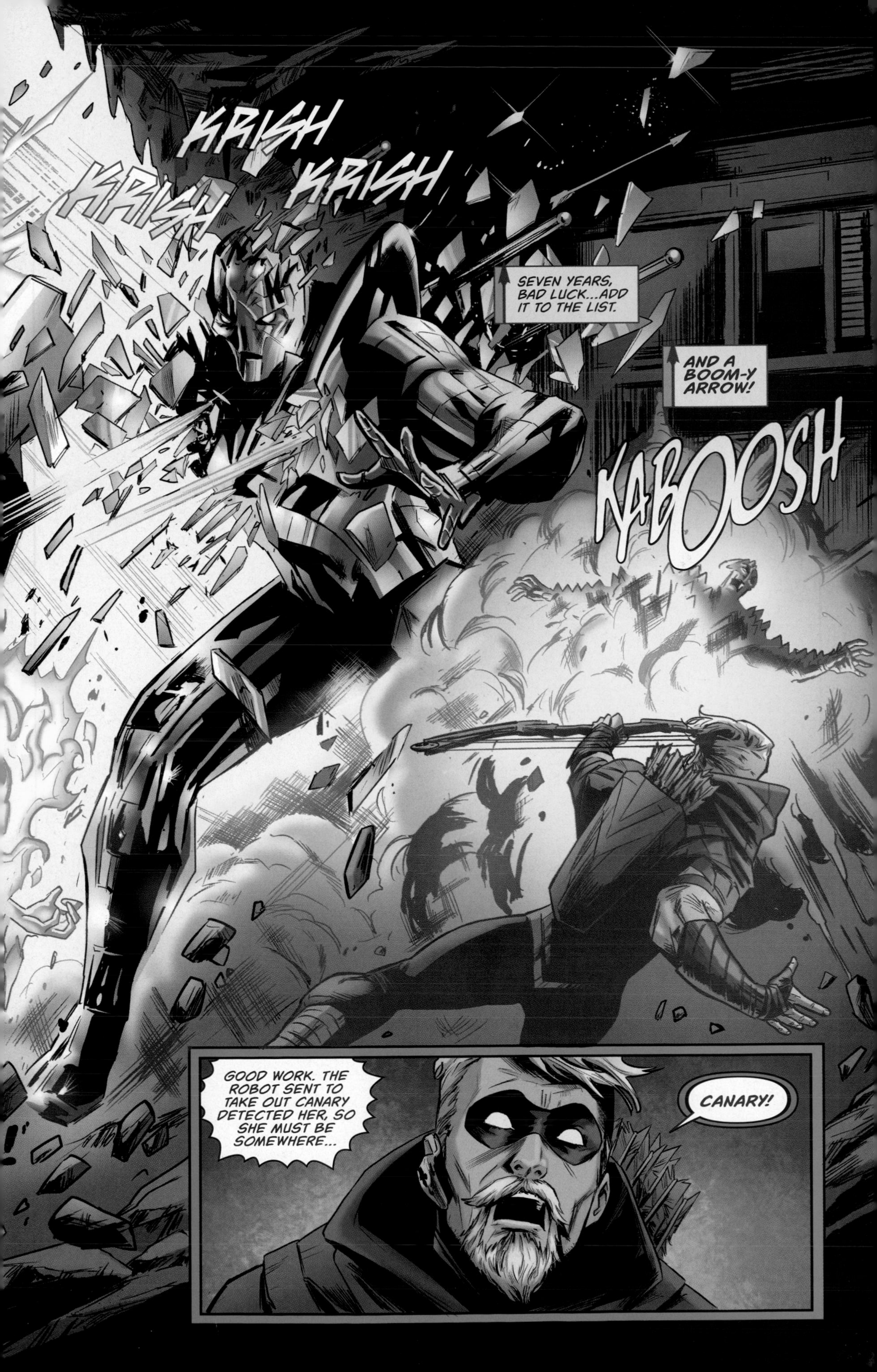
KRISH
KRISH
KRISH
SEVEN YEARS, BAD LUCK...ADD IT TO THE LIST.
AND A BOOM-Y ARROW!
KABOOSH
GOOD WORK. THE ROBOT SENT TO TAKE OUT CANARY DETECTED HER, SO SHE MUST BE SOMEWHERE...
CANARY!

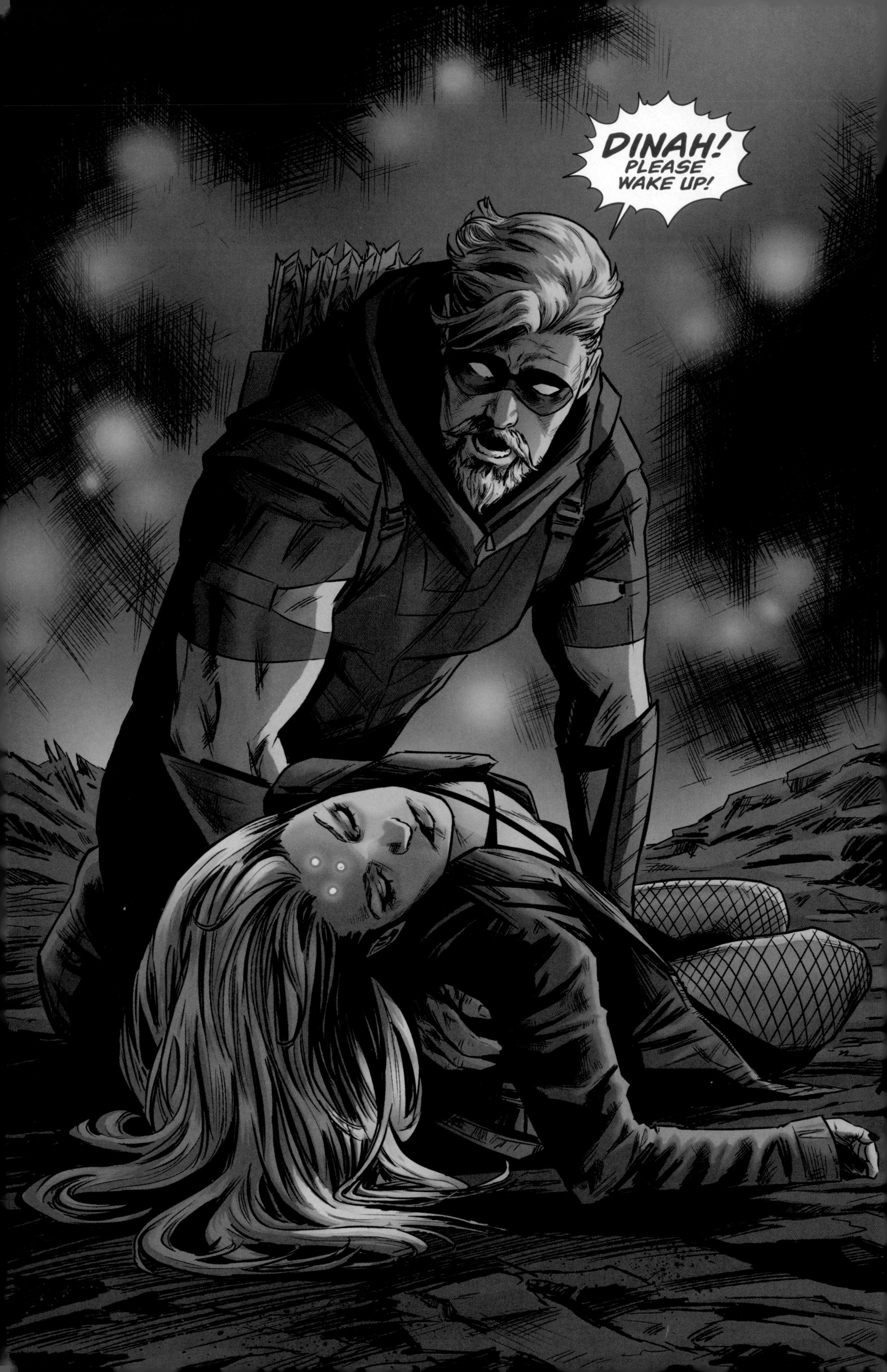
DINAH! PLEASE WAKE UP!

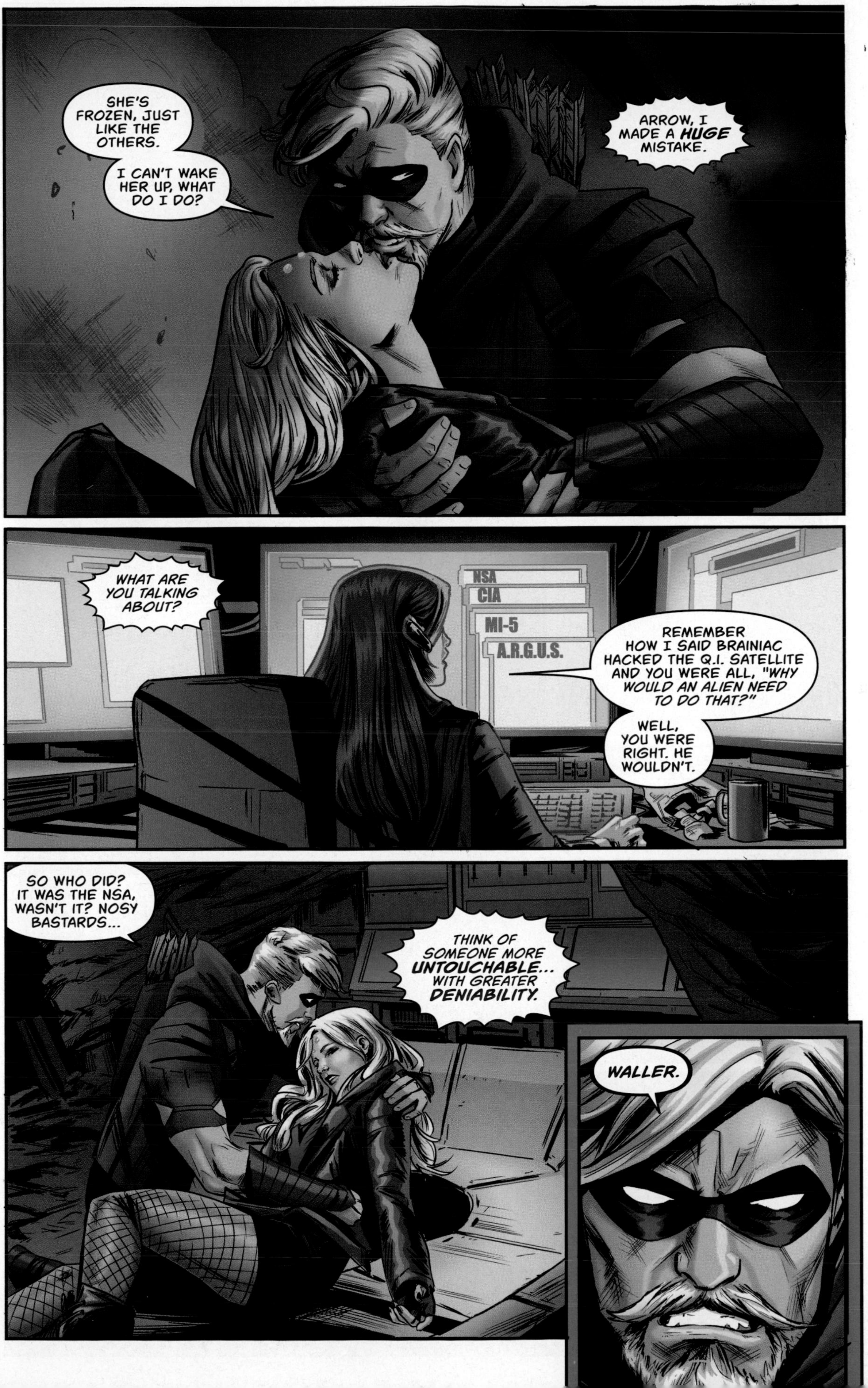
SHE'S FROZEN, JUST LIKE THE OTHERS.
I CAN'T WAKE HER UP, WHAT DO I DO?
ARROW, I MADE A HUGE MISTAKE.
WHAT ARE YOU TALKING ABOUT?
NSA
CIA
MI-5
A.R.G.U.S.
REMEMBER HOW I SAID BRAINIAC HACKED THE Q.I. SATELLITE AND YOU WERE ALL, "WHY WOULD AN ALIEN NEED TO DO THAT?"
WELL, YOU WERE RIGHT. HE WOULDN'T.
SO WHO DID? IT WAS THE NSA, WASN'T IT? NOSY BASTARDS...
THINK OF SOMEONE MORE UNTOUCHABLE... WITH GREATER DENIABILITY.
WALLER.

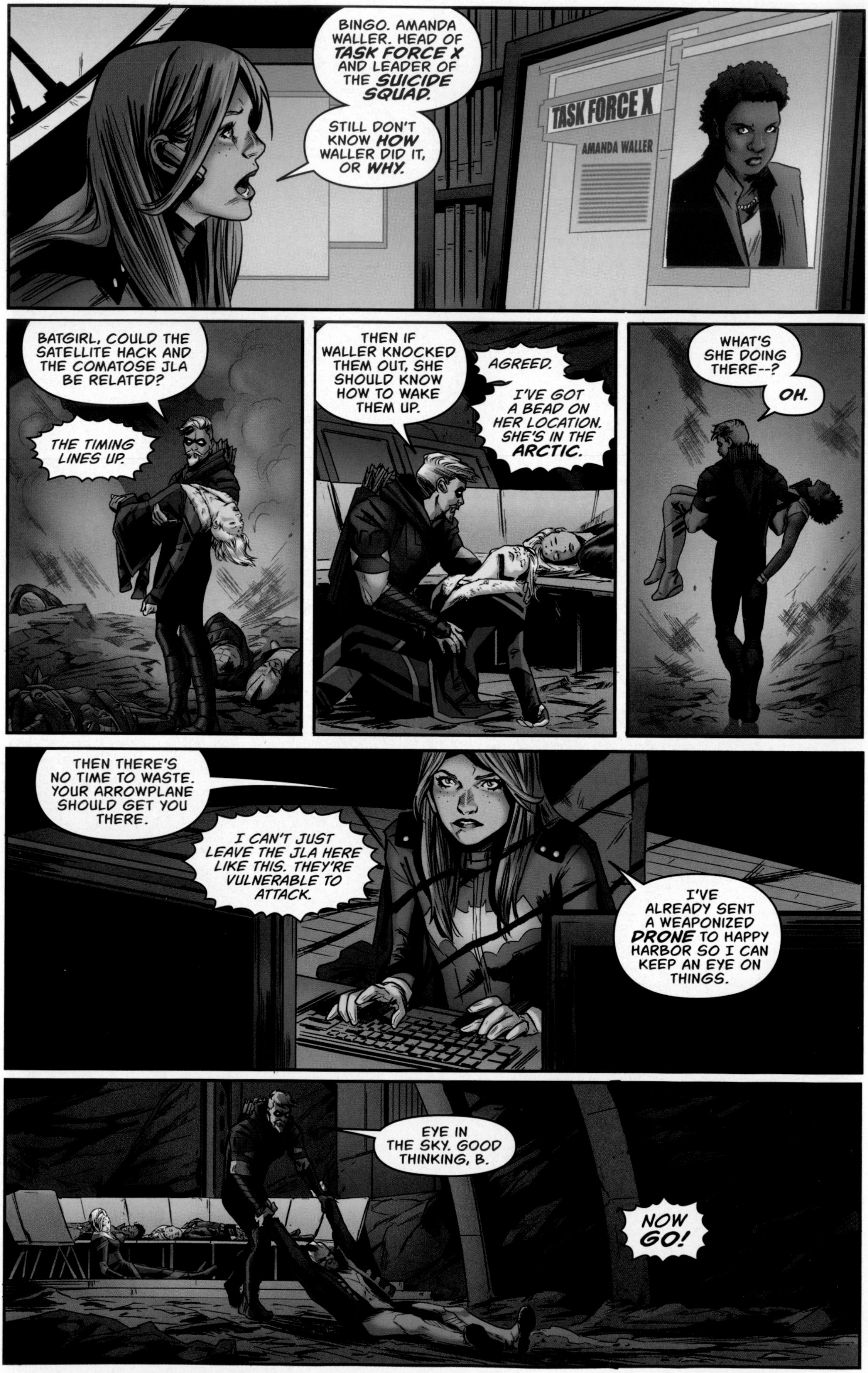
BINGO. AMANDA WALLER. HEAD OF TASK FORCE X AND LEADER OF THE SUICIDE SQUAD.
STILL DON'T KNOW HOW WALLER DID IT, OR WHY.
TASK FORCE X
AMANDA WALLER
BATGIRL, COULD THE SATELLITE HACK AND THE COMATOSE JLA BE RELATED?
THE TIMING LINES UP.
THEN IF WALLER KNOCKED THEM OUT, SHE SHOULD KNOW HOW TO WAKE THEM UP.
AGREED.
I'VE GOT A BEAD ON HER LOCATION. SHE'S IN THE ARCTIC.
WHAT'S SHE DOING THERE--?
OH.
THEN THERE'S NO TIME TO WASTE. YOUR ARROWPLANE SHOULD GET YOU THERE.
I CAN'T JUST LEAVE THE JLA HERE LIKE THIS. THEY'RE VULNERABLE TO ATTACK.
I'VE ALREADY SENT A WEAPONIZED DRONE TO HAPPY HARBOR SO I CAN KEEP AN EYE ON THINGS.
EYE IN THE SKY. GOOD THINKING, B.
NOW GO!

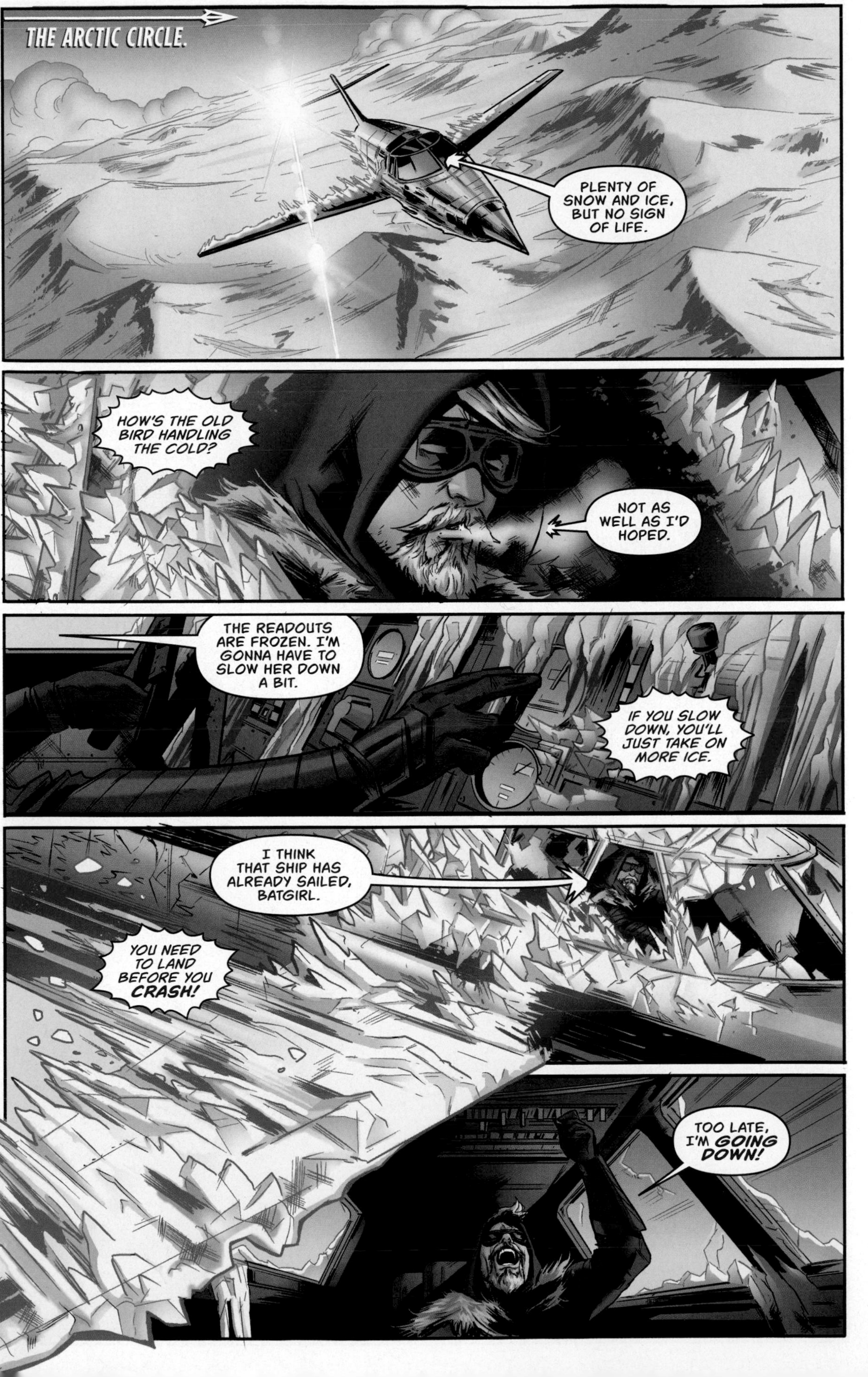
THE ARCTIC CIRCLE.
PLENTY OF SNOW AND ICE, BUT NO SIGN OF LIFE.
HOW'S THE OLD BIRD HANDLING THE COLD?
NOT AS WELL AS I'D HOPED.
THE READOUTS ARE FROZEN. I'M GONNA HAVE TO SLOW HER DOWN A BIT.
IF YOU SLOW DOWN, YOU'LL JUST TAKE ON MORE ICE.
I THINK THAT SHIP HAS ALREADY SAILED, BATGIRL.
YOU NEED TO LAND BEFORE YOU CRASH!
TOO LATE, I'M GOING DOWN!

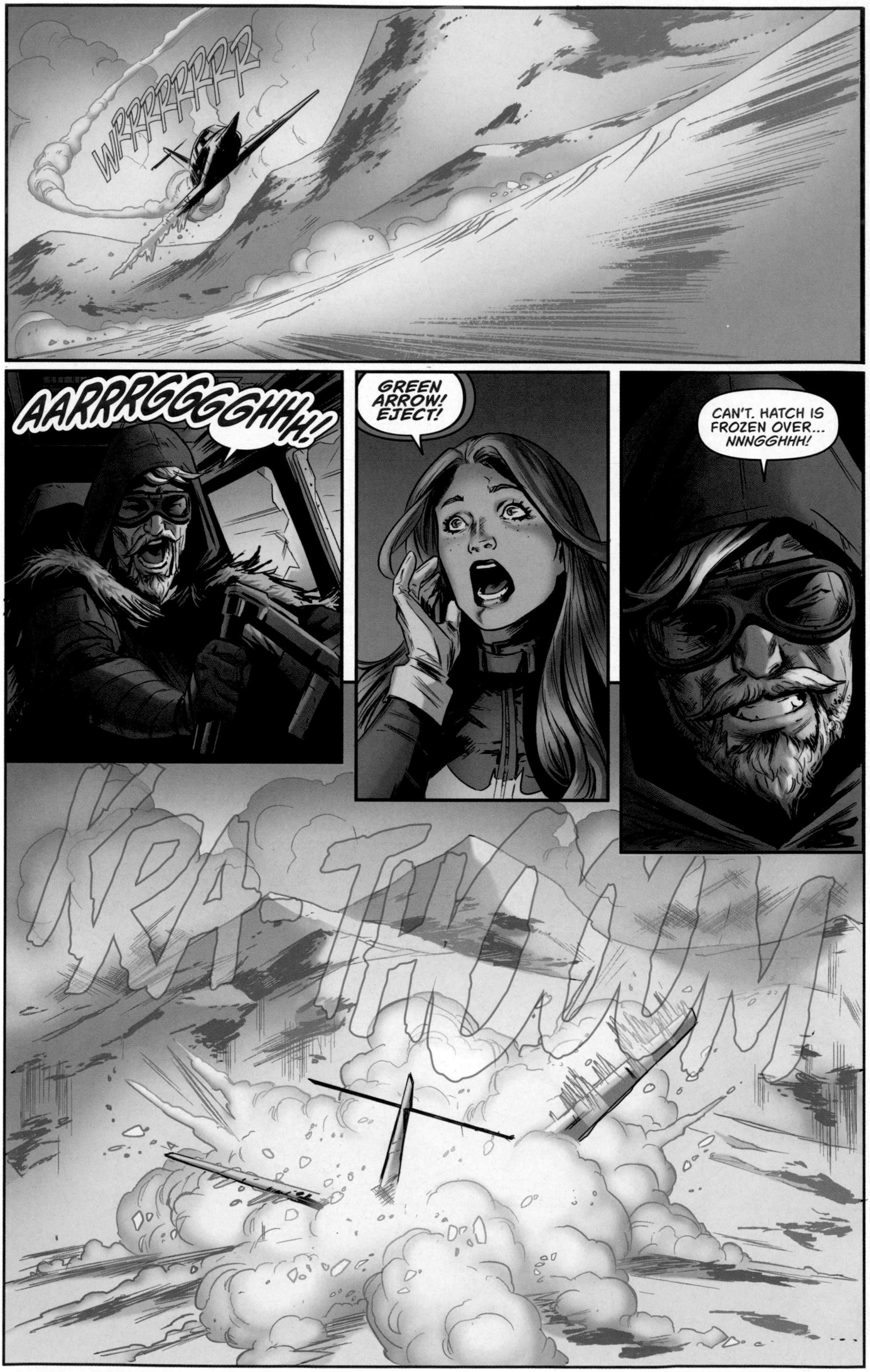
WRRRRRRRR
AARRRGGGGHHH!
GREEN ARROW! EJECT!
CAN'T. HATCH IS FROZEN OVER... NNNGGHHH!
KRA-THOOM

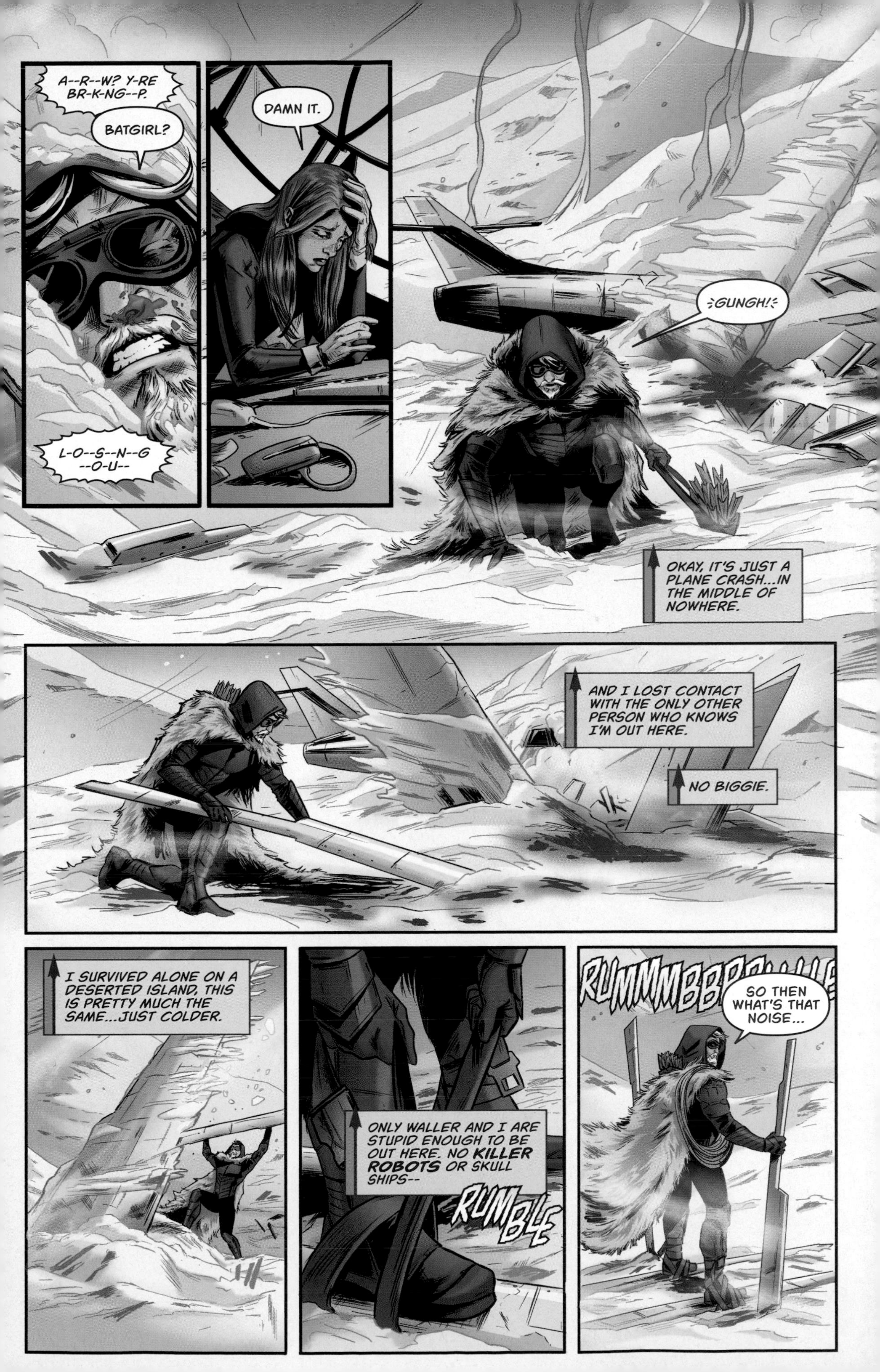

A--R--W? Y-RE BR-K-NG--P.
BATGIRL?
L-O--S--N--G --O-U--
DAMN IT.
GUNGH!
OKAY, IT'S JUST A PLANE CRASH...IN THE MIDDLE OF NOWHERE.
AND I LOST CONTACT WITH THE ONLY OTHER PERSON WHO KNOWS I'M OUT HERE.
NO BIGGIE.
I SURVIVED ALONE ON A DESERTED ISLAND, THIS IS PRETTY MUCH THE SAME...JUST COLDER.
ONLY WALLER AND I ARE STUPID ENOUGH TO BE OUT HERE. NO **KILLER ROBOTS** OR SKULL SHIPS--
RUMBLE
SO THEN WHAT'S THAT NOISE...

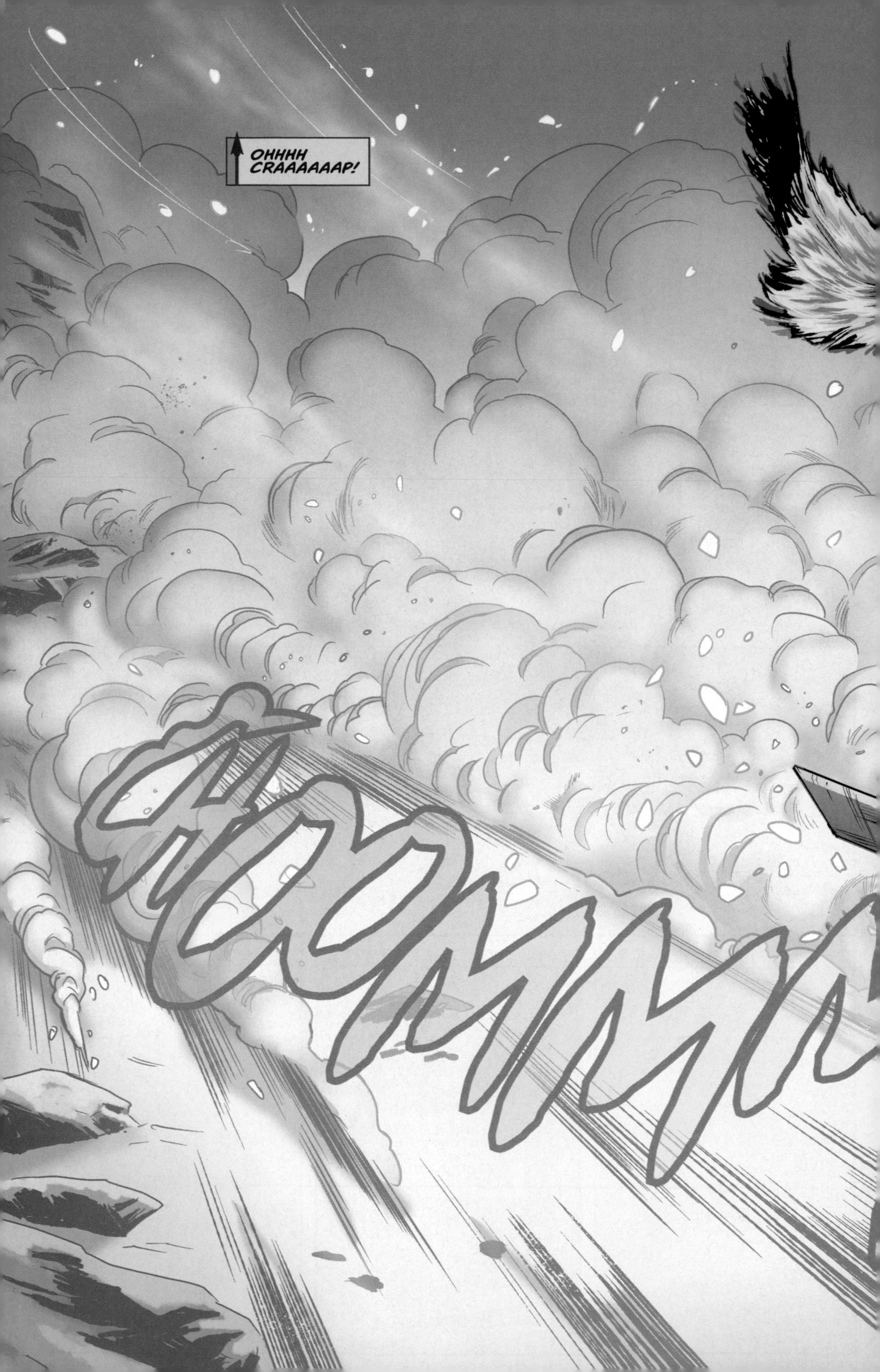
OHHHH CRAAAAAP!

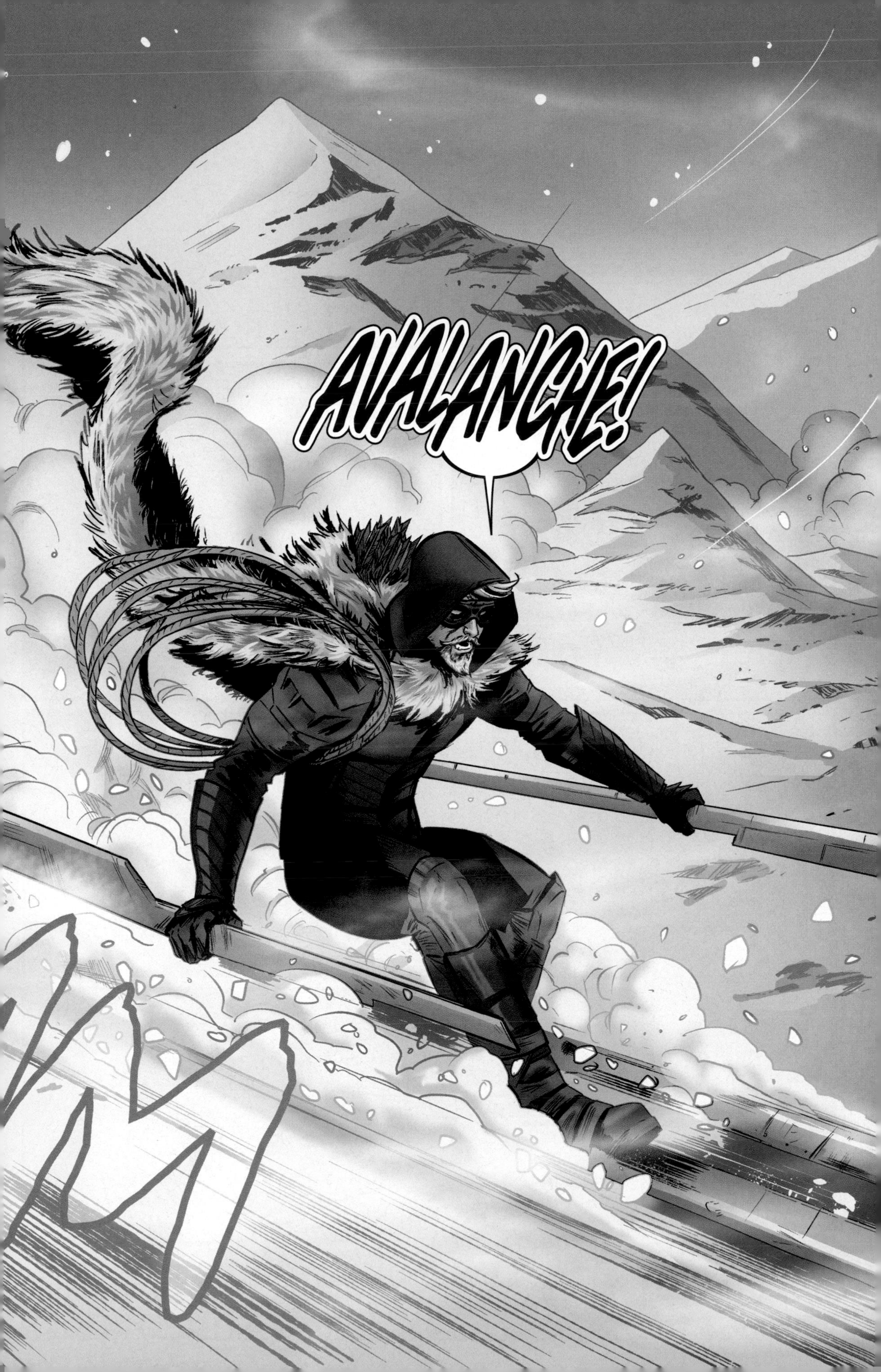
AVALANCHE!

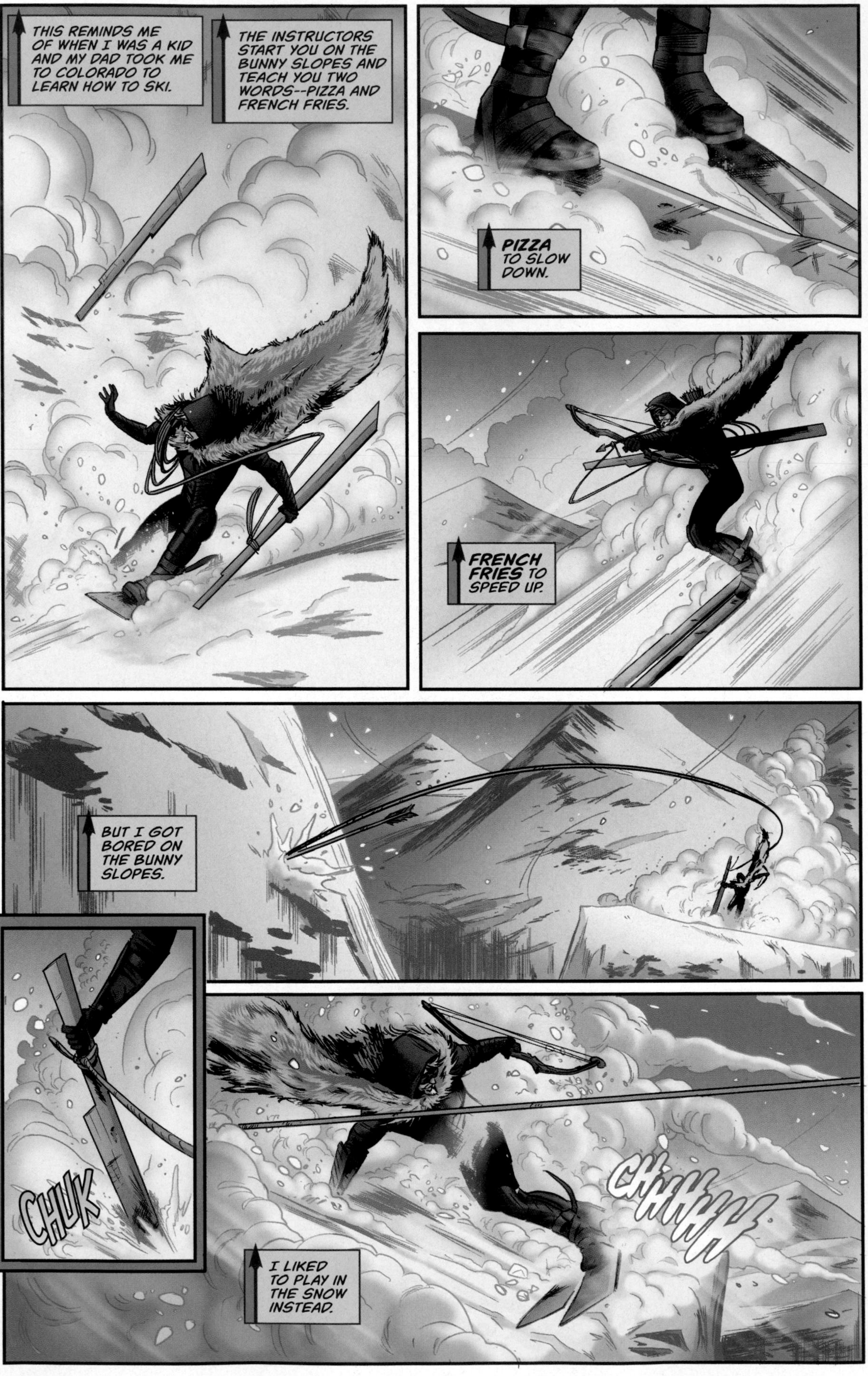
THIS REMINDS ME OF WHEN I WAS A KID AND MY DAD TOOK ME TO COLORADO TO LEARN HOW TO SKI.
THE INSTRUCTORS START YOU ON THE BUNNY SLOPES AND TEACH YOU TWO WORDS--PIZZA AND FRENCH FRIES.
PIZZA TO SLOW DOWN.
FRENCH FRIES TO SPEED UP.
BUT I GOT BORED ON THE BUNNY SLOPES.
CHUK
CHHHHH
I LIKED TO PLAY IN THE SNOW INSTEAD.

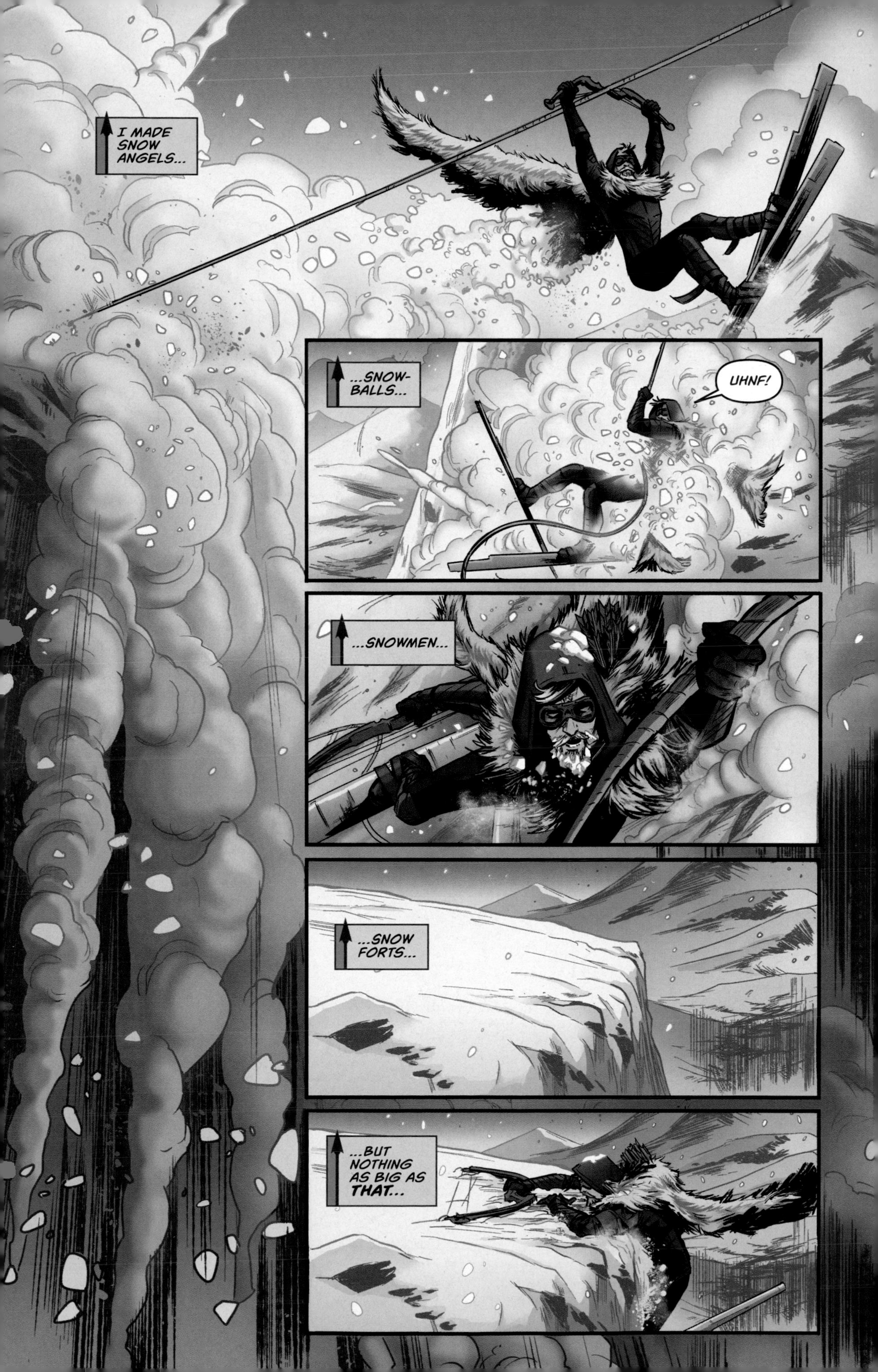
I MADE SNOW ANGELS...
...SNOW-BALLS...
UHNF!
...SNOWMEN...
...SNOW FORTS...
...BUT NOTHING AS BIG AS THAT...

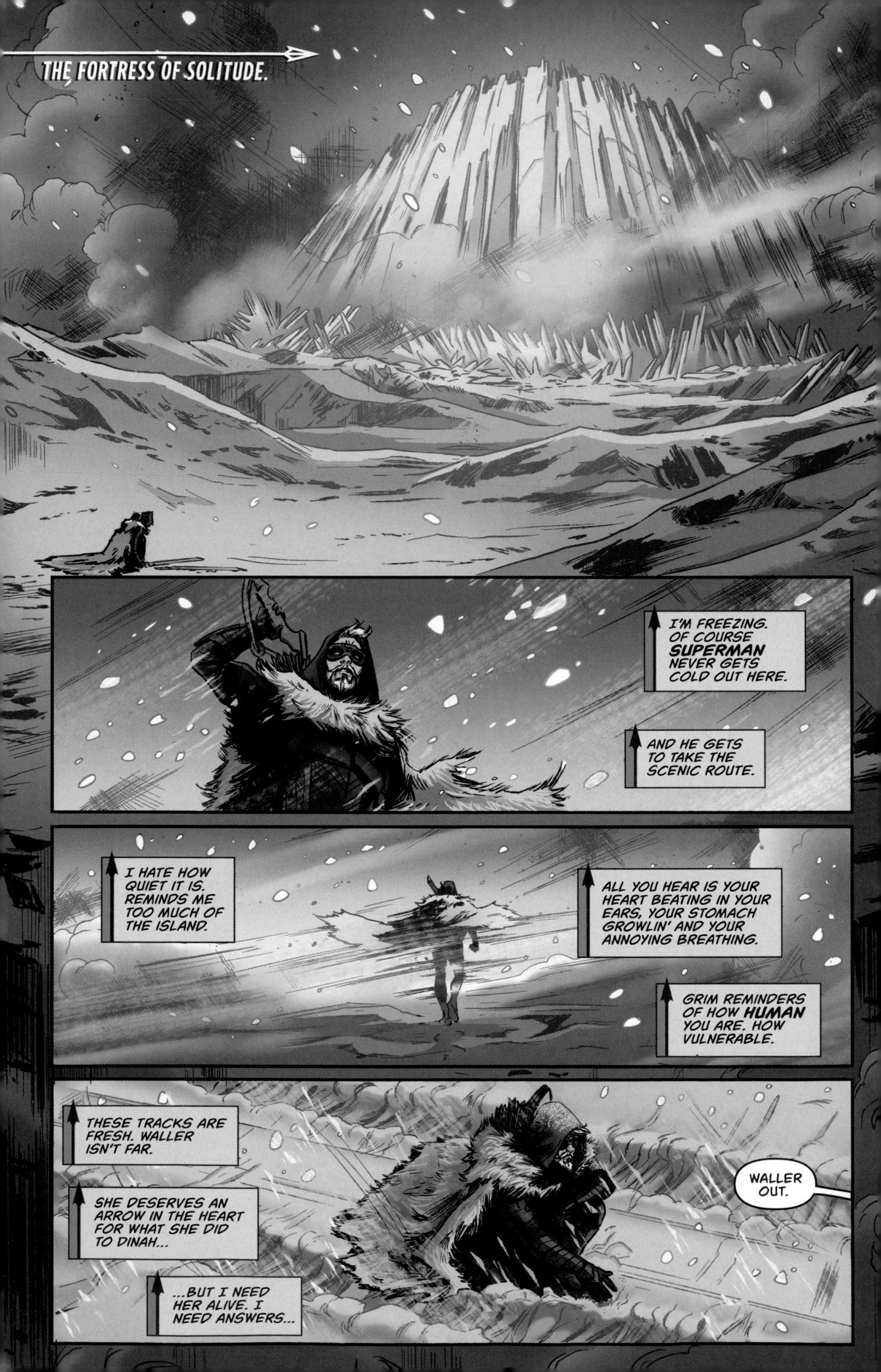
THE FORTRESS OF SOLITUDE.
I'M FREEZING. OF COURSE SUPERMAN NEVER GETS COLD OUT HERE.
AND HE GETS TO TAKE THE SCENIC ROUTE.
I HATE HOW QUIET IT IS. REMINDS ME TOO MUCH OF THE ISLAND.
ALL YOU HEAR IS YOUR HEART BEATING IN YOUR EARS, YOUR STOMACH GROWLIN' AND YOUR ANNOYING BREATHING.
GRIM REMINDERS OF HOW HUMAN YOU ARE. HOW VULNERABLE.
THESE TRACKS ARE FRESH. WALLER ISN'T FAR.
SHE DESERVES AN ARROW IN THE HEART FOR WHAT SHE DID TO DINAH...
...BUT I NEED HER ALIVE. I NEED ANSWERS...
WALLER OUT.

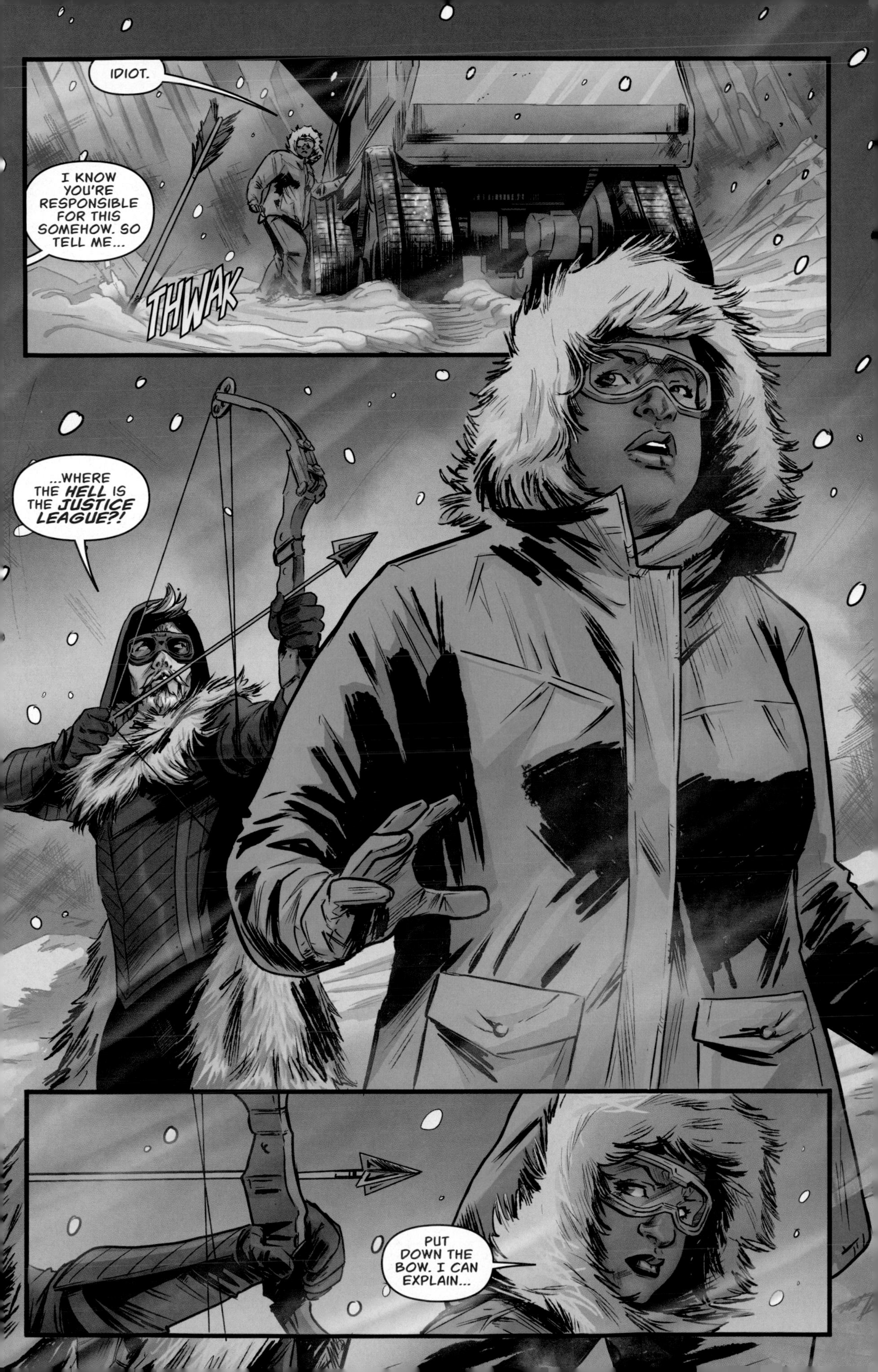
IDIOT.
I KNOW YOU'RE RESPONSIBLE FOR THIS SOMEHOW. SO TELL ME...
THWAK
...WHERE THE *HELL* IS THE *JUSTICE LEAGUE?!*
PUT DOWN THE BOW. I CAN EXPLAIN...

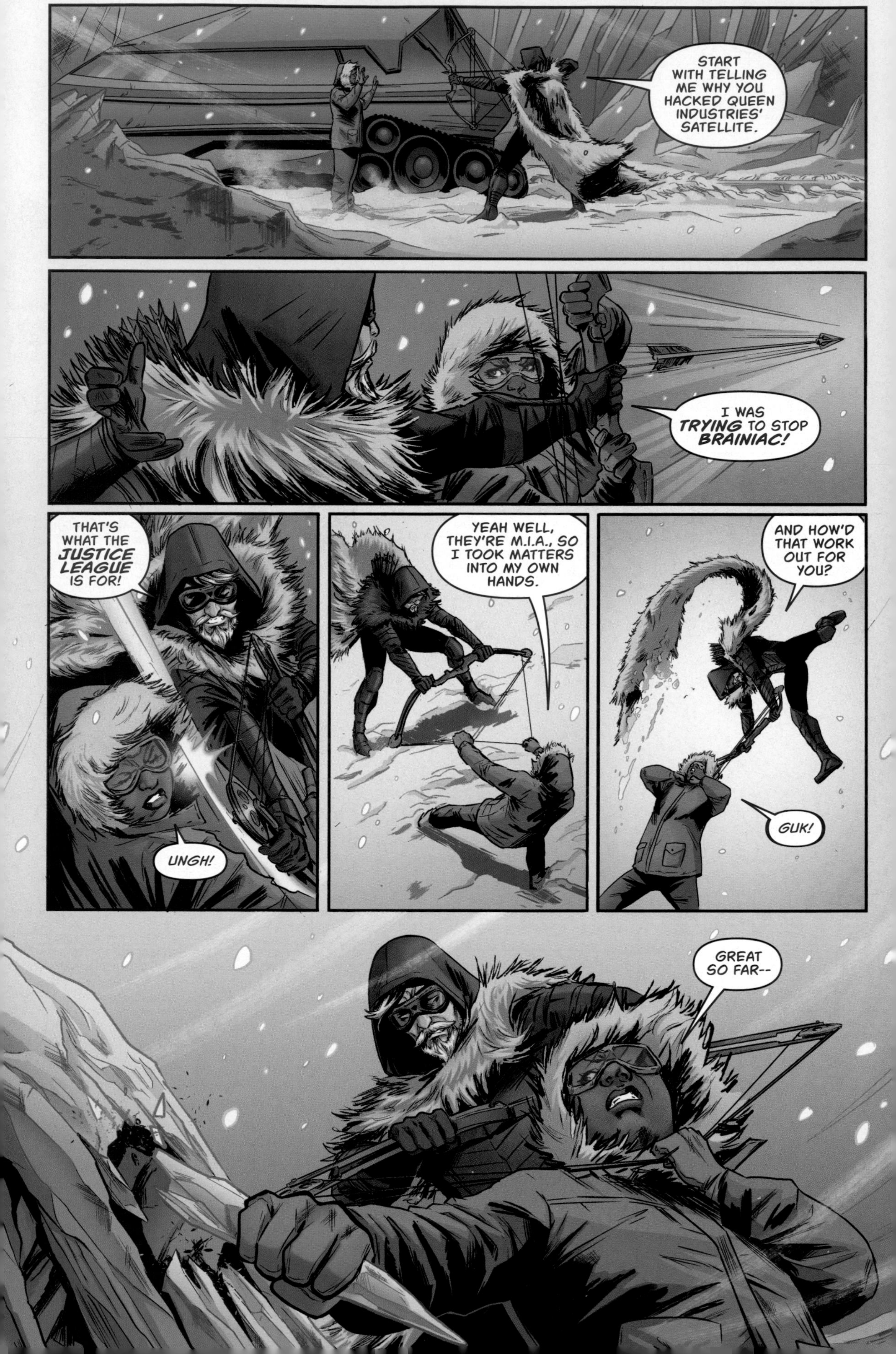
START WITH TELLING ME WHY YOU HACKED QUEEN INDUSTRIES' SATELLITE.
I WAS *TRYING* TO STOP *BRAINIAC!*
THAT'S WHAT THE *JUSTICE LEAGUE* IS FOR!
UNGH!
YEAH WELL, THEY'RE M.I.A., SO I TOOK MATTERS INTO MY OWN HANDS.
AND HOW'D THAT WORK OUT FOR YOU?
GUK!
GREAT SO FAR--

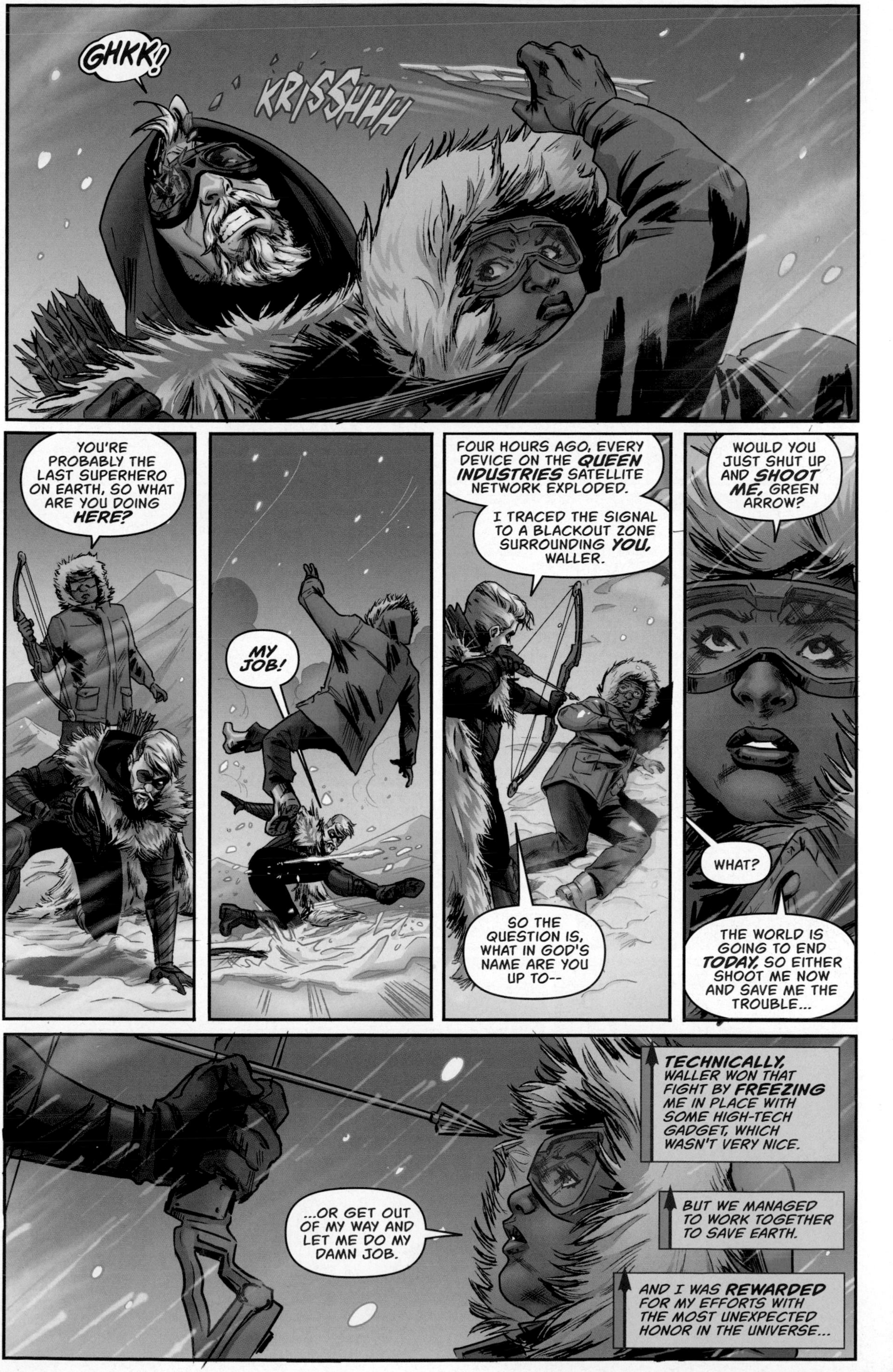
GHKK!
KRISSHHH
YOU'RE PROBABLY THE LAST SUPERHERO ON EARTH, SO WHAT ARE YOU DOING HERE?
MY JOB!
FOUR HOURS AGO, EVERY DEVICE ON THE QUEEN INDUSTRIES SATELLITE NETWORK EXPLODED.
I TRACED THE SIGNAL TO A BLACKOUT ZONE SURROUNDING YOU, WALLER.
SO THE QUESTION IS, WHAT IN GOD'S NAME ARE YOU UP TO--
WOULD YOU JUST SHUT UP AND SHOOT ME, GREEN ARROW?
WHAT?
THE WORLD IS GOING TO END TODAY, SO EITHER SHOOT ME NOW AND SAVE ME THE TROUBLE...
...OR GET OUT OF MY WAY AND LET ME DO MY DAMN JOB.
TECHNICALLY, WALLER WON THAT FIGHT BY FREEZING ME IN PLACE WITH SOME HIGH-TECH GADGET, WHICH WASN'T VERY NICE.
BUT WE MANAGED TO WORK TOGETHER TO SAVE EARTH.
AND I WAS REWARDED FOR MY EFFORTS WITH THE MOST UNEXPECTED HONOR IN THE UNIVERSE...

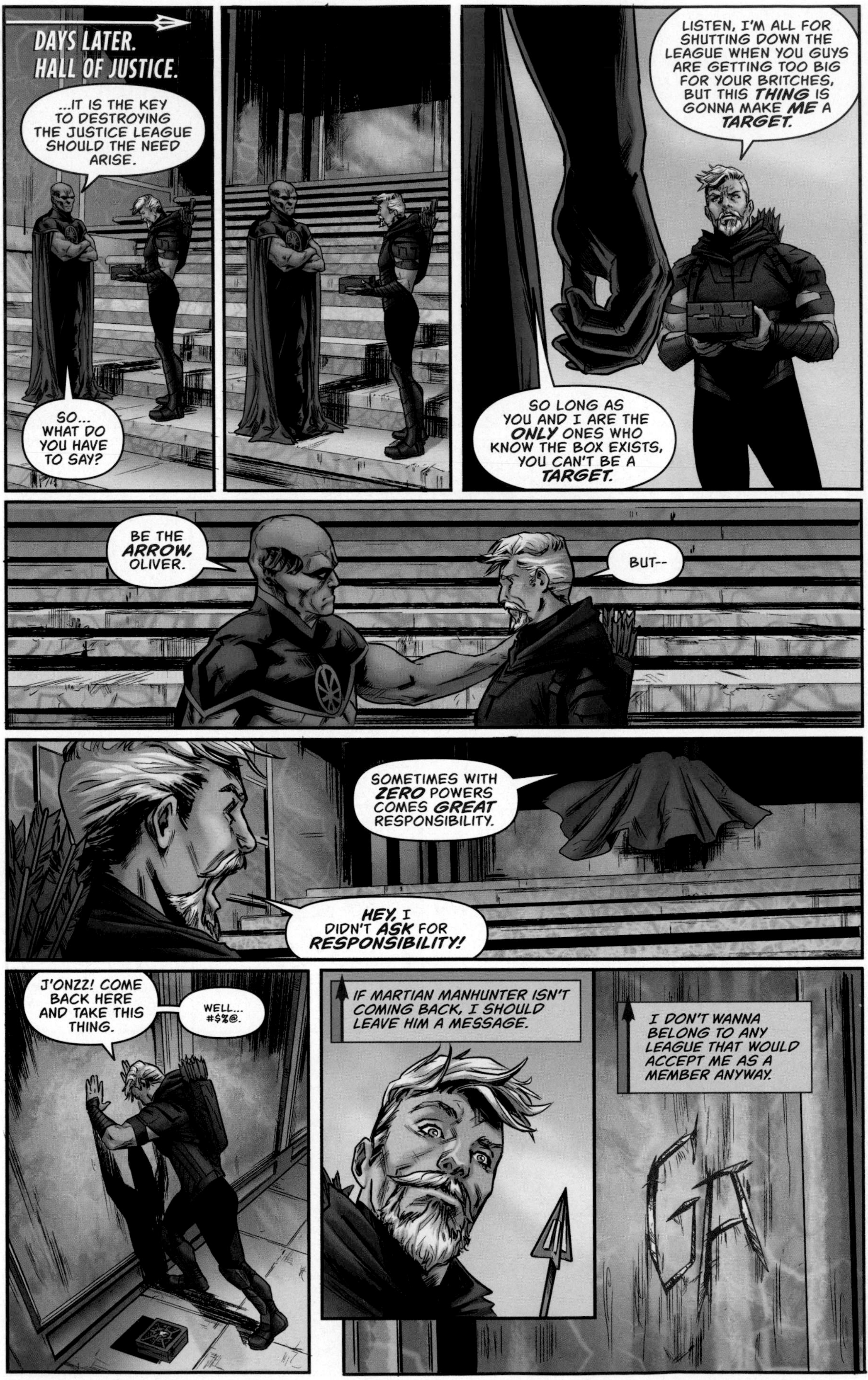
DAYS LATER. HALL OF JUSTICE.
...IT IS THE KEY TO DESTROYING THE JUSTICE LEAGUE SHOULD THE NEED ARISE.
SO... WHAT DO YOU HAVE TO SAY?
LISTEN, I'M ALL FOR SHUTTING DOWN THE LEAGUE WHEN YOU GUYS ARE GETTING TOO BIG FOR YOUR BRITCHES, BUT THIS THING IS GONNA MAKE ME A TARGET.
SO LONG AS YOU AND I ARE THE ONLY ONES WHO KNOW THE BOX EXISTS, YOU CAN'T BE A TARGET.
BE THE ARROW, OLIVER.
BUT--
SOMETIMES WITH ZERO POWERS COMES GREAT RESPONSIBILITY.
HEY, I DIDN'T ASK FOR RESPONSIBILITY!
J'ONZZ! COME BACK HERE AND TAKE THIS THING.
WELL... #$%@.
IF MARTIAN MANHUNTER ISN'T COMING BACK, I SHOULD LEAVE HIM A MESSAGE.
I DON'T WANNA BELONG TO ANY LEAGUE THAT WOULD ACCEPT ME AS A MEMBER ANYWAY.
GA

MARTIAN MANHUNTER JUST DUMPED THIS ALL-POWERFUL ON/OFF SWITCH IN MY LAP WITHOUT GIVING ME ANY IDEA WHAT'S INSIDE IT OR WHAT IT DOES.

THE ONLY THING J'ONZZ GAVE ME THAT I WANTED WAS MY PRETTY BIRD.

GASOLINE & SERVICE

AFTER WE SAVED THE WORLD, HE WAS ABLE TO WAKE DINAH AND THE OTHERS UP.

7.50¢

I'VE ALWAYS BEEN A LITTLE JEALOUS OF SUPERHEROES WITH META-POWERS.

BUT NOW, WITH THIS JUNK IN THE TRUNK, I'VE GOT A POWER GREATER THAN **EVERYONE** IN THE JUSTICE LEAGUE COMBINED...

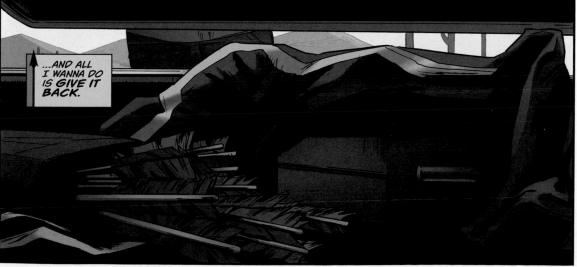

...AND ALL I WANNA DO IS **GIVE IT BACK.**

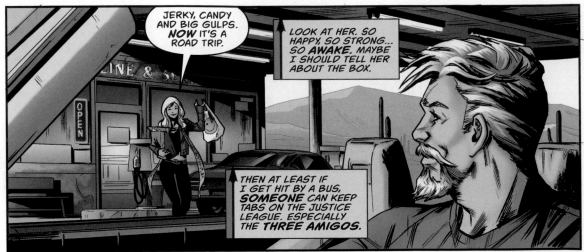

JERKY, CANDY AND BIG GULPS. *NOW* IT'S A ROAD TRIP.

LOOK AT HER. SO HAPPY, SO STRONG... SO *AWAKE.* MAYBE I SHOULD TELL HER ABOUT THE BOX.

THEN AT LEAST IF I GET HIT BY A BUS, *SOMEONE* CAN KEEP TABS ON THE JUSTICE LEAGUE. ESPECIALLY THE *THREE AMIGOS.*

BUT THE LAST THING I WANT IS TO PUT DINAH IN DANGER. SHE DOESN'T DESERVE TO BE A TARGET, TOO.

I GOT YOUR FAVORITES. WHAT'S THE MATTER?

NOTHING, JUST EXCITED TO GET BACK HOME. BUCKLE UP!

HEY, WHY ARE WE DRIVING? I THOUGHT YOU SAID THE *ARROWPLANE* WAS BACK IN ACTION.

IT WAS... BUT I'VE GOT PLANS FOR AN UPGRADE.

I'VE NEVER KEPT A SECRET FROM DINAH-- OKAY, THAT'S A LIE, I NEVER TOLD HER THAT SHE FARTS IN HER SLEEP SOMETIMES--BUT *THIS?*

BURY THE LEDE, OLLIE. ANYTHING ELSE YOU WANNA TELL ME?

NOPE. YOU'RE UP TO SPEED NOW, SLEEPING BEAUTY.

I'M SO SCREWED.

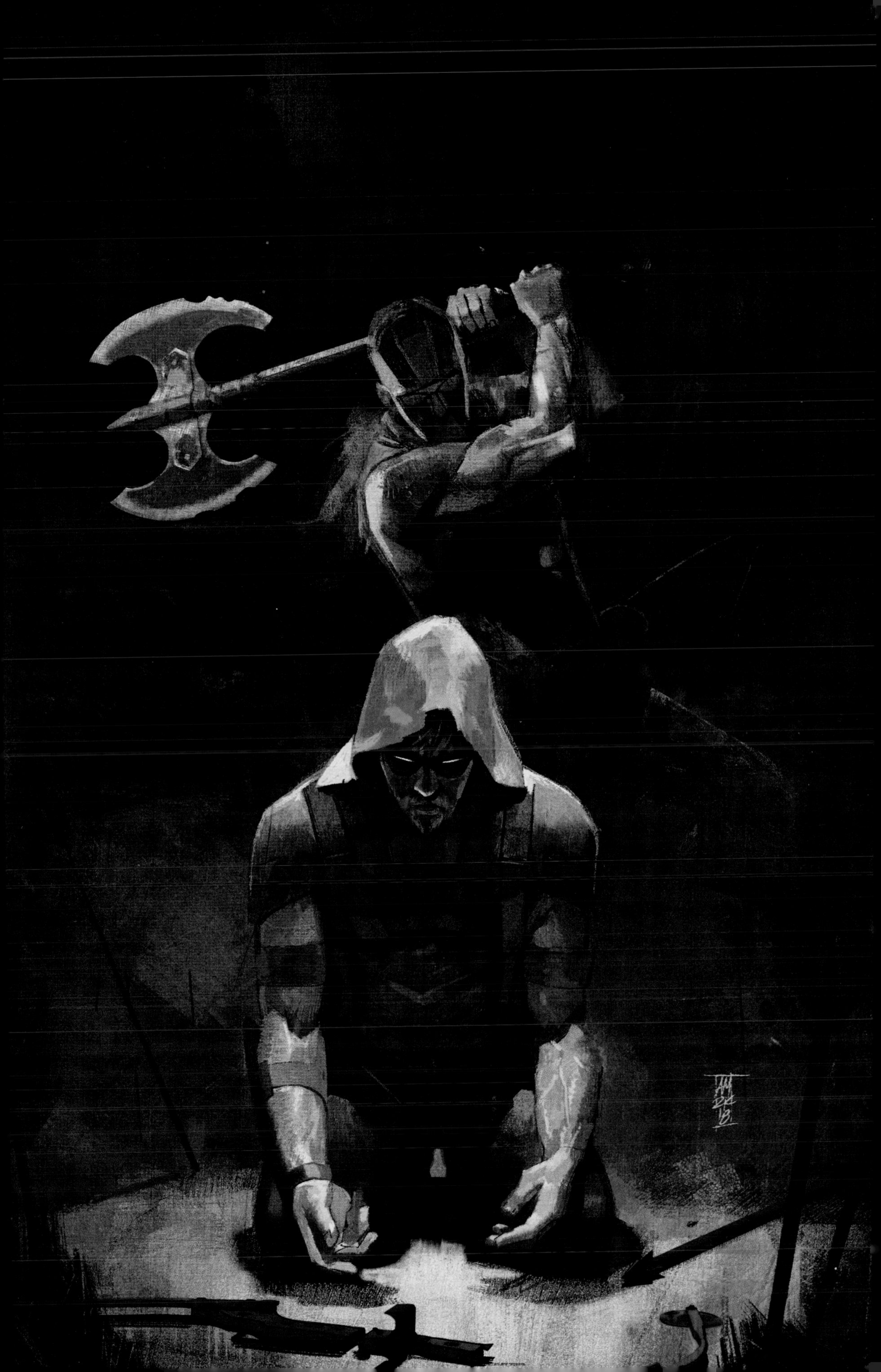

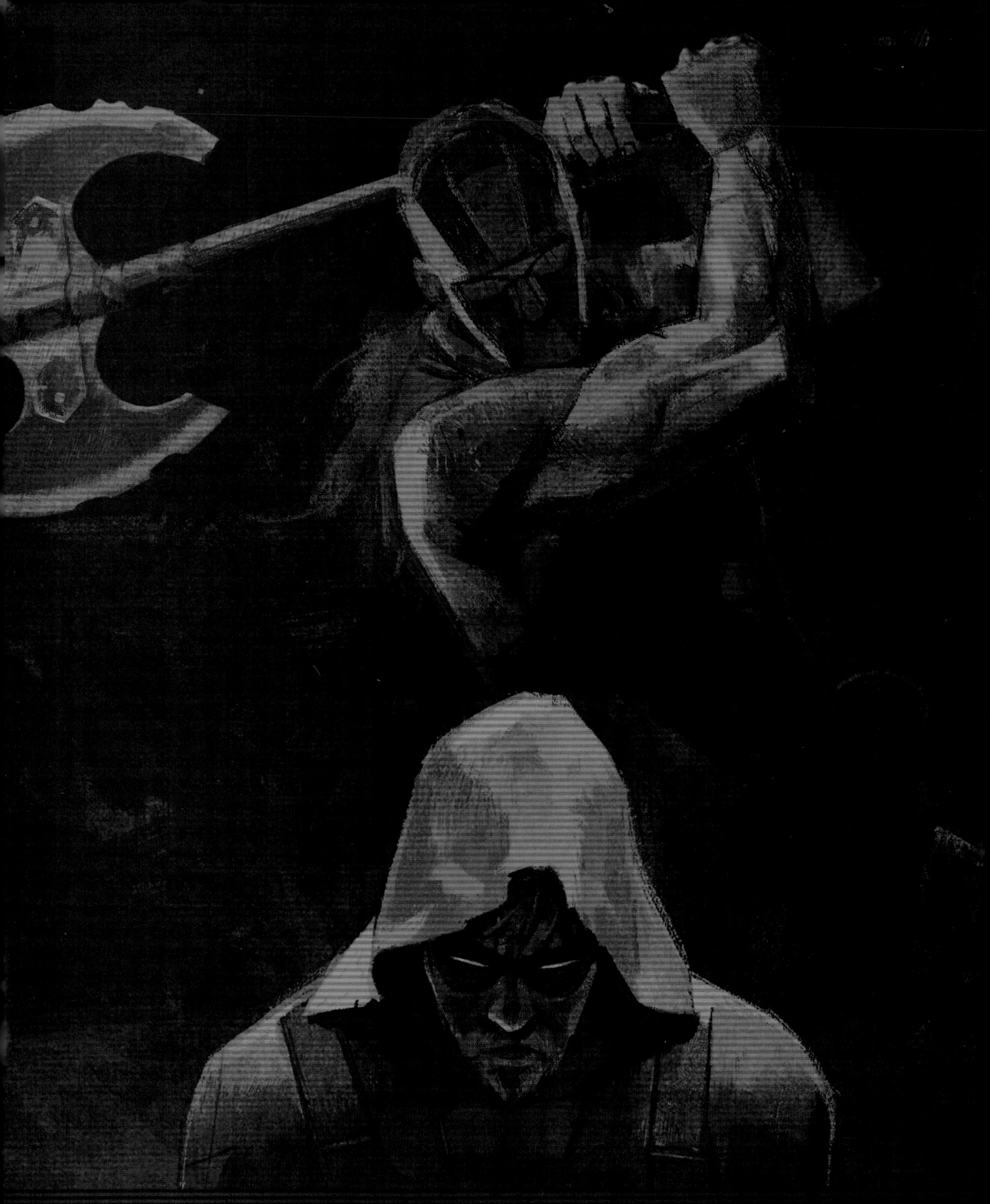

GREEN ARROW

#43

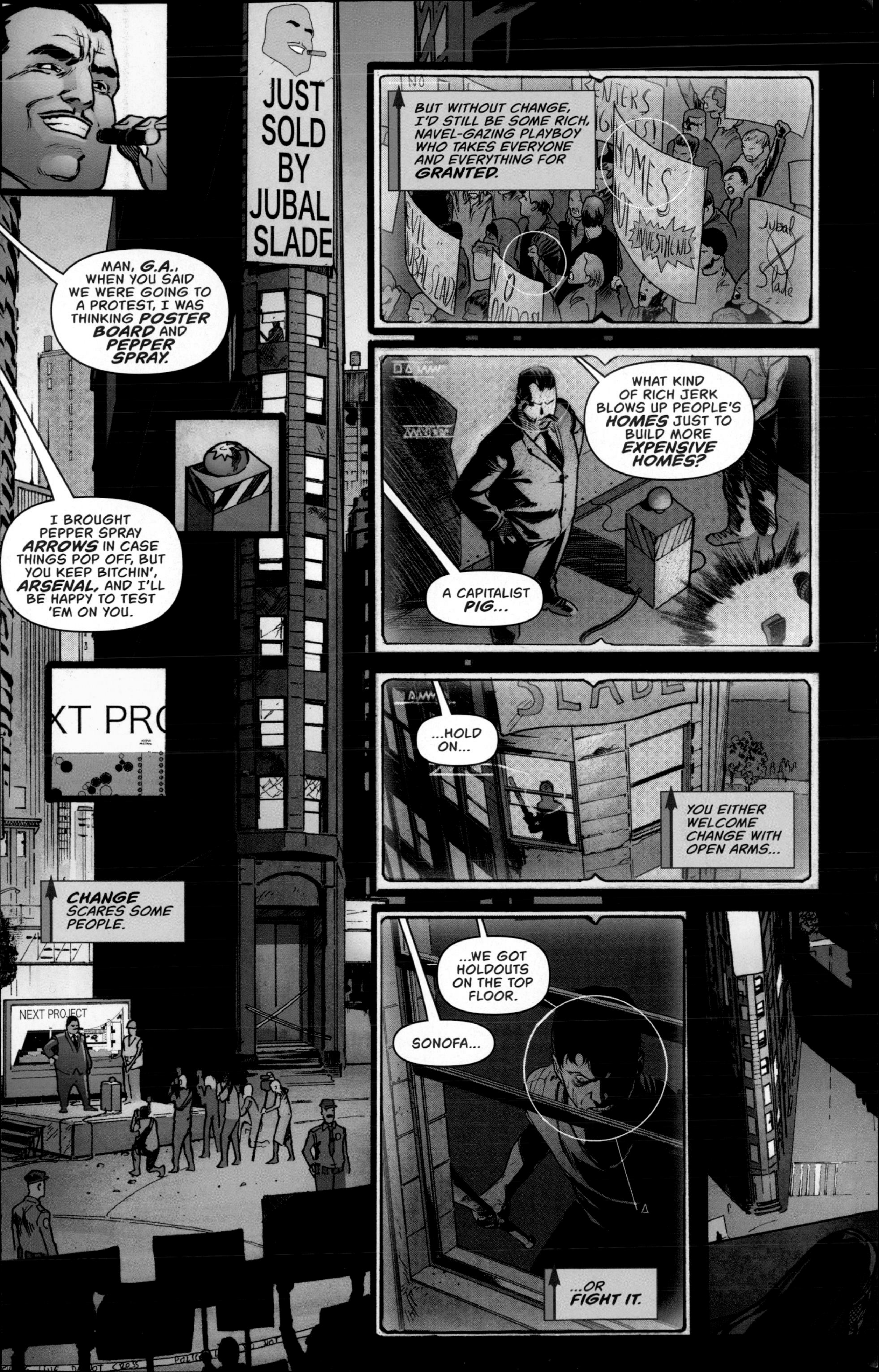

JUST SOLD BY JUBAL SLADE
MAN, G.A., WHEN YOU SAID WE WERE GOING TO A PROTEST, I WAS THINKING POSTER BOARD AND PEPPER SPRAY.
I BROUGHT PEPPER SPRAY ARROWS IN CASE THINGS POP OFF, BUT YOU KEEP BITCHIN', ARSENAL, AND I'LL BE HAPPY TO TEST 'EM ON YOU.
XT PRO
CHANGE SCARES SOME PEOPLE.
NEXT PROJECT
BUT WITHOUT CHANGE, I'D STILL BE SOME RICH, NAVEL-GAZING PLAYBOY WHO TAKES EVERYONE AND EVERYTHING FOR GRANTED.
HOMES NOT INVESTMENTS
Jubal Slade
WHAT KIND OF RICH JERK BLOWS UP PEOPLE'S HOMES JUST TO BUILD MORE EXPENSIVE HOMES?
A CAPITALIST PIG...
SLADE
...HOLD ON...
YOU EITHER WELCOME CHANGE WITH OPEN ARMS...
...WE GOT HOLDOUTS ON THE TOP FLOOR.
SONOFA...
...OR FIGHT IT.

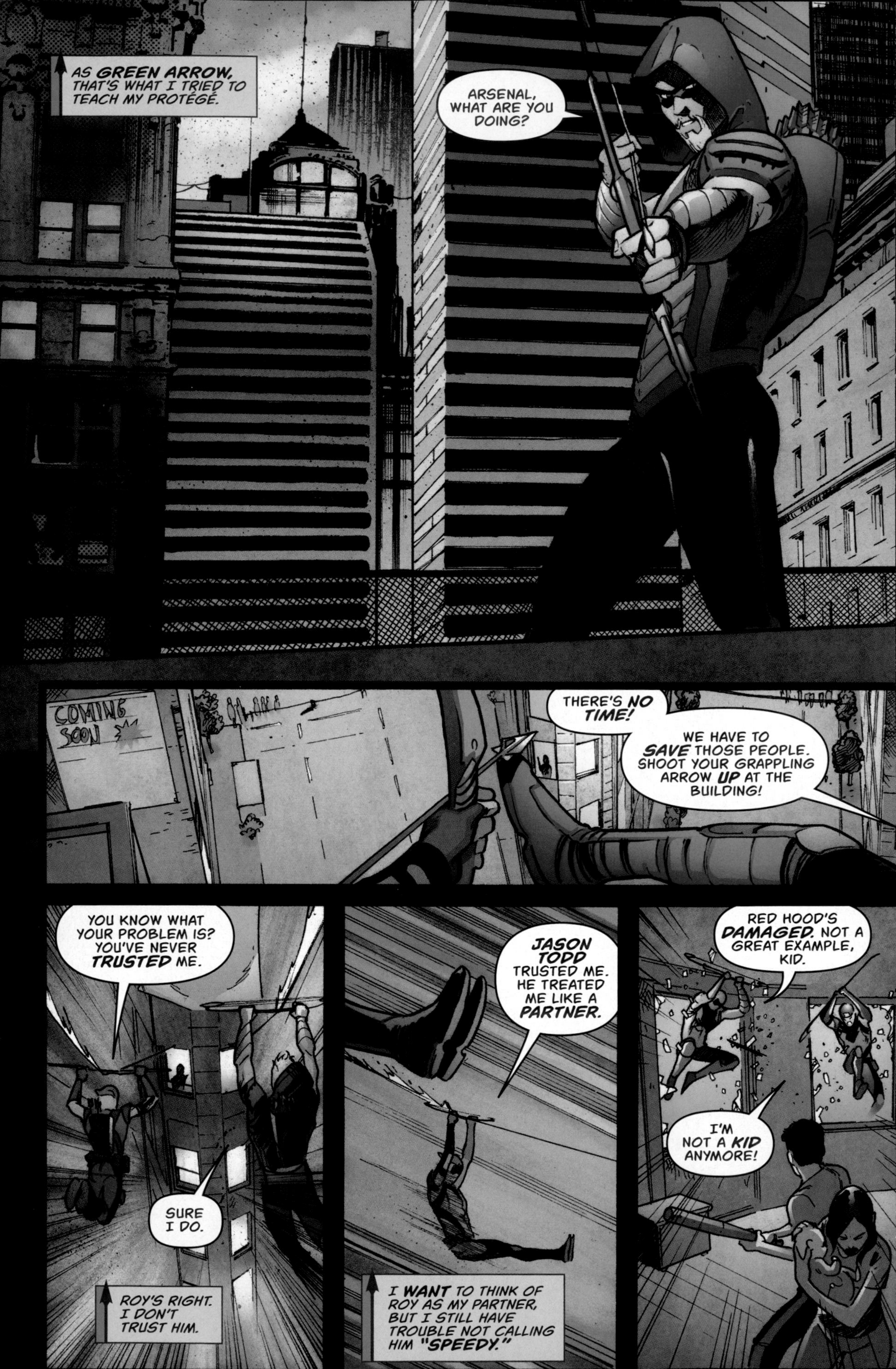
AS GREEN ARROW, THAT'S WHAT I TRIED TO TEACH MY PROTÉGÉ.
ARSENAL, WHAT ARE YOU DOING?
COMING SOON
THERE'S NO TIME!
WE HAVE TO SAVE THOSE PEOPLE. SHOOT YOUR GRAPPLING ARROW UP AT THE BUILDING!
YOU KNOW WHAT YOUR PROBLEM IS? YOU'VE NEVER TRUSTED ME.
SURE I DO.
ROY'S RIGHT. I DON'T TRUST HIM.
JASON TODD TRUSTED ME. HE TREATED ME LIKE A PARTNER.
I WANT TO THINK OF ROY AS MY PARTNER, BUT I STILL HAVE TROUBLE NOT CALLING HIM "SPEEDY."
RED HOOD'S DAMAGED. NOT A GREAT EXAMPLE, KID.
I'M NOT A KID ANYMORE!

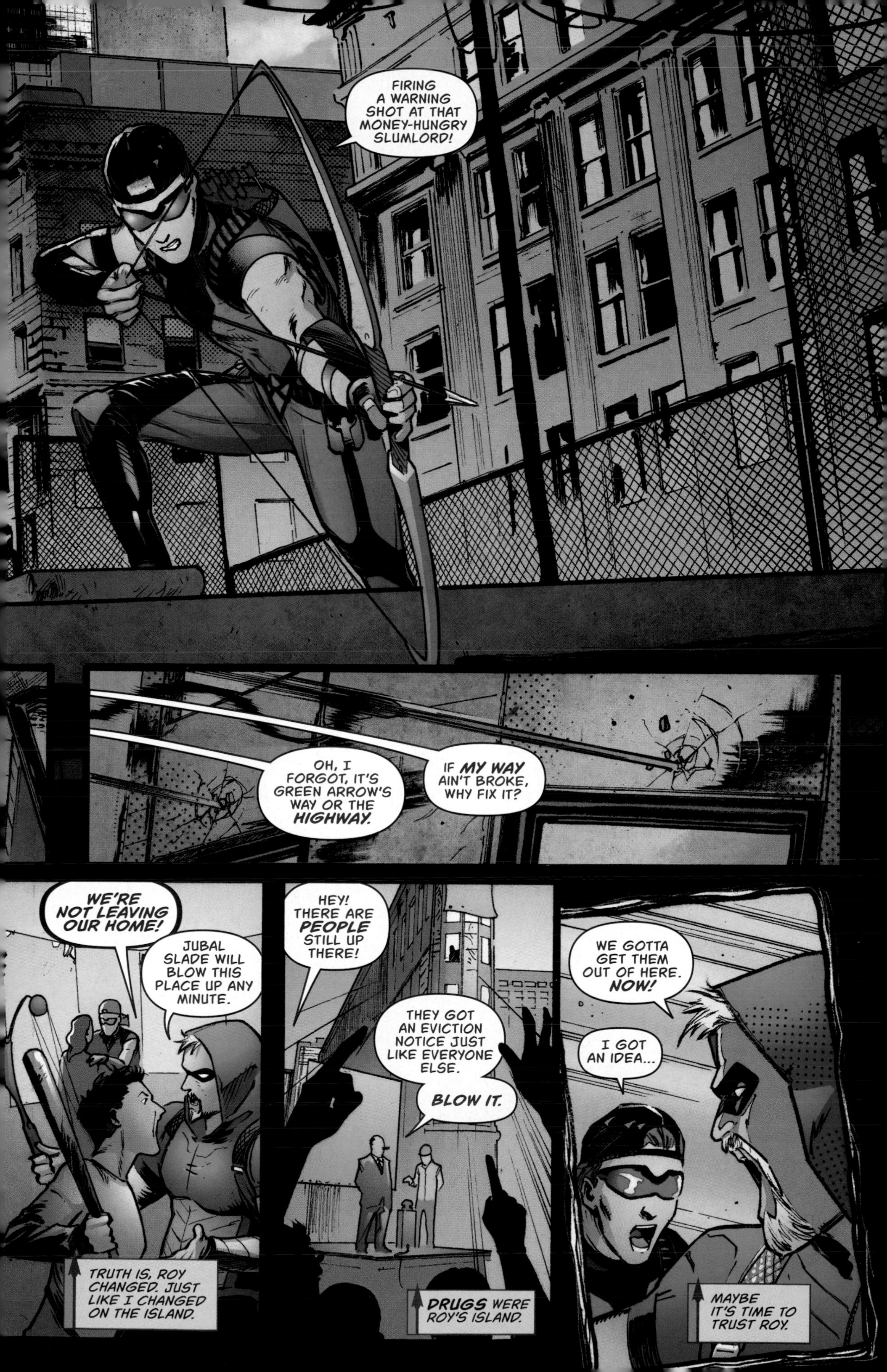
FIRING A WARNING SHOT AT THAT MONEY-HUNGRY SLUMLORD!
OH, I FORGOT, IT'S GREEN ARROW'S WAY OR THE HIGHWAY.
IF MY WAY AIN'T BROKE, WHY FIX IT?
WE'RE NOT LEAVING OUR HOME!
JUBAL SLADE WILL BLOW THIS PLACE UP ANY MINUTE.
TRUTH IS, ROY CHANGED. JUST LIKE I CHANGED ON THE ISLAND.
HEY! THERE ARE PEOPLE STILL UP THERE!
THEY GOT AN EVICTION NOTICE JUST LIKE EVERYONE ELSE.
BLOW IT.
DRUGS WERE ROY'S ISLAND.
WE GOTTA GET THEM OUT OF HERE. NOW!
I GOT AN IDEA...
MAYBE IT'S TIME TO TRUST ROY.

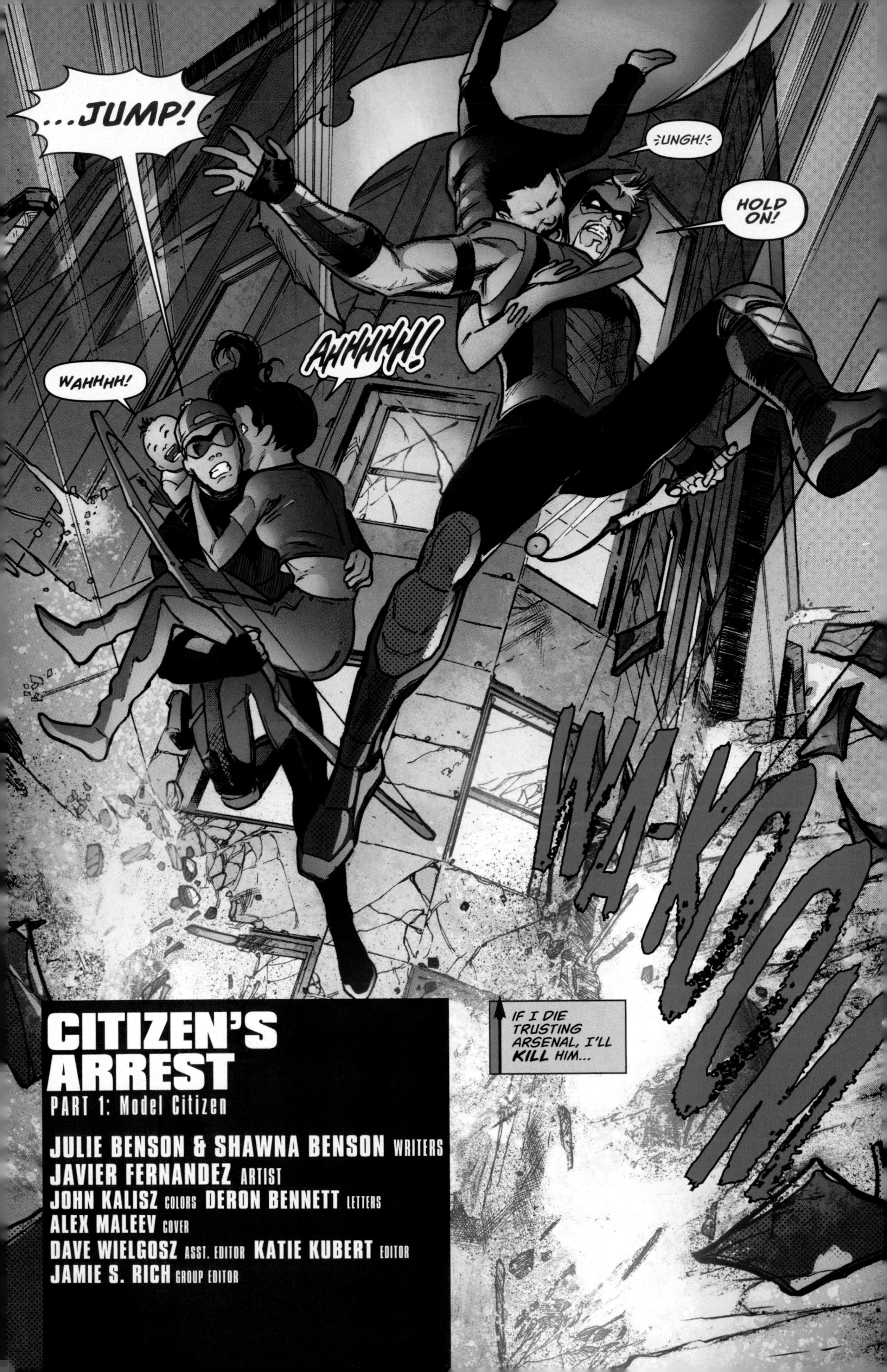
...JUMP!
UNGH!
HOLD ON!
WAHHHH!
AHHHHH!
IF I DIE TRUSTING ARSENAL, I'LL KILL HIM...

CITIZEN'S ARREST

PART 1: Model Citizen

JULIE BENSON & SHAWNA BENSON WRITERS
JAVIER FERNANDEZ ARTIST
JOHN KALISZ COLORS DERON BENNETT LETTERS
ALEX MALEEV COVER
DAVE WIELGOSZ ASST. EDITOR KATIE KUBERT EDITOR
JAMIE S. RICH GROUP EDITOR

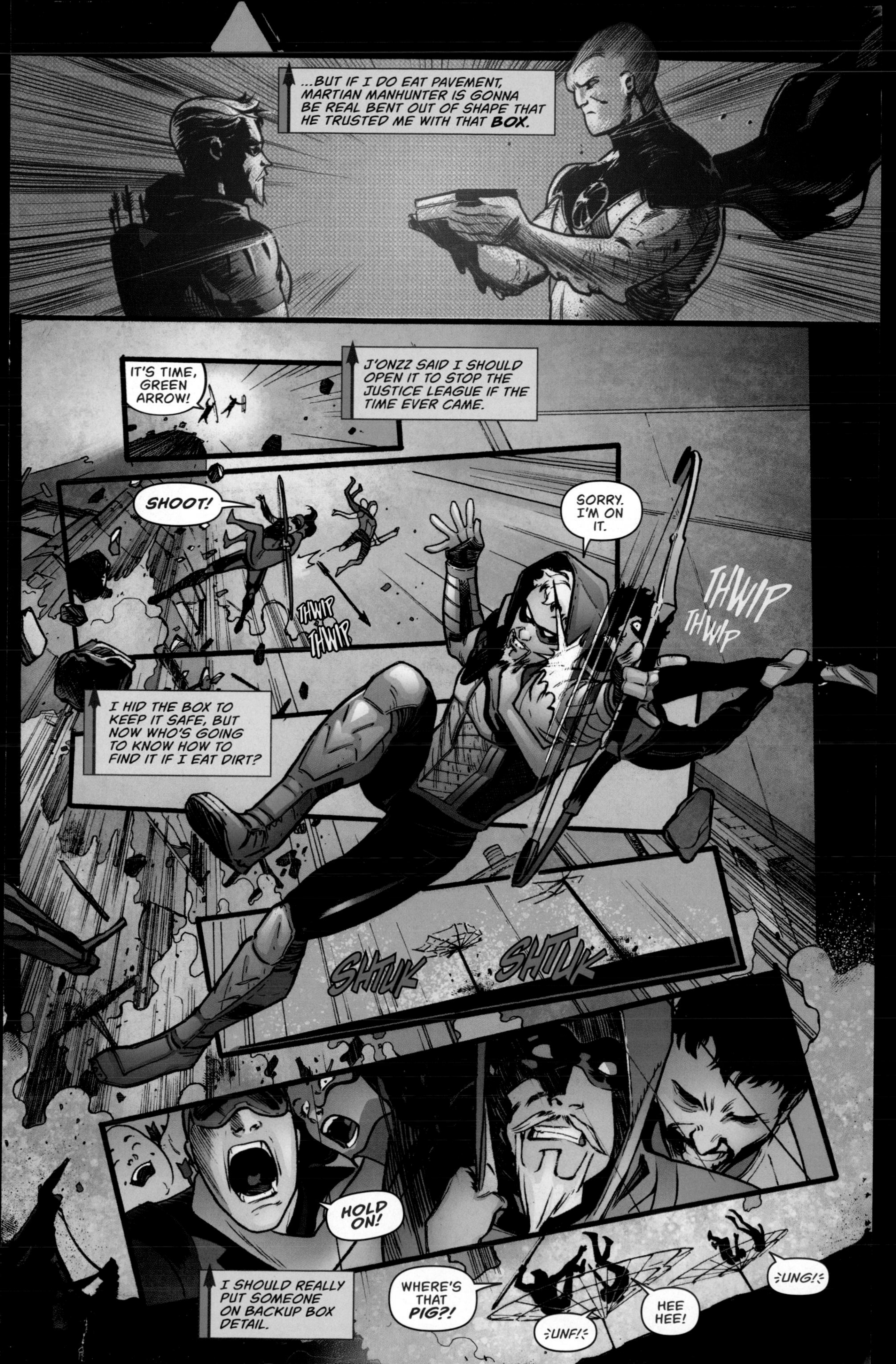
...BUT IF I DO EAT PAVEMENT, MARTIAN MANHUNTER IS GONNA BE REAL BENT OUT OF SHAPE THAT HE TRUSTED ME WITH THAT BOX.
IT'S TIME, GREEN ARROW!
J'ONZZ SAID I SHOULD OPEN IT TO STOP THE JUSTICE LEAGUE IF THE TIME EVER CAME.
SHOOT!
SORRY. I'M ON IT.
THWIP THWIP
THWIP THWIP
I HID THE BOX TO KEEP IT SAFE, BUT NOW WHO'S GOING TO KNOW HOW TO FIND IT IF I EAT DIRT?
SHTUK SHTUK
HOLD ON!
I SHOULD REALLY PUT SOMEONE ON BACKUP BOX DETAIL.
WHERE'S THAT PIG?!
UNF!
HEE HEE!
UNG!

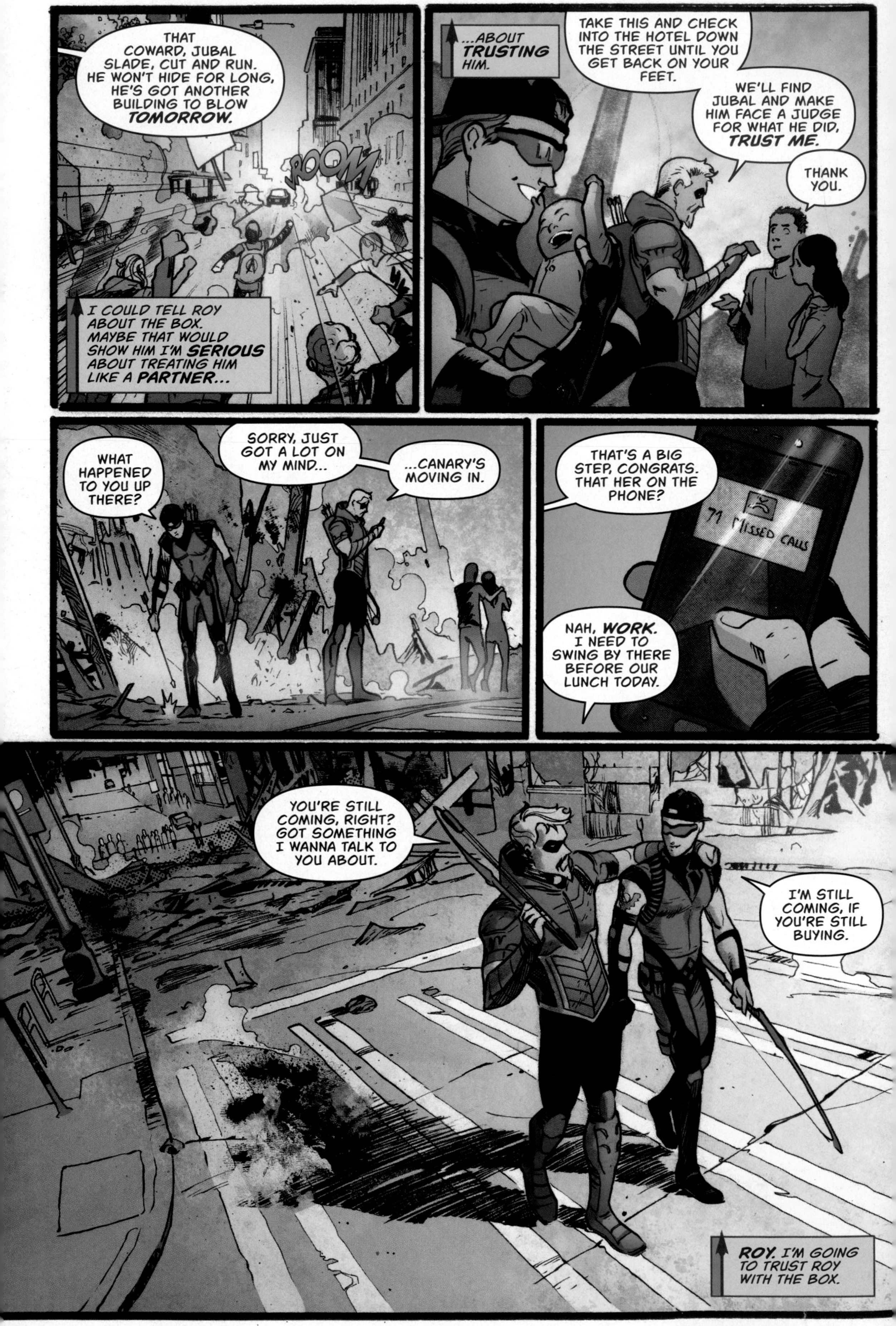
THAT COWARD, JUBAL SLADE, CUT AND RUN. HE WON'T HIDE FOR LONG, HE'S GOT ANOTHER BUILDING TO BLOW TOMORROW.
ROOM
I COULD TELL ROY ABOUT THE BOX. MAYBE THAT WOULD SHOW HIM I'M SERIOUS ABOUT TREATING HIM LIKE A PARTNER...
...ABOUT TRUSTING HIM.
TAKE THIS AND CHECK INTO THE HOTEL DOWN THE STREET UNTIL YOU GET BACK ON YOUR FEET.
WE'LL FIND JUBAL AND MAKE HIM FACE A JUDGE FOR WHAT HE DID, TRUST ME.
THANK YOU.
WHAT HAPPENED TO YOU UP THERE?
SORRY, JUST GOT A LOT ON MY MIND...
...CANARY'S MOVING IN.
THAT'S A BIG STEP, CONGRATS. THAT HER ON THE PHONE?
71 MISSED CALLS
NAH, WORK. I NEED TO SWING BY THERE BEFORE OUR LUNCH TODAY.
YOU'RE STILL COMING, RIGHT? GOT SOMETHING I WANNA TALK TO YOU ABOUT.
I'M STILL COMING, IF YOU'RE STILL BUYING.
ROY. I'M GOING TO TRUST ROY WITH THE BOX.

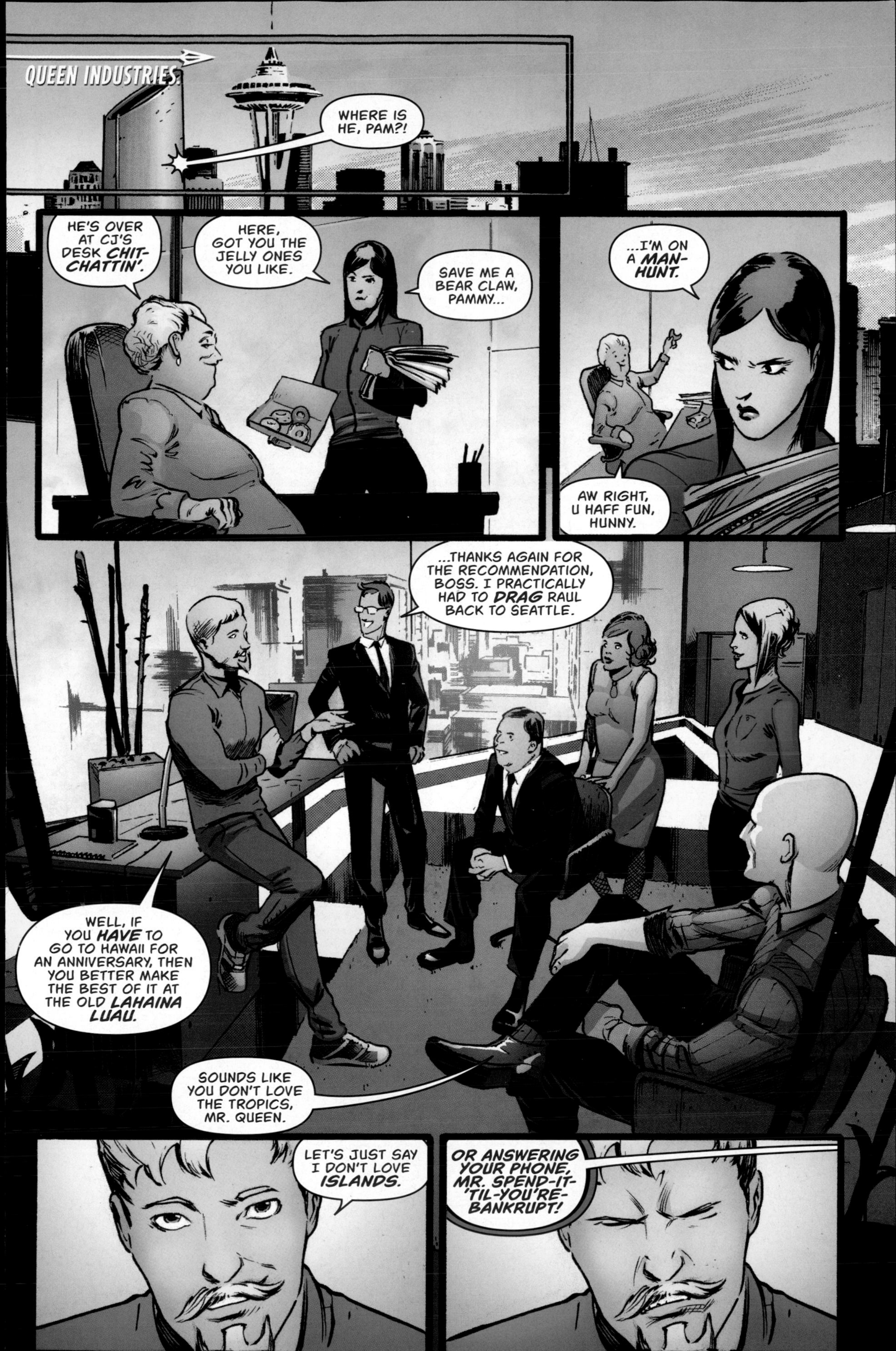
QUEEN INDUSTRIES:
WHERE IS HE, PAM?!
HE'S OVER AT CJ'S DESK CHIT-CHATTIN'.
HERE, GOT YOU THE JELLY ONES YOU LIKE.
SAVE ME A BEAR CLAW, PAMMY...
...I'M ON A MAN-HUNT.
AW RIGHT, U HAFF FUN, HUNNY.
...THANKS AGAIN FOR THE RECOMMENDATION, BOSS. I PRACTICALLY HAD TO DRAG RAUL BACK TO SEATTLE.
WELL, IF YOU HAVE TO GO TO HAWAII FOR AN ANNIVERSARY, THEN YOU BETTER MAKE THE BEST OF IT AT THE OLD LAHAINA LUAU.
SOUNDS LIKE YOU DON'T LOVE THE TROPICS, MR. QUEEN.
LET'S JUST SAY I DON'T LOVE ISLANDS.
OR ANSWERING YOUR PHONE, MR. SPEND-IT-'TIL-YOU'RE-BANKRUPT!

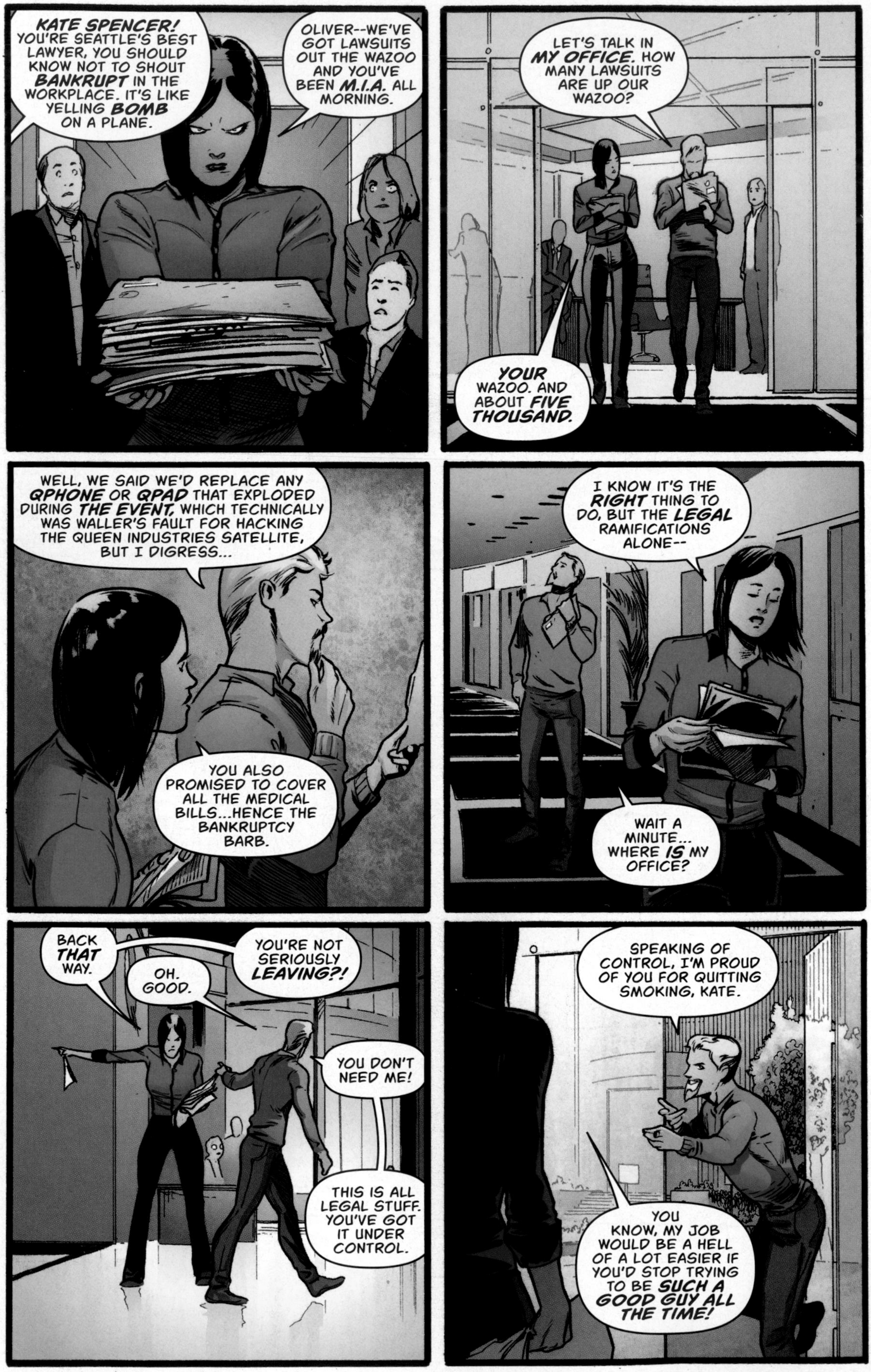
KATE SPENCER! YOU'RE SEATTLE'S BEST LAWYER, YOU SHOULD KNOW NOT TO SHOUT BANKRUPT IN THE WORKPLACE. IT'S LIKE YELLING BOMB ON A PLANE.
OLIVER--WE'VE GOT LAWSUITS OUT THE WAZOO AND YOU'VE BEEN M.I.A. ALL MORNING.
LET'S TALK IN MY OFFICE. HOW MANY LAWSUITS ARE UP OUR WAZOO?
YOUR WAZOO. AND ABOUT FIVE THOUSAND.
WELL, WE SAID WE'D REPLACE ANY QPHONE OR QPAD THAT EXPLODED DURING THE EVENT, WHICH TECHNICALLY WAS WALLER'S FAULT FOR HACKING THE QUEEN INDUSTRIES SATELLITE, BUT I DIGRESS...
YOU ALSO PROMISED TO COVER ALL THE MEDICAL BILLS...HENCE THE BANKRUPTCY BARB.
I KNOW IT'S THE RIGHT THING TO DO, BUT THE LEGAL RAMIFICATIONS ALONE--
WAIT A MINUTE... WHERE IS MY OFFICE?
BACK THAT WAY.
OH. GOOD.
YOU'RE NOT SERIOUSLY LEAVING?!
YOU DON'T NEED ME!
THIS IS ALL LEGAL STUFF. YOU'VE GOT IT UNDER CONTROL.
SPEAKING OF CONTROL, I'M PROUD OF YOU FOR QUITTING SMOKING, KATE.
YOU KNOW, MY JOB WOULD BE A HELL OF A LOT EASIER IF YOU'D STOP TRYING TO BE SUCH A GOOD GUY ALL THE TIME!

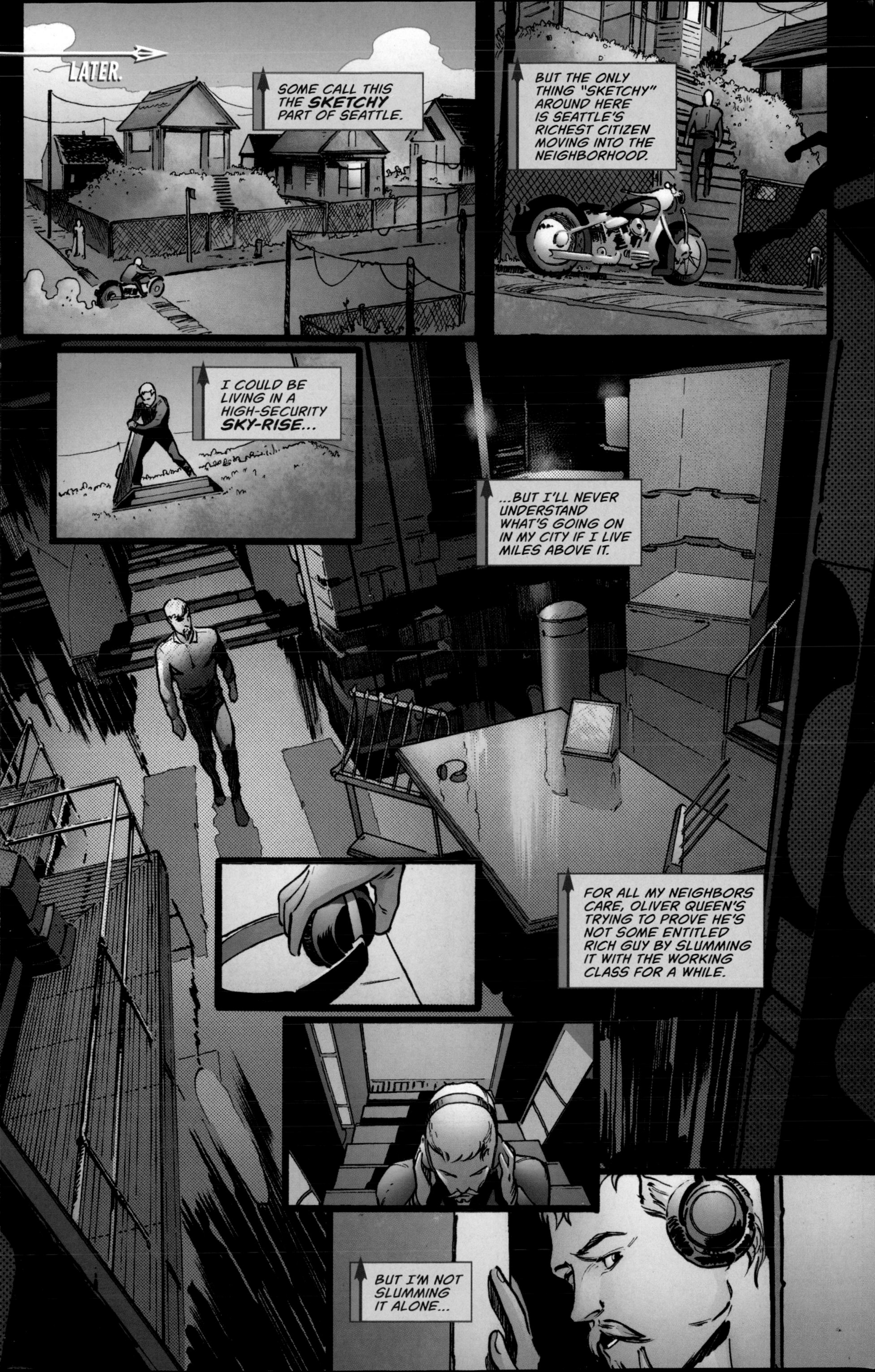
LATER.
SOME CALL THIS THE SKETCHY PART OF SEATTLE.
BUT THE ONLY THING "SKETCHY" AROUND HERE IS SEATTLE'S RICHEST CITIZEN MOVING INTO THE NEIGHBORHOOD.
I COULD BE LIVING IN A HIGH-SECURITY SKY-RISE...
...BUT I'LL NEVER UNDERSTAND WHAT'S GOING ON IN MY CITY IF I LIVE MILES ABOVE IT.
FOR ALL MY NEIGHBORS CARE, OLIVER QUEEN'S TRYING TO PROVE HE'S NOT SOME ENTITLED RICH GUY BY SLUMMING IT WITH THE WORKING CLASS FOR A WHILE.
BUT I'M NOT SLUMMING IT ALONE...

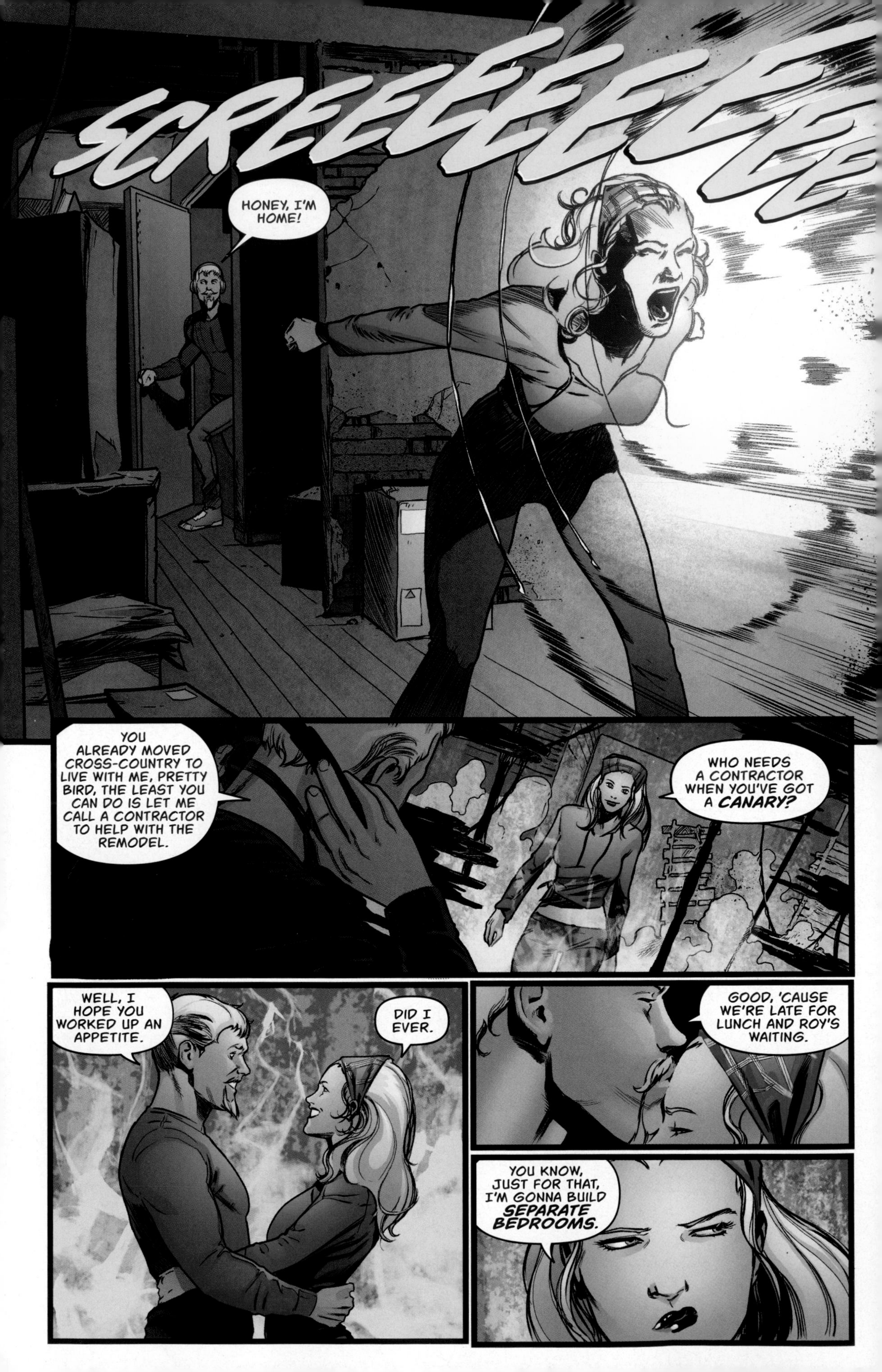
SCREEEEEEEE
HONEY, I'M HOME!
YOU ALREADY MOVED CROSS-COUNTRY TO LIVE WITH ME, PRETTY BIRD, THE LEAST YOU CAN DO IS LET ME CALL A CONTRACTOR TO HELP WITH THE REMODEL.
WHO NEEDS A CONTRACTOR WHEN YOU'VE GOT A CANARY?
WELL, I HOPE YOU WORKED UP AN APPETITE.
DID I EVER.
GOOD, 'CAUSE WE'RE LATE FOR LUNCH AND ROY'S WAITING.
YOU KNOW, JUST FOR THAT, I'M GONNA BUILD SEPARATE BEDROOMS.

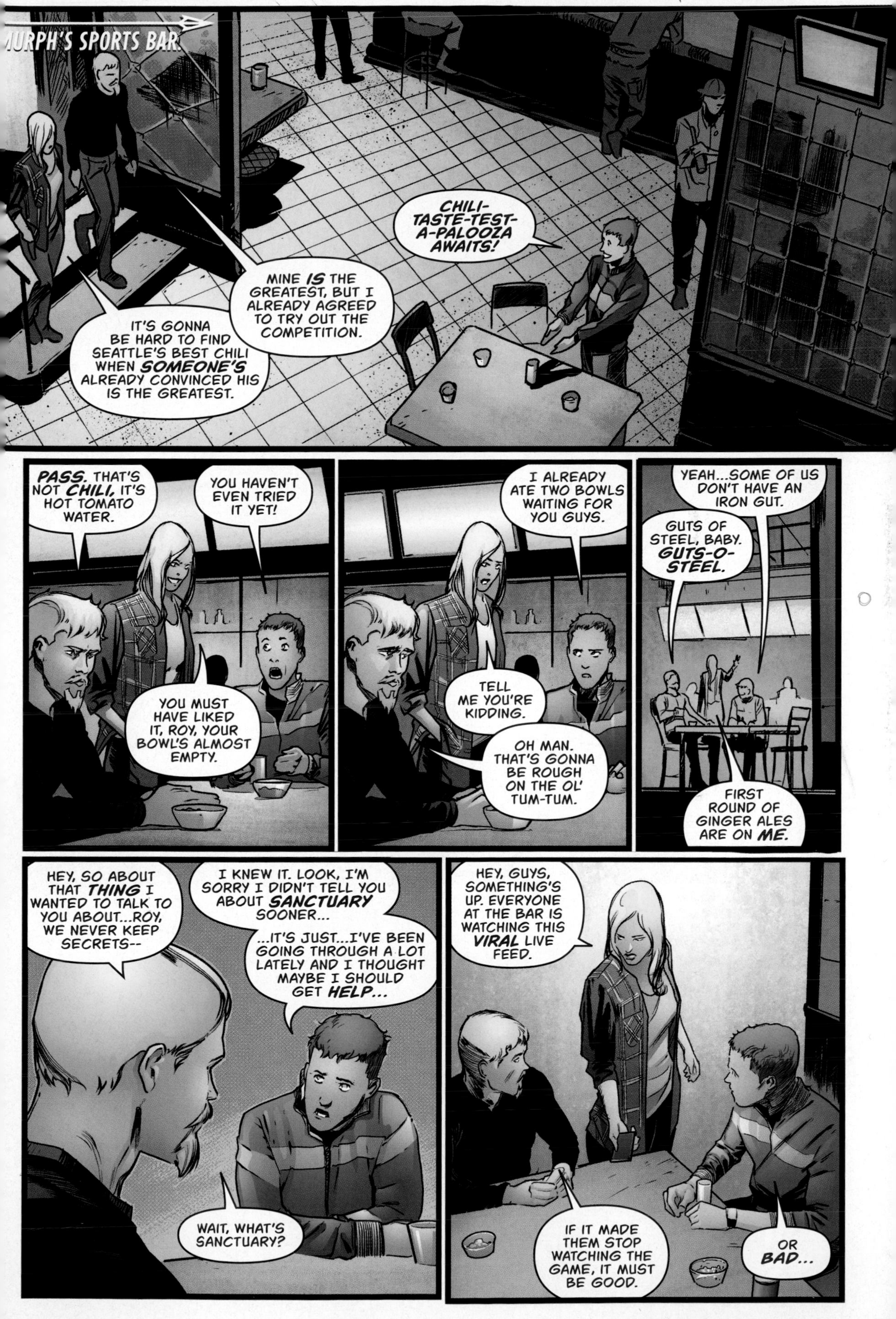
MURPH'S SPORTS BAR.
CHILI-TASTE-TEST-A-PALOOZA AWAITS!
IT'S GONNA BE HARD TO FIND SEATTLE'S BEST CHILI WHEN SOMEONE'S ALREADY CONVINCED HIS IS THE GREATEST.
MINE IS THE GREATEST, BUT I ALREADY AGREED TO TRY OUT THE COMPETITION.
PASS. THAT'S NOT CHILI, IT'S HOT TOMATO WATER.
YOU HAVEN'T EVEN TRIED IT YET!
YOU MUST HAVE LIKED IT, ROY, YOUR BOWL'S ALMOST EMPTY.
I ALREADY ATE TWO BOWLS WAITING FOR YOU GUYS.
TELL ME YOU'RE KIDDING.
OH MAN. THAT'S GONNA BE ROUGH ON THE OL' TUM-TUM.
YEAH...SOME OF US DON'T HAVE AN IRON GUT.
GUTS OF STEEL, BABY. GUTS-O-STEEL.
FIRST ROUND OF GINGER ALES ARE ON ME.
HEY, SO ABOUT THAT THING I WANTED TO TALK TO YOU ABOUT...ROY, WE NEVER KEEP SECRETS--
I KNEW IT. LOOK, I'M SORRY I DIDN'T TELL YOU ABOUT SANCTUARY SOONER...
...IT'S JUST...I'VE BEEN GOING THROUGH A LOT LATELY AND I THOUGHT MAYBE I SHOULD GET HELP...
WAIT, WHAT'S SANCTUARY?
HEY, GUYS, SOMETHING'S UP. EVERYONE AT THE BAR IS WATCHING THIS VIRAL LIVE FEED.
IF IT MADE THEM STOP WATCHING THE GAME, IT MUST BE GOOD.
OR BAD...

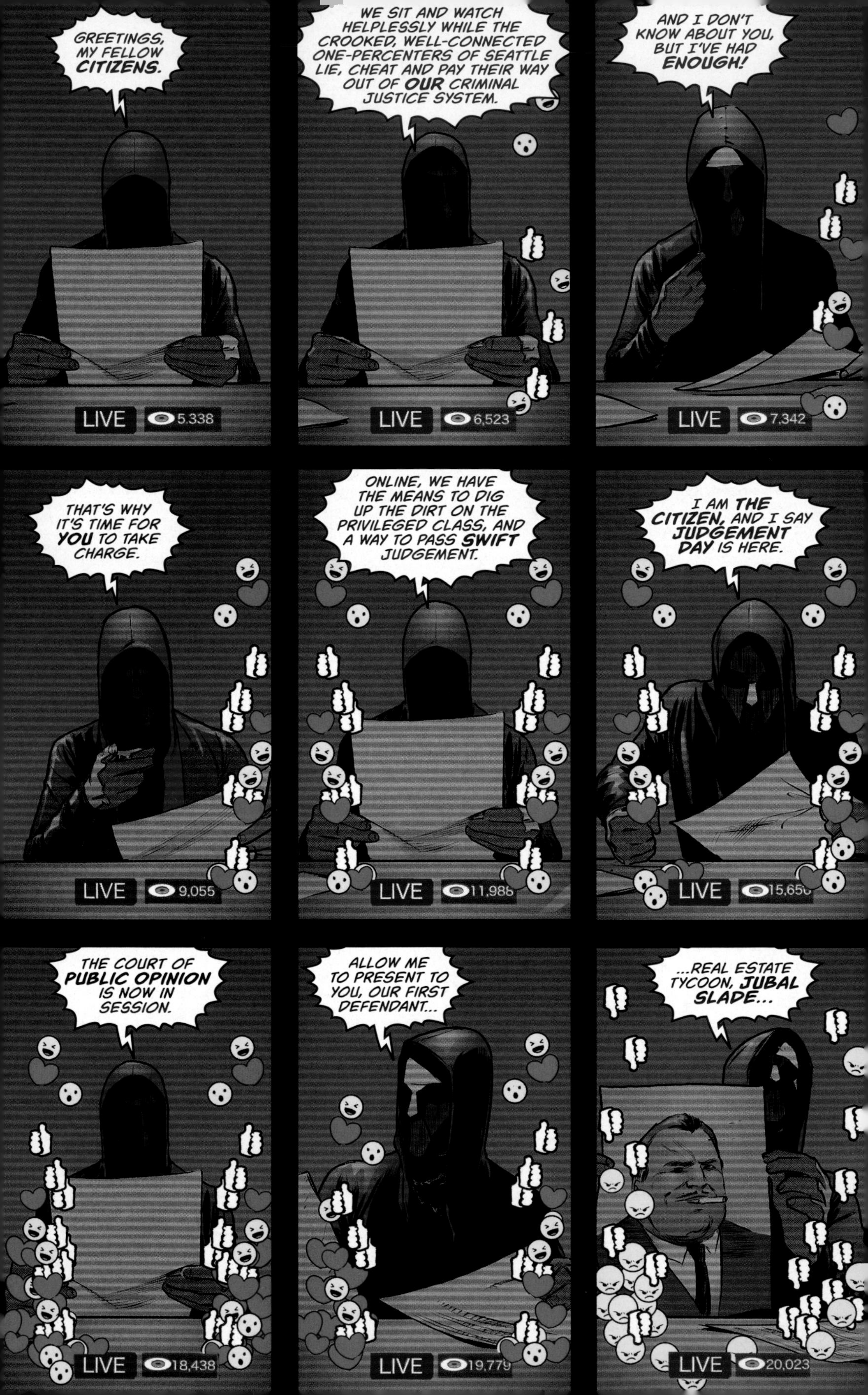
GREETINGS, MY FELLOW CITIZENS.
LIVE 5.338
WE SIT AND WATCH HELPLESSLY WHILE THE CROOKED, WELL-CONNECTED ONE-PERCENTERS OF SEATTLE LIE, CHEAT AND PAY THEIR WAY OUT OF OUR CRIMINAL JUSTICE SYSTEM.
LIVE 6,523
AND I DON'T KNOW ABOUT YOU, BUT I'VE HAD ENOUGH!
LIVE 7,342
THAT'S WHY IT'S TIME FOR YOU TO TAKE CHARGE.
LIVE 9,055
ONLINE, WE HAVE THE MEANS TO DIG UP THE DIRT ON THE PRIVILEGED CLASS, AND A WAY TO PASS SWIFT JUDGEMENT.
LIVE 11,988
I AM THE CITIZEN, AND I SAY JUDGEMENT DAY IS HERE.
LIVE 15,650
THE COURT OF PUBLIC OPINION IS NOW IN SESSION.
LIVE 18,438
ALLOW ME TO PRESENT TO YOU, OUR FIRST DEFENDANT...
LIVE 19,779
...REAL ESTATE TYCOON, JUBAL SLADE...
LIVE 20,023

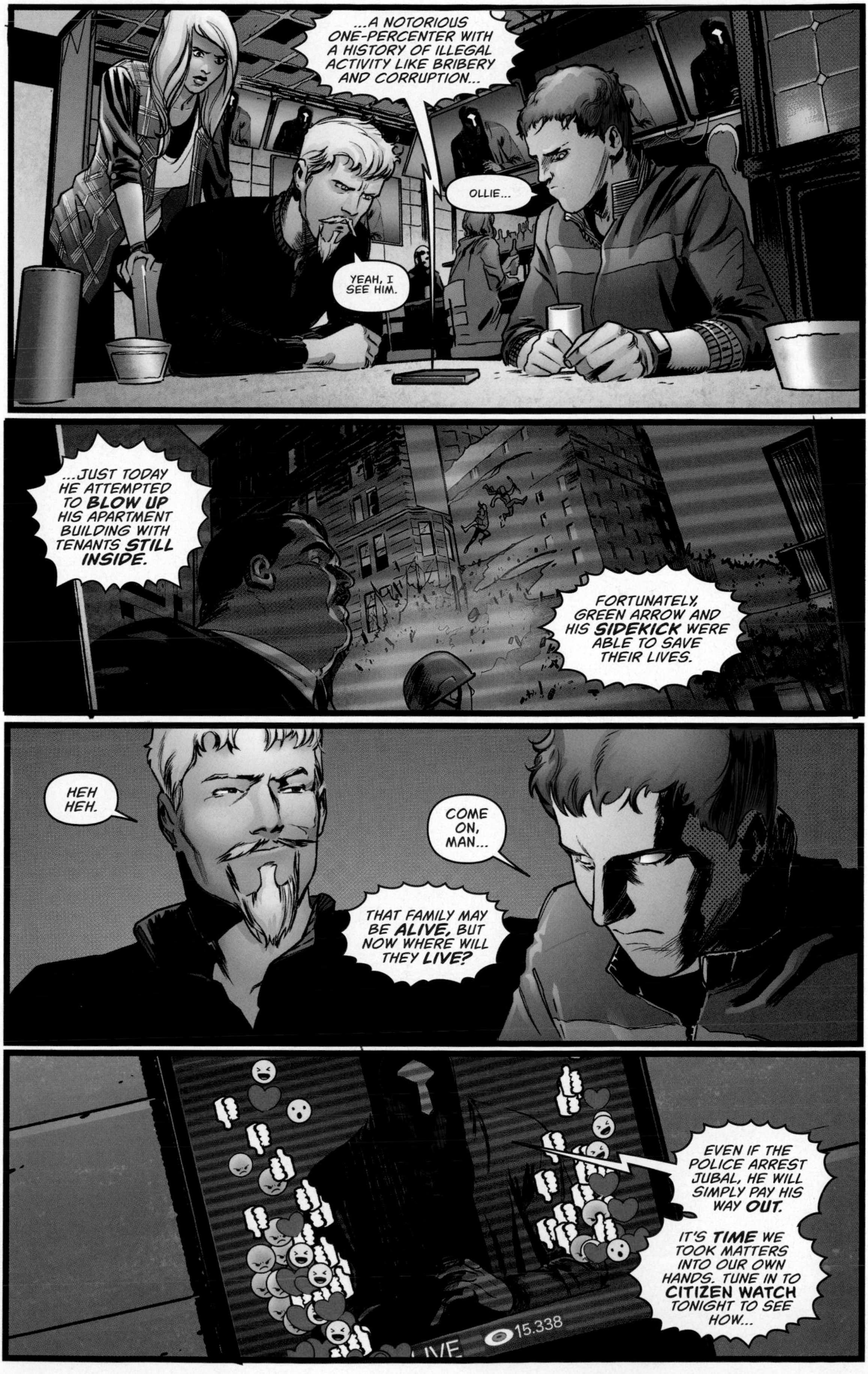
...A NOTORIOUS ONE-PERCENTER WITH A HISTORY OF ILLEGAL ACTIVITY LIKE BRIBERY AND CORRUPTION...
OLLIE...
YEAH, I SEE HIM.
...JUST TODAY HE ATTEMPTED TO BLOW UP HIS APARTMENT BUILDING WITH TENANTS STILL INSIDE.
FORTUNATELY, GREEN ARROW AND HIS SIDEKICK WERE ABLE TO SAVE THEIR LIVES.
HEH HEH.
COME ON, MAN...
THAT FAMILY MAY BE ALIVE, BUT NOW WHERE WILL THEY LIVE?
EVEN IF THE POLICE ARREST JUBAL, HE WILL SIMPLY PAY HIS WAY OUT.
IT'S TIME WE TOOK MATTERS INTO OUR OWN HANDS. TUNE IN TO CITIZEN WATCH TONIGHT TO SEE HOW...
15.338

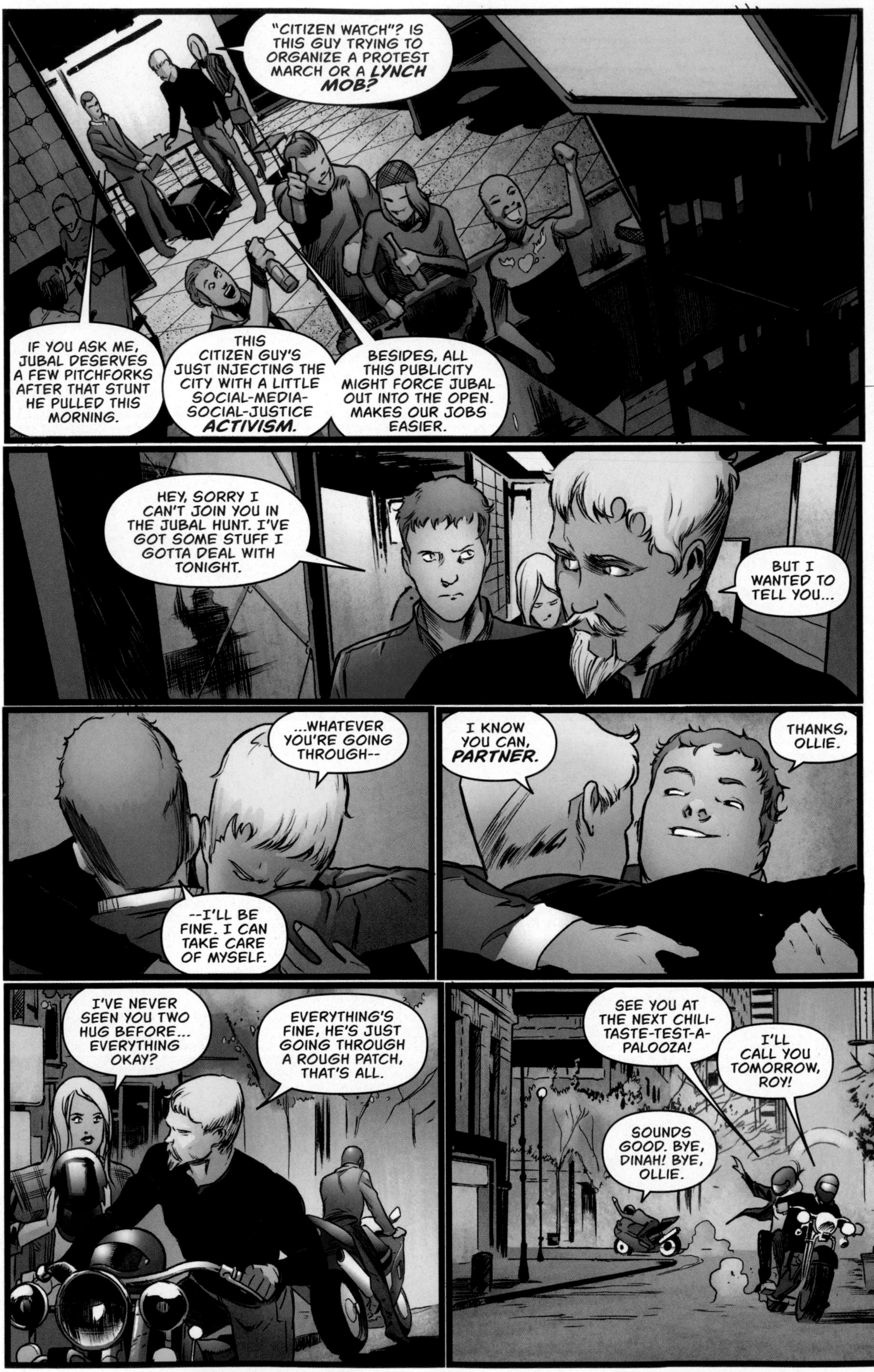
"CITIZEN WATCH"? IS THIS GUY TRYING TO ORGANIZE A PROTEST MARCH OR A LYNCH MOB?
IF YOU ASK ME, JUBAL DESERVES A FEW PITCHFORKS AFTER THAT STUNT HE PULLED THIS MORNING.
THIS CITIZEN GUY'S JUST INJECTING THE CITY WITH A LITTLE SOCIAL-MEDIA-SOCIAL-JUSTICE ACTIVISM.
BESIDES, ALL THIS PUBLICITY MIGHT FORCE JUBAL OUT INTO THE OPEN. MAKES OUR JOBS EASIER.
HEY, SORRY I CAN'T JOIN YOU IN THE JUBAL HUNT. I'VE GOT SOME STUFF I GOTTA DEAL WITH TONIGHT.
BUT I WANTED TO TELL YOU...
...WHATEVER YOU'RE GOING THROUGH--
--I'LL BE FINE. I CAN TAKE CARE OF MYSELF.
I KNOW YOU CAN, PARTNER.
THANKS, OLLIE.
I'VE NEVER SEEN YOU TWO HUG BEFORE... EVERYTHING OKAY?
EVERYTHING'S FINE, HE'S JUST GOING THROUGH A ROUGH PATCH, THAT'S ALL.
SEE YOU AT THE NEXT CHILI-TASTE-TEST-A-PALOOZA!
I'LL CALL YOU TOMORROW, ROY!
SOUNDS GOOD. BYE, DINAH! BYE, OLLIE.

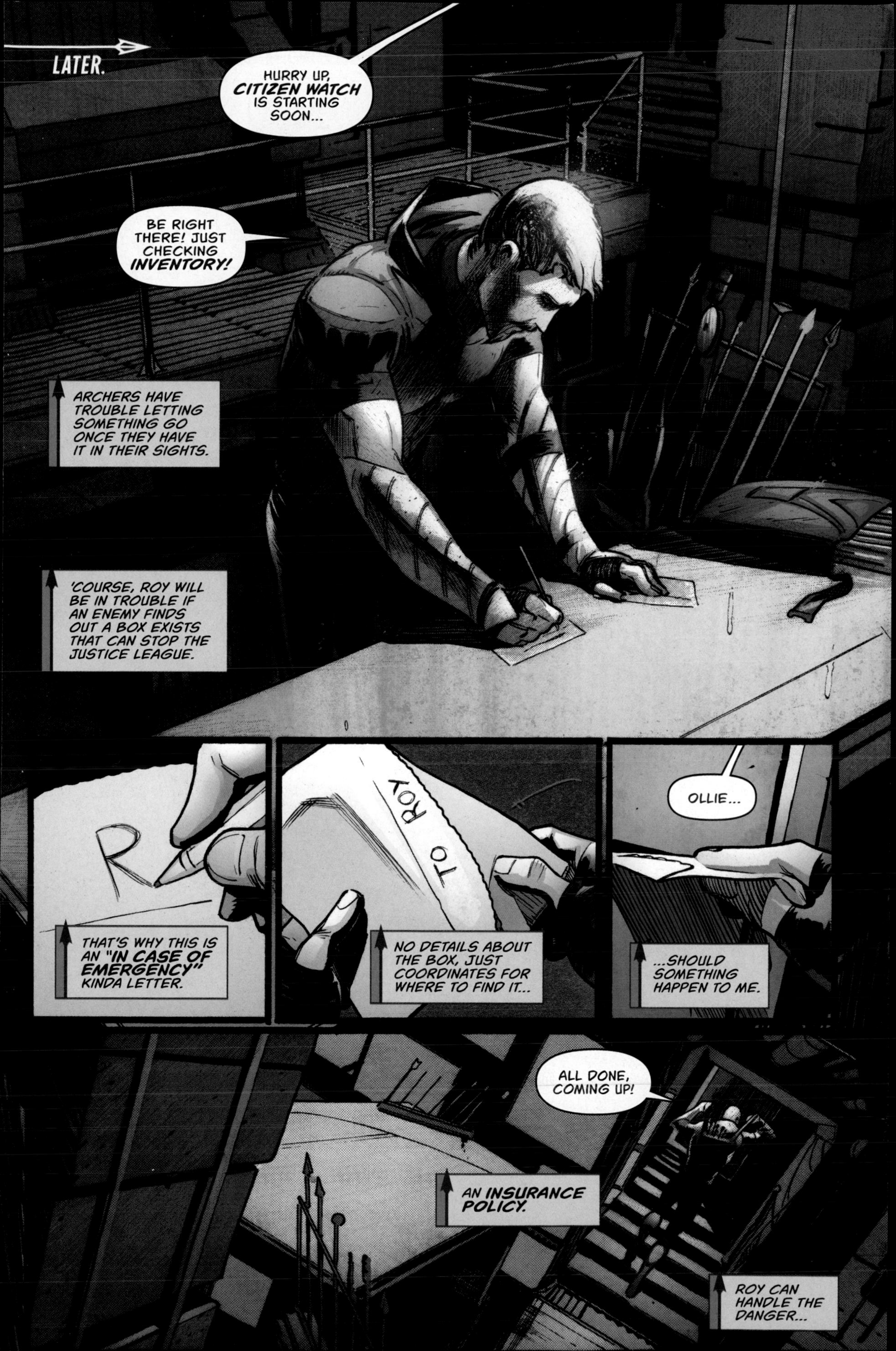
LATER.
HURRY UP, CITIZEN WATCH IS STARTING SOON...
BE RIGHT THERE! JUST CHECKING INVENTORY!
ARCHERS HAVE TROUBLE LETTING SOMETHING GO ONCE THEY HAVE IT IN THEIR SIGHTS.
'COURSE, ROY WILL BE IN TROUBLE IF AN ENEMY FINDS OUT A BOX EXISTS THAT CAN STOP THE JUSTICE LEAGUE.
R
THAT'S WHY THIS IS AN "IN CASE OF EMERGENCY" KINDA LETTER.
TO ROY
NO DETAILS ABOUT THE BOX, JUST COORDINATES FOR WHERE TO FIND IT...
OLLIE...
...SHOULD SOMETHING HAPPEN TO ME.
ALL DONE, COMING UP!
AN INSURANCE POLICY.
ROY CAN HANDLE THE DANGER...

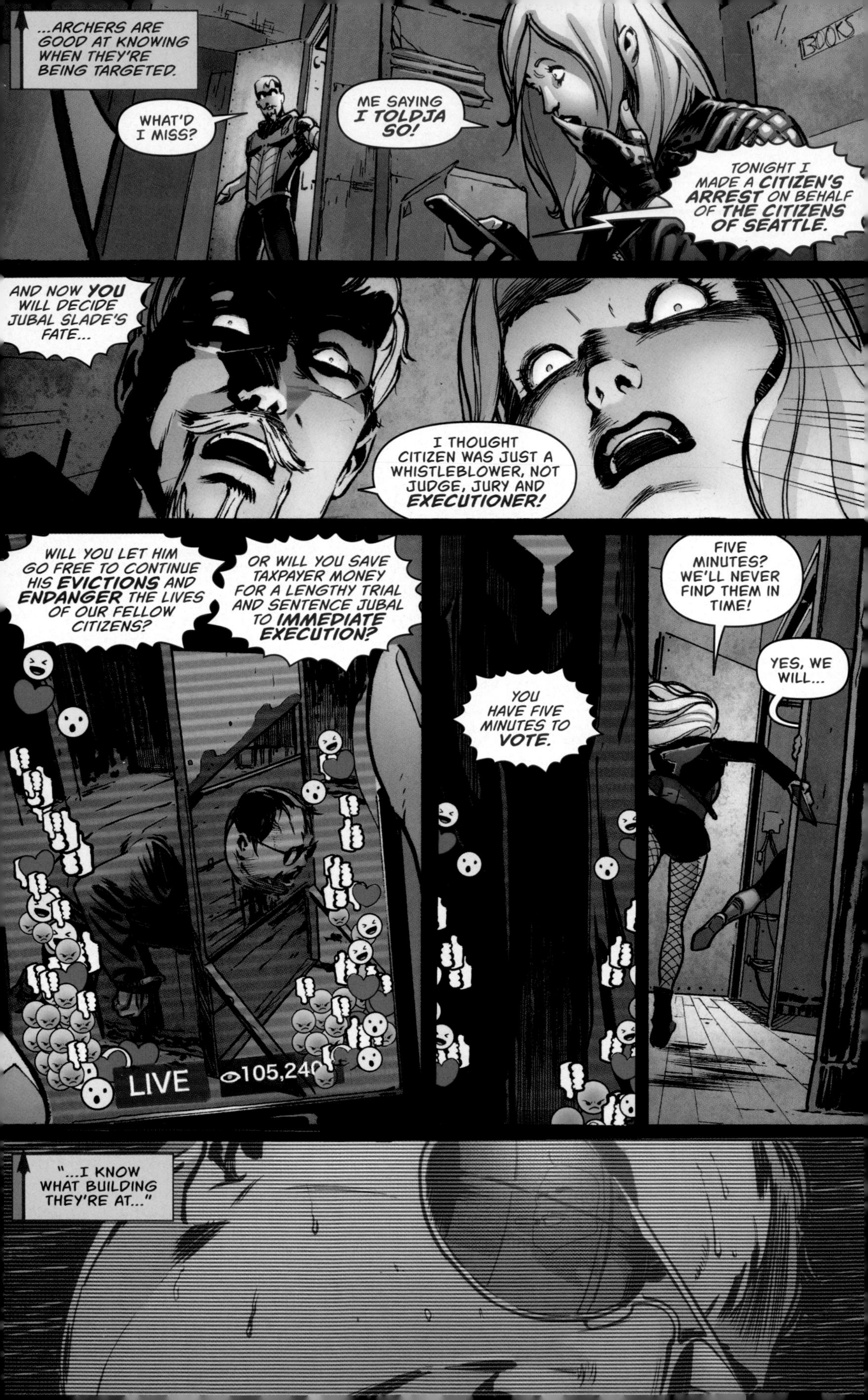
...ARCHERS ARE GOOD AT KNOWING WHEN THEY'RE BEING TARGETED.
WHAT'D I MISS?
ME SAYING I TOLDJA SO!
TONIGHT I MADE A CITIZEN'S ARREST ON BEHALF OF THE CITIZENS OF SEATTLE.
AND NOW YOU WILL DECIDE JUBAL SLADE'S FATE...
I THOUGHT CITIZEN WAS JUST A WHISTLEBLOWER, NOT JUDGE, JURY AND EXECUTIONER!
WILL YOU LET HIM GO FREE TO CONTINUE HIS EVICTIONS AND ENDANGER THE LIVES OF OUR FELLOW CITIZENS?
OR WILL YOU SAVE TAXPAYER MONEY FOR A LENGTHY TRIAL AND SENTENCE JUBAL TO IMMEDIATE EXECUTION?
LIVE
105,240
YOU HAVE FIVE MINUTES TO VOTE.
FIVE MINUTES? WE'LL NEVER FIND THEM IN TIME!
YES, WE WILL...
"...I KNOW WHAT BUILDING THEY'RE AT..."

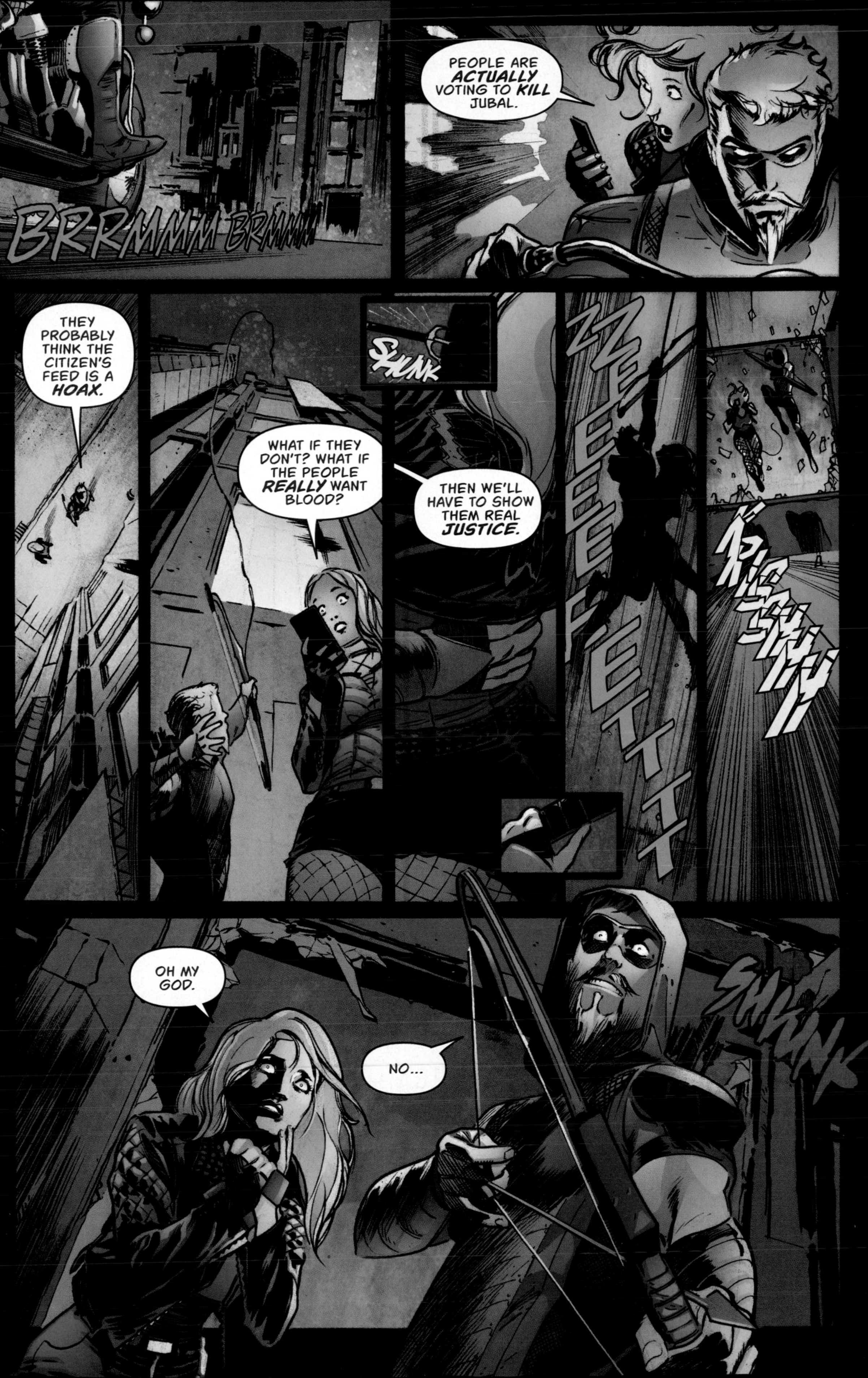
BRRMMMM BRMMMM
PEOPLE ARE ACTUALLY VOTING TO KILL JUBAL.
THEY PROBABLY THINK THE CITIZEN'S FEED IS A HOAX.
SHUNK
WHAT IF THEY DON'T? WHAT IF THE PEOPLE REALLY WANT BLOOD?
THEN WE'LL HAVE TO SHOW THEM REAL JUSTICE.
ZZEEEEEETTTTT
KRISSHHH
OH MY GOD.
NO...
SHUNK

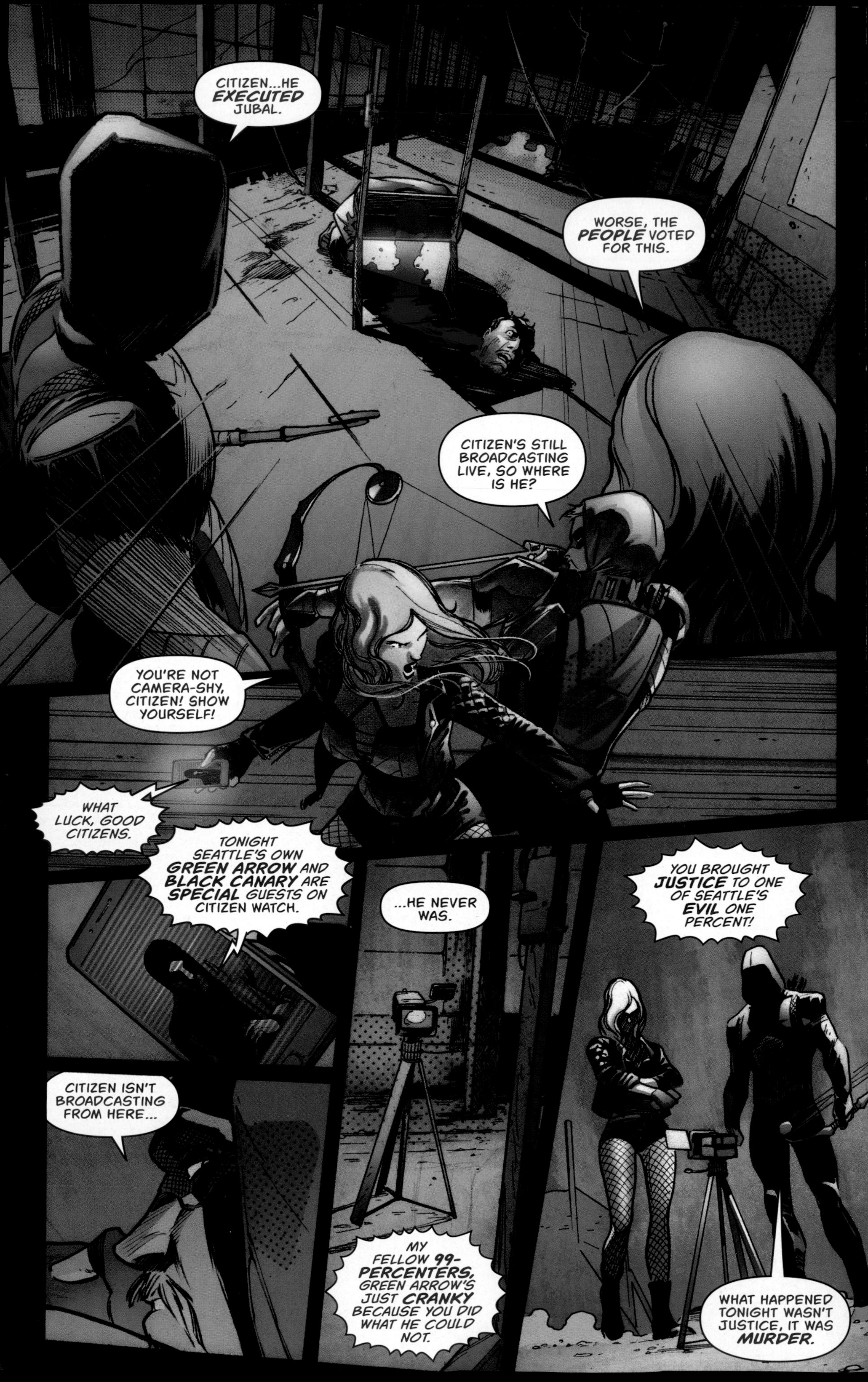
CITIZEN...HE EXECUTED JUBAL.
WORSE, THE PEOPLE VOTED FOR THIS.
CITIZEN'S STILL BROADCASTING LIVE, SO WHERE IS HE?
YOU'RE NOT CAMERA-SHY, CITIZEN! SHOW YOURSELF!
WHAT LUCK, GOOD CITIZENS.
TONIGHT SEATTLE'S OWN GREEN ARROW AND BLACK CANARY ARE SPECIAL GUESTS ON CITIZEN WATCH.
CITIZEN ISN'T BROADCASTING FROM HERE...
...HE NEVER WAS.
MY FELLOW 99-PERCENTERS, GREEN ARROW'S JUST CRANKY BECAUSE YOU DID WHAT HE COULD NOT.
YOU BROUGHT JUSTICE TO ONE OF SEATTLE'S EVIL ONE PERCENT!
WHAT HAPPENED TONIGHT WASN'T JUSTICE, IT WAS MURDER.

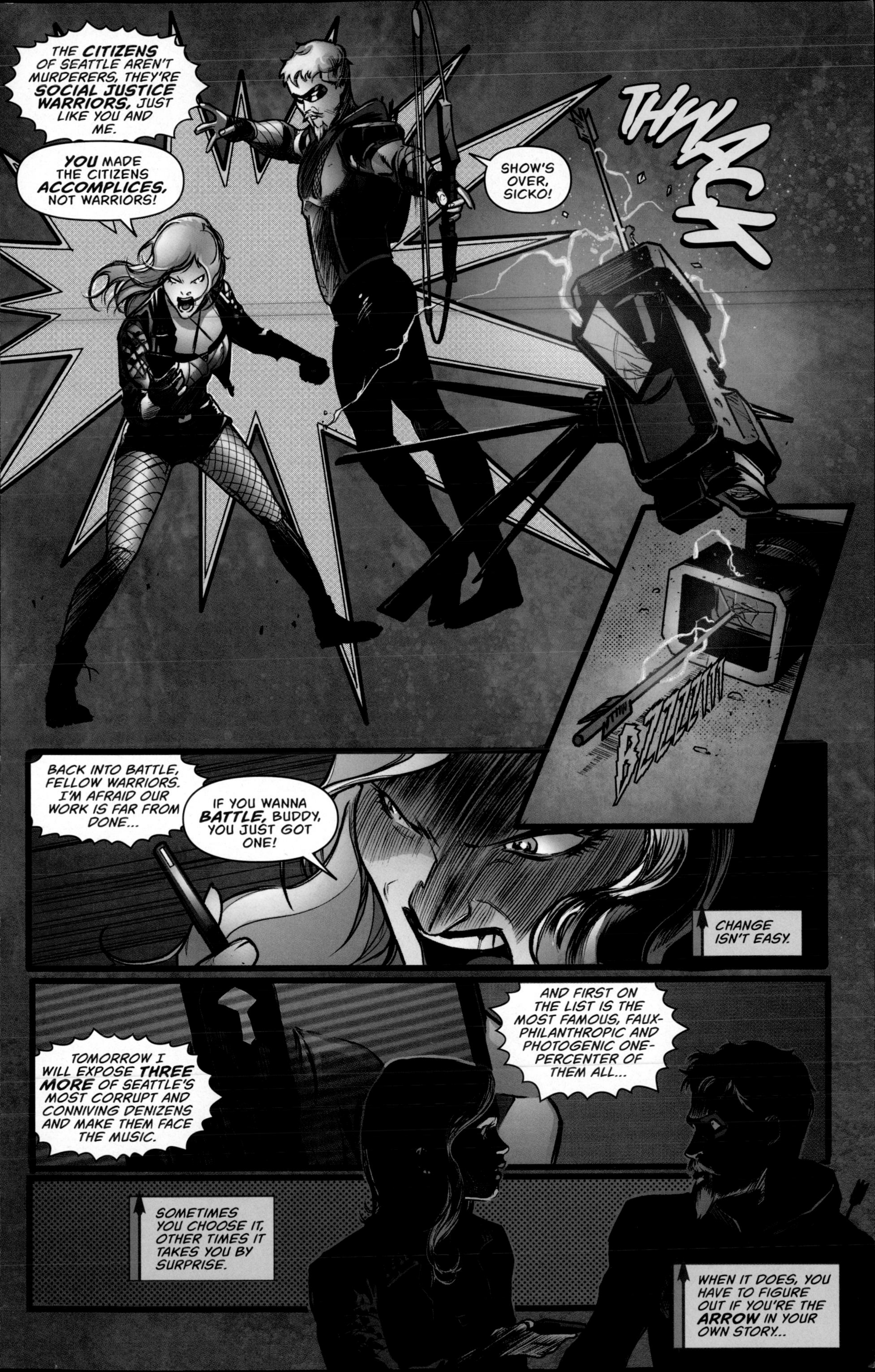
THE CITIZENS OF SEATTLE AREN'T MURDERERS, THEY'RE SOCIAL JUSTICE WARRIORS, JUST LIKE YOU AND ME.
YOU MADE THE CITIZENS ACCOMPLICES, NOT WARRIORS!
SHOW'S OVER, SICKO!
THWACK
BZZZZT
BACK INTO BATTLE, FELLOW WARRIORS. I'M AFRAID OUR WORK IS FAR FROM DONE...
IF YOU WANNA BATTLE, BUDDY, YOU JUST GOT ONE!
CHANGE ISN'T EASY.
TOMORROW I WILL EXPOSE THREE MORE OF SEATTLE'S MOST CORRUPT AND CONNIVING DENIZENS AND MAKE THEM FACE THE MUSIC.
AND FIRST ON THE LIST IS THE MOST FAMOUS, FAUX-PHILANTHROPIC AND PHOTOGENIC ONE-PERCENTER OF THEM ALL...
SOMETIMES YOU CHOOSE IT, OTHER TIMES IT TAKES YOU BY SURPRISE.
WHEN IT DOES, YOU HAVE TO FIGURE OUT IF YOU'RE THE ARROW IN YOUR OWN STORY...

Queen Foundation hits
fundraising go
...OLIVER QUEEN!
The Absentee CEO, OLIVER
Queen Industries
OLIVER QUEEN mingles but isn't single!
OLIVER QUEEN - IN TROUBLE AGAIN!
...OR THE TARGET.

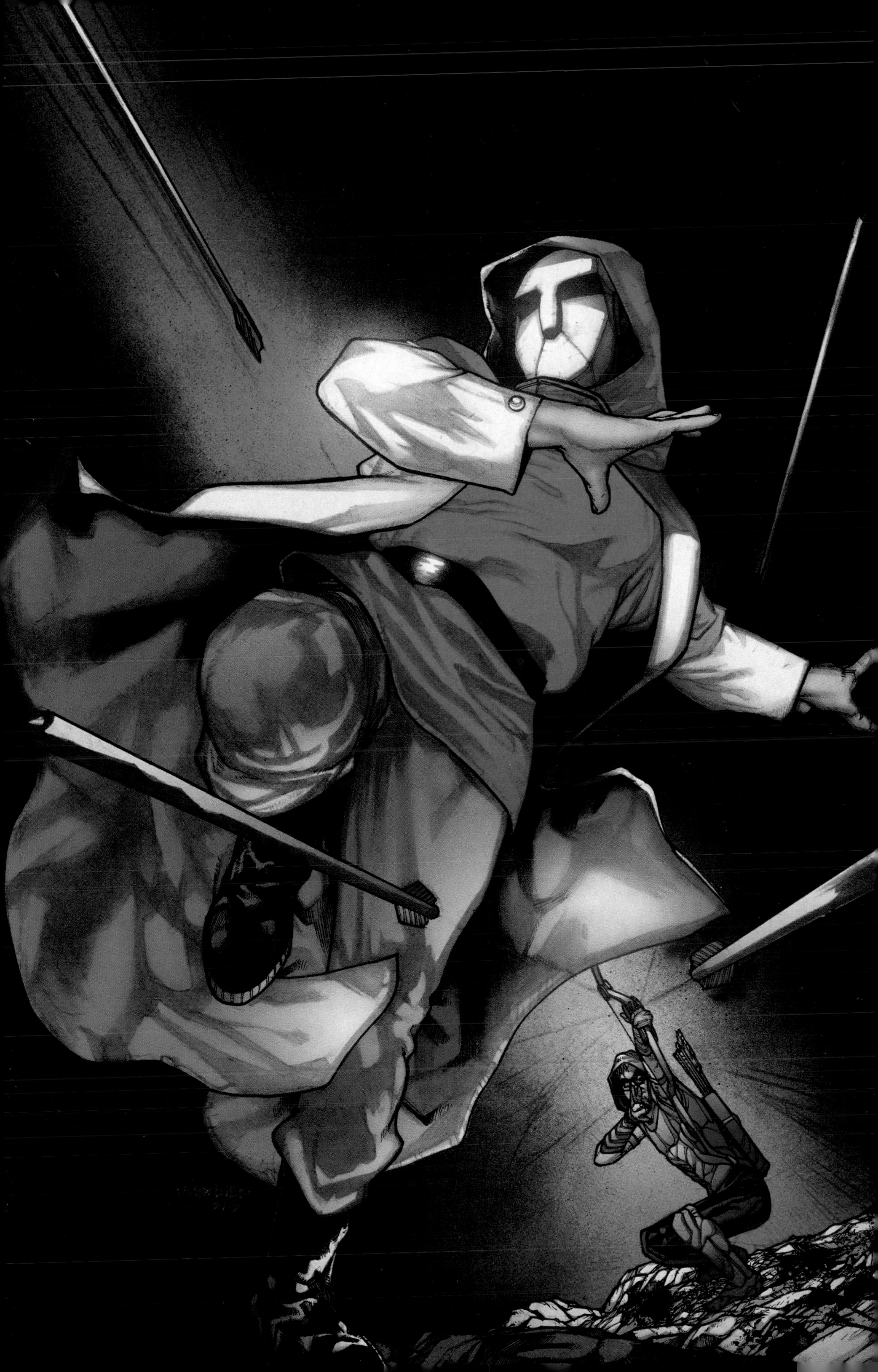

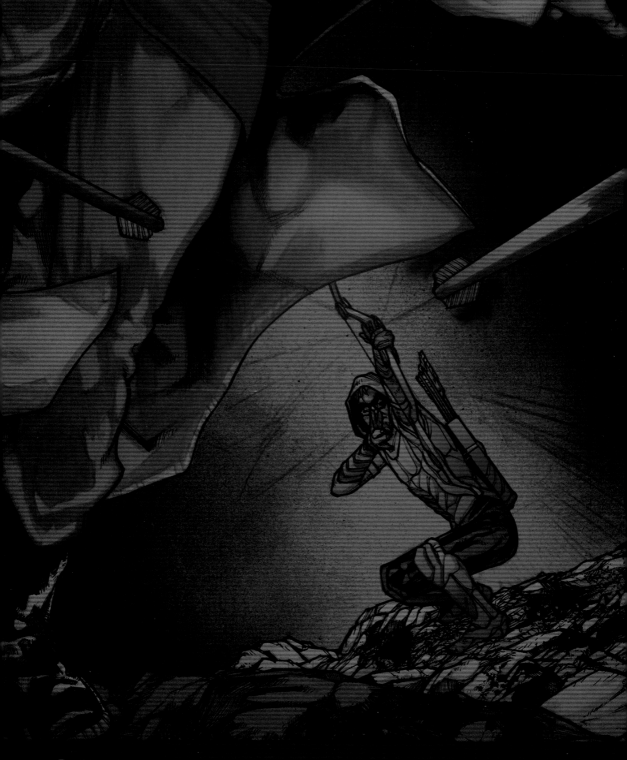

GREEN ARROW
#44

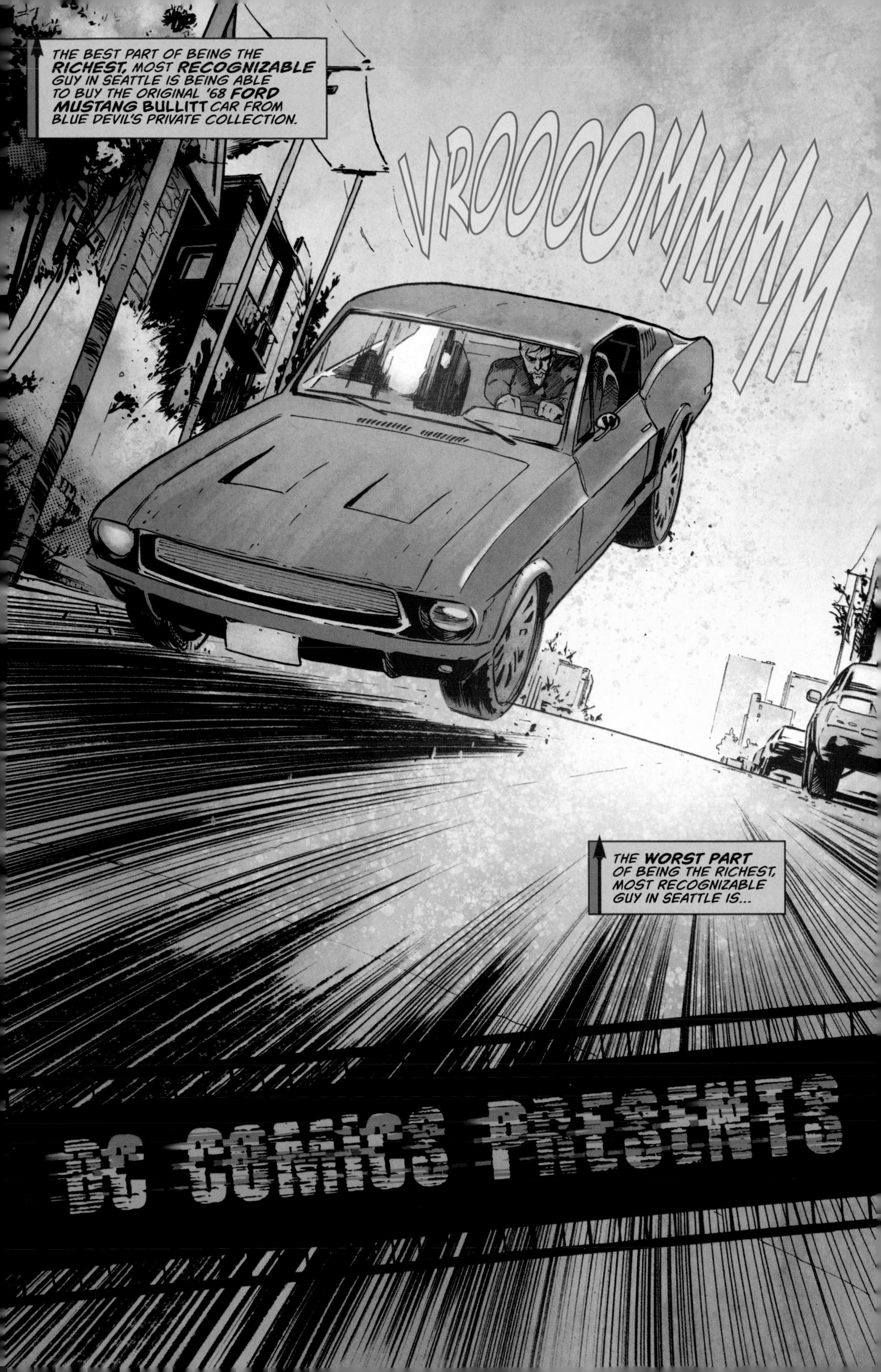
THE BEST PART OF BEING THE RICHEST, MOST RECOGNIZABLE GUY IN SEATTLE IS BEING ABLE TO BUY THE ORIGINAL '68 FORD MUSTANG BULLITT CAR FROM BLUE DEVIL'S PRIVATE COLLECTION.
VROOOOMMMMM
THE WORST PART OF BEING THE RICHEST, MOST RECOGNIZABLE GUY IN SEATTLE IS...
DC COMICS PRESENTS

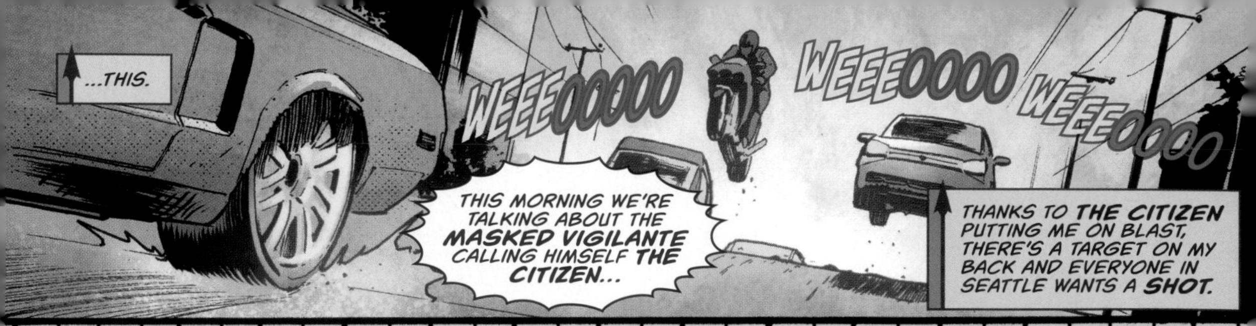
...THIS.
WEEEOOOOO
WEEEOOOO
WEEEOOOO
THIS MORNING WE'RE TALKING ABOUT THE MASKED VIGILANTE CALLING HIMSELF THE CITIZEN...
THANKS TO THE CITIZEN PUTTING ME ON BLAST, THERE'S A TARGET ON MY BACK AND EVERYONE IN SEATTLE WANTS A SHOT.

CITIZEN'S ARREST PART 2: Model Citizen

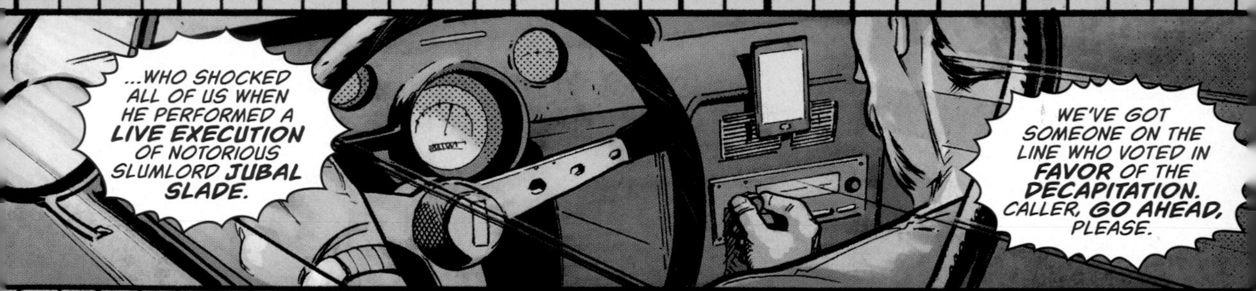
...WHO SHOCKED ALL OF US WHEN HE PERFORMED A LIVE EXECUTION OF NOTORIOUS SLUMLORD JUBAL SLADE.
WE'VE GOT SOMEONE ON THE LINE WHO VOTED IN FAVOR OF THE DECAPITATION. CALLER, GO AHEAD, PLEASE.

JULIE BENSON & SHAWNA BENSON WRITERS JAVIER FERNANDEZ ARTIST

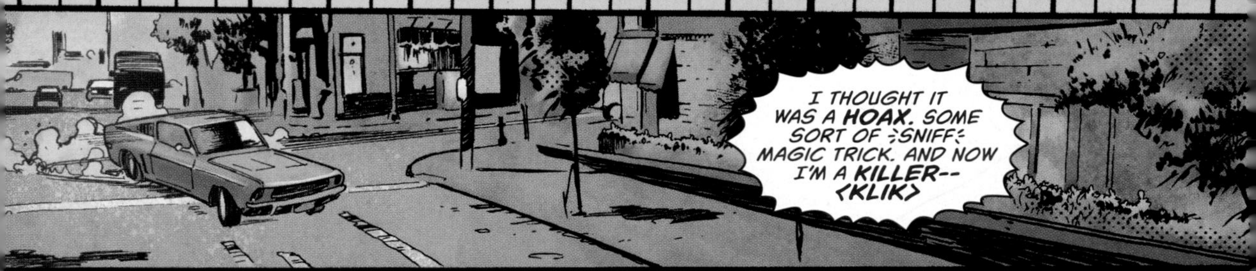
I THOUGHT IT WAS A HOAX. SOME SORT OF *SNIFF* MAGIC TRICK. AND NOW I'M A KILLER-- <KLIK>

JOHN KALISZ COLORS DERON BENNETT LETTERS ALEX MALEEV COVER

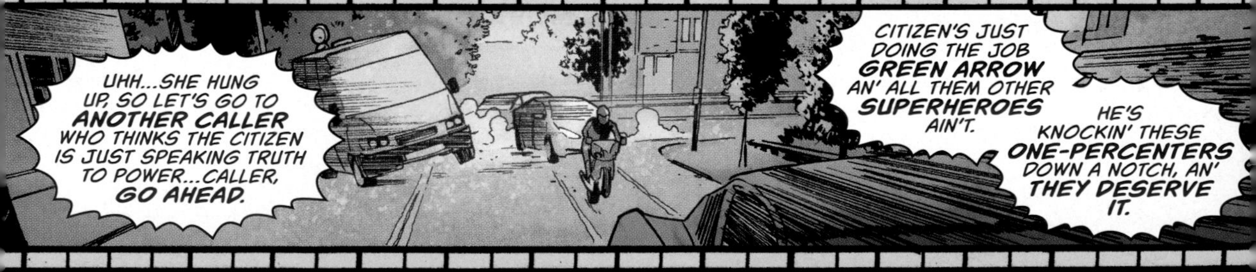
UHH...SHE HUNG UP, SO LET'S GO TO ANOTHER CALLER WHO THINKS THE CITIZEN IS JUST SPEAKING TRUTH TO POWER...CALLER, GO AHEAD.
CITIZEN'S JUST DOING THE JOB GREEN ARROW AN' ALL THEM OTHER SUPERHEROES AIN'T.
HE'S KNOCKIN' THESE ONE-PERCENTERS DOWN A NOTCH, AN' THEY DESERVE IT.

DAVE WIELGOSZ ASST. EDITOR KATIE KUBERT EDITOR JAMIE S. RICH GROUP EDITOR

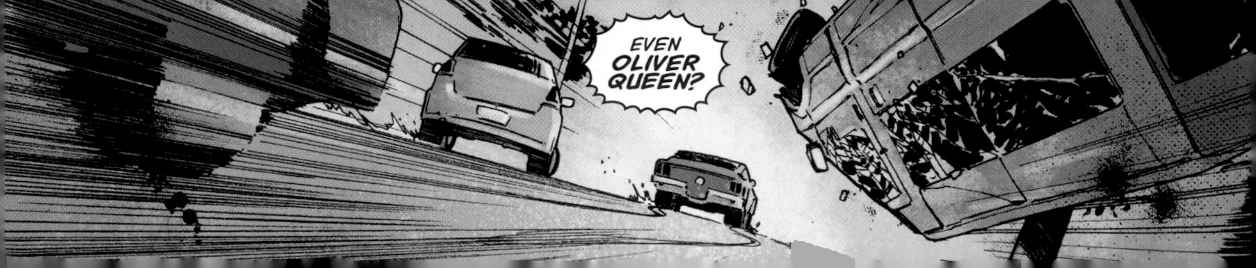
EVEN OLIVER QUEEN?

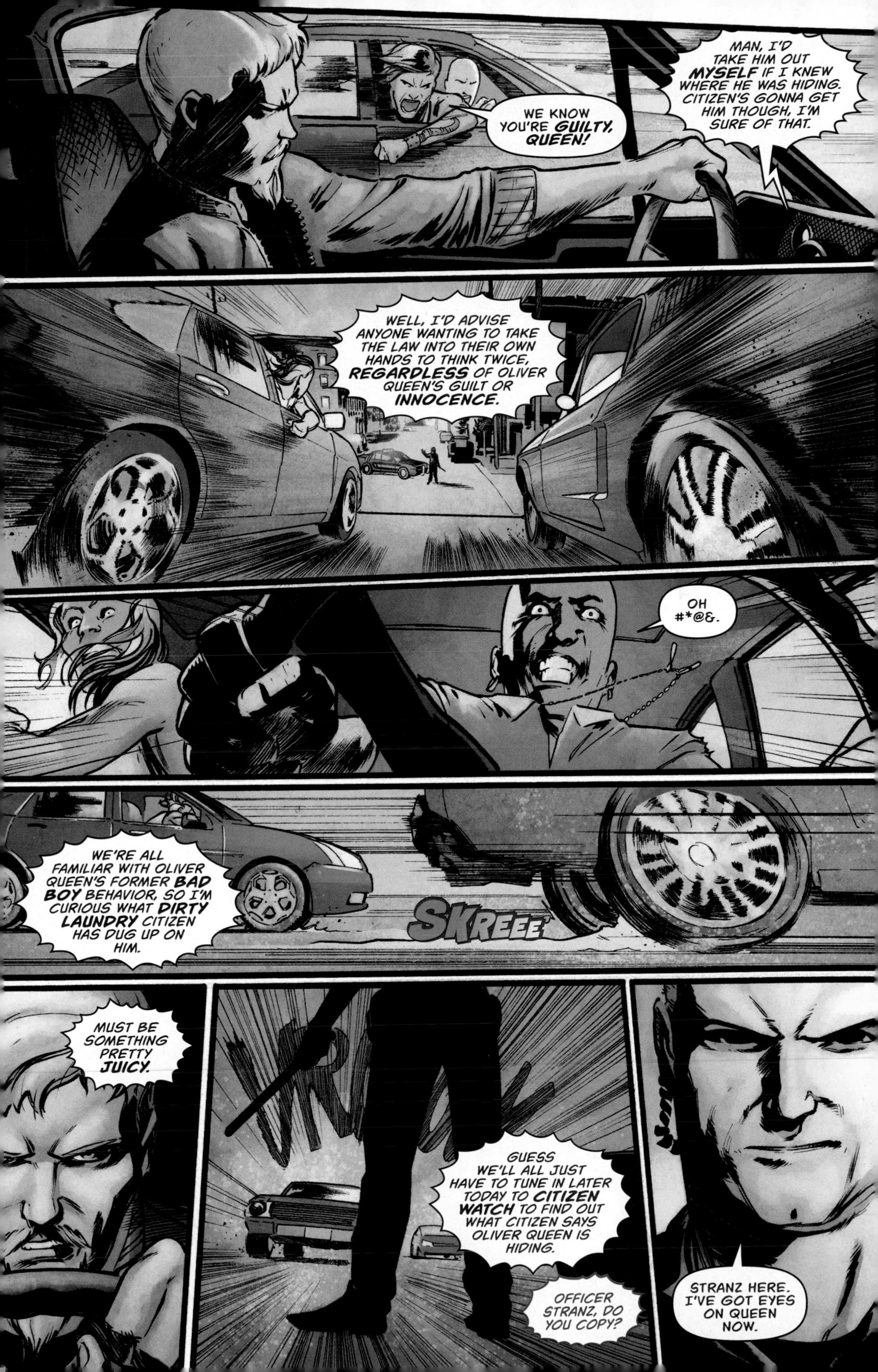
WE KNOW YOU'RE GUILTY, QUEEN!
MAN, I'D TAKE HIM OUT MYSELF IF I KNEW WHERE HE WAS HIDING. CITIZEN'S GONNA GET HIM THOUGH, I'M SURE OF THAT.
WELL, I'D ADVISE ANYONE WANTING TO TAKE THE LAW INTO THEIR OWN HANDS TO THINK TWICE, REGARDLESS OF OLIVER QUEEN'S GUILT OR INNOCENCE.
OH #*@&.
WE'RE ALL FAMILIAR WITH OLIVER QUEEN'S FORMER BAD BOY BEHAVIOR, SO I'M CURIOUS WHAT DIRTY LAUNDRY CITIZEN HAS DUG UP ON HIM.
SKREEE
MUST BE SOMETHING PRETTY JUICY.
GUESS WE'LL ALL JUST HAVE TO TUNE IN LATER TODAY TO CITIZEN WATCH TO FIND OUT WHAT CITIZEN SAYS OLIVER QUEEN IS HIDING.
OFFICER STRANZ, DO YOU COPY?
STRANZ HERE. I'VE GOT EYES ON QUEEN NOW.

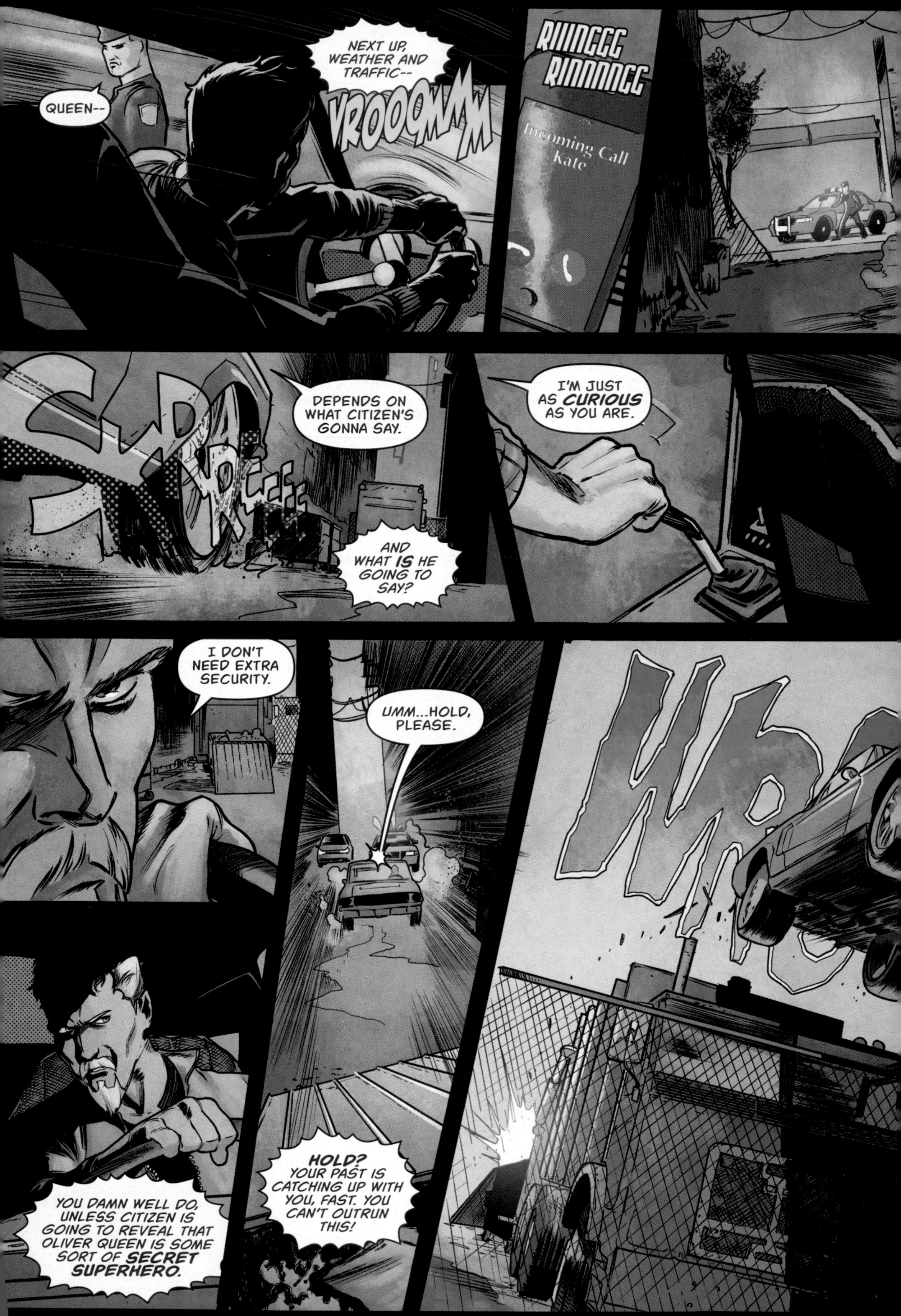
NEXT UP, WEATHER AND TRAFFIC--
QUEEN--
VROOOMM
RIIINGGG RINNNNGG
Incoming Call Kate
DEPENDS ON WHAT CITIZEN'S GONNA SAY.
AND WHAT IS HE GOING TO SAY?
I'M JUST AS CURIOUS AS YOU ARE.
I DON'T NEED EXTRA SECURITY.
YOU DAMN WELL DO, UNLESS CITIZEN IS GOING TO REVEAL THAT OLIVER QUEEN IS SOME SORT OF SECRET SUPERHERO.
UMM...HOLD, PLEASE.
HOLD? YOUR PAST IS CATCHING UP WITH YOU, FAST. YOU CAN'T OUTRUN THIS!

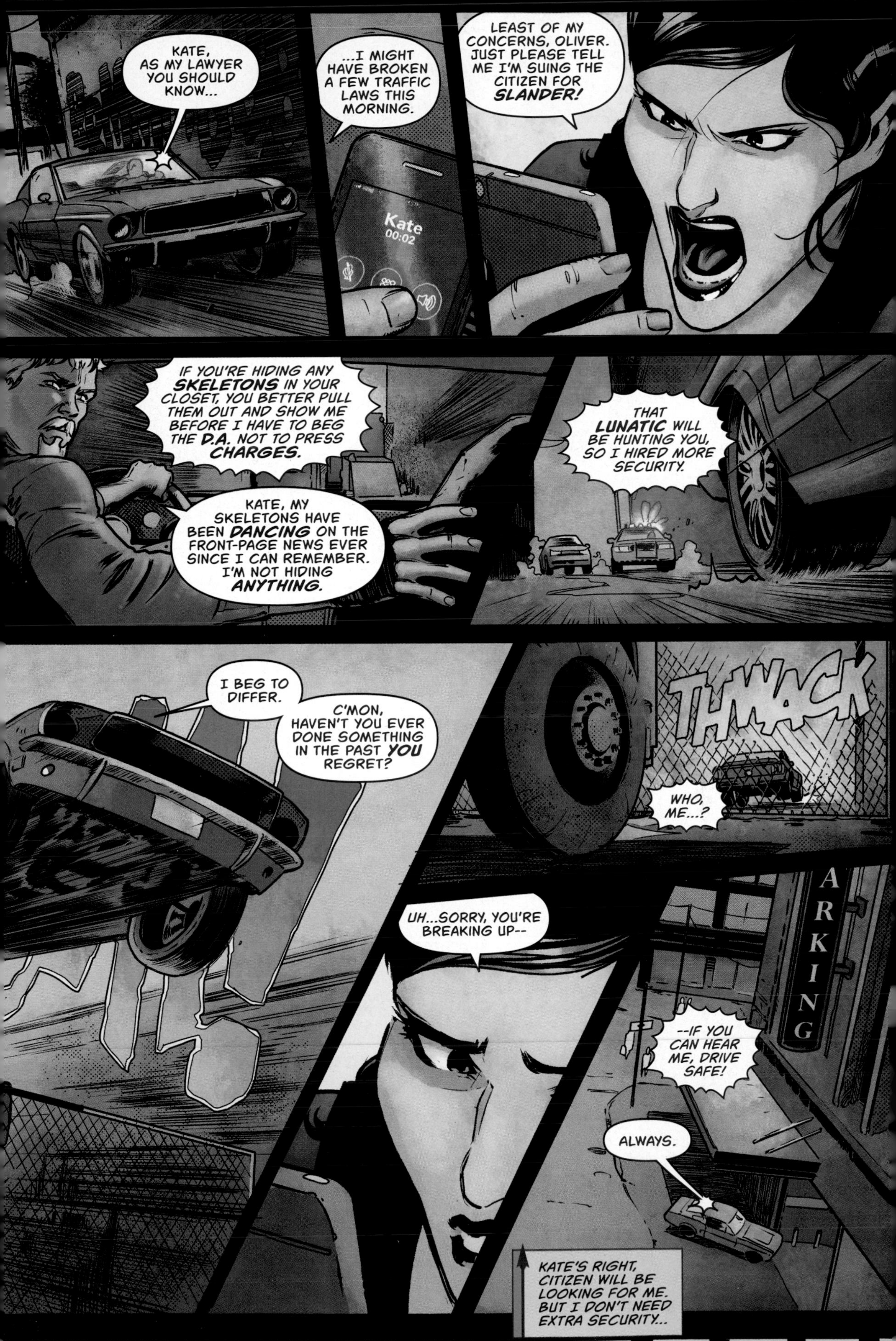
KATE, AS MY LAWYER YOU SHOULD KNOW...
...I MIGHT HAVE BROKEN A FEW TRAFFIC LAWS THIS MORNING.
Kate 00:02
LEAST OF MY CONCERNS, OLIVER. JUST PLEASE TELL ME I'M SUING THE CITIZEN FOR SLANDER!
IF YOU'RE HIDING ANY SKELETONS IN YOUR CLOSET, YOU BETTER PULL THEM OUT AND SHOW ME BEFORE I HAVE TO BEG THE D.A. NOT TO PRESS CHARGES.
KATE, MY SKELETONS HAVE BEEN DANCING ON THE FRONT-PAGE NEWS EVER SINCE I CAN REMEMBER. I'M NOT HIDING ANYTHING.
THAT LUNATIC WILL BE HUNTING YOU, SO I HIRED MORE SECURITY.
I BEG TO DIFFER.
C'MON, HAVEN'T YOU EVER DONE SOMETHING IN THE PAST YOU REGRET?
THWACK
WHO, ME...?
UH...SORRY, YOU'RE BREAKING UP--
ARKING
--IF YOU CAN HEAR ME, DRIVE SAFE!
ALWAYS.
KATE'S RIGHT, CITIZEN WILL BE LOOKING FOR ME. BUT I DON'T NEED EXTRA SECURITY...

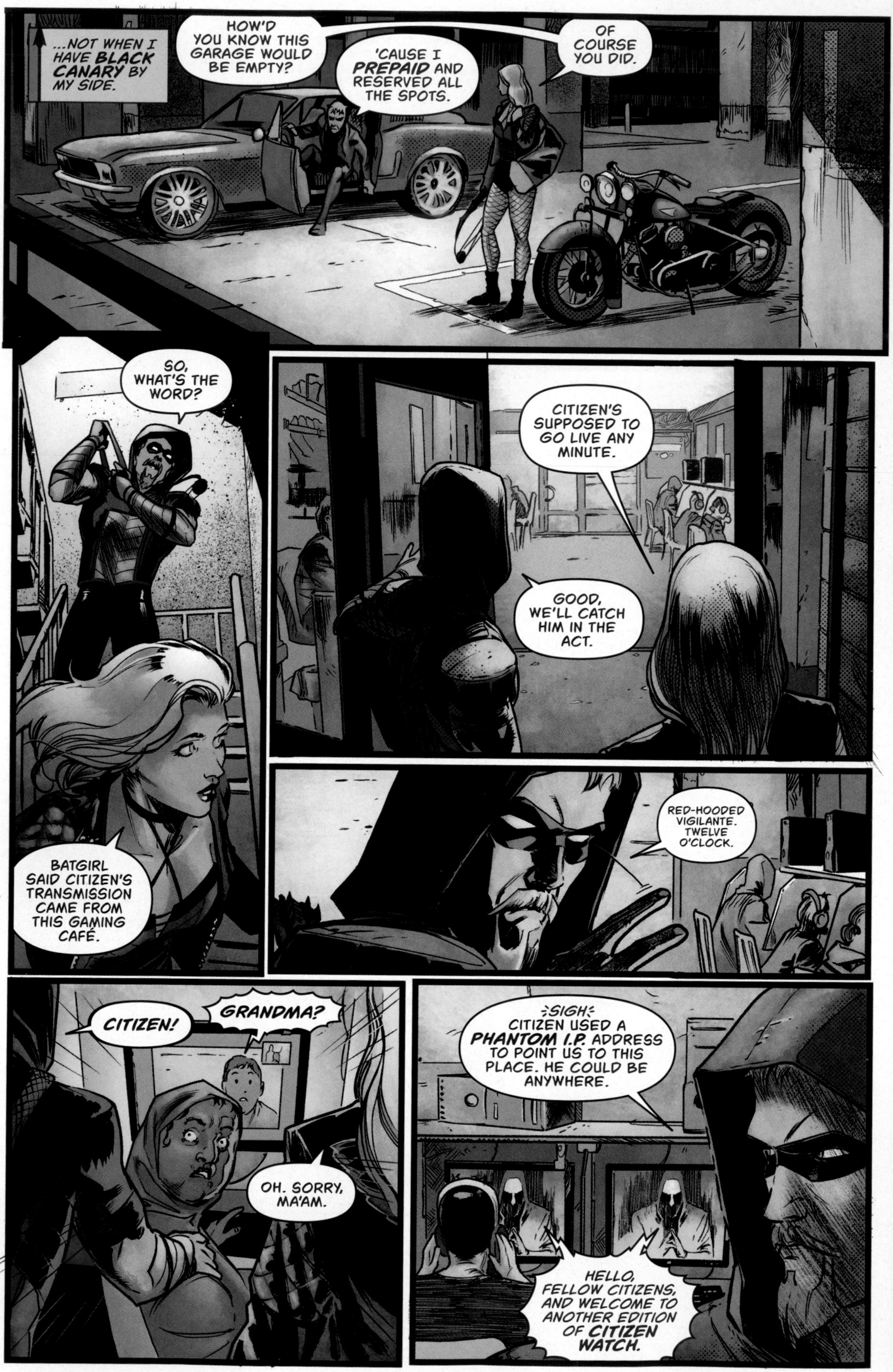

...NOT WHEN I HAVE BLACK CANARY BY MY SIDE.
HOW'D YOU KNOW THIS GARAGE WOULD BE EMPTY?
'CAUSE I PREPAID AND RESERVED ALL THE SPOTS.
OF COURSE YOU DID.
SO, WHAT'S THE WORD?
BATGIRL SAID CITIZEN'S TRANSMISSION CAME FROM THIS GAMING CAFÉ.
CITIZEN'S SUPPOSED TO GO LIVE ANY MINUTE.
GOOD, WE'LL CATCH HIM IN THE ACT.
RED-HOODED VIGILANTE. TWELVE O'CLOCK.
CITIZEN!
GRANDMA?
OH. SORRY, MA'AM.
SIGH CITIZEN USED A PHANTOM I.P. ADDRESS TO POINT US TO THIS PLACE. HE COULD BE ANYWHERE.
HELLO, FELLOW CITIZENS, AND WELCOME TO ANOTHER EDITION OF CITIZEN WATCH.

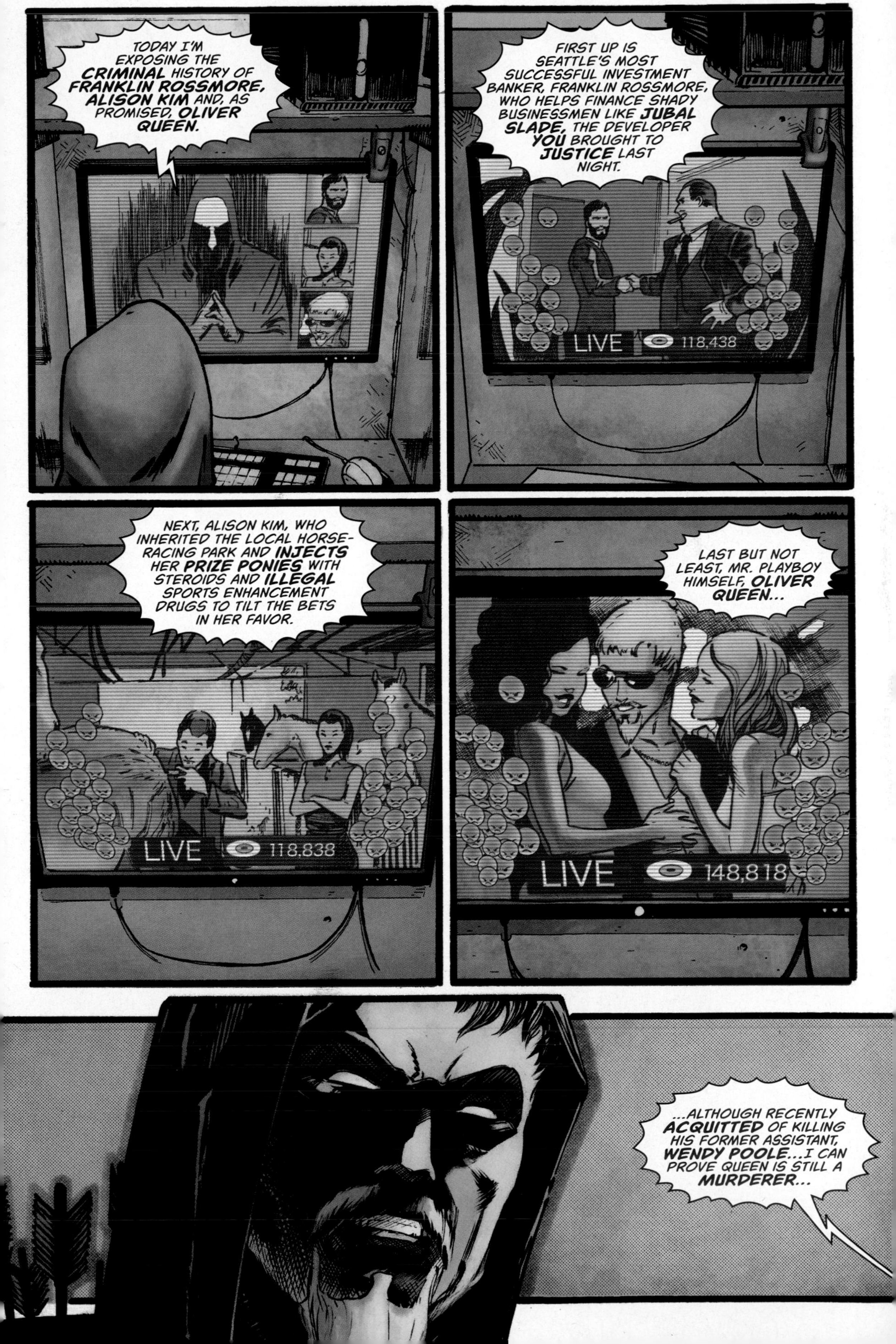
TODAY I'M EXPOSING THE CRIMINAL HISTORY OF FRANKLIN ROSSMORE, ALISON KIM AND, AS PROMISED, OLIVER QUEEN.
FIRST UP IS SEATTLE'S MOST SUCCESSFUL INVESTMENT BANKER, FRANKLIN ROSSMORE, WHO HELPS FINANCE SHADY BUSINESSMEN LIKE JUBAL SLADE, THE DEVELOPER YOU BROUGHT TO JUSTICE LAST NIGHT.
LIVE 118,438
NEXT, ALISON KIM, WHO INHERITED THE LOCAL HORSE-RACING PARK AND INJECTS HER PRIZE PONIES WITH STEROIDS AND ILLEGAL SPORTS ENHANCEMENT DRUGS TO TILT THE BETS IN HER FAVOR.
LIVE 118,838
LAST BUT NOT LEAST, MR. PLAYBOY HIMSELF, OLIVER QUEEN...
LIVE 148,818
...ALTHOUGH RECENTLY ACQUITTED OF KILLING HIS FORMER ASSISTANT, WENDY POOLE...I CAN PROVE QUEEN IS STILL A MURDERER...

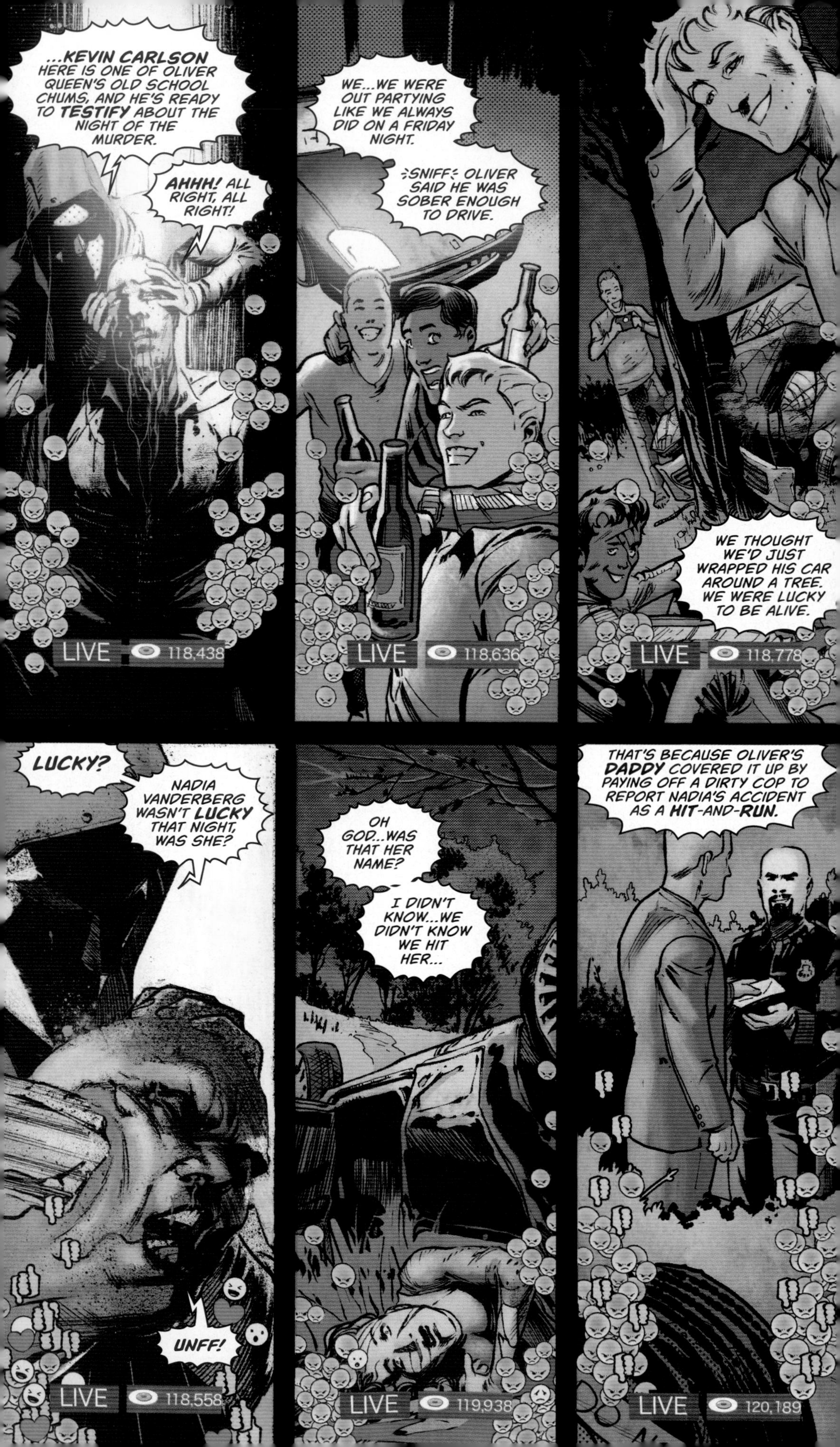
...KEVIN CARLSON HERE IS ONE OF OLIVER QUEEN'S OLD SCHOOL CHUMS, AND HE'S READY TO TESTIFY ABOUT THE NIGHT OF THE MURDER.
AHHH! ALL RIGHT, ALL RIGHT!
LIVE 118,438
WE...WE WERE OUT PARTYING LIKE WE ALWAYS DID ON A FRIDAY NIGHT.
SNIFF OLIVER SAID HE WAS SOBER ENOUGH TO DRIVE.
LIVE 118,636
WE THOUGHT WE'D JUST WRAPPED HIS CAR AROUND A TREE. WE WERE LUCKY TO BE ALIVE.
LIVE 118,778
LUCKY?
NADIA VANDERBERG WASN'T LUCKY THAT NIGHT, WAS SHE?
UNFF!
LIVE 118,558
OH GOD...WAS THAT HER NAME?
I DIDN'T KNOW...WE DIDN'T KNOW WE HIT HER...
LIVE 119,938
THAT'S BECAUSE OLIVER'S DADDY COVERED IT UP BY PAYING OFF A DIRTY COP TO REPORT NADIA'S ACCIDENT AS A HIT-AND-RUN.
LIVE 120,189

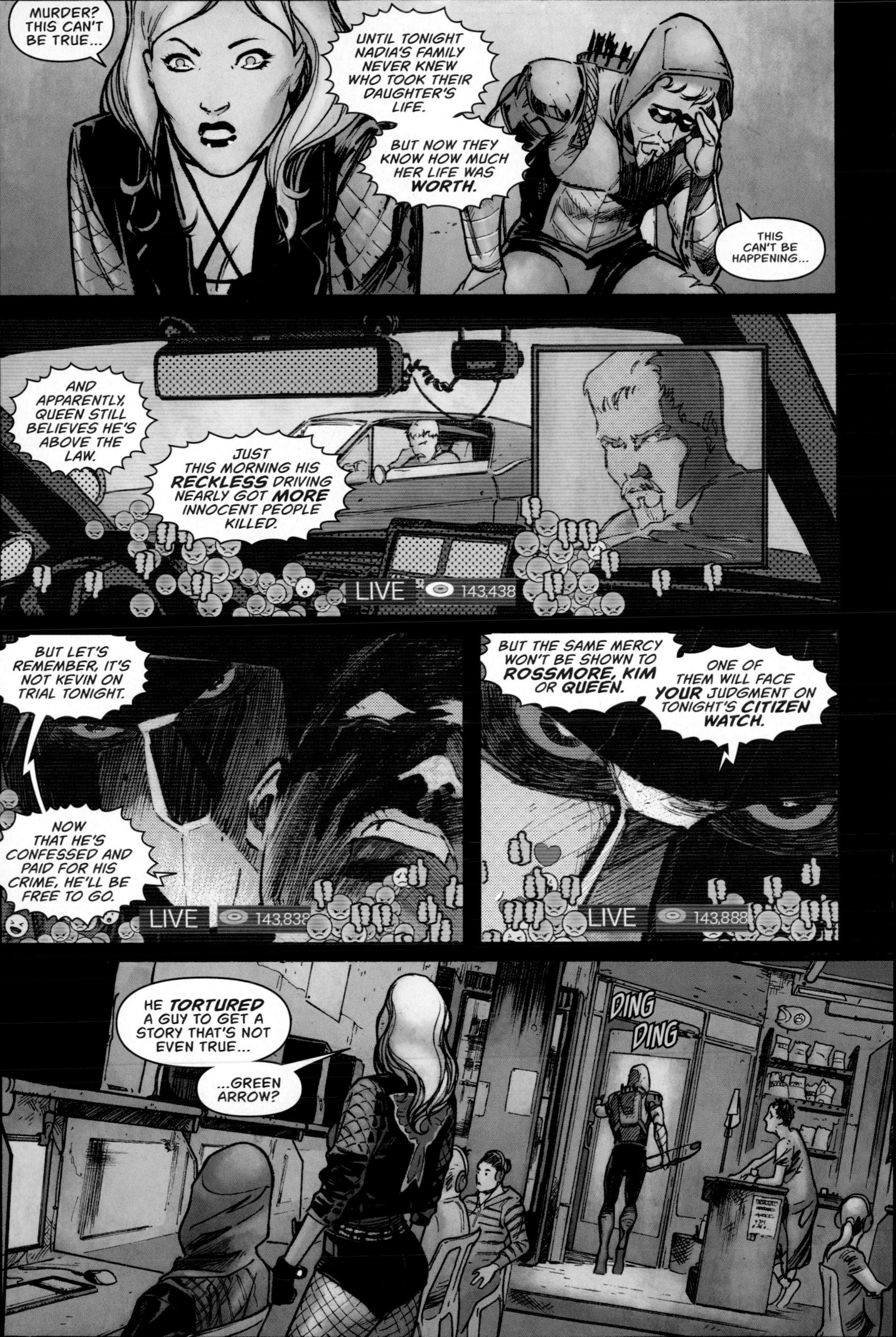
MURDER? THIS CAN'T BE TRUE...
UNTIL TONIGHT NADIA'S FAMILY NEVER KNEW WHO TOOK THEIR DAUGHTER'S LIFE.
BUT NOW THEY KNOW HOW MUCH HER LIFE WAS WORTH.
THIS CAN'T BE HAPPENING...
AND APPARENTLY, QUEEN STILL BELIEVES HE'S ABOVE THE LAW.
JUST THIS MORNING HIS RECKLESS DRIVING NEARLY GOT MORE INNOCENT PEOPLE KILLED.
LIVE 143,438
BUT LET'S REMEMBER, IT'S NOT KEVIN ON TRIAL TONIGHT.
NOW THAT HE'S CONFESSED AND PAID FOR HIS CRIME, HE'LL BE FREE TO GO.
LIVE 143,838
BUT THE SAME MERCY WON'T BE SHOWN TO ROSSMORE, KIM OR QUEEN.
ONE OF THEM WILL FACE YOUR JUDGMENT ON TONIGHT'S CITIZEN WATCH.
LIVE 143,888
HE TORTURED A GUY TO GET A STORY THAT'S NOT EVEN TRUE...
...GREEN ARROW?
DING DING

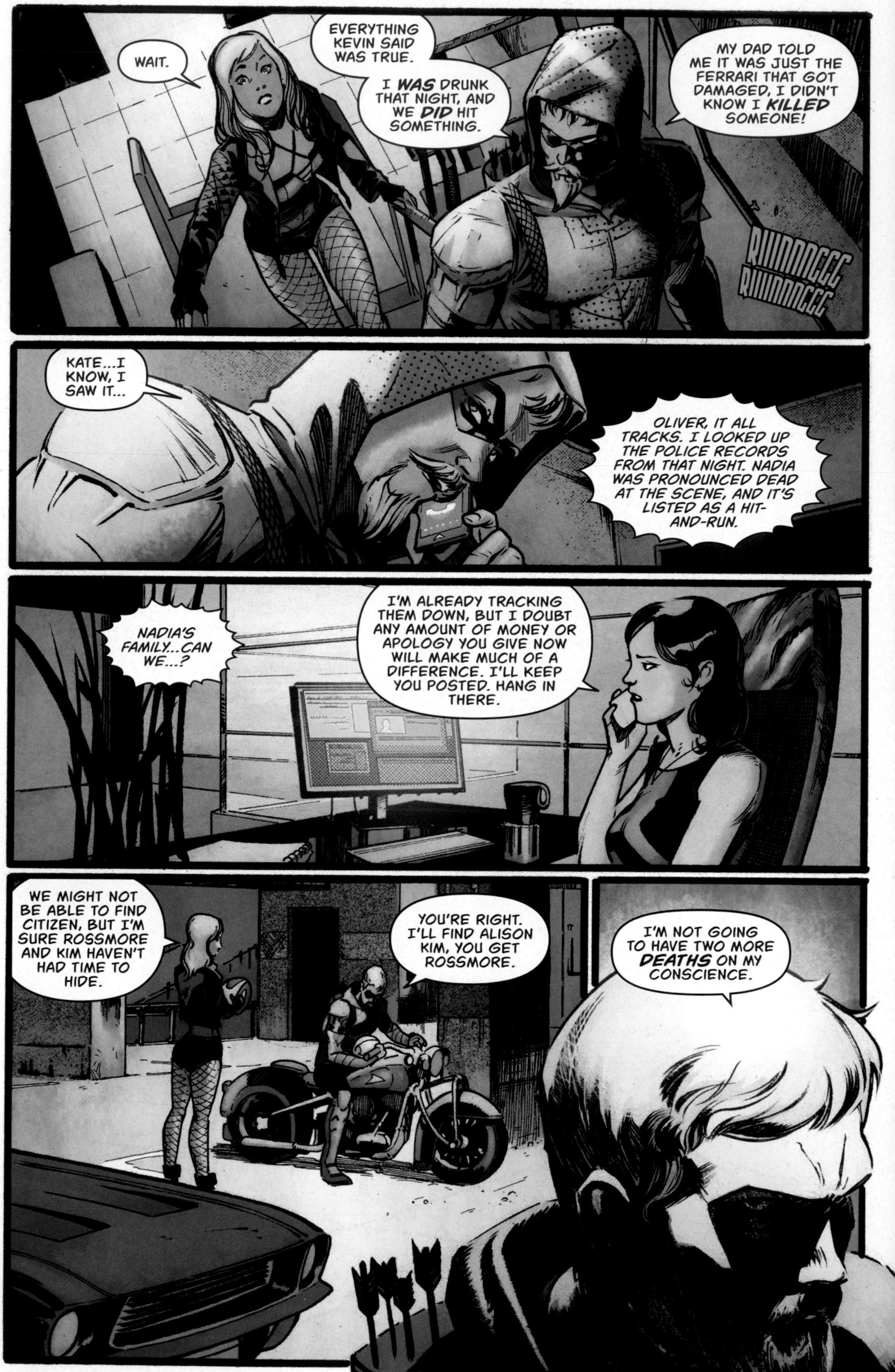
WAIT.
EVERYTHING KEVIN SAID WAS TRUE.
I *WAS* DRUNK THAT NIGHT, AND WE *DID* HIT SOMETHING.
MY DAD TOLD ME IT WAS JUST THE FERRARI THAT GOT DAMAGED, I DIDN'T KNOW I *KILLED* SOMEONE!
KATE...I KNOW, I SAW IT...
OLIVER, IT ALL TRACKS. I LOOKED UP THE POLICE RECORDS FROM THAT NIGHT. NADIA WAS PRONOUNCED DEAD AT THE SCENE, AND IT'S LISTED AS A HIT-AND-RUN.
NADIA'S FAMILY...CAN WE...?
I'M ALREADY TRACKING THEM DOWN, BUT I DOUBT ANY AMOUNT OF MONEY OR APOLOGY YOU GIVE NOW WILL MAKE MUCH OF A DIFFERENCE. I'LL KEEP YOU POSTED. HANG IN THERE.
WE MIGHT NOT BE ABLE TO FIND CITIZEN, BUT I'M SURE ROSSMORE AND KIM HAVEN'T HAD TIME TO HIDE.
YOU'RE RIGHT. I'LL FIND ALISON KIM, YOU GET ROSSMORE.
I'M NOT GOING TO HAVE TWO MORE *DEATHS* ON MY CONSCIENCE.

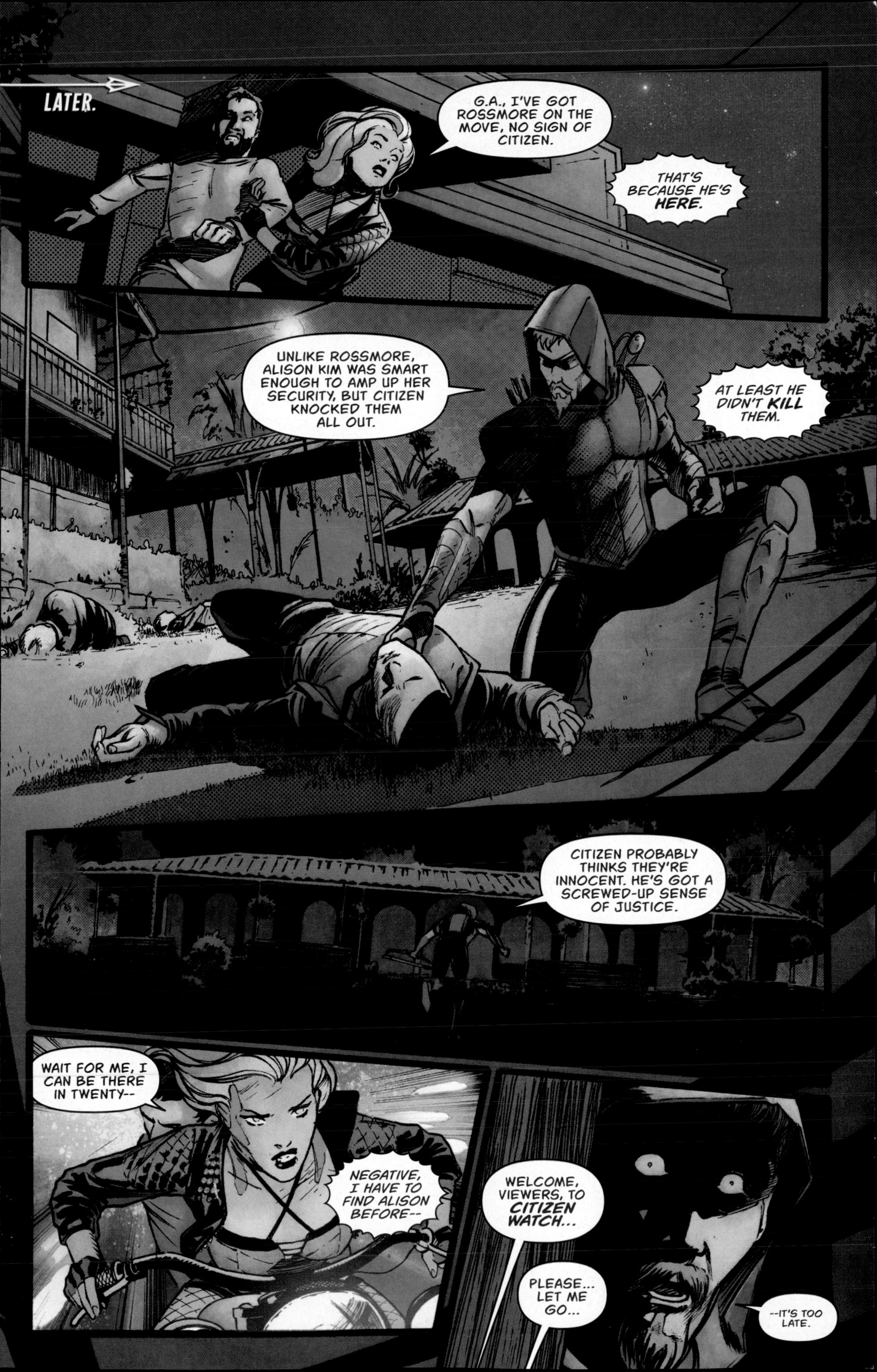

LATER.
G.A., I'VE GOT ROSSMORE ON THE MOVE, NO SIGN OF CITIZEN.
THAT'S BECAUSE HE'S HERE.
UNLIKE ROSSMORE, ALISON KIM WAS SMART ENOUGH TO AMP UP HER SECURITY, BUT CITIZEN KNOCKED THEM ALL OUT.
AT LEAST HE DIDN'T KILL THEM.
CITIZEN PROBABLY THINKS THEY'RE INNOCENT. HE'S GOT A SCREWED-UP SENSE OF JUSTICE.
WAIT FOR ME, I CAN BE THERE IN TWENTY--
NEGATIVE, I HAVE TO FIND ALISON BEFORE--
WELCOME, VIEWERS, TO CITIZEN WATCH...
PLEASE... LET ME GO...
--IT'S TOO LATE.

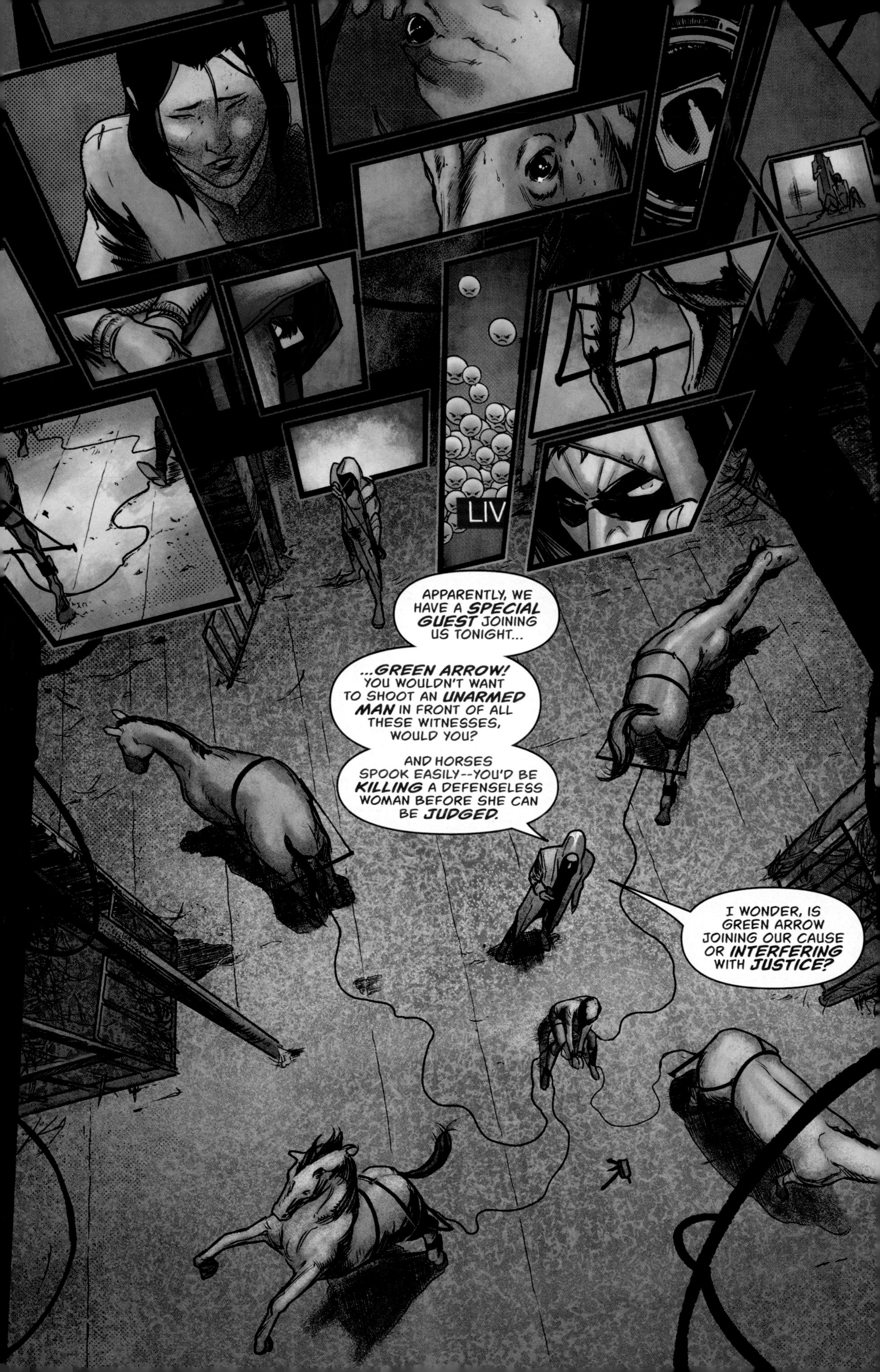
LIV
APPARENTLY, WE HAVE A SPECIAL GUEST JOINING US TONIGHT...
...GREEN ARROW! YOU WOULDN'T WANT TO SHOOT AN UNARMED MAN IN FRONT OF ALL THESE WITNESSES, WOULD YOU?
AND HORSES SPOOK EASILY--YOU'D BE KILLING A DEFENSELESS WOMAN BEFORE SHE CAN BE JUDGED.
I WONDER, IS GREEN ARROW JOINING OUR CAUSE OR INTERFERING WITH JUSTICE?

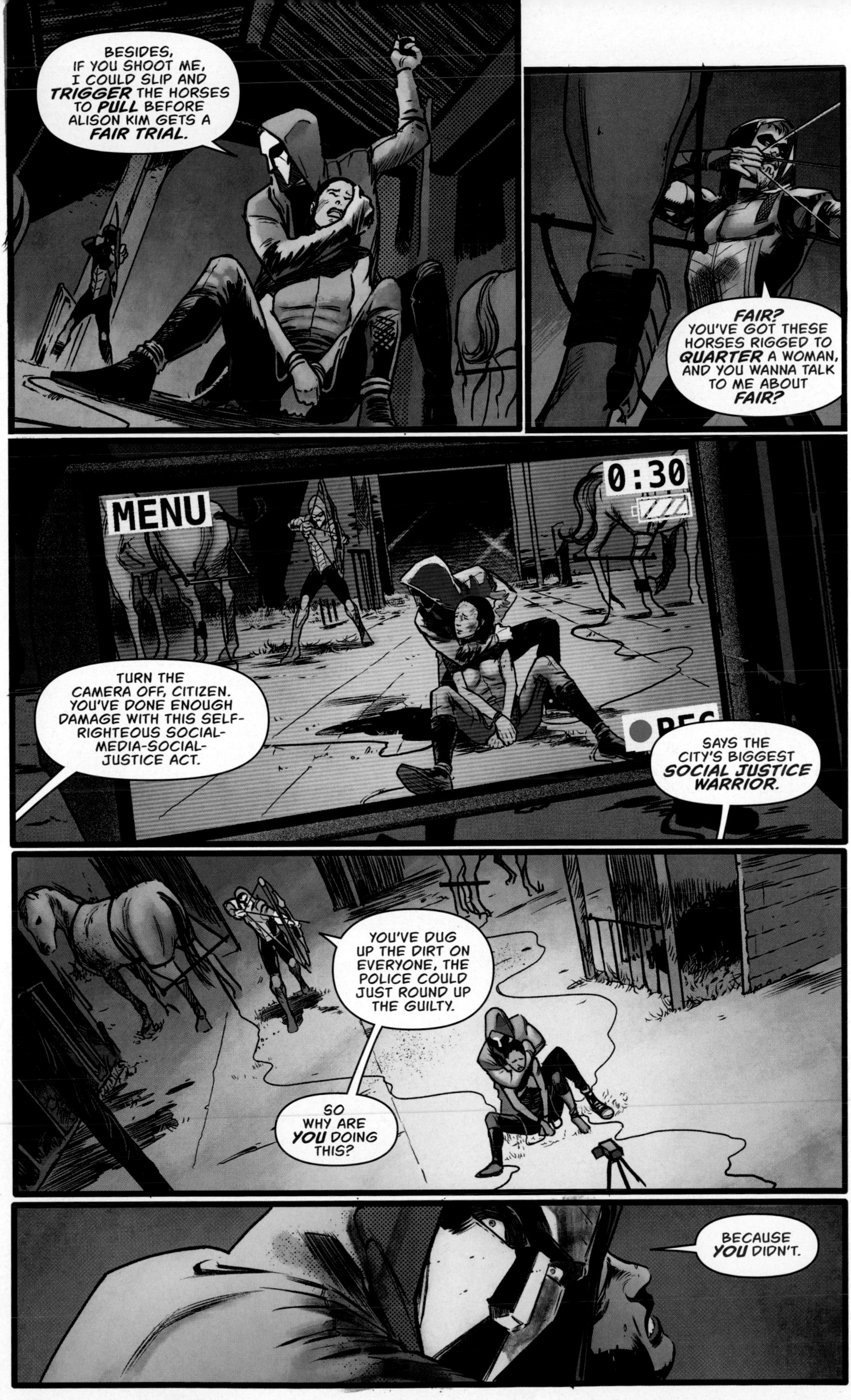

BESIDES, IF YOU SHOOT ME, I COULD SLIP AND TRIGGER THE HORSES TO PULL BEFORE ALISON KIM GETS A FAIR TRIAL.
FAIR? YOU'VE GOT THESE HORSES RIGGED TO QUARTER A WOMAN, AND YOU WANNA TALK TO ME ABOUT FAIR?
MENU
0:30
TURN THE CAMERA OFF, CITIZEN. YOU'VE DONE ENOUGH DAMAGE WITH THIS SELF-RIGHTEOUS SOCIAL-MEDIA-SOCIAL-JUSTICE ACT.
SAYS THE CITY'S BIGGEST SOCIAL JUSTICE WARRIOR.
YOU'VE DUG UP THE DIRT ON EVERYONE, THE POLICE COULD JUST ROUND UP THE GUILTY.
SO WHY ARE YOU DOING THIS?
BECAUSE YOU DIDN'T.

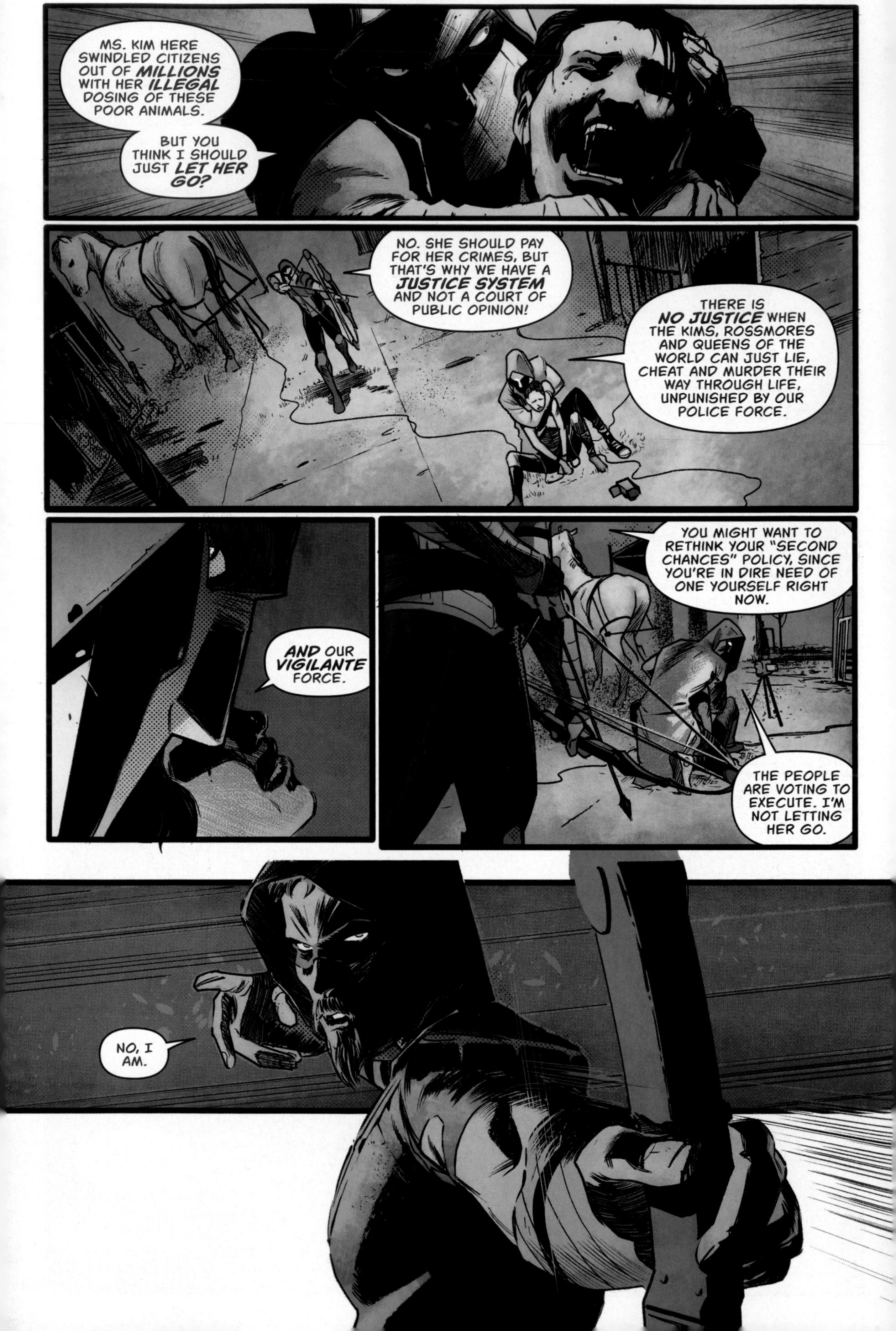
MS. KIM HERE SWINDLED CITIZENS OUT OF MILLIONS WITH HER ILLEGAL DOSING OF THESE POOR ANIMALS.
BUT YOU THINK I SHOULD JUST LET HER GO?
NO. SHE SHOULD PAY FOR HER CRIMES, BUT THAT'S WHY WE HAVE A JUSTICE SYSTEM AND NOT A COURT OF PUBLIC OPINION!
THERE IS NO JUSTICE WHEN THE KIMS, ROSSMORES AND QUEENS OF THE WORLD CAN JUST LIE, CHEAT AND MURDER THEIR WAY THROUGH LIFE, UNPUNISHED BY OUR POLICE FORCE.
AND OUR VIGILANTE FORCE.
YOU MIGHT WANT TO RETHINK YOUR "SECOND CHANCES" POLICY, SINCE YOU'RE IN DIRE NEED OF ONE YOURSELF RIGHT NOW.
THE PEOPLE ARE VOTING TO EXECUTE. I'M NOT LETTING HER GO.
NO, I AM.

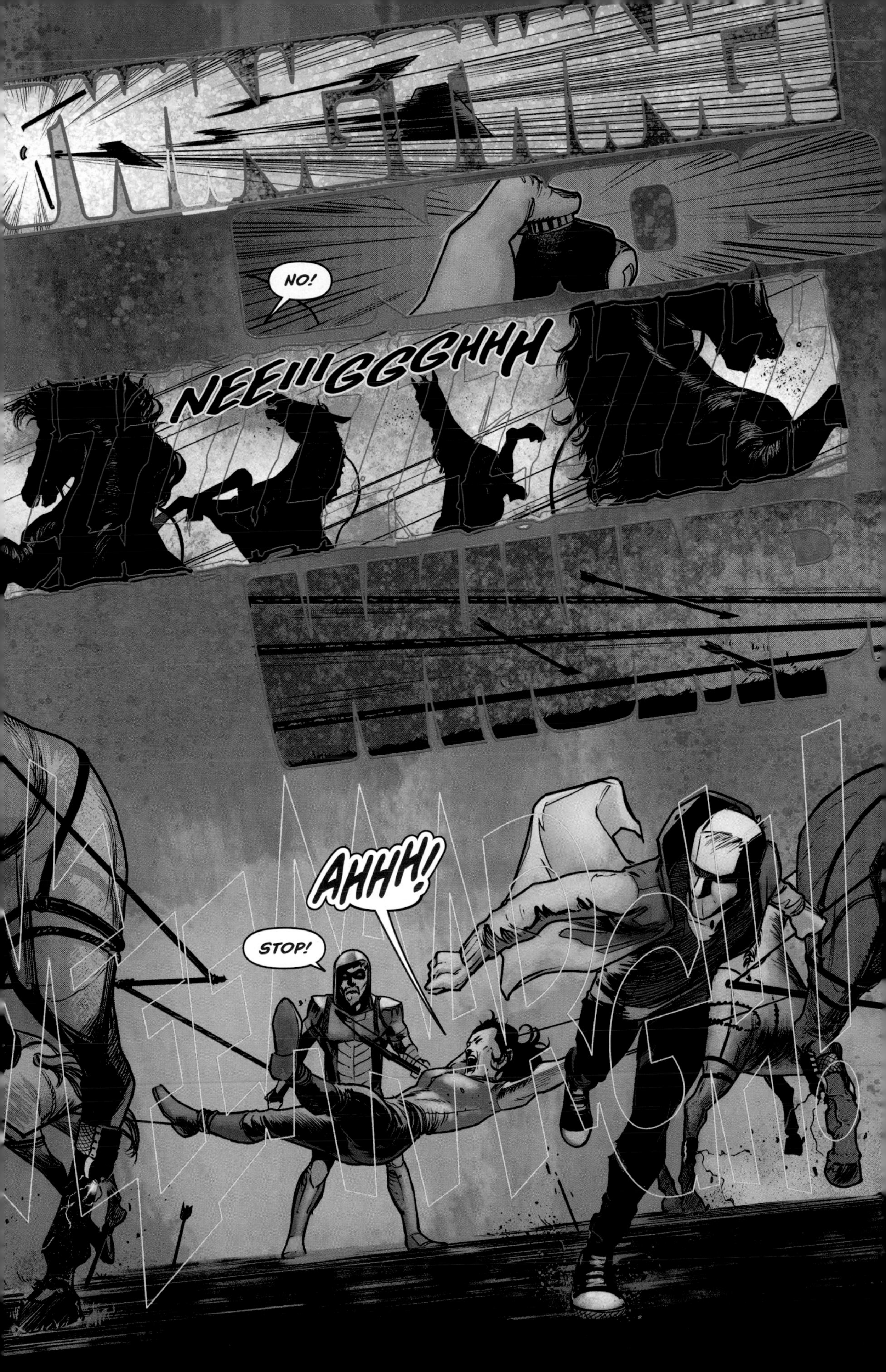
NO!
NEEIIIGGGHHH
AHHH!
STOP!

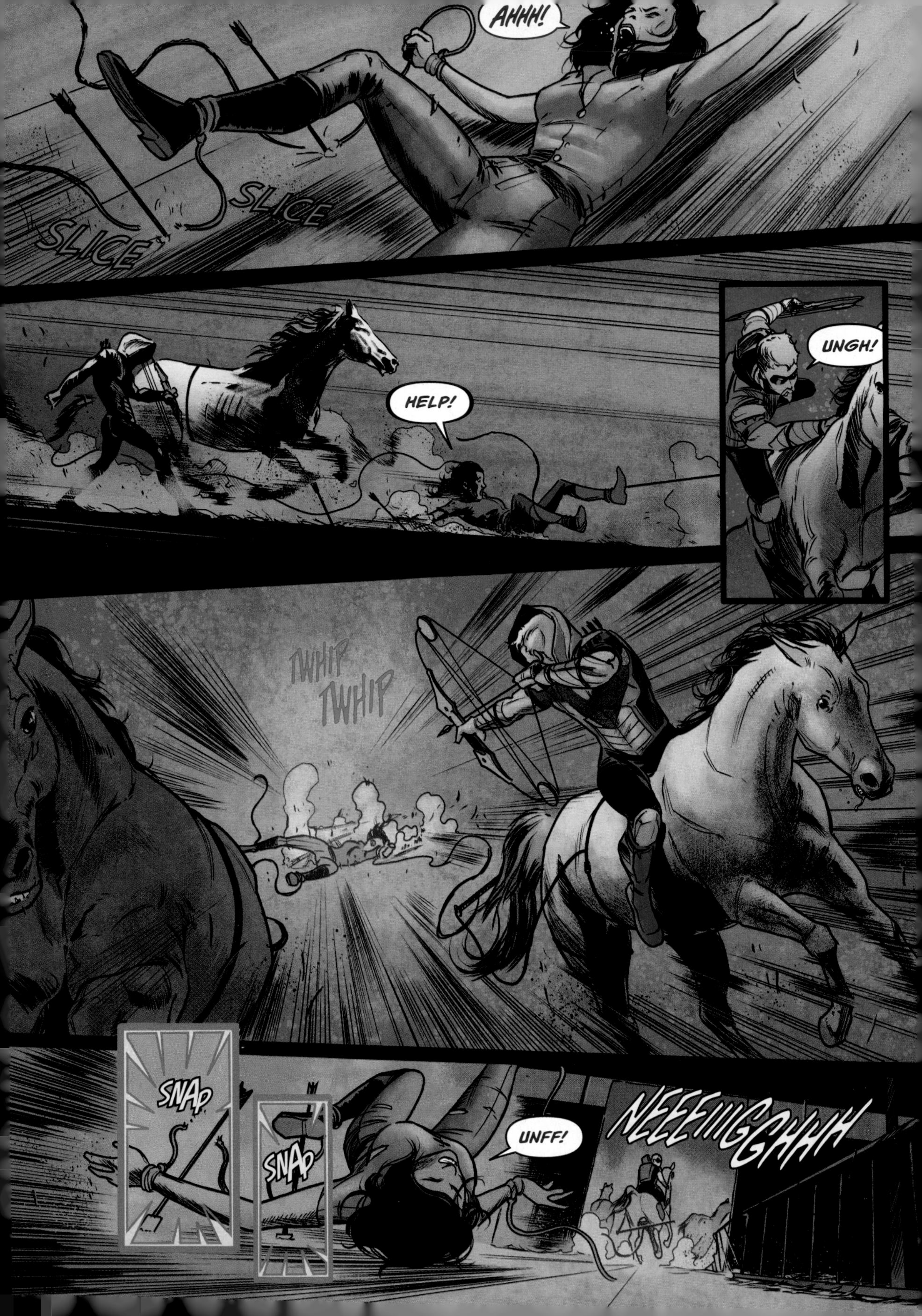

AHHH!
SLICE
SLICE
HELP!
UNGH!
TWHIP
TWHIP
SNAP
SNAP
UNFF!
NEEEIIIGGHHH

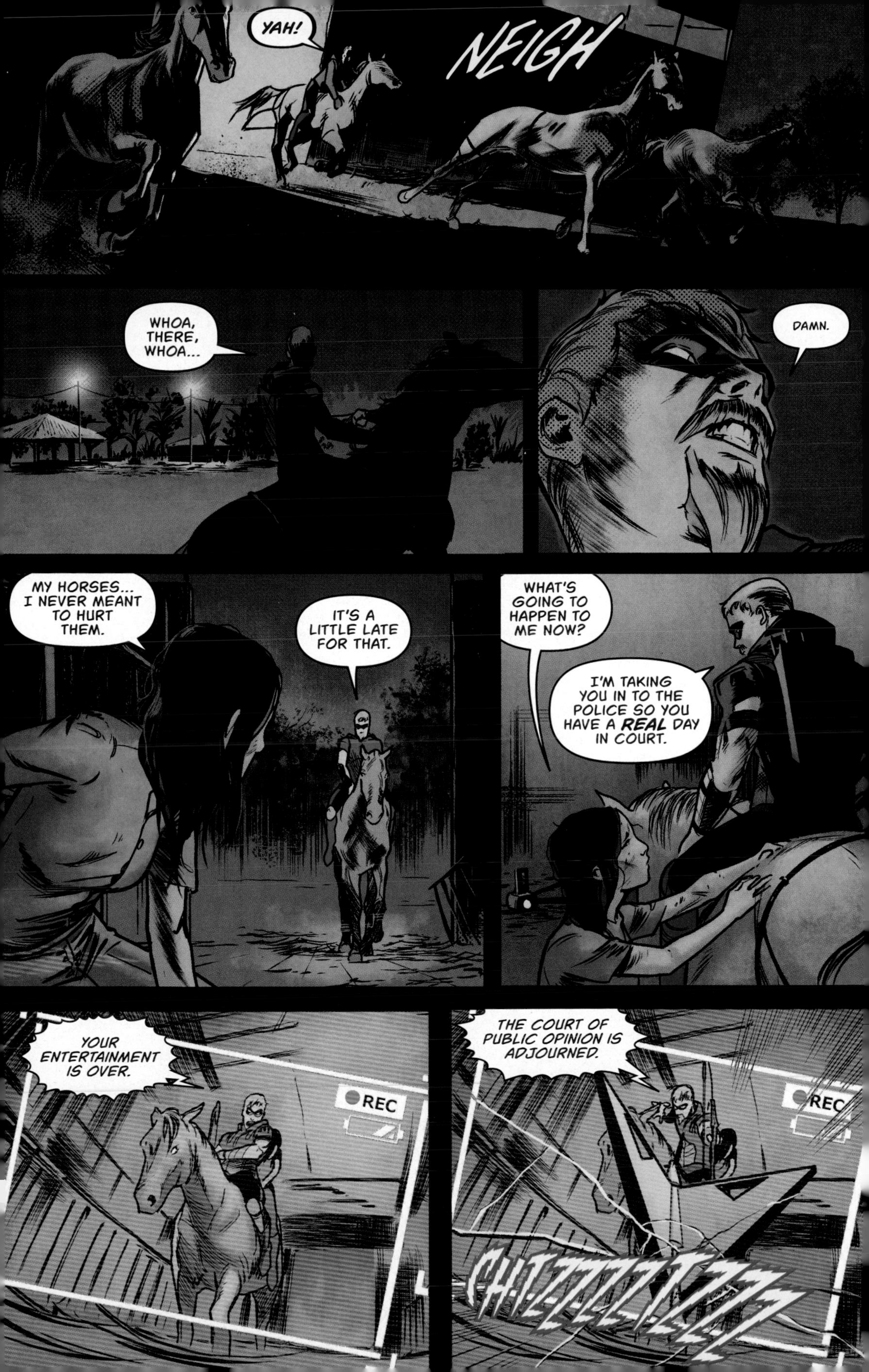
YAH!
NEIGH
WHOA, THERE, WHOA...
DAMN.
MY HORSES... I NEVER MEANT TO HURT THEM.
IT'S A LITTLE LATE FOR THAT.
WHAT'S GOING TO HAPPEN TO ME NOW?
I'M TAKING YOU IN TO THE POLICE SO YOU HAVE A **REAL** DAY IN COURT.
YOUR ENTERTAINMENT IS OVER.
REC
THE COURT OF PUBLIC OPINION IS ADJOURNED.
REC
CHZZZZZZZ

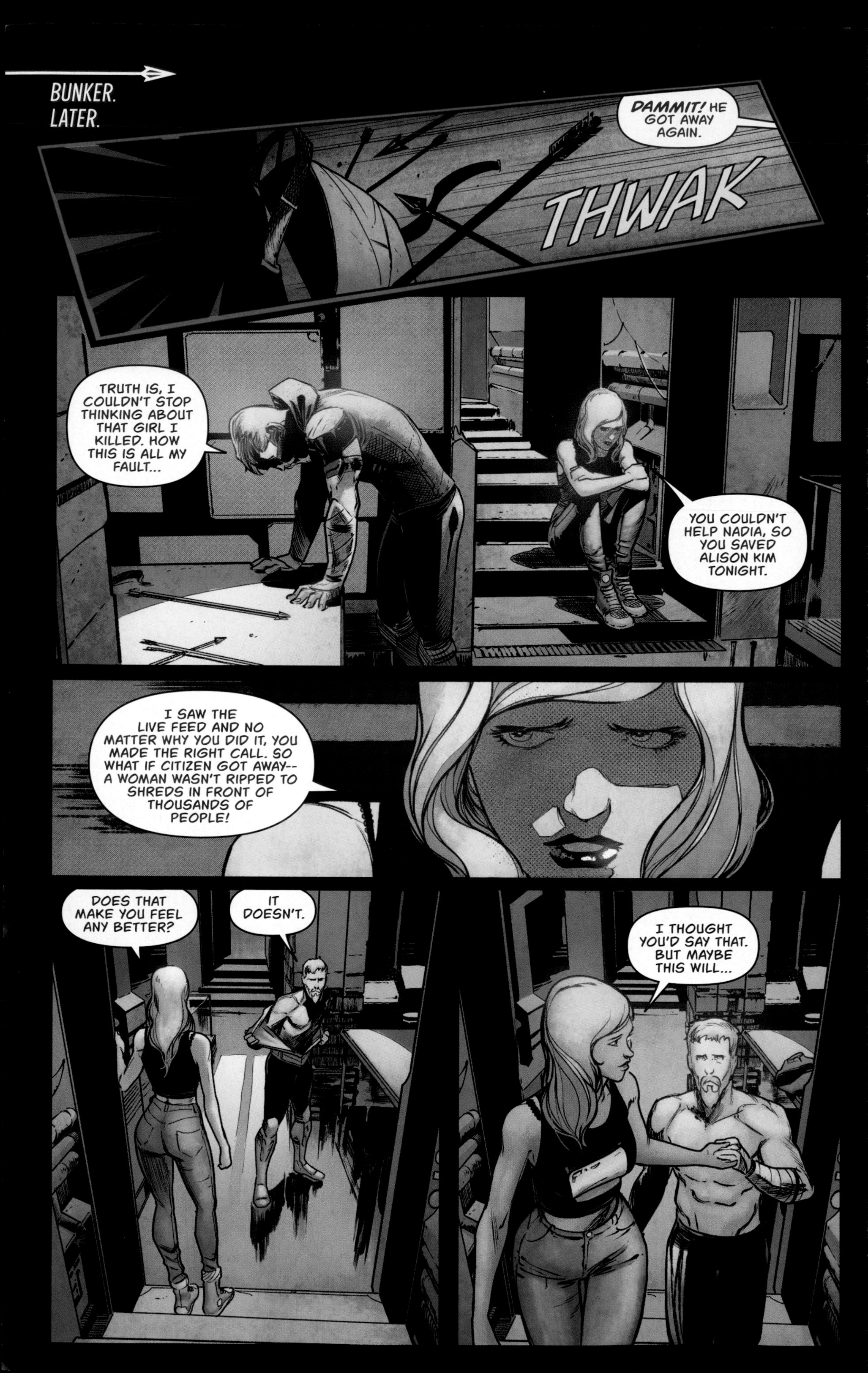
BUNKER. LATER.
DAMMIT! HE GOT AWAY AGAIN.
THWAK
TRUTH IS, I COULDN'T STOP THINKING ABOUT THAT GIRL I KILLED. HOW THIS IS ALL MY FAULT...
YOU COULDN'T HELP NADIA, SO YOU SAVED ALISON KIM TONIGHT.
I SAW THE LIVE FEED AND NO MATTER WHY YOU DID IT, YOU MADE THE RIGHT CALL. SO WHAT IF CITIZEN GOT AWAY-- A WOMAN WASN'T RIPPED TO SHREDS IN FRONT OF THOUSANDS OF PEOPLE!
DOES THAT MAKE YOU FEEL ANY BETTER?
IT DOESN'T.
I THOUGHT YOU'D SAY THAT. BUT MAYBE THIS WILL...

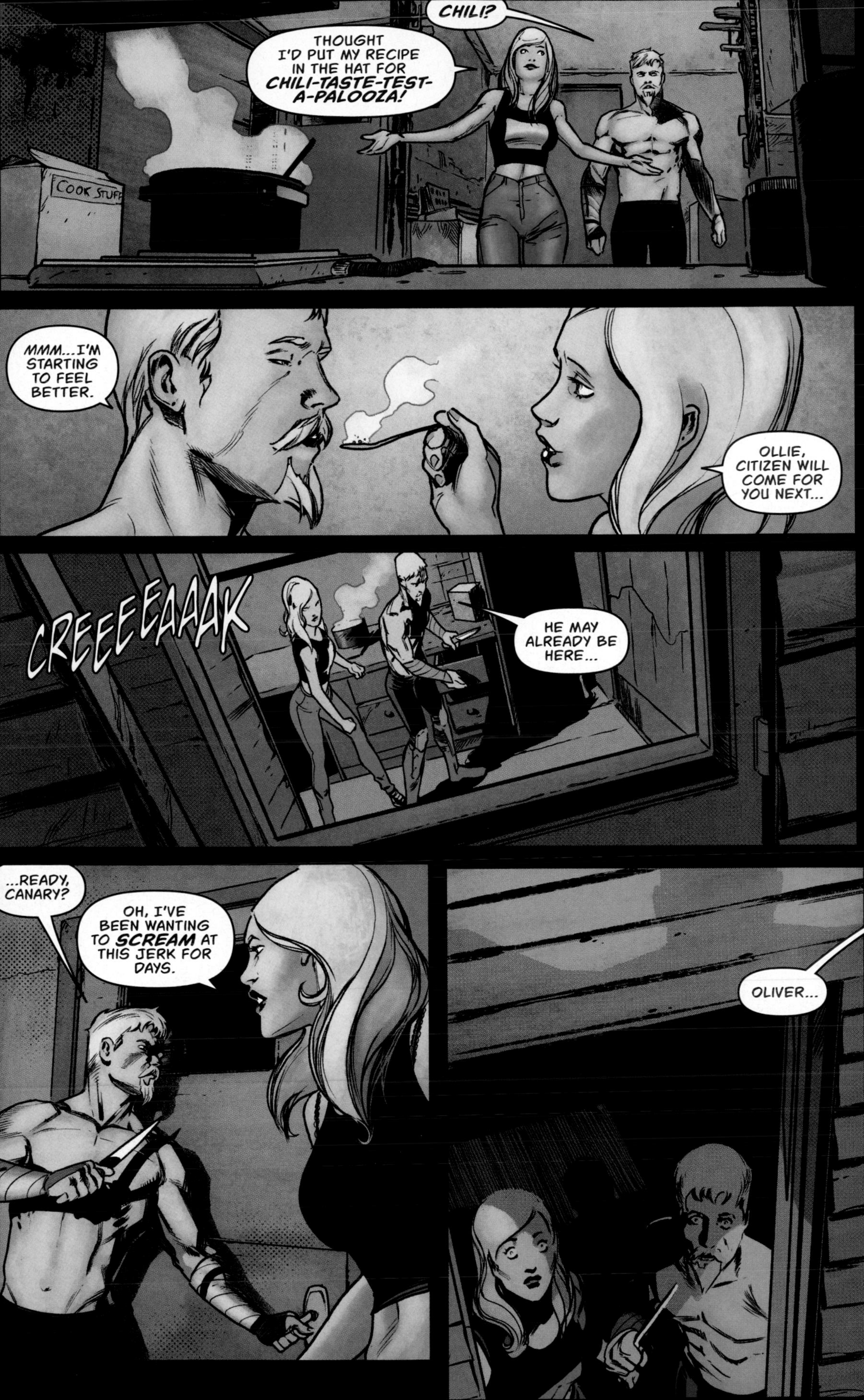
CHILI!?
THOUGHT I'D PUT MY RECIPE IN THE HAT FOR CHILI-TASTE-TEST-A-PALOOZA!
COOK STUFF
MMM...I'M STARTING TO FEEL BETTER.
OLLIE, CITIZEN WILL COME FOR YOU NEXT...
CREEEEAAAK
HE MAY ALREADY BE HERE...
...READY, CANARY?
OH, I'VE BEEN WANTING TO SCREAM AT THIS JERK FOR DAYS.
OLIVER...

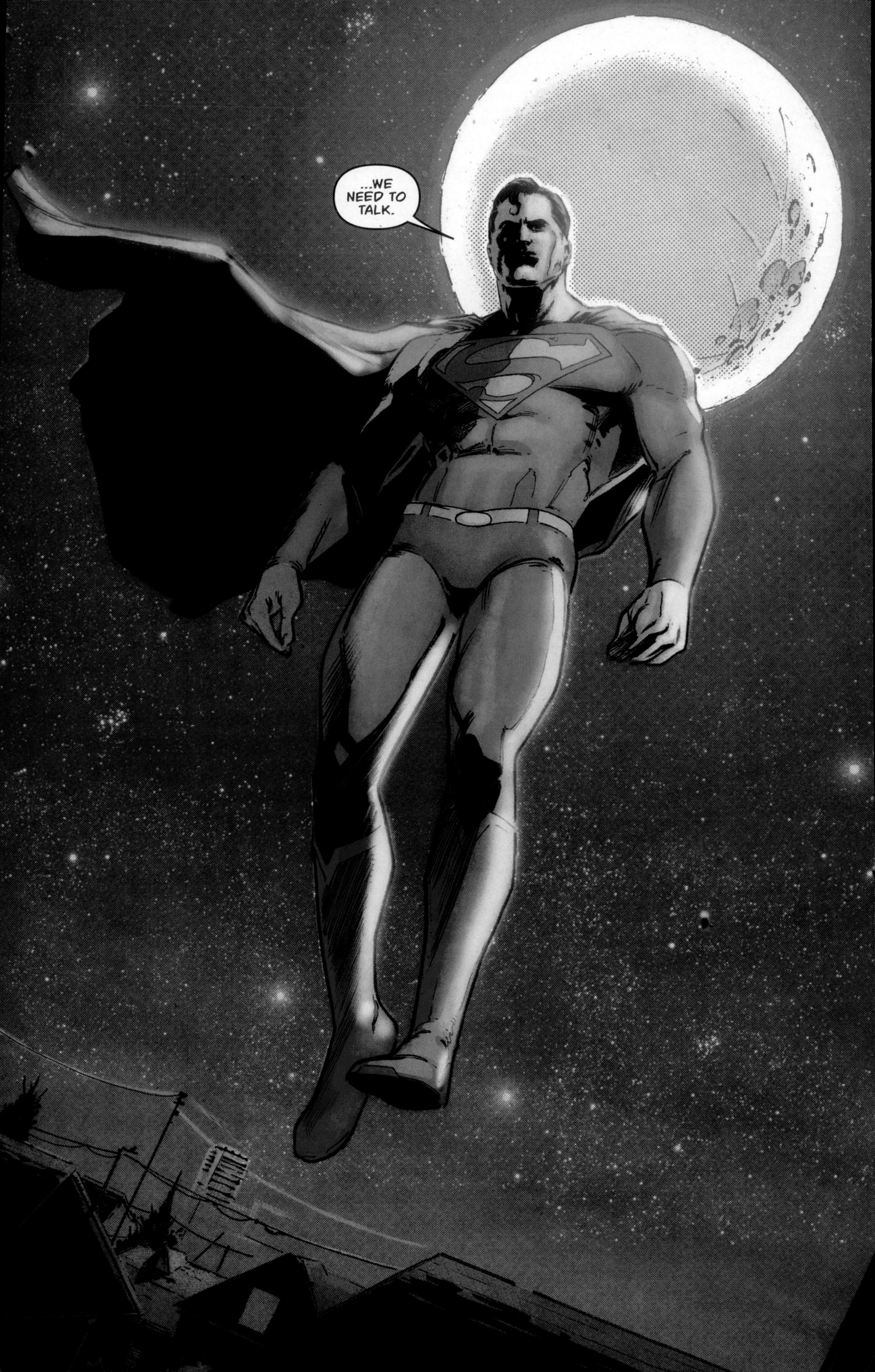
...WE NEED TO TALK.

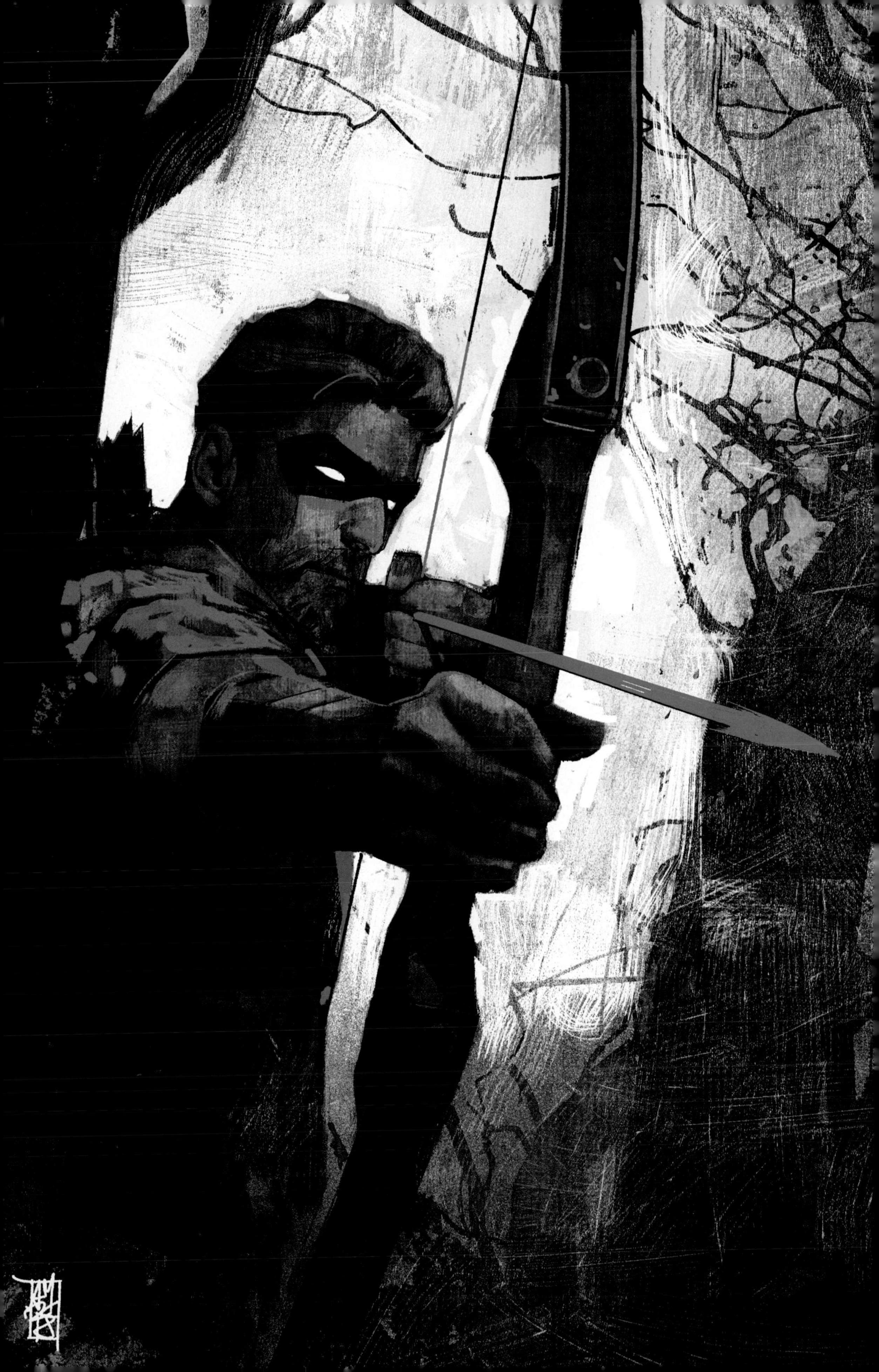

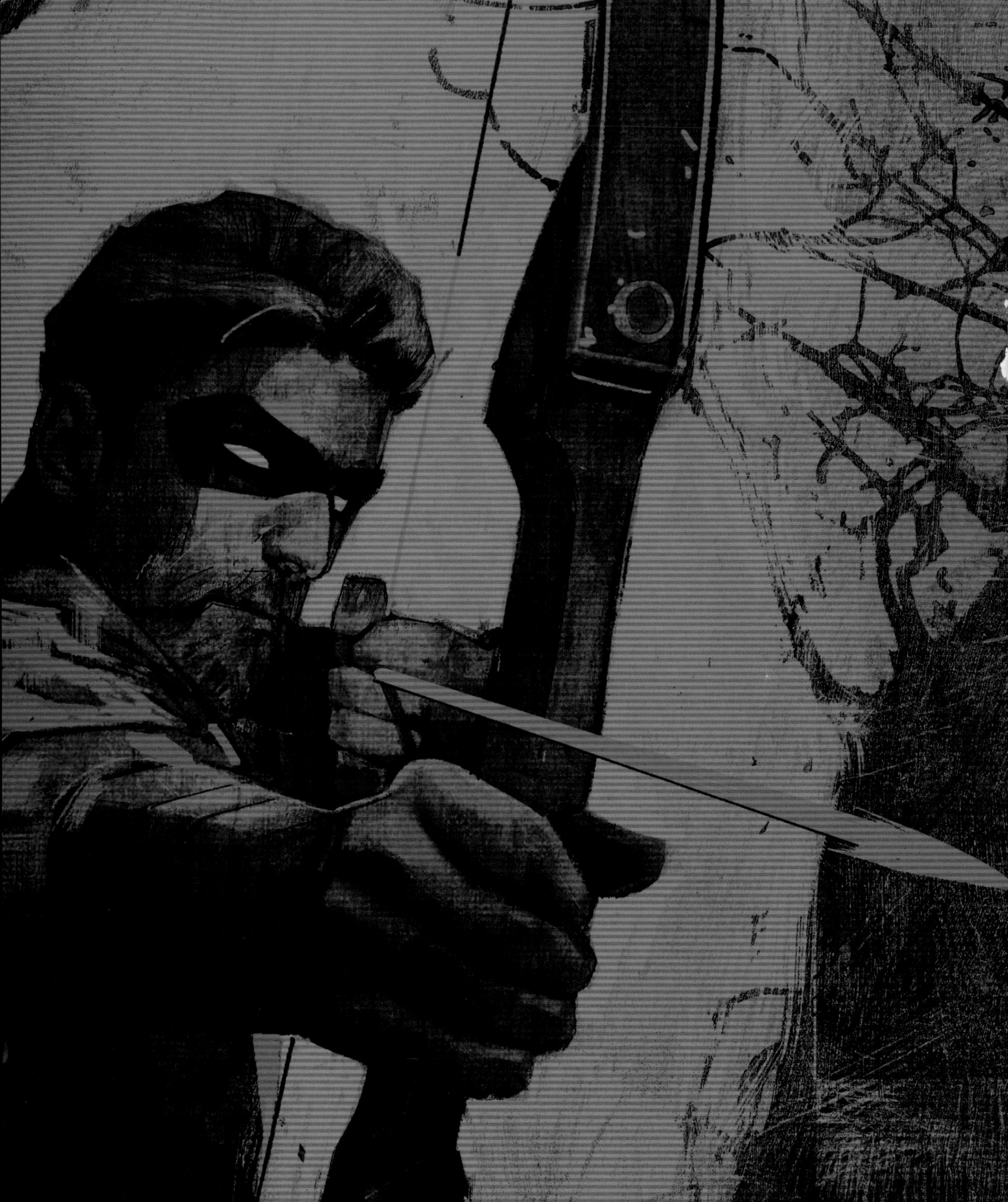

GREEN ARROW
#45

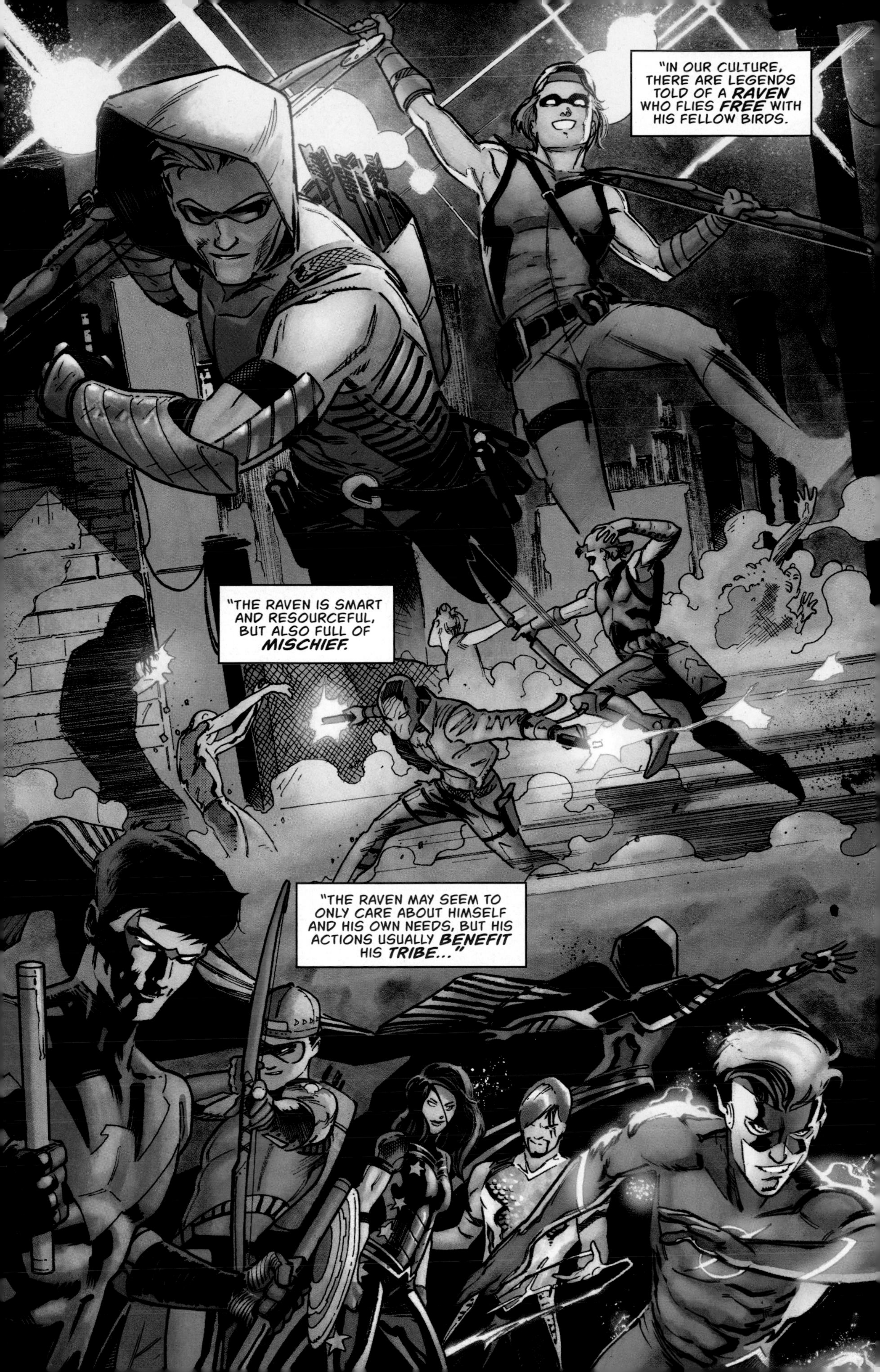
"IN OUR CULTURE, THERE ARE LEGENDS TOLD OF A **RAVEN** WHO FLIES **FREE** WITH HIS FELLOW BIRDS.
"THE RAVEN IS SMART AND RESOURCEFUL, BUT ALSO FULL OF **MISCHIEF.**
"THE RAVEN MAY SEEM TO ONLY CARE ABOUT HIMSELF AND HIS OWN NEEDS, BUT HIS ACTIONS USUALLY **BENEFIT** HIS **TRIBE...**"

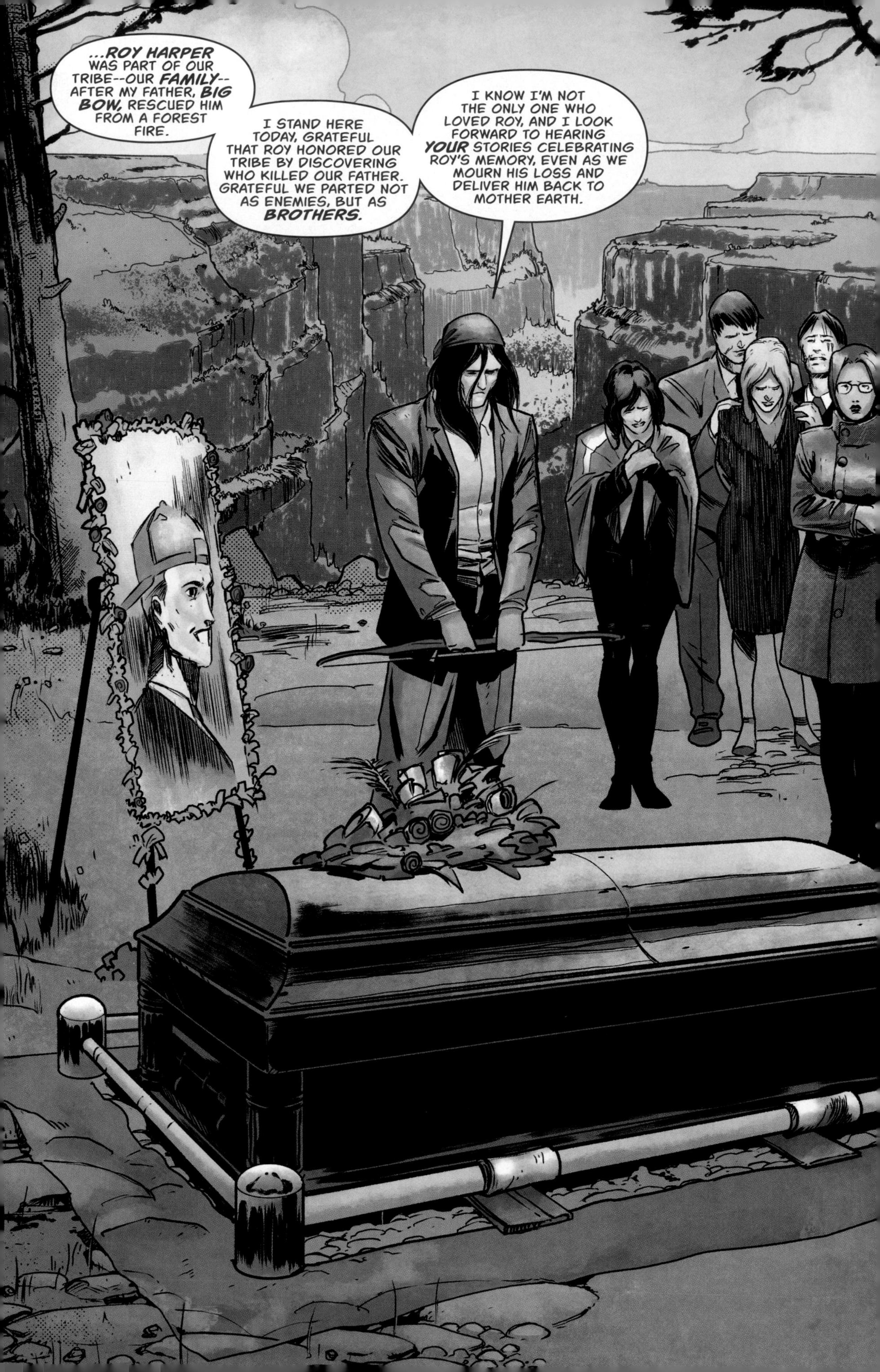
...ROY HARPER WAS PART OF OUR TRIBE--OUR FAMILY--AFTER MY FATHER, BIG BOW, RESCUED HIM FROM A FOREST FIRE.
I STAND HERE TODAY, GRATEFUL THAT ROY HONORED OUR TRIBE BY DISCOVERING WHO KILLED OUR FATHER. GRATEFUL WE PARTED NOT AS ENEMIES, BUT AS BROTHERS.
I KNOW I'M NOT THE ONLY ONE WHO LOVED ROY, AND I LOOK FORWARD TO HEARING YOUR STORIES CELEBRATING ROY'S MEMORY, EVEN AS WE MOURN HIS LOSS AND DELIVER HIM BACK TO MOTHER EARTH.

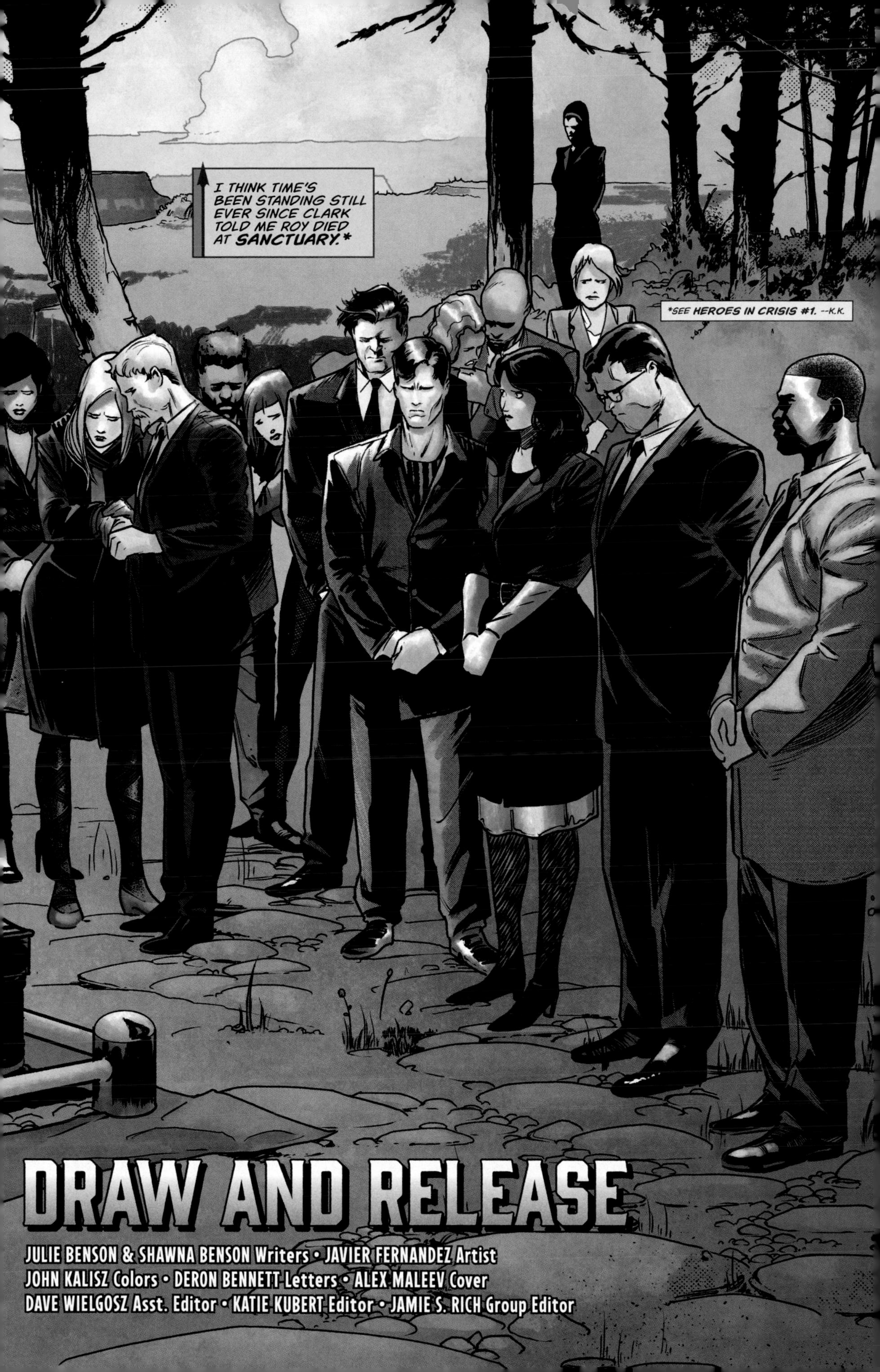
I THINK TIME'S BEEN STANDING STILL EVER SINCE CLARK TOLD ME ROY DIED AT SANCTUARY.*
*SEE HEROES IN CRISIS #1. --K.K.
DRAW AND RELEASE
JULIE BENSON & SHAWNA BENSON Writers • JAVIER FERNANDEZ Artist
JOHN KALISZ Colors • DERON BENNETT Letters • ALEX MALEEV Cover
DAVE WIELGOSZ Asst. Editor • KATIE KUBERT Editor • JAMIE S. RICH Group Editor

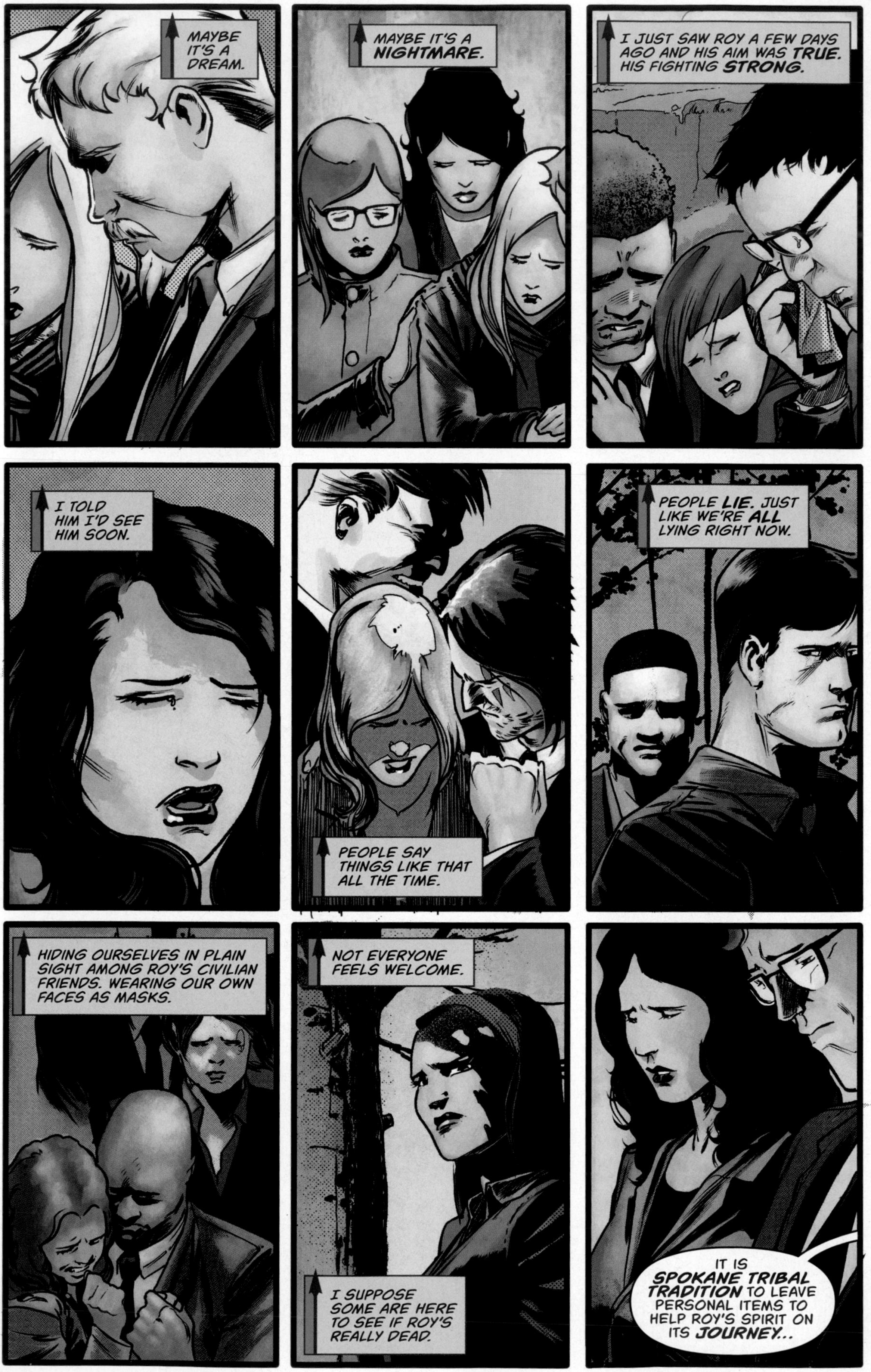
MAYBE IT'S A DREAM.
MAYBE IT'S A NIGHTMARE.
I JUST SAW ROY A FEW DAYS AGO AND HIS AIM WAS TRUE. HIS FIGHTING STRONG.
I TOLD HIM I'D SEE HIM SOON.
PEOPLE SAY THINGS LIKE THAT ALL THE TIME.
PEOPLE LIE. JUST LIKE WE'RE ALL LYING RIGHT NOW.
HIDING OURSELVES IN PLAIN SIGHT AMONG ROY'S CIVILIAN FRIENDS. WEARING OUR OWN FACES AS MASKS.
NOT EVERYONE FEELS WELCOME.
I SUPPOSE SOME ARE HERE TO SEE IF ROY'S REALLY DEAD.
IT IS SPOKANE TRIBAL TRADITION TO LEAVE PERSONAL ITEMS TO HELP ROY'S SPIRIT ON ITS JOURNEY...

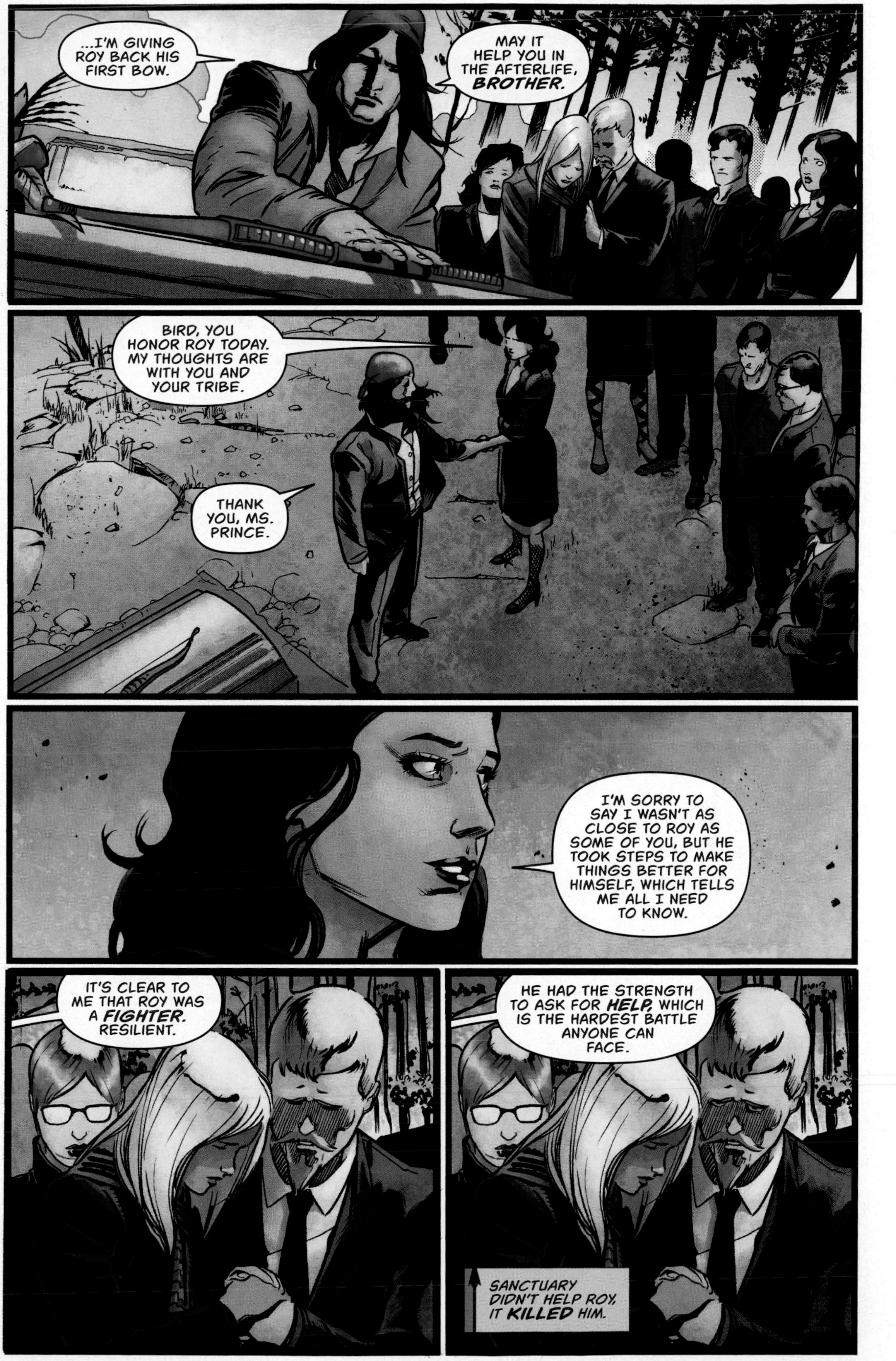
...I'M GIVING ROY BACK HIS FIRST BOW.
MAY IT HELP YOU IN THE AFTERLIFE, BROTHER.
BIRD, YOU HONOR ROY TODAY. MY THOUGHTS ARE WITH YOU AND YOUR TRIBE.
THANK YOU, MS. PRINCE.
I'M SORRY TO SAY I WASN'T AS CLOSE TO ROY AS SOME OF YOU, BUT HE TOOK STEPS TO MAKE THINGS BETTER FOR HIMSELF, WHICH TELLS ME ALL I NEED TO KNOW.
IT'S CLEAR TO ME THAT ROY WAS A FIGHTER. RESILIENT.
HE HAD THE STRENGTH TO ASK FOR HELP, WHICH IS THE HARDEST BATTLE ANYONE CAN FACE.
SANCTUARY DIDN'T HELP ROY, IT KILLED HIM.

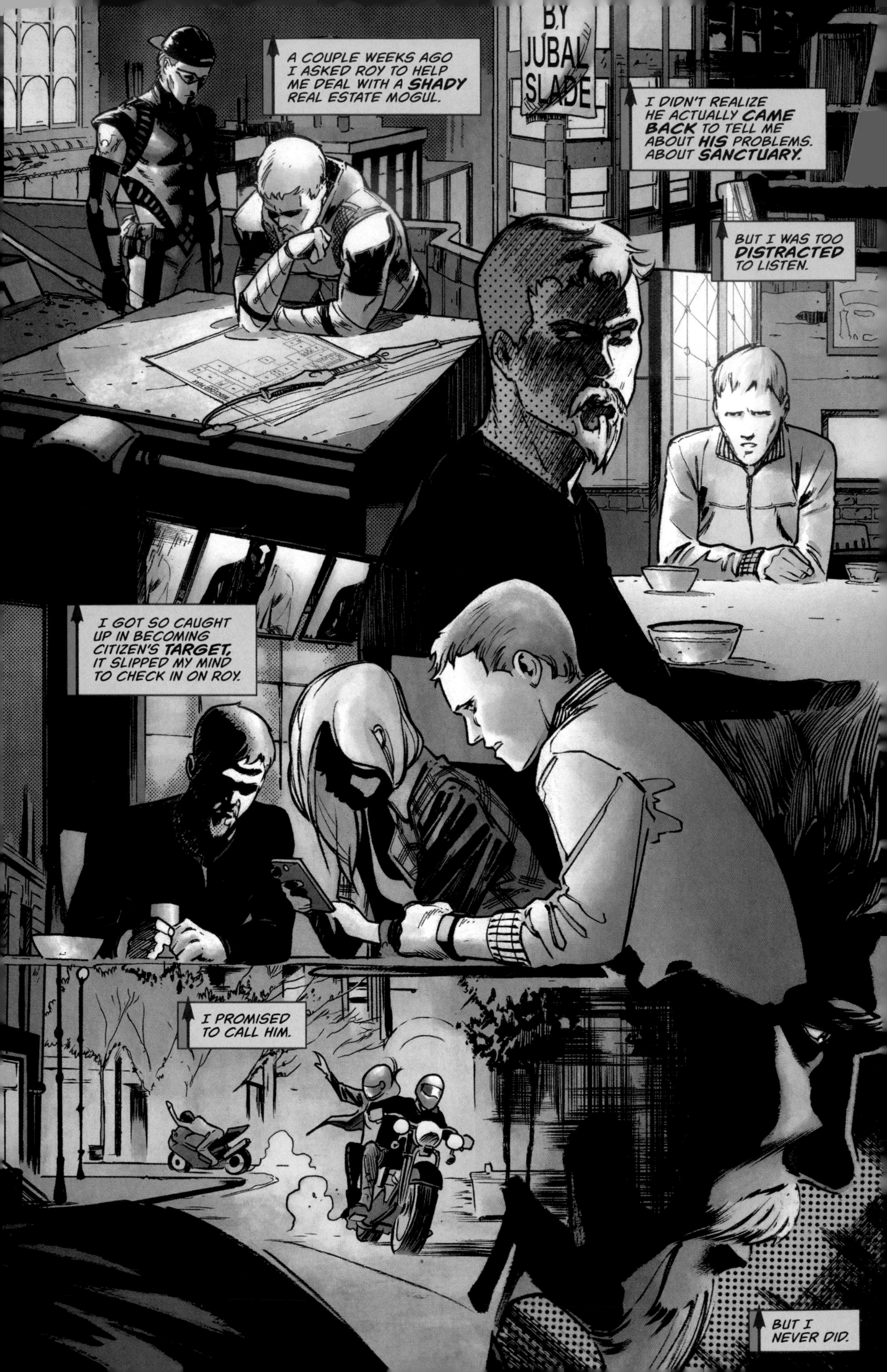
A COUPLE WEEKS AGO I ASKED ROY TO HELP ME DEAL WITH A SHADY REAL ESTATE MOGUL.
BY JUBAL SLADE
I DIDN'T REALIZE HE ACTUALLY CAME BACK TO TELL ME ABOUT HIS PROBLEMS. ABOUT SANCTUARY.
BUT I WAS TOO DISTRACTED TO LISTEN.
I GOT SO CAUGHT UP IN BECOMING CITIZEN'S TARGET, IT SLIPPED MY MIND TO CHECK IN ON ROY.
I PROMISED TO CALL HIM.
BUT I NEVER DID.

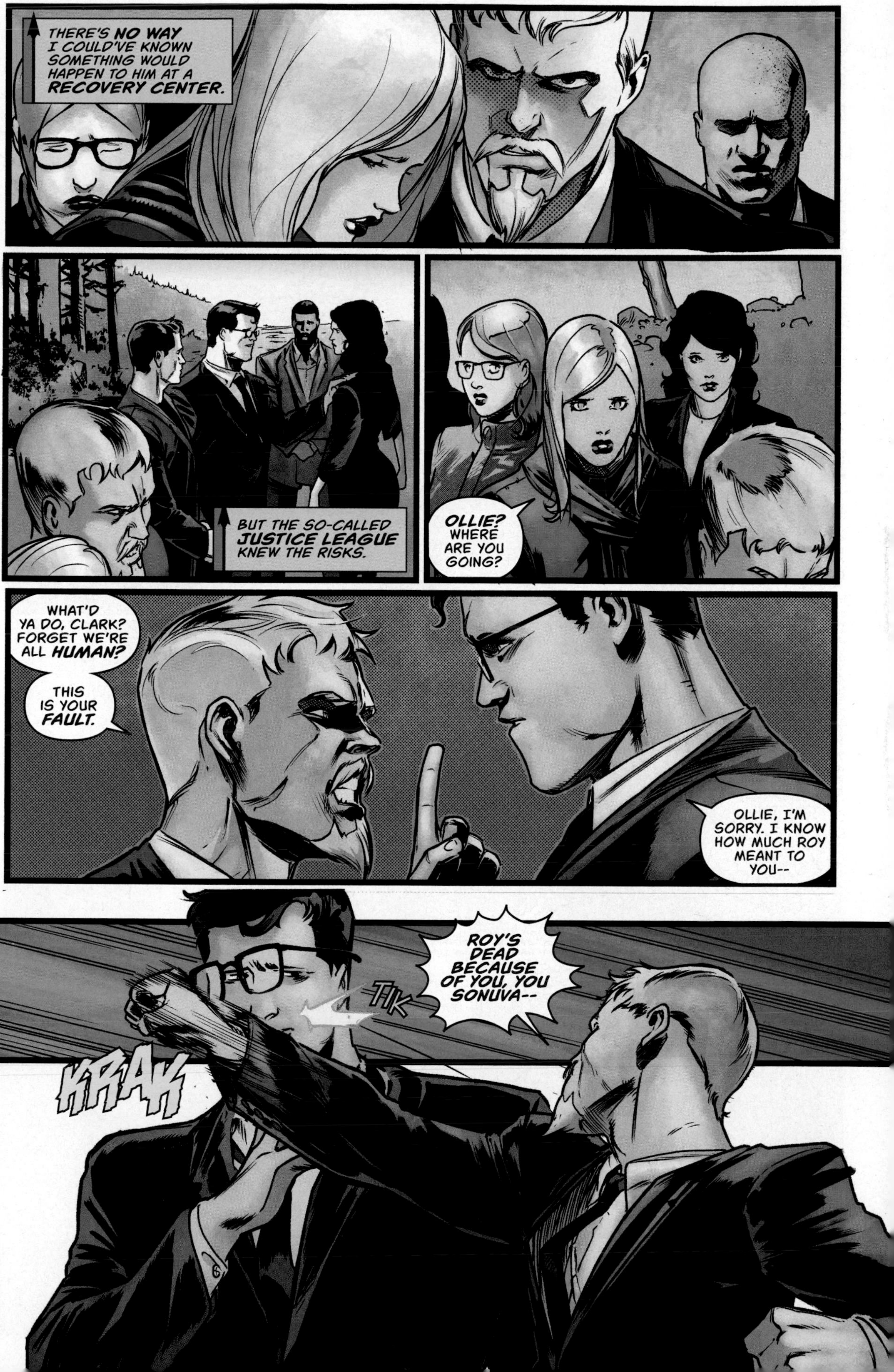

THERE'S NO WAY I COULD'VE KNOWN SOMETHING WOULD HAPPEN TO HIM AT A RECOVERY CENTER.
BUT THE SO-CALLED JUSTICE LEAGUE KNEW THE RISKS.
OLLIE? WHERE ARE YOU GOING?
WHAT'D YA DO, CLARK? FORGET WE'RE ALL HUMAN?
THIS IS YOUR FAULT.
OLLIE, I'M SORRY. I KNOW HOW MUCH ROY MEANT TO YOU--
ROY'S DEAD BECAUSE OF YOU, YOU SONUVA--
TIK
KRAK

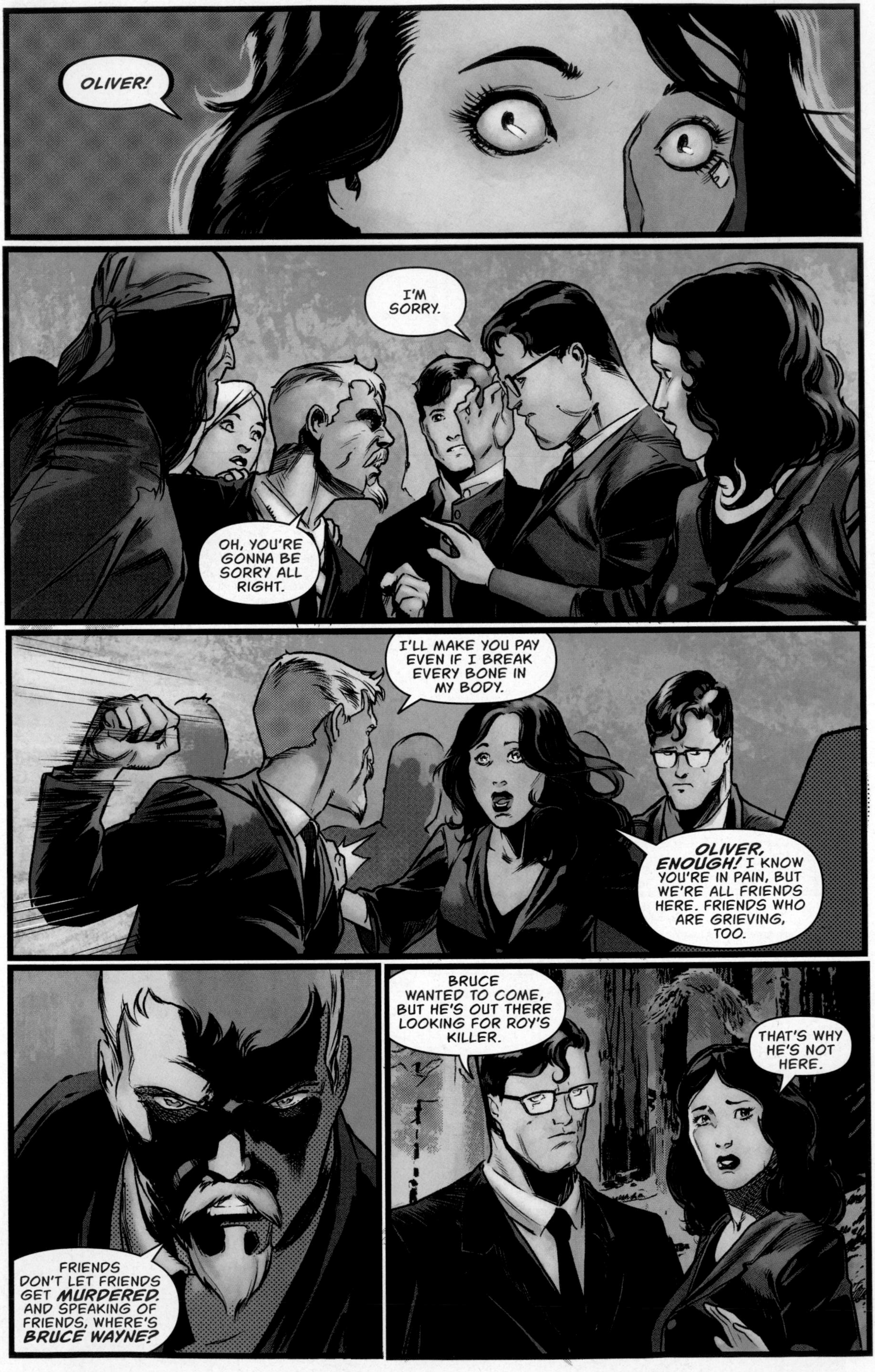
OLIVER!
I'M SORRY.
OH, YOU'RE GONNA BE SORRY ALL RIGHT.
I'LL MAKE YOU PAY EVEN IF I BREAK EVERY BONE IN MY BODY.
OLIVER, ENOUGH! I KNOW YOU'RE IN PAIN, BUT WE'RE ALL FRIENDS HERE. FRIENDS WHO ARE GRIEVING, TOO.
FRIENDS DON'T LET FRIENDS GET MURDERED. AND SPEAKING OF FRIENDS, WHERE'S BRUCE WAYNE?
BRUCE WANTED TO COME, BUT HE'S OUT THERE LOOKING FOR ROY'S KILLER.
THAT'S WHY HE'S NOT HERE.

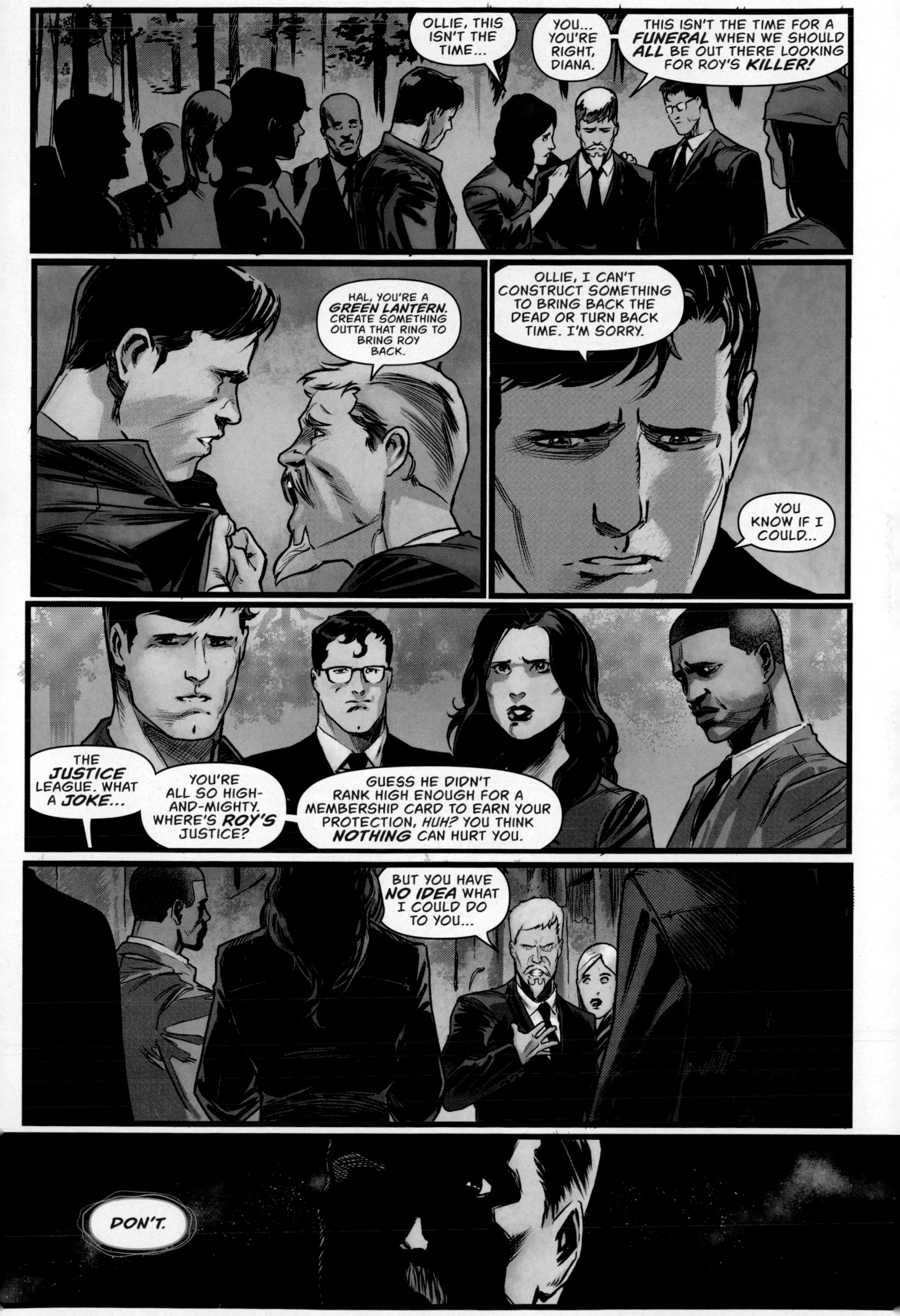
OLLIE, THIS ISN'T THE TIME...
YOU... YOU'RE RIGHT, DIANA.
THIS ISN'T THE TIME FOR A FUNERAL WHEN WE SHOULD ALL BE OUT THERE LOOKING FOR ROY'S KILLER!
HAL, YOU'RE A GREEN LANTERN. CREATE SOMETHING OUTTA THAT RING TO BRING ROY BACK.
OLLIE, I CAN'T CONSTRUCT SOMETHING TO BRING BACK THE DEAD OR TURN BACK TIME. I'M SORRY.
YOU KNOW IF I COULD...
THE JUSTICE LEAGUE. WHAT A JOKE...
YOU'RE ALL SO HIGH-AND-MIGHTY. WHERE'S ROY'S JUSTICE?
GUESS HE DIDN'T RANK HIGH ENOUGH FOR A MEMBERSHIP CARD TO EARN YOUR PROTECTION, HUH? YOU THINK NOTHING CAN HURT YOU.
BUT YOU HAVE NO IDEA WHAT I COULD DO TO YOU...
DON'T.

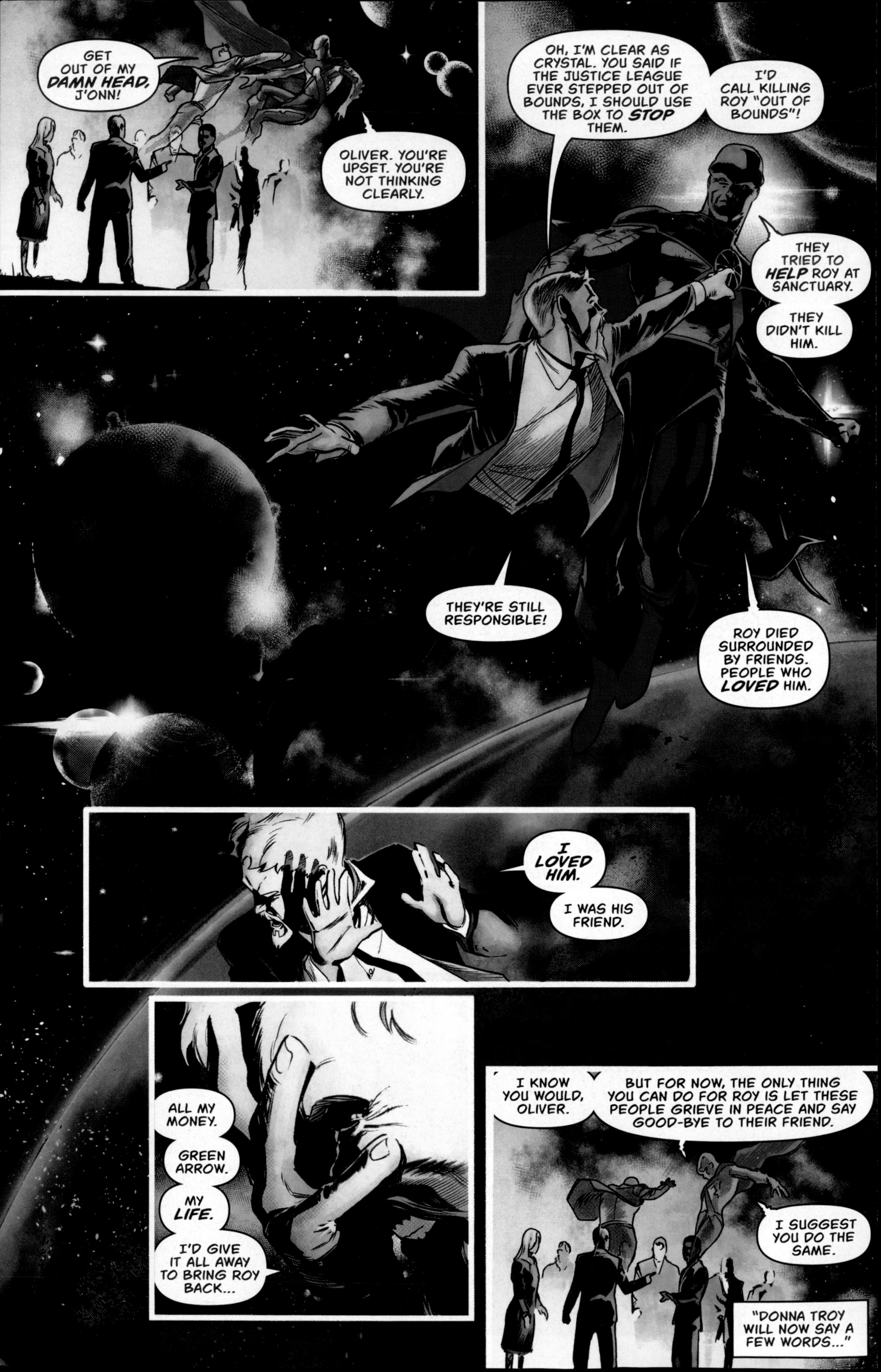
GET OUT OF MY DAMN HEAD, J'ONN!
OLIVER. YOU'RE UPSET. YOU'RE NOT THINKING CLEARLY.
OH, I'M CLEAR AS CRYSTAL. YOU SAID IF THE JUSTICE LEAGUE EVER STEPPED OUT OF BOUNDS, I SHOULD USE THE BOX TO STOP THEM.
I'D CALL KILLING ROY "OUT OF BOUNDS"!
THEY TRIED TO HELP ROY AT SANCTUARY.
THEY DIDN'T KILL HIM.
THEY'RE STILL RESPONSIBLE!
ROY DIED SURROUNDED BY FRIENDS. PEOPLE WHO LOVED HIM.
I LOVED HIM.
I WAS HIS FRIEND.
ALL MY MONEY.
GREEN ARROW.
MY LIFE.
I'D GIVE IT ALL AWAY TO BRING ROY BACK...
I KNOW YOU WOULD, OLIVER.
BUT FOR NOW, THE ONLY THING YOU CAN DO FOR ROY IS LET THESE PEOPLE GRIEVE IN PEACE AND SAY GOOD-BYE TO THEIR FRIEND.
I SUGGEST YOU DO THE SAME.
"DONNA TROY WILL NOW SAY A FEW WORDS..."

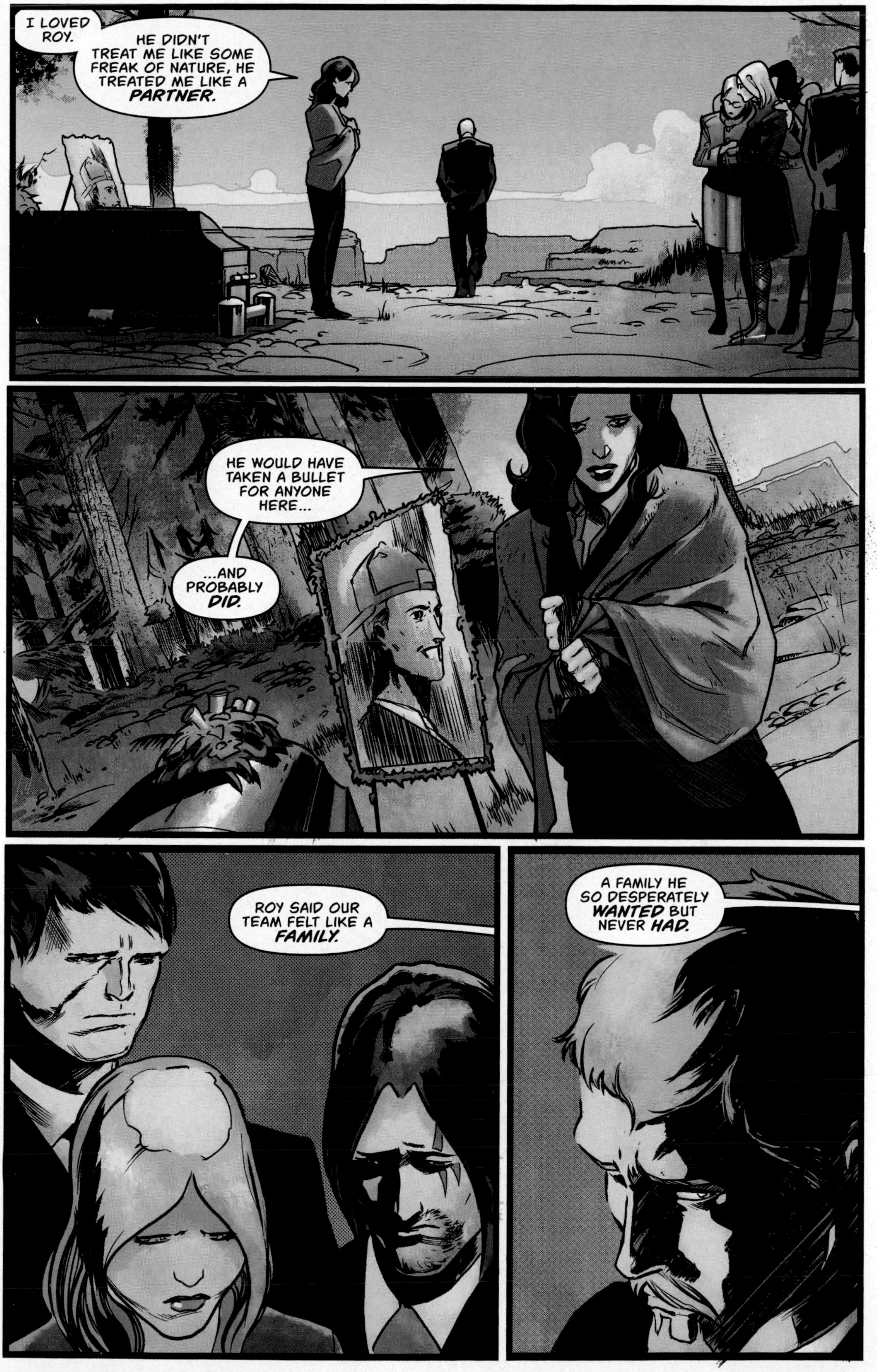
I LOVED ROY.
HE DIDN'T TREAT ME LIKE SOME FREAK OF NATURE, HE TREATED ME LIKE A PARTNER.
HE WOULD HAVE TAKEN A BULLET FOR ANYONE HERE...
...AND PROBABLY DID.
ROY SAID OUR TEAM FELT LIKE A FAMILY.
A FAMILY HE SO DESPERATELY WANTED BUT NEVER HAD.

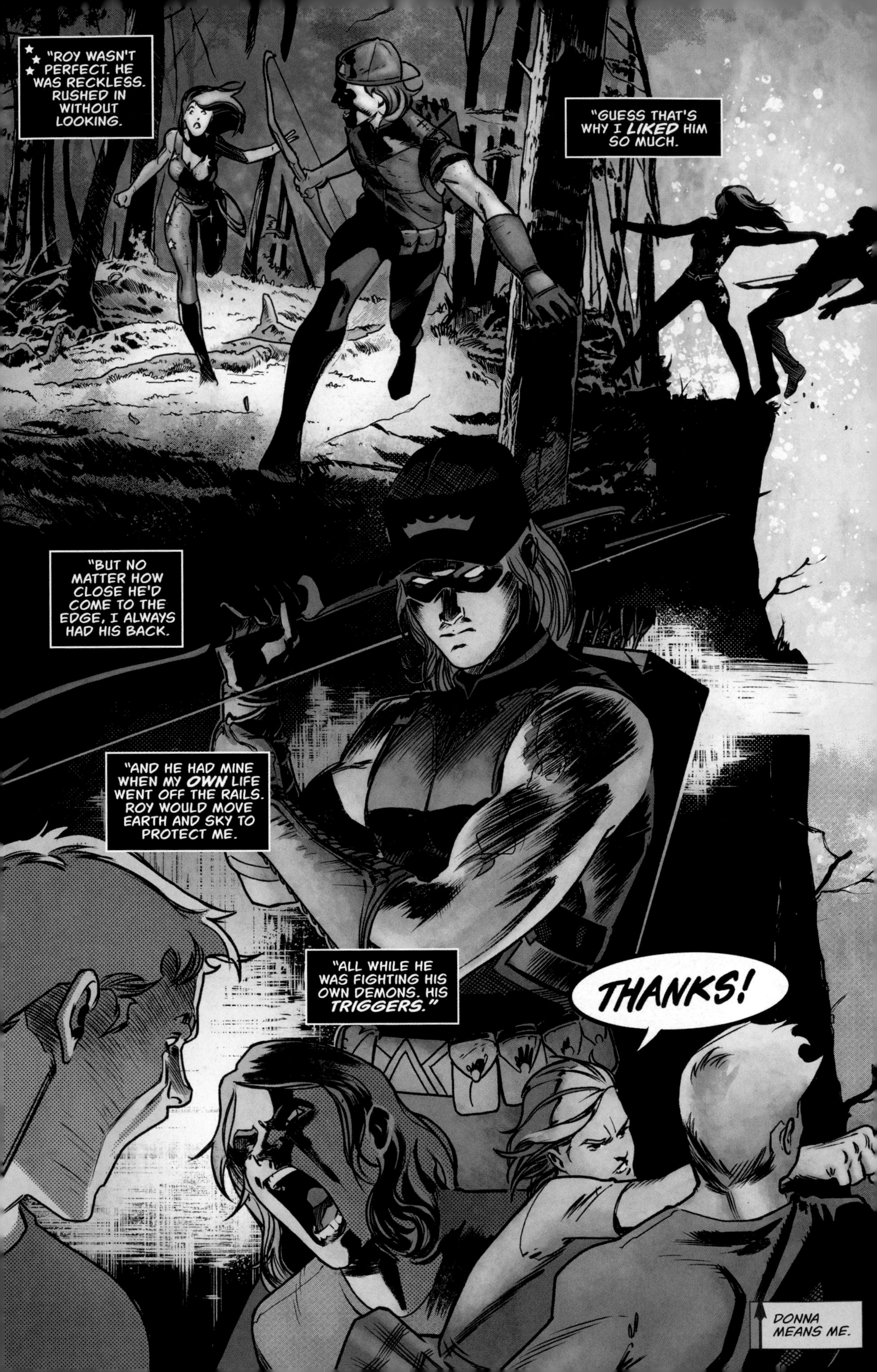
"ROY WASN'T PERFECT. HE WAS RECKLESS. RUSHED IN WITHOUT LOOKING.
"GUESS THAT'S WHY I LIKED HIM SO MUCH.
"BUT NO MATTER HOW CLOSE HE'D COME TO THE EDGE, I ALWAYS HAD HIS BACK.
"AND HE HAD MINE WHEN MY OWN LIFE WENT OFF THE RAILS. ROY WOULD MOVE EARTH AND SKY TO PROTECT ME.
"ALL WHILE HE WAS FIGHTING HIS OWN DEMONS. HIS TRIGGERS."
THANKS!
DONNA MEANS ME.

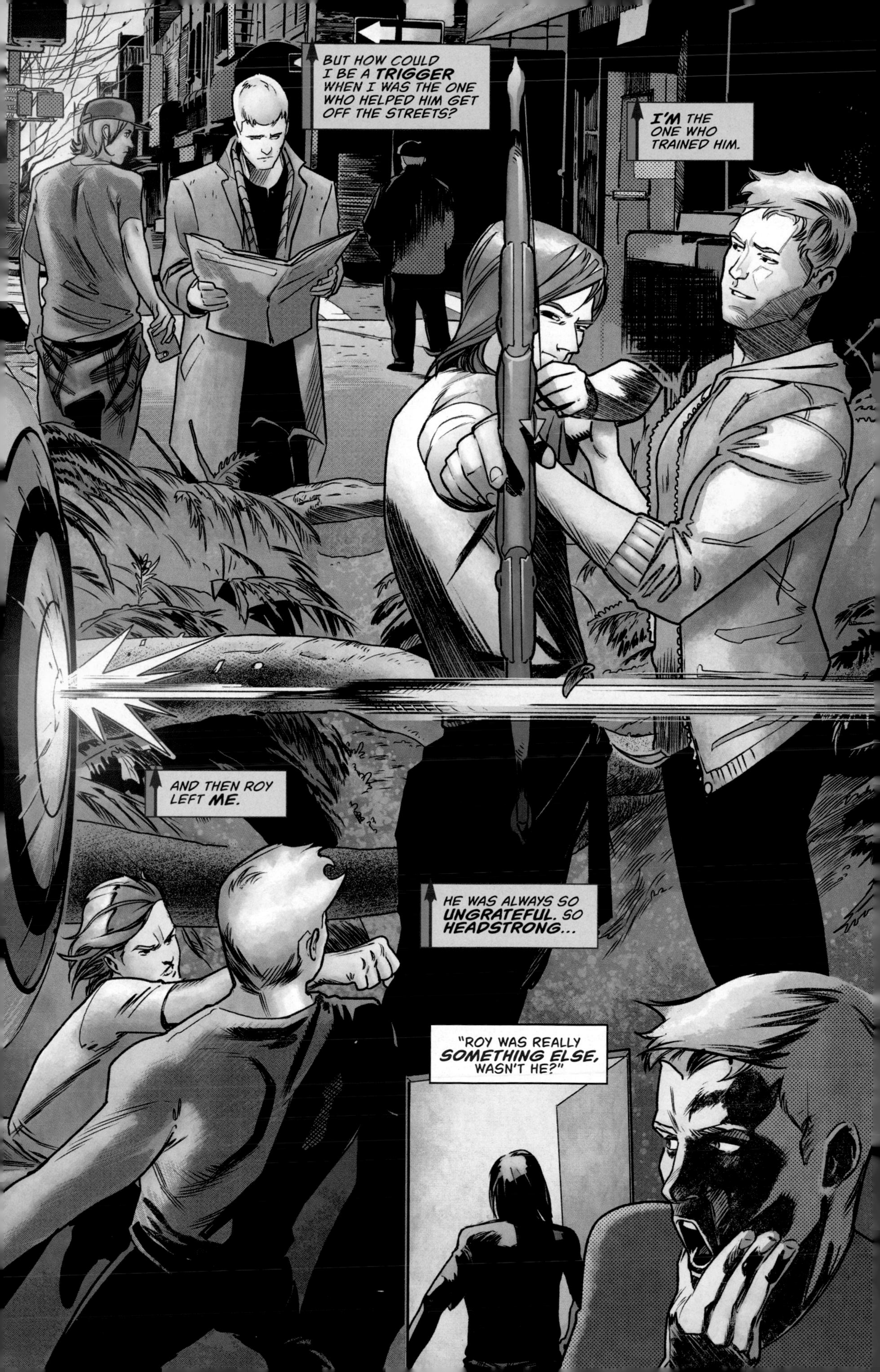
BUT HOW COULD I BE A TRIGGER WHEN I WAS THE ONE WHO HELPED HIM GET OFF THE STREETS?
I'M THE ONE WHO TRAINED HIM.
AND THEN ROY LEFT ME.
HE WAS ALWAYS SO UNGRATEFUL. SO HEADSTRONG...
"ROY WAS REALLY SOMETHING ELSE, WASN'T HE?"

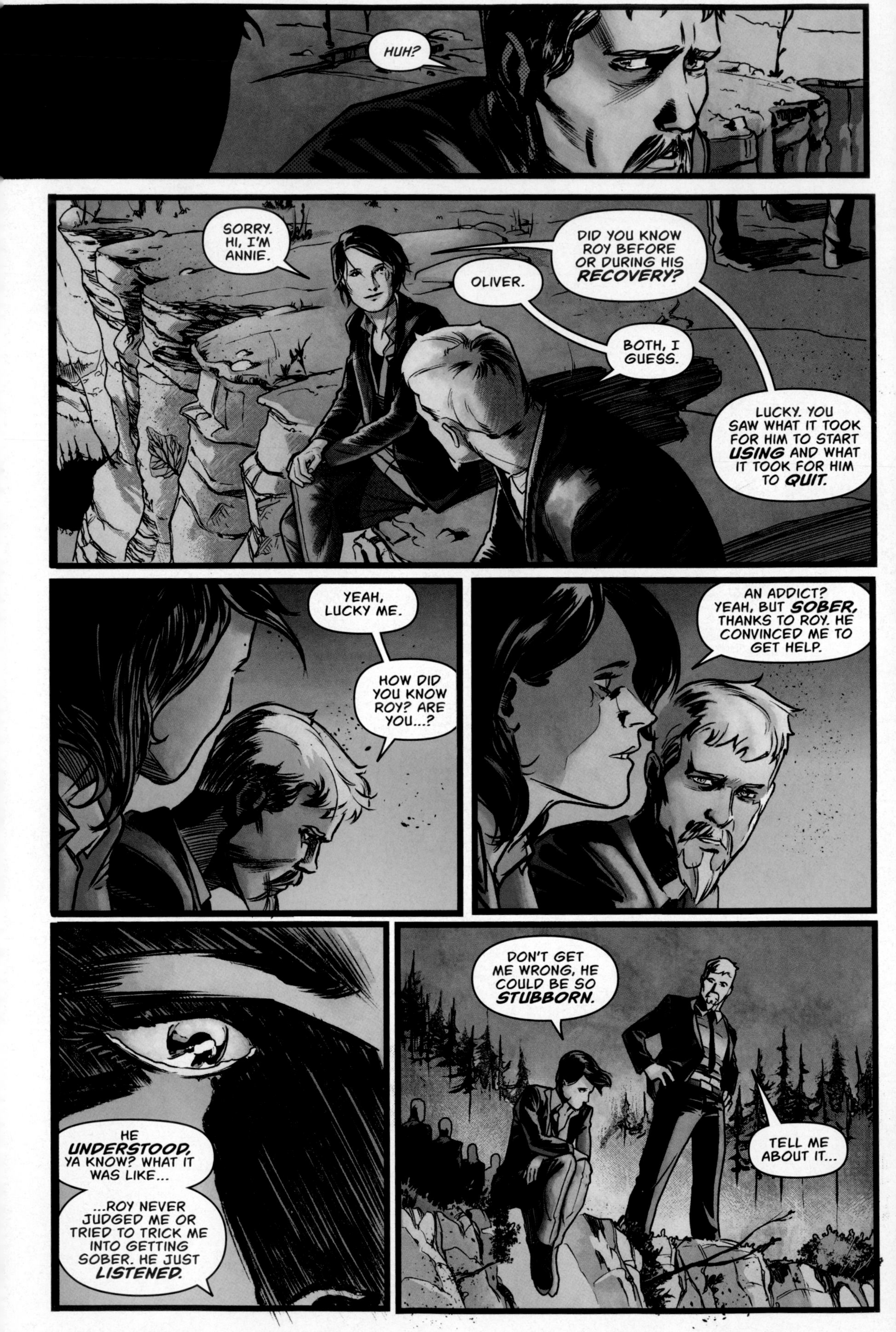
HUH?
SORRY. HI, I'M ANNIE.
OLIVER.
DID YOU KNOW ROY BEFORE OR DURING HIS RECOVERY?
BOTH, I GUESS.
LUCKY. YOU SAW WHAT IT TOOK FOR HIM TO START USING AND WHAT IT TOOK FOR HIM TO QUIT.
YEAH, LUCKY ME.
HOW DID YOU KNOW ROY? ARE YOU...?
AN ADDICT? YEAH, BUT SOBER, THANKS TO ROY. HE CONVINCED ME TO GET HELP.
HE UNDERSTOOD, YA KNOW? WHAT IT WAS LIKE...
...ROY NEVER JUDGED ME OR TRIED TO TRICK ME INTO GETTING SOBER. HE JUST LISTENED.
DON'T GET ME WRONG, HE COULD BE SO STUBBORN.
TELL ME ABOUT IT...

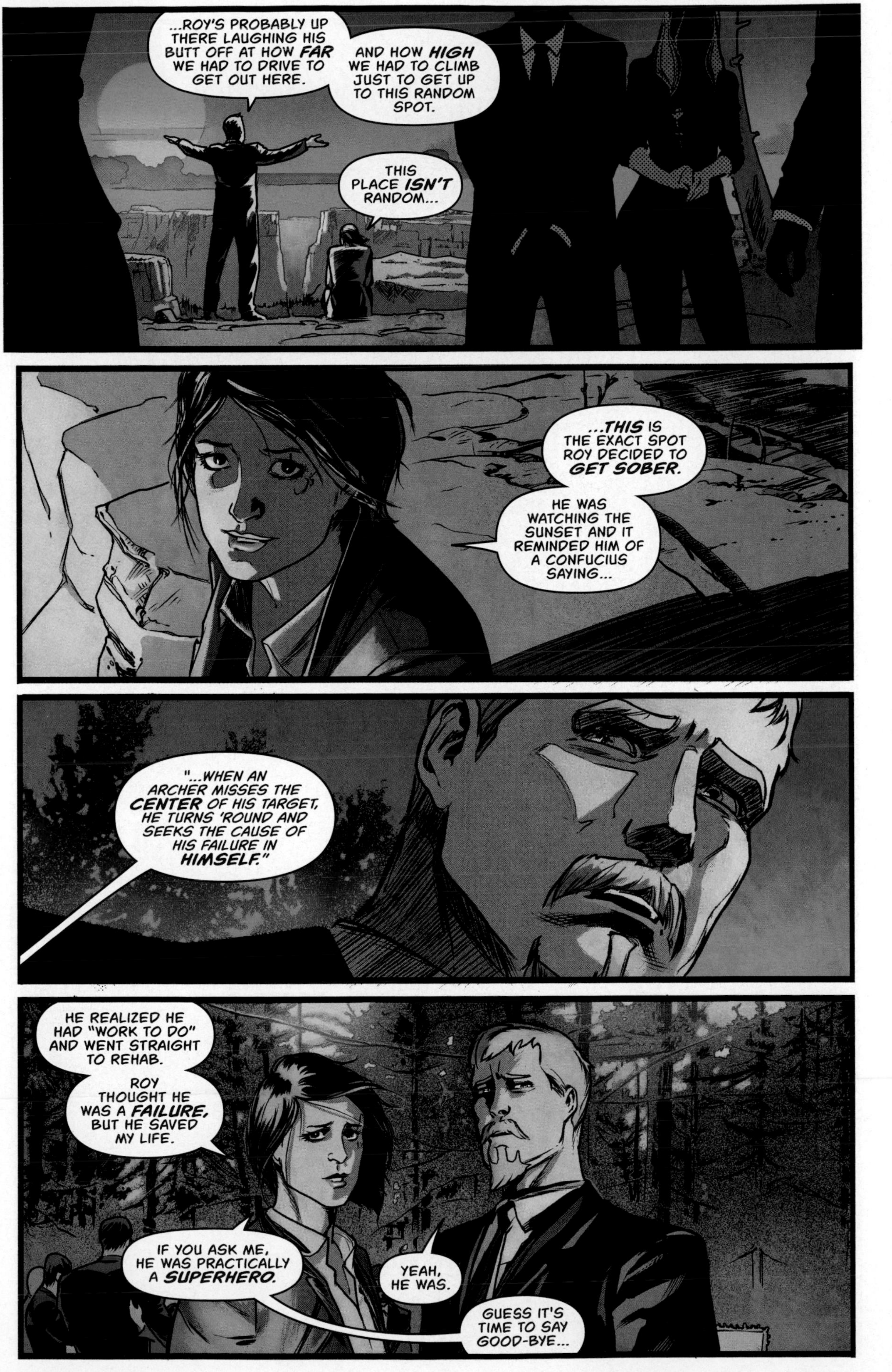
...ROY'S PROBABLY UP THERE LAUGHING HIS BUTT OFF AT HOW FAR WE HAD TO DRIVE TO GET OUT HERE.
AND HOW HIGH WE HAD TO CLIMB JUST TO GET UP TO THIS RANDOM SPOT.
THIS PLACE ISN'T RANDOM...
...THIS IS THE EXACT SPOT ROY DECIDED TO GET SOBER.
HE WAS WATCHING THE SUNSET AND IT REMINDED HIM OF A CONFUCIUS SAYING...
"...WHEN AN ARCHER MISSES THE CENTER OF HIS TARGET, HE TURNS 'ROUND AND SEEKS THE CAUSE OF HIS FAILURE IN HIMSELF."
HE REALIZED HE HAD "WORK TO DO" AND WENT STRAIGHT TO REHAB.
ROY THOUGHT HE WAS A FAILURE, BUT HE SAVED MY LIFE.
IF YOU ASK ME, HE WAS PRACTICALLY A SUPERHERO.
YEAH, HE WAS.
GUESS IT'S TIME TO SAY GOOD-BYE...

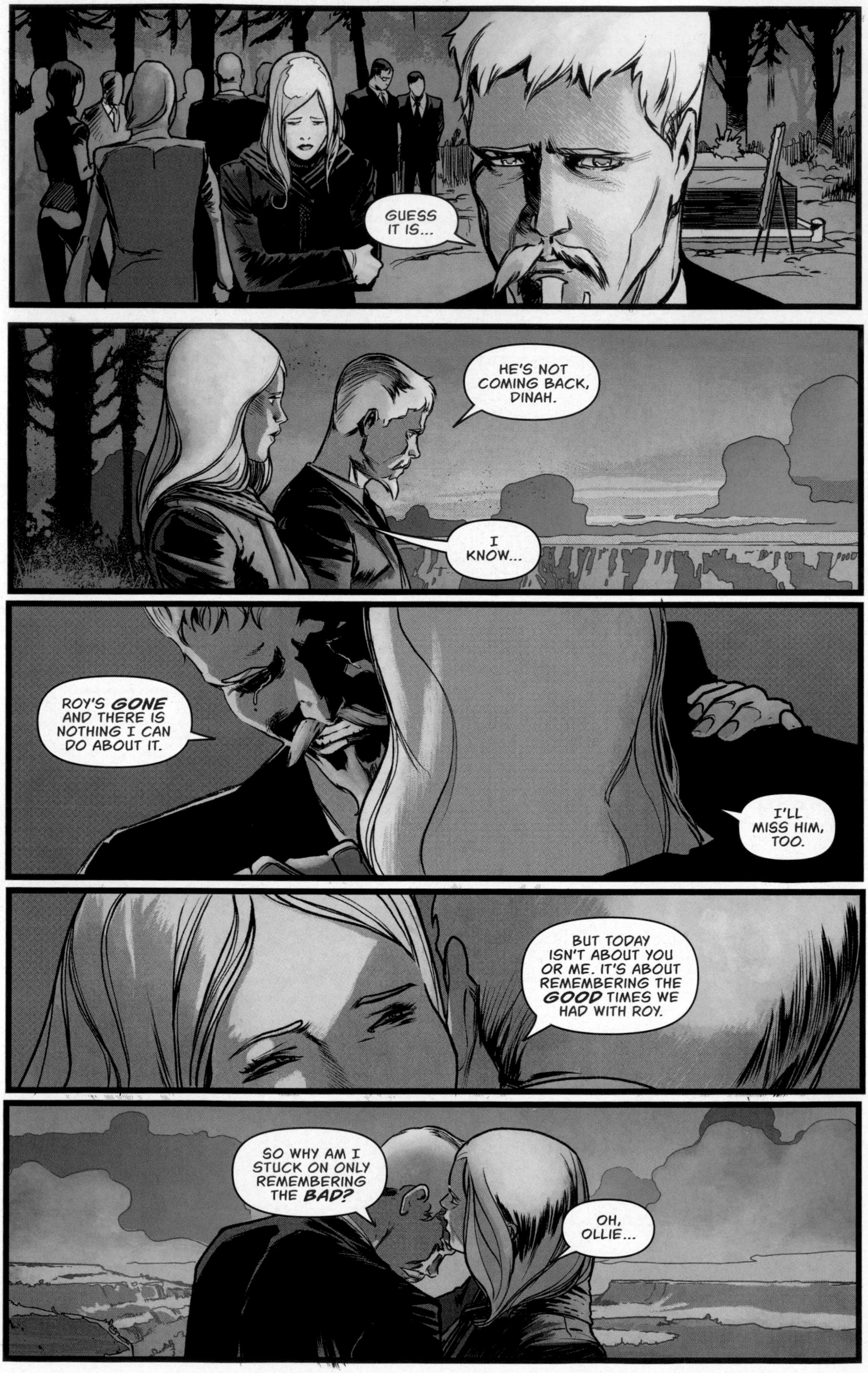
GUESS IT IS...
HE'S NOT COMING BACK, DINAH.
I KNOW...
ROY'S **GONE** AND THERE IS NOTHING I CAN DO ABOUT IT.
I'LL MISS HIM, TOO.
BUT TODAY ISN'T ABOUT YOU OR ME. IT'S ABOUT REMEMBERING THE **GOOD** TIMES WE HAD WITH ROY.
SO WHY AM I STUCK ON ONLY REMEMBERING THE **BAD?**
OH, OLLIE...

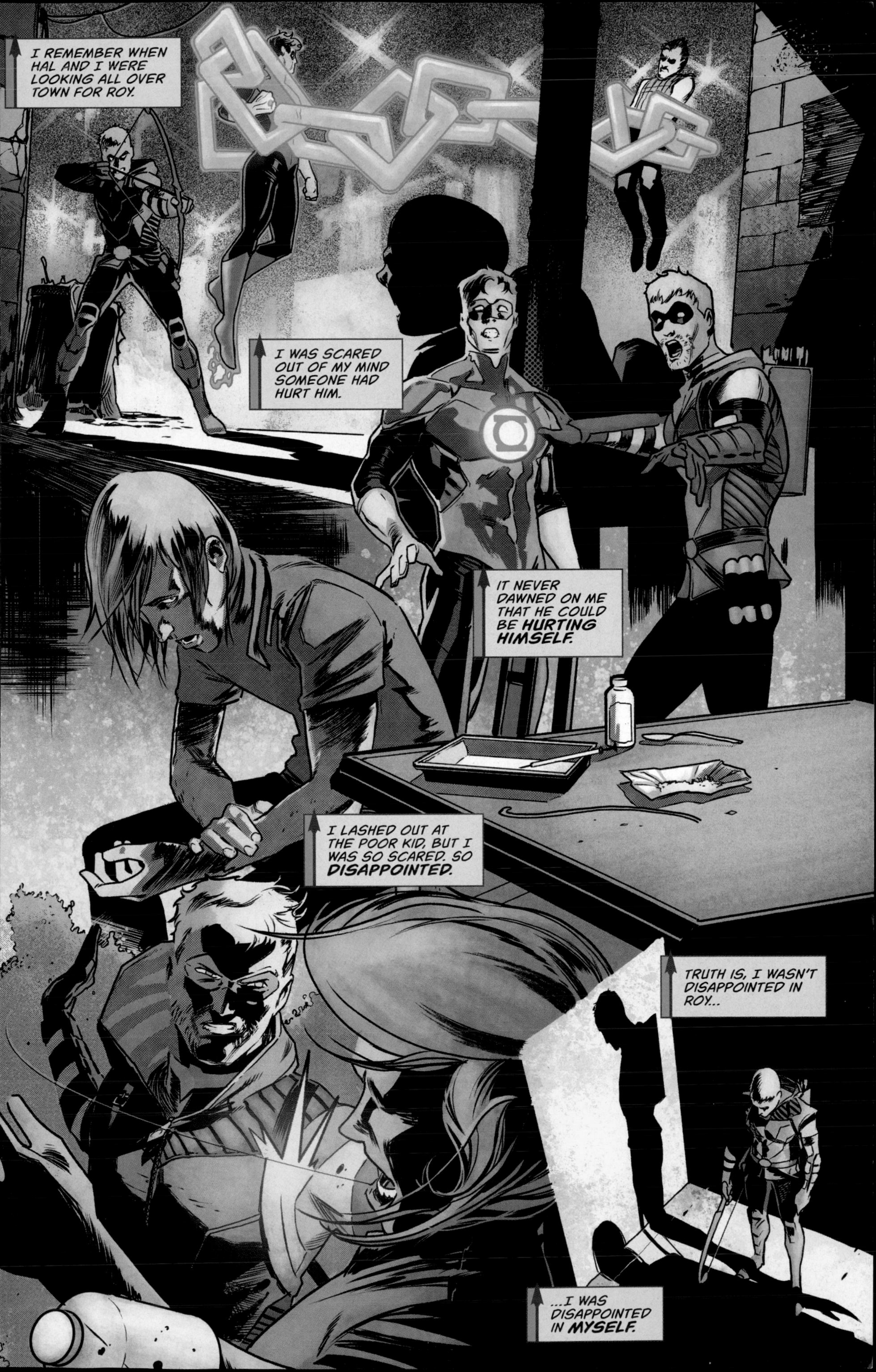
I REMEMBER WHEN HAL AND I WERE LOOKING ALL OVER TOWN FOR ROY.
I WAS SCARED OUT OF MY MIND SOMEONE HAD HURT HIM.
IT NEVER DAWNED ON ME THAT HE COULD BE HURTING HIMSELF.
I LASHED OUT AT THE POOR KID, BUT I WAS SO SCARED. SO DISAPPOINTED.
TRUTH IS, I WASN'T DISAPPOINTED IN ROY...
...I WAS DISAPPOINTED IN MYSELF.

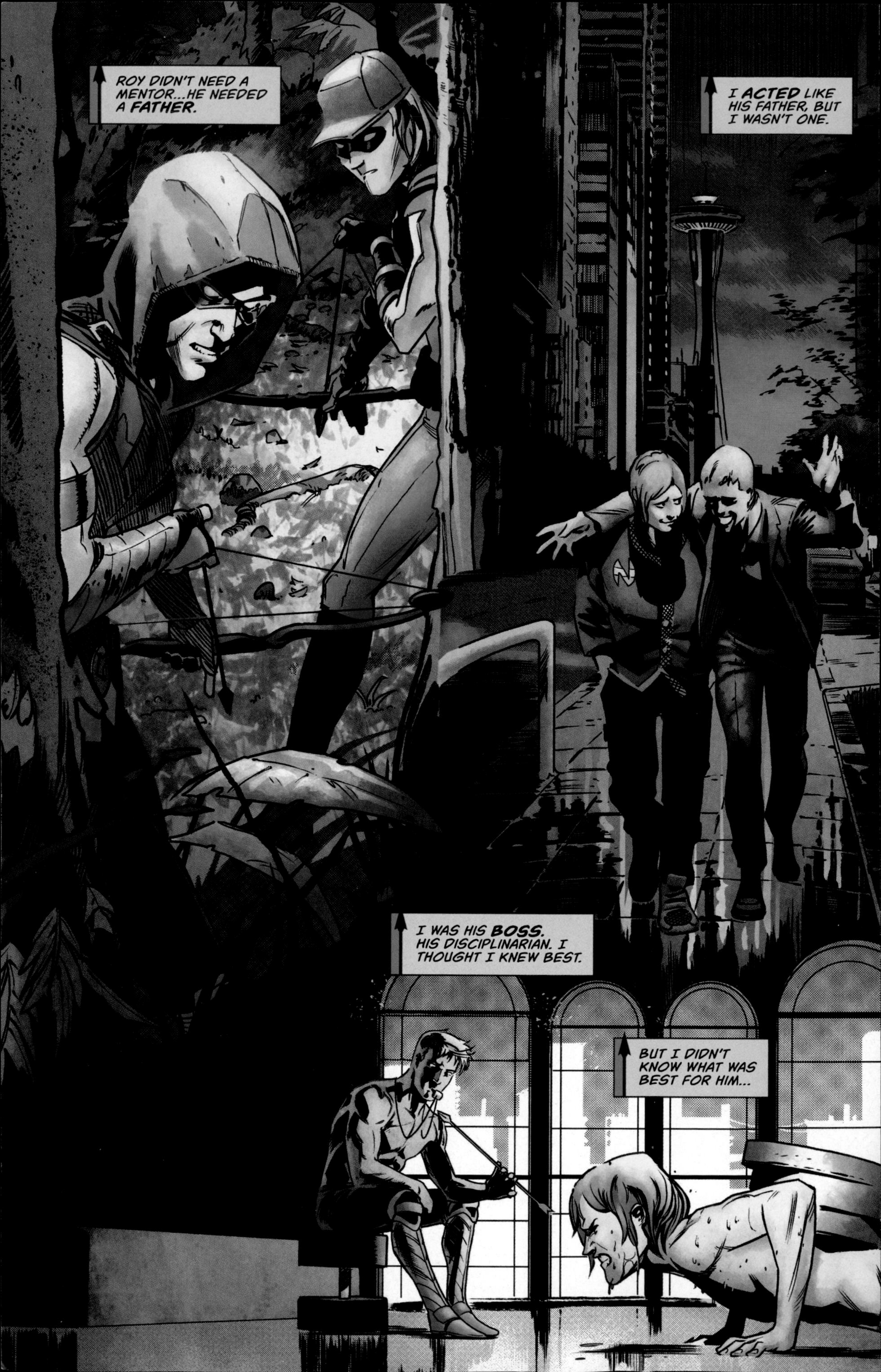
ROY DIDN'T NEED A MENTOR...HE NEEDED A FATHER.
I ACTED LIKE HIS FATHER, BUT I WASN'T ONE.
I WAS HIS BOSS. HIS DISCIPLINARIAN. I THOUGHT I KNEW BEST.
BUT I DIDN'T KNOW WHAT WAS BEST FOR HIM...

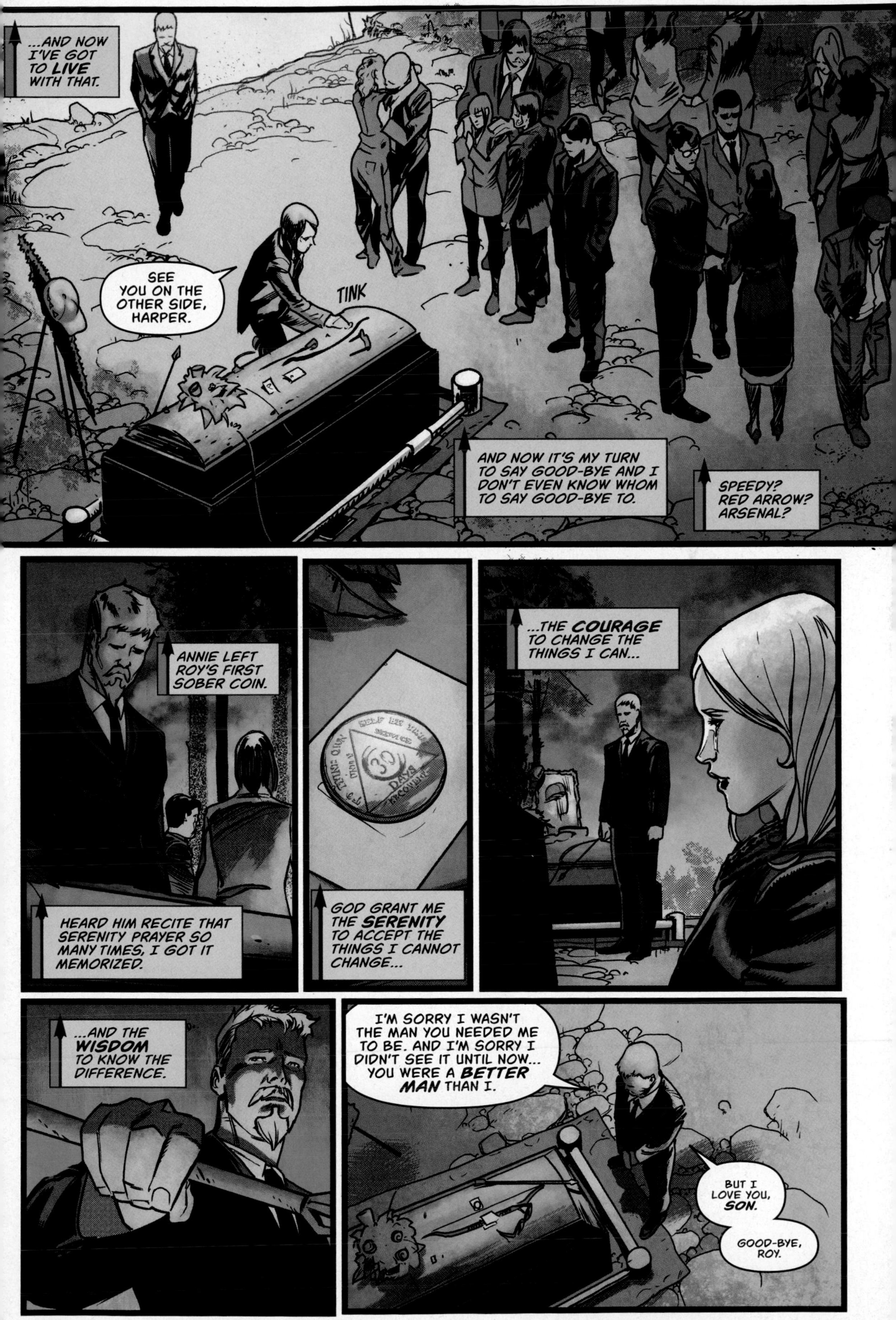

...AND NOW I'VE GOT TO LIVE WITH THAT.
SEE YOU ON THE OTHER SIDE, HARPER.
TINK
AND NOW IT'S MY TURN TO SAY GOOD-BYE AND I DON'T EVEN KNOW WHOM TO SAY GOOD-BYE TO.
SPEEDY? RED ARROW? ARSENAL?
ANNIE LEFT ROY'S FIRST SOBER COIN.
HEARD HIM RECITE THAT SERENITY PRAYER SO MANY TIMES, I GOT IT MEMORIZED.
GOD GRANT ME THE SERENITY TO ACCEPT THE THINGS I CANNOT CHANGE...
...THE COURAGE TO CHANGE THE THINGS I CAN...
...AND THE WISDOM TO KNOW THE DIFFERENCE.
I'M SORRY I WASN'T THE MAN YOU NEEDED ME TO BE. AND I'M SORRY I DIDN'T SEE IT UNTIL NOW... YOU WERE A BETTER MAN THAN I.
BUT I LOVE YOU, SON.
GOOD-BYE, ROY.

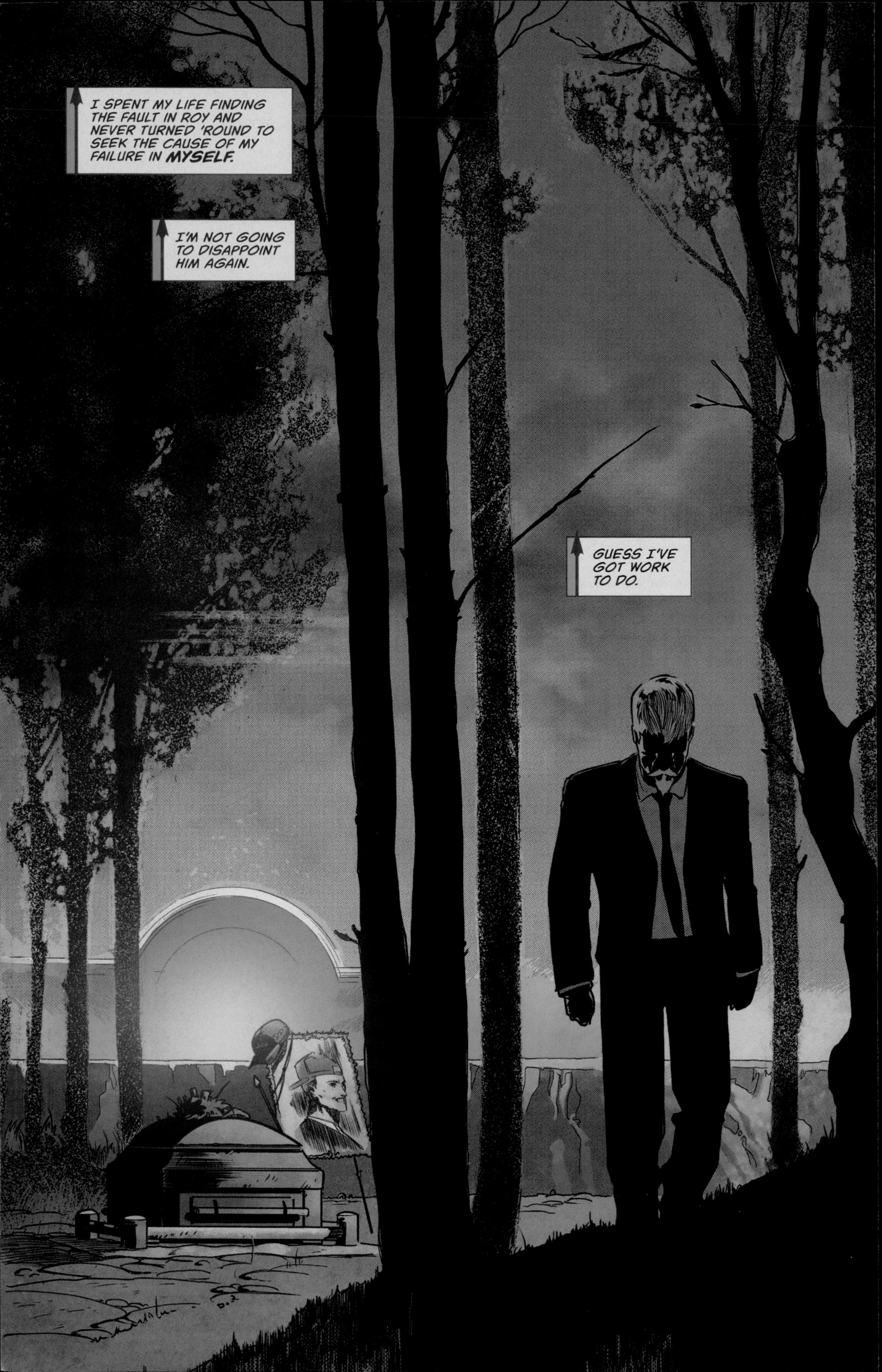
I SPENT MY LIFE FINDING THE FAULT IN ROY AND NEVER TURNED 'ROUND TO SEEK THE CAUSE OF MY FAILURE IN MYSELF.
I'M NOT GOING TO DISAPPOINT HIM AGAIN.
GUESS I'VE GOT WORK TO DO.

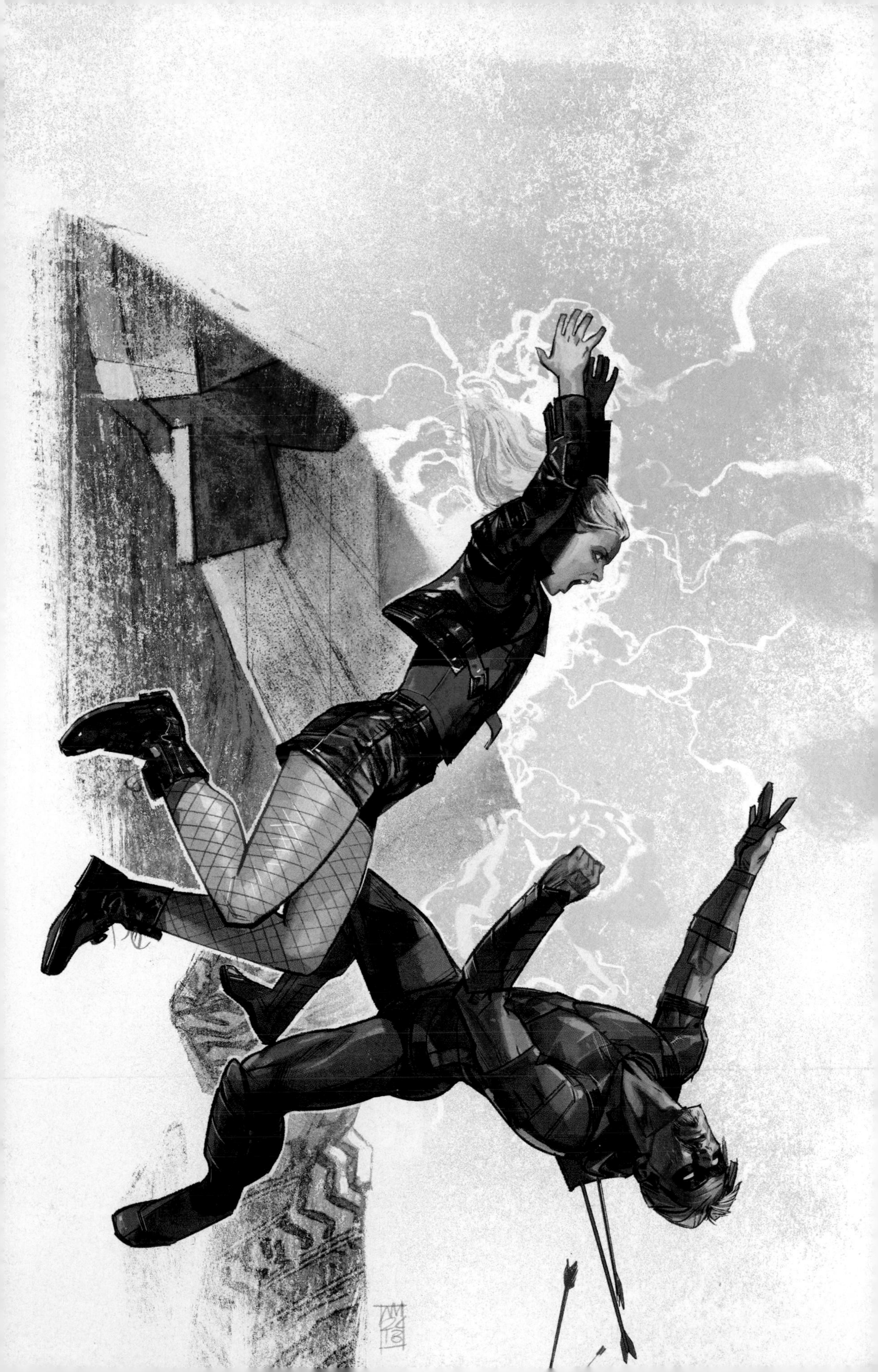

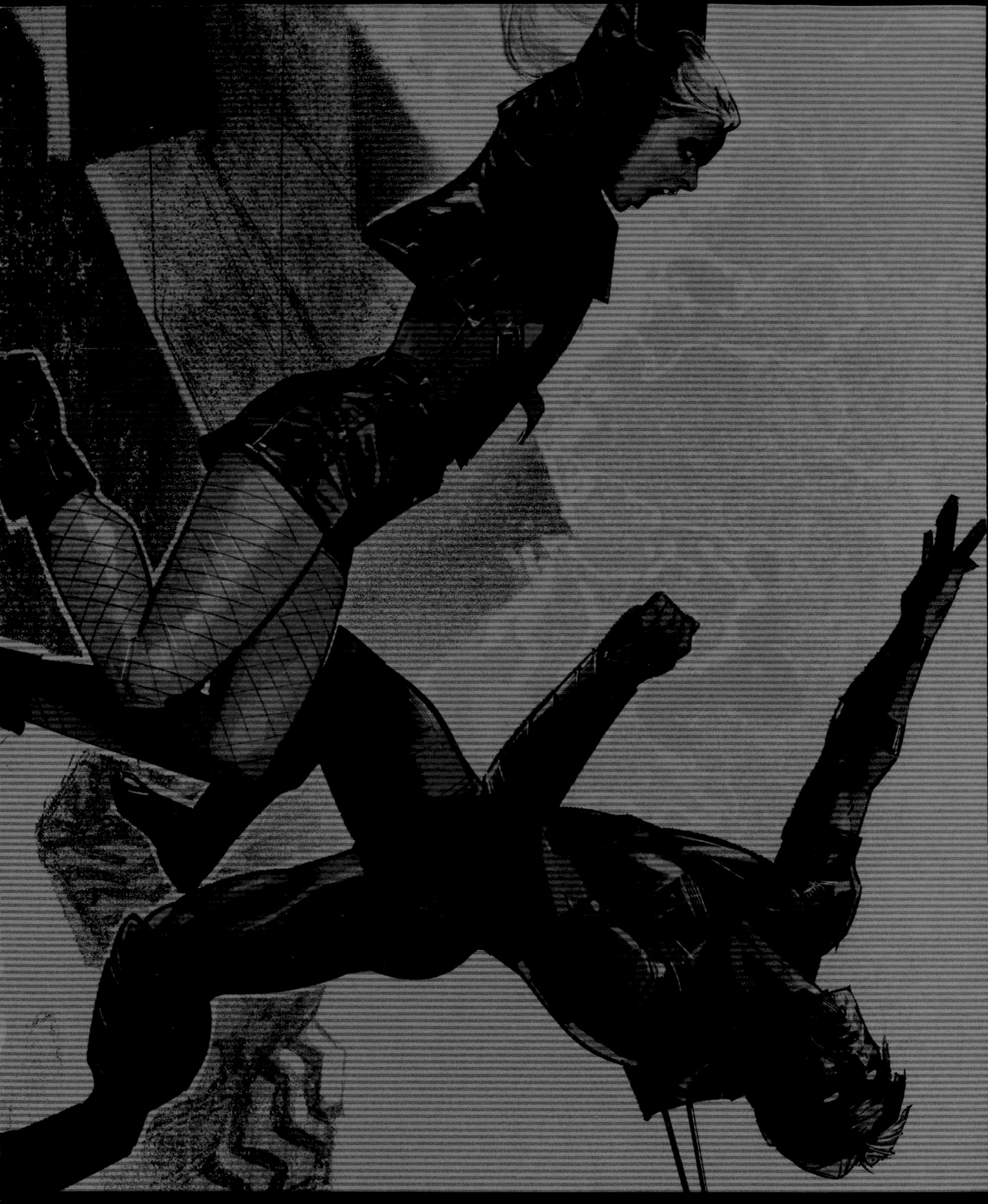

GREEN ARROW

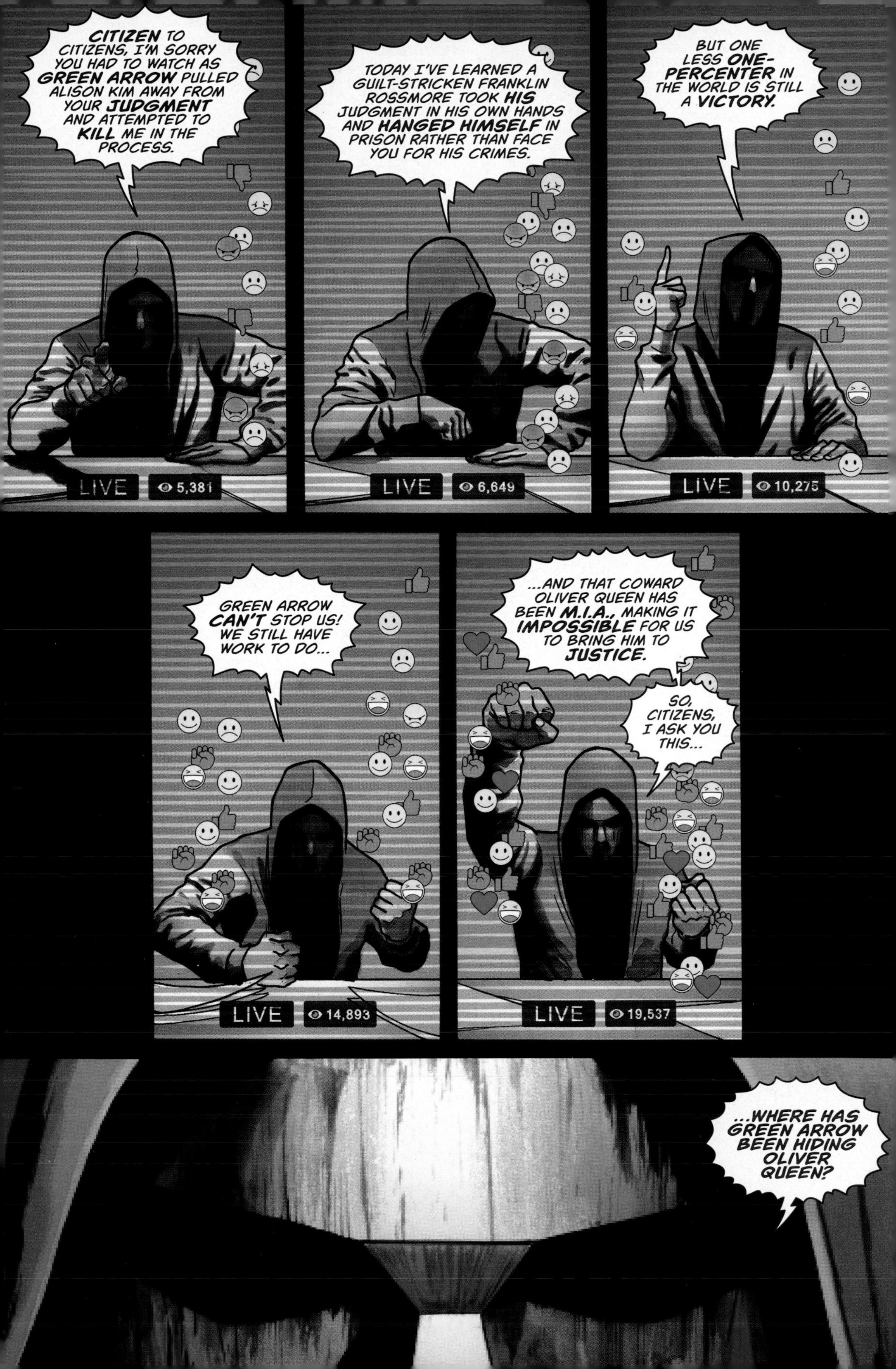
CITIZEN TO CITIZENS, I'M SORRY YOU HAD TO WATCH AS GREEN ARROW PULLED ALISON KIM AWAY FROM YOUR JUDGMENT AND ATTEMPTED TO KILL ME IN THE PROCESS.
LIVE
5,381
TODAY I'VE LEARNED A GUILT-STRICKEN FRANKLIN ROSSMORE TOOK HIS JUDGMENT IN HIS OWN HANDS AND HANGED HIMSELF IN PRISON RATHER THAN FACE YOU FOR HIS CRIMES.
LIVE
6,649
BUT ONE LESS ONE-PERCENTER IN THE WORLD IS STILL A VICTORY.
LIVE
10,275
GREEN ARROW CAN'T STOP US! WE STILL HAVE WORK TO DO...
LIVE
14,893
...AND THAT COWARD OLIVER QUEEN HAS BEEN M.I.A., MAKING IT IMPOSSIBLE FOR US TO BRING HIM TO JUSTICE.
SO, CITIZENS, I ASK YOU THIS...
LIVE
19,537
...WHERE HAS GREEN ARROW BEEN HIDING OLIVER QUEEN?

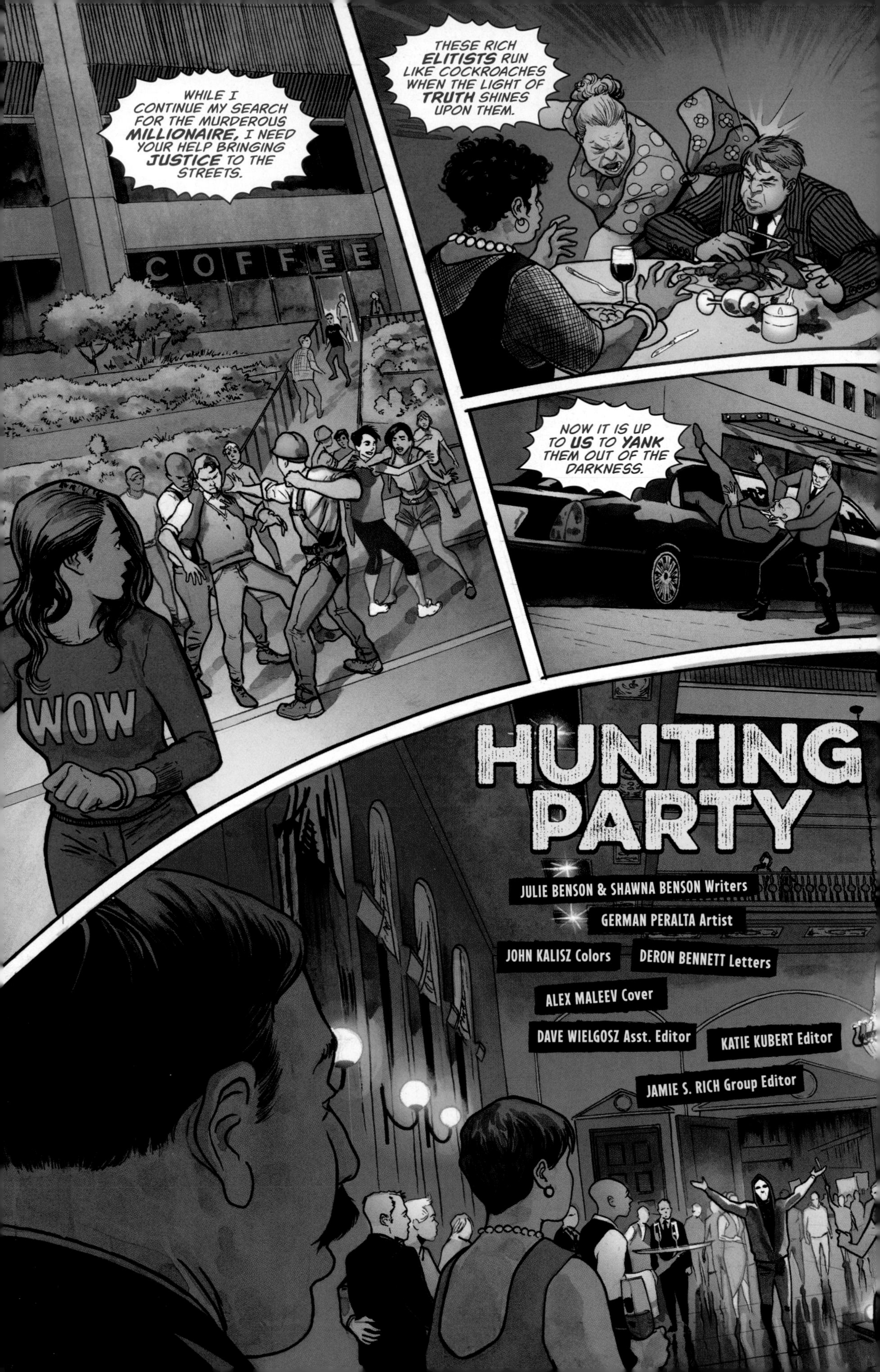
WHILE I CONTINUE MY SEARCH FOR THE MURDEROUS MILLIONAIRE, I NEED YOUR HELP BRINGING JUSTICE TO THE STREETS.
COFFEE
THESE RICH ELITISTS RUN LIKE COCKROACHES WHEN THE LIGHT OF TRUTH SHINES UPON THEM.
NOW IT IS UP TO US TO YANK THEM OUT OF THE DARKNESS.
WOW
HUNTING PARTY
JULIE BENSON & SHAWNA BENSON Writers
GERMAN PERALTA Artist
JOHN KALISZ Colors
DERON BENNETT Letters
ALEX MALEEV Cover
DAVE WIELGOSZ Asst. Editor
KATIE KUBERT Editor
JAMIE S. RICH Group Editor

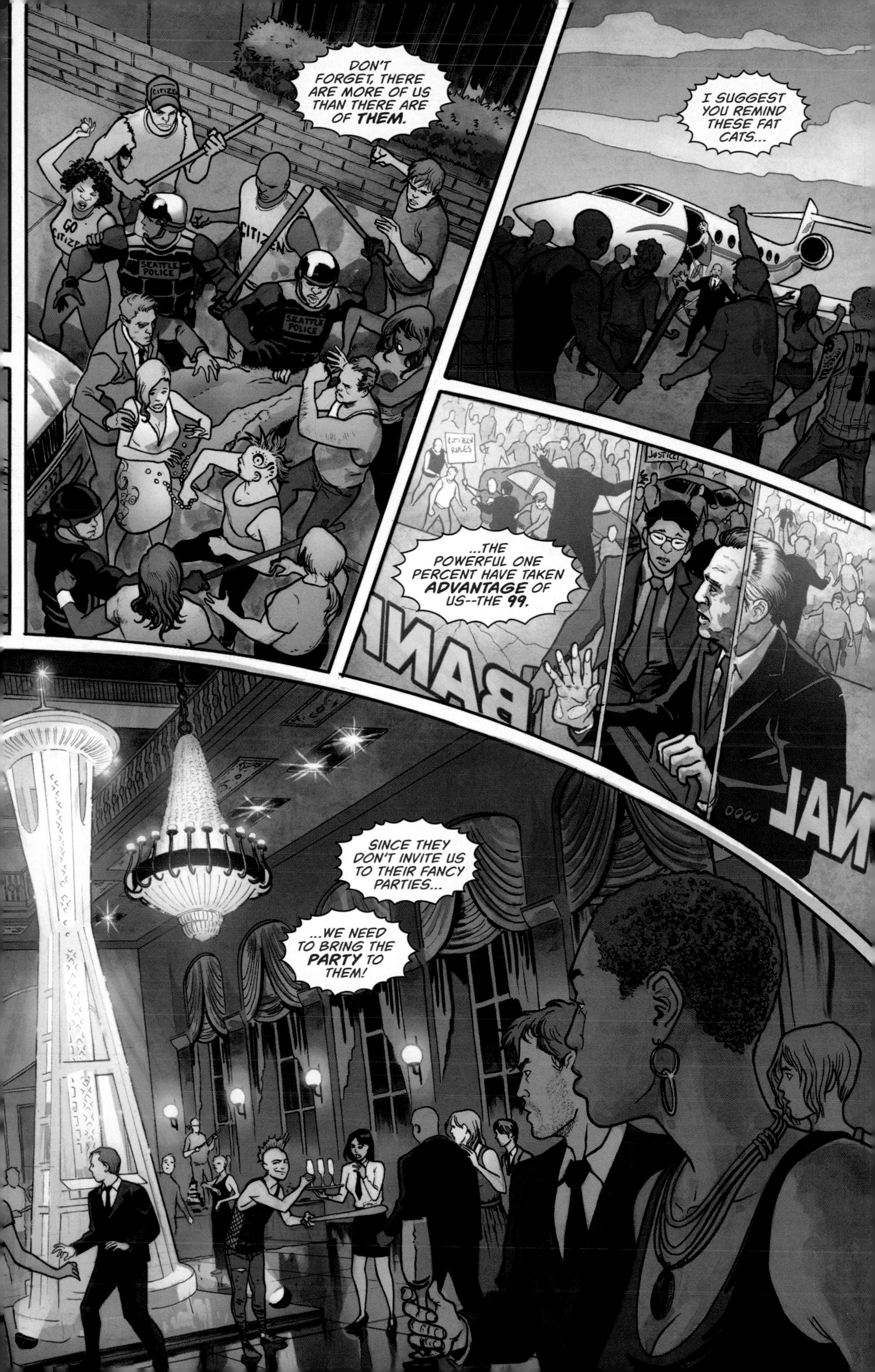

DON'T FORGET, THERE ARE MORE OF US THAN THERE ARE OF **THEM.**
CITIZEN
GO CITIZEN
CITIZEN
SEATTLE POLICE
SEATTLE POLICE
I SUGGEST YOU REMIND THESE FAT CATS...
CITIZEN RULES
JUSTICE!
...THE POWERFUL ONE PERCENT HAVE TAKEN **ADVANTAGE** OF US--THE **99.**
SINCE THEY DON'T INVITE US TO THEIR FANCY PARTIES...
...WE NEED TO BRING THE **PARTY** TO THEM!

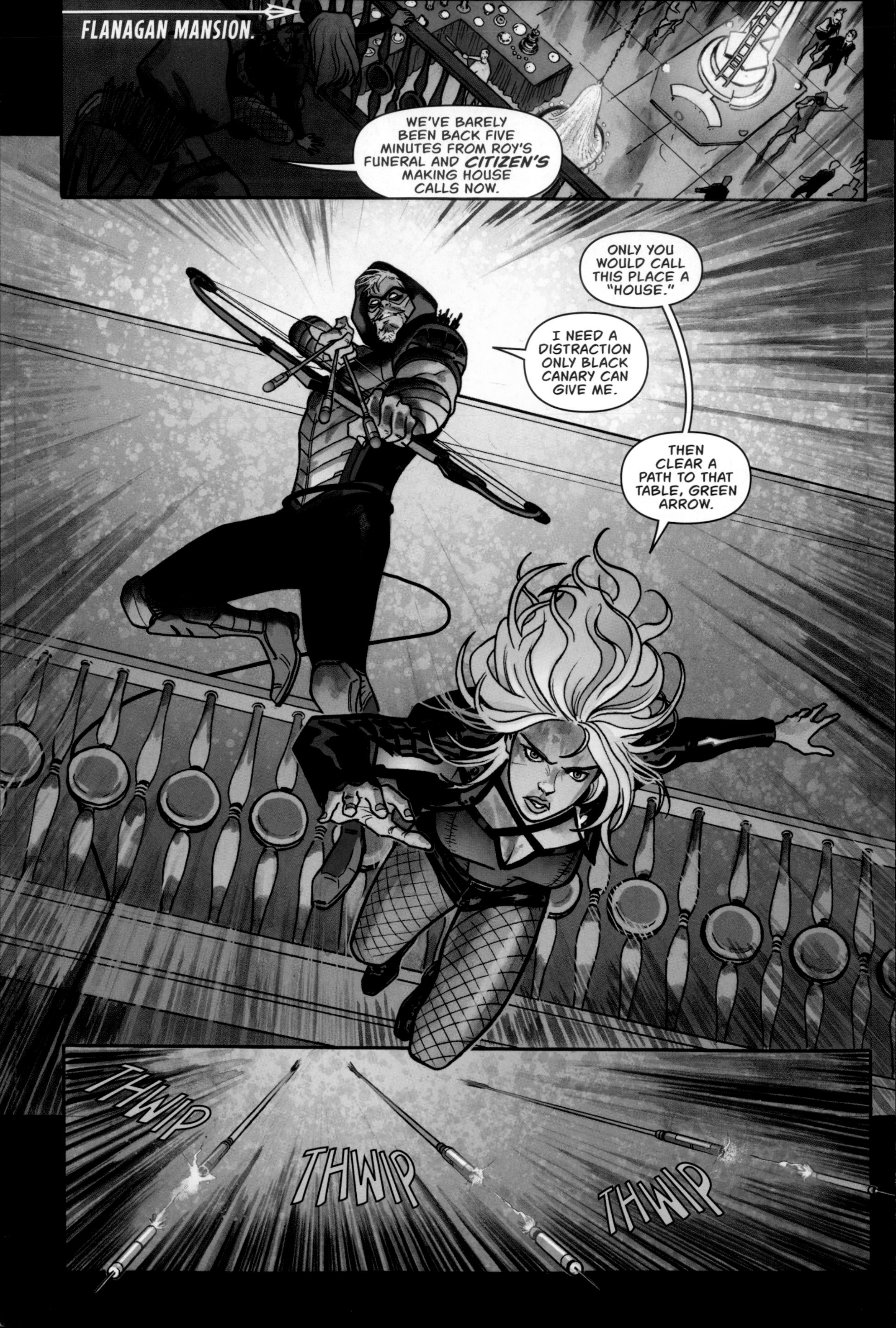
FLANAGAN MANSION.
WE'VE BARELY BEEN BACK FIVE MINUTES FROM ROY'S FUNERAL AND CITIZEN'S MAKING HOUSE CALLS NOW.
ONLY YOU WOULD CALL THIS PLACE A "HOUSE."
I NEED A DISTRACTION ONLY BLACK CANARY CAN GIVE ME.
THEN CLEAR A PATH TO THAT TABLE, GREEN ARROW.
THWIP
THWIP
THWIP

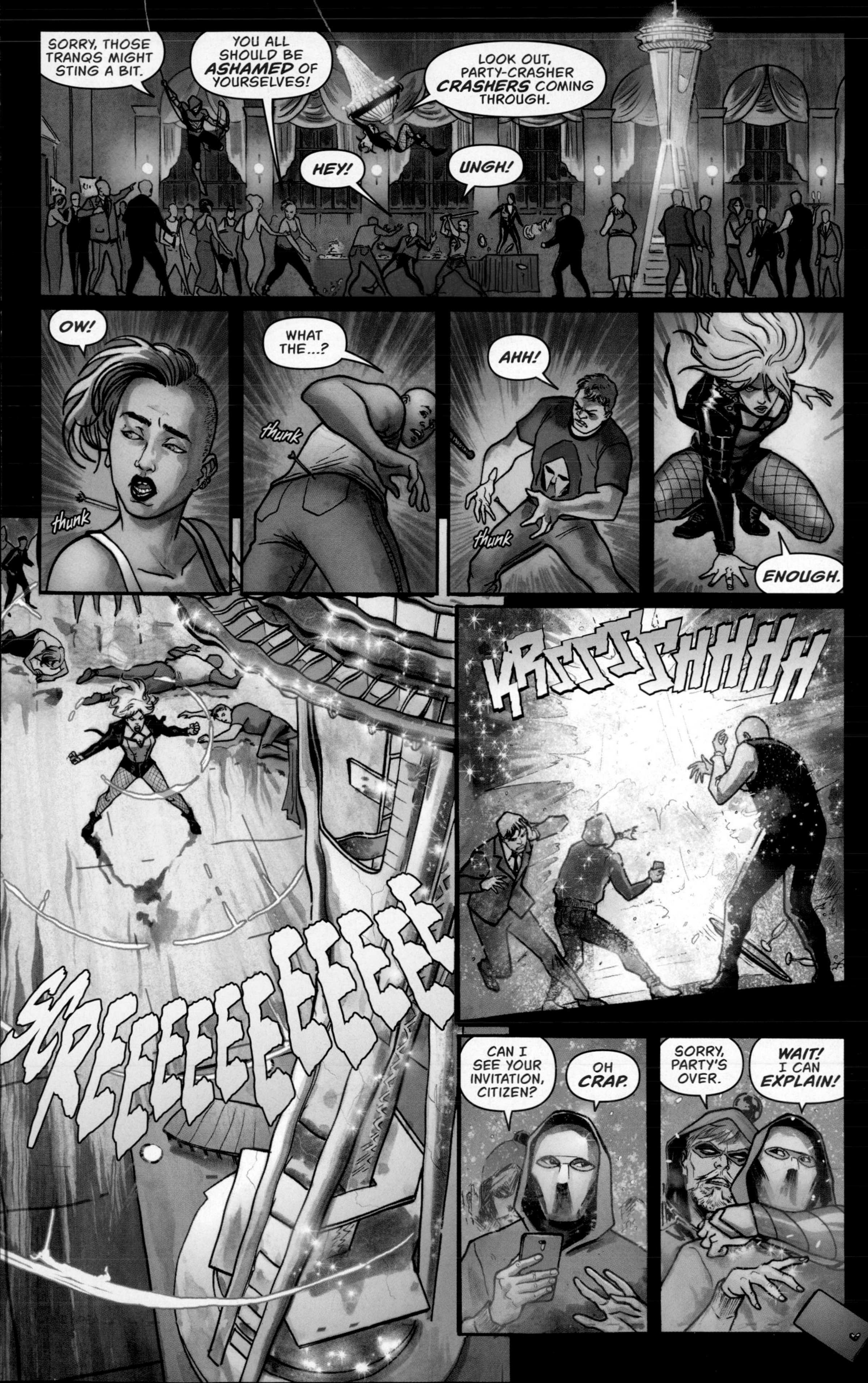
SORRY, THOSE TRANQS MIGHT STING A BIT.
YOU ALL SHOULD BE ASHAMED OF YOURSELVES!
LOOK OUT, PARTY-CRASHER CRASHERS COMING THROUGH.
HEY!
UNGH!
OW!
thunk
WHAT THE...?
thunk
AHH!
thunk
ENOUGH.
SCREEEEEEEEEEE
KRSSSHHHHH
CAN I SEE YOUR INVITATION, CITIZEN?
OH CRAP.
SORRY, PARTY'S OVER.
WAIT! I CAN EXPLAIN!

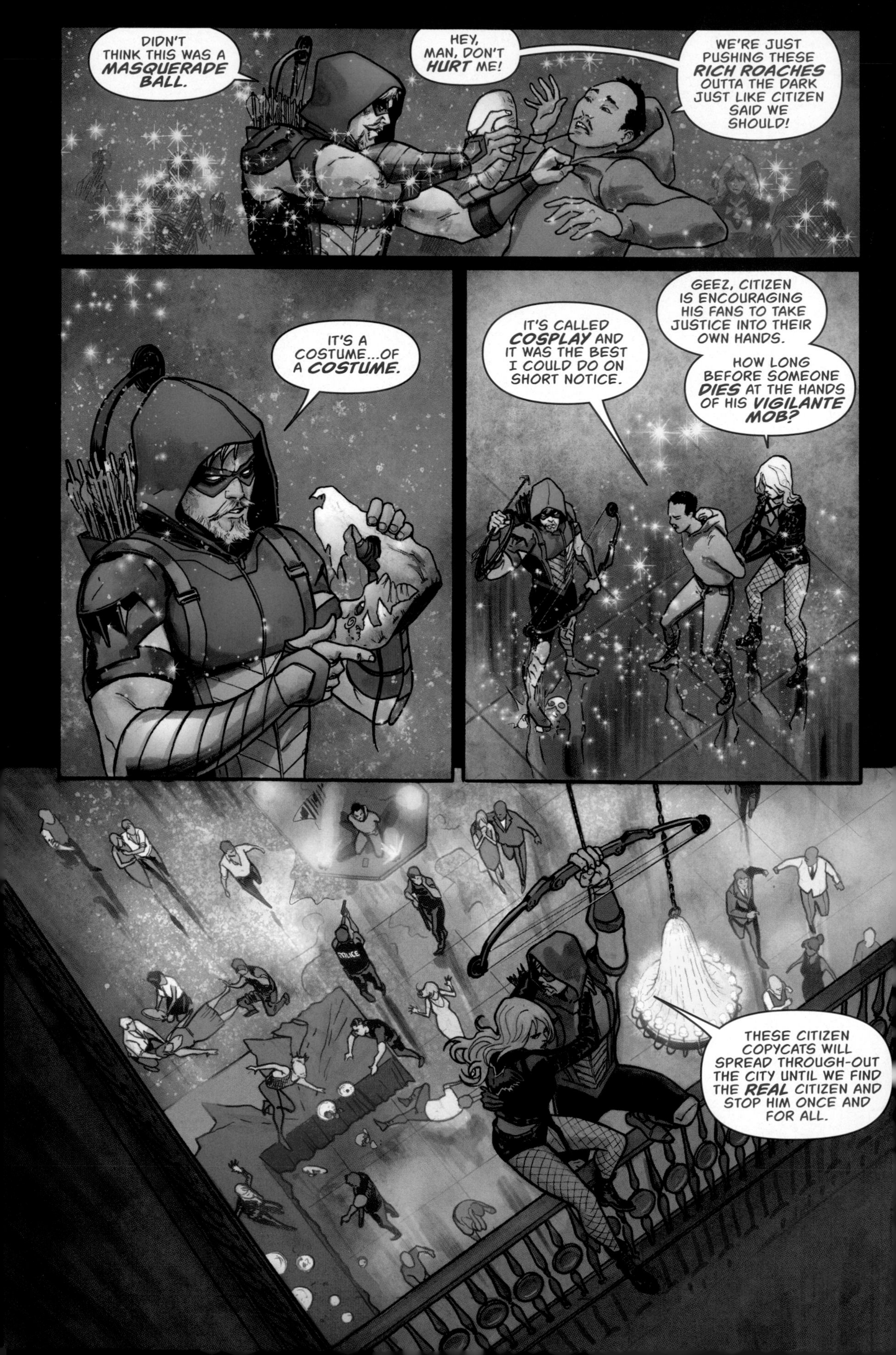
DIDN'T THINK THIS WAS A MASQUERADE BALL.
HEY, MAN, DON'T HURT ME!
WE'RE JUST PUSHING THESE RICH ROACHES OUTTA THE DARK JUST LIKE CITIZEN SAID WE SHOULD!
IT'S A COSTUME...OF A COSTUME.
IT'S CALLED COSPLAY AND IT WAS THE BEST I COULD DO ON SHORT NOTICE.
GEEZ, CITIZEN IS ENCOURAGING HIS FANS TO TAKE JUSTICE INTO THEIR OWN HANDS.
HOW LONG BEFORE SOMEONE DIES AT THE HANDS OF HIS VIGILANTE MOB?
THESE CITIZEN COPYCATS WILL SPREAD THROUGH-OUT THE CITY UNTIL WE FIND THE REAL CITIZEN AND STOP HIM ONCE AND FOR ALL.

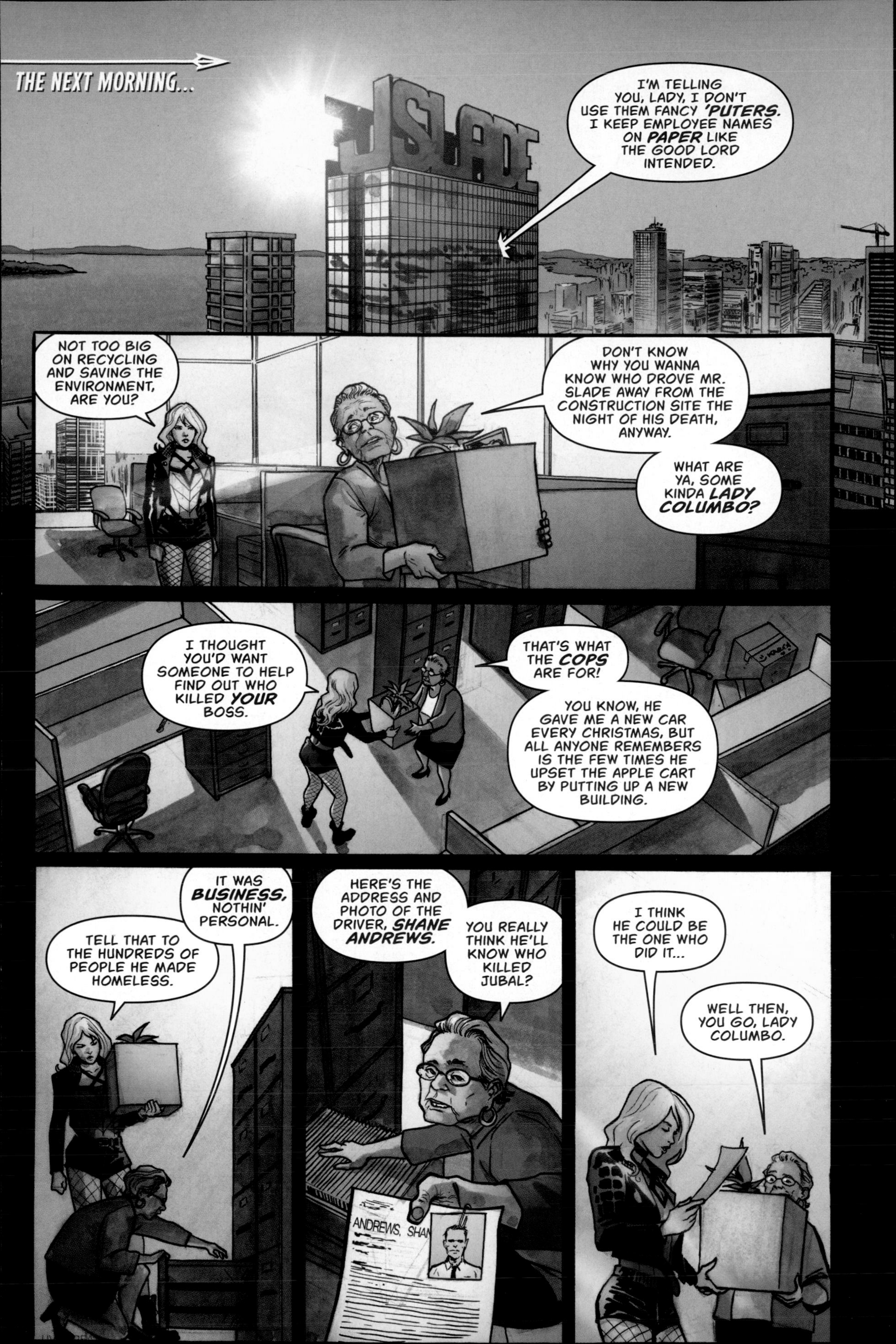

THE NEXT MORNING...
SLADE
I'M TELLING YOU, LADY, I DON'T USE THEM FANCY 'PUTERS. I KEEP EMPLOYEE NAMES ON PAPER LIKE THE GOOD LORD INTENDED.
NOT TOO BIG ON RECYCLING AND SAVING THE ENVIRONMENT, ARE YOU?
DON'T KNOW WHY YOU WANNA KNOW WHO DROVE MR. SLADE AWAY FROM THE CONSTRUCTION SITE THE NIGHT OF HIS DEATH, ANYWAY.
WHAT ARE YA, SOME KINDA LADY COLUMBO?
I THOUGHT YOU'D WANT SOMEONE TO HELP FIND OUT WHO KILLED YOUR BOSS.
THAT'S WHAT THE COPS ARE FOR!
YOU KNOW, HE GAVE ME A NEW CAR EVERY CHRISTMAS, BUT ALL ANYONE REMEMBERS IS THE FEW TIMES HE UPSET THE APPLE CART BY PUTTING UP A NEW BUILDING.
TELL THAT TO THE HUNDREDS OF PEOPLE HE MADE HOMELESS.
IT WAS BUSINESS, NOTHIN' PERSONAL.
HERE'S THE ADDRESS AND PHOTO OF THE DRIVER, SHANE ANDREWS.
YOU REALLY THINK HE'LL KNOW WHO KILLED JUBAL?
ANDREWS, SHAN
I THINK HE COULD BE THE ONE WHO DID IT...
WELL THEN, YOU GO, LADY COLUMBO.

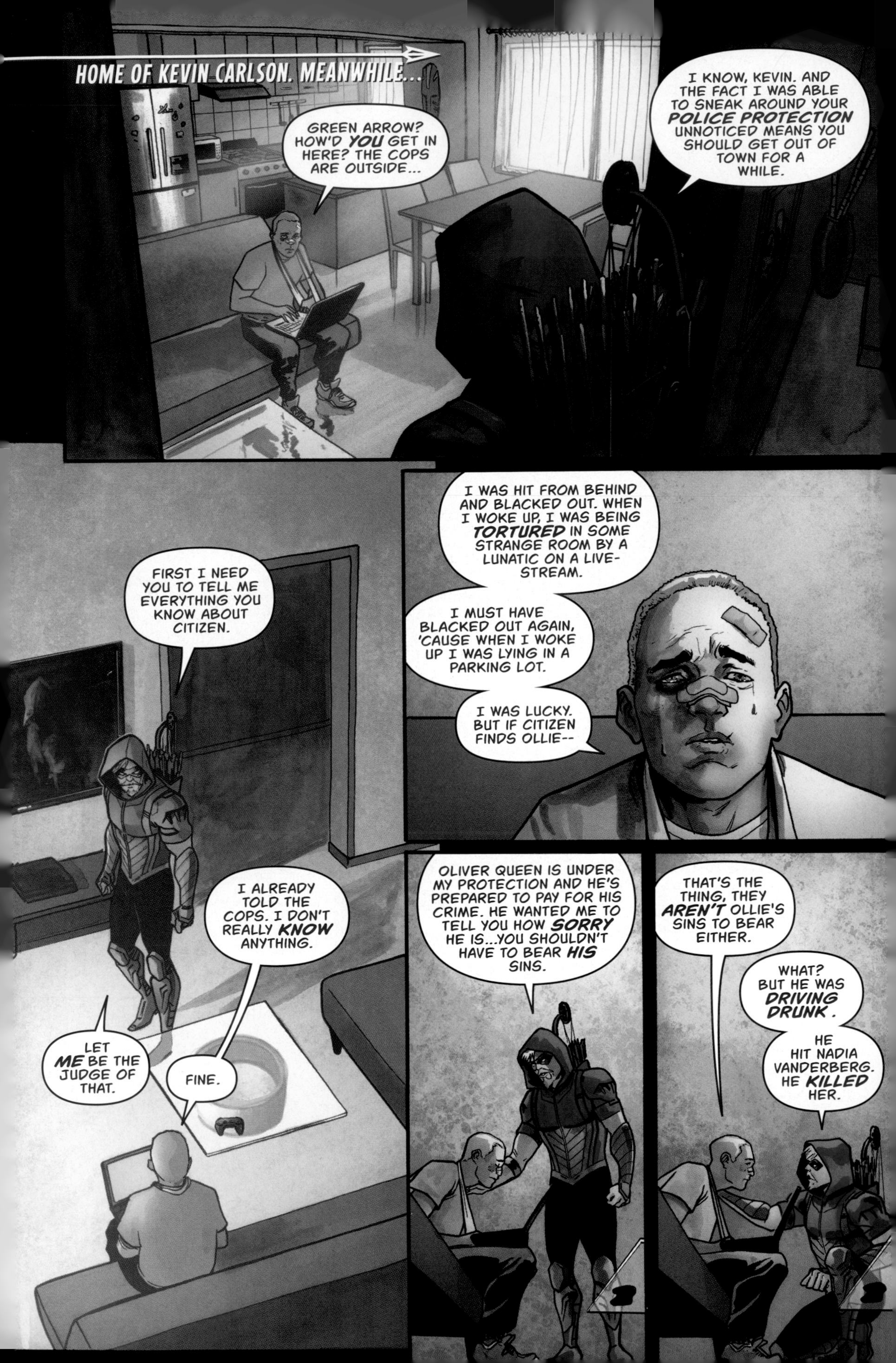
HOME OF KEVIN CARLSON. MEANWHILE...
GREEN ARROW? HOW'D YOU GET IN HERE? THE COPS ARE OUTSIDE...
I KNOW, KEVIN. AND THE FACT I WAS ABLE TO SNEAK AROUND YOUR POLICE PROTECTION UNNOTICED MEANS YOU SHOULD GET OUT OF TOWN FOR A WHILE.
FIRST I NEED YOU TO TELL ME EVERYTHING YOU KNOW ABOUT CITIZEN.
I ALREADY TOLD THE COPS. I DON'T REALLY KNOW ANYTHING.
LET ME BE THE JUDGE OF THAT.
FINE.
I WAS HIT FROM BEHIND AND BLACKED OUT. WHEN I WOKE UP, I WAS BEING TORTURED IN SOME STRANGE ROOM BY A LUNATIC ON A LIVE-STREAM.
I MUST HAVE BLACKED OUT AGAIN, 'CAUSE WHEN I WOKE UP I WAS LYING IN A PARKING LOT.
I WAS LUCKY. BUT IF CITIZEN FINDS OLLIE--
OLIVER QUEEN IS UNDER MY PROTECTION AND HE'S PREPARED TO PAY FOR HIS CRIME. HE WANTED ME TO TELL YOU HOW SORRY HE IS...YOU SHOULDN'T HAVE TO BEAR HIS SINS.
THAT'S THE THING, THEY AREN'T OLLIE'S SINS TO BEAR EITHER.
WHAT? BUT HE WAS DRIVING DRUNK.
HE HIT NADIA VANDERBERG. HE KILLED HER.

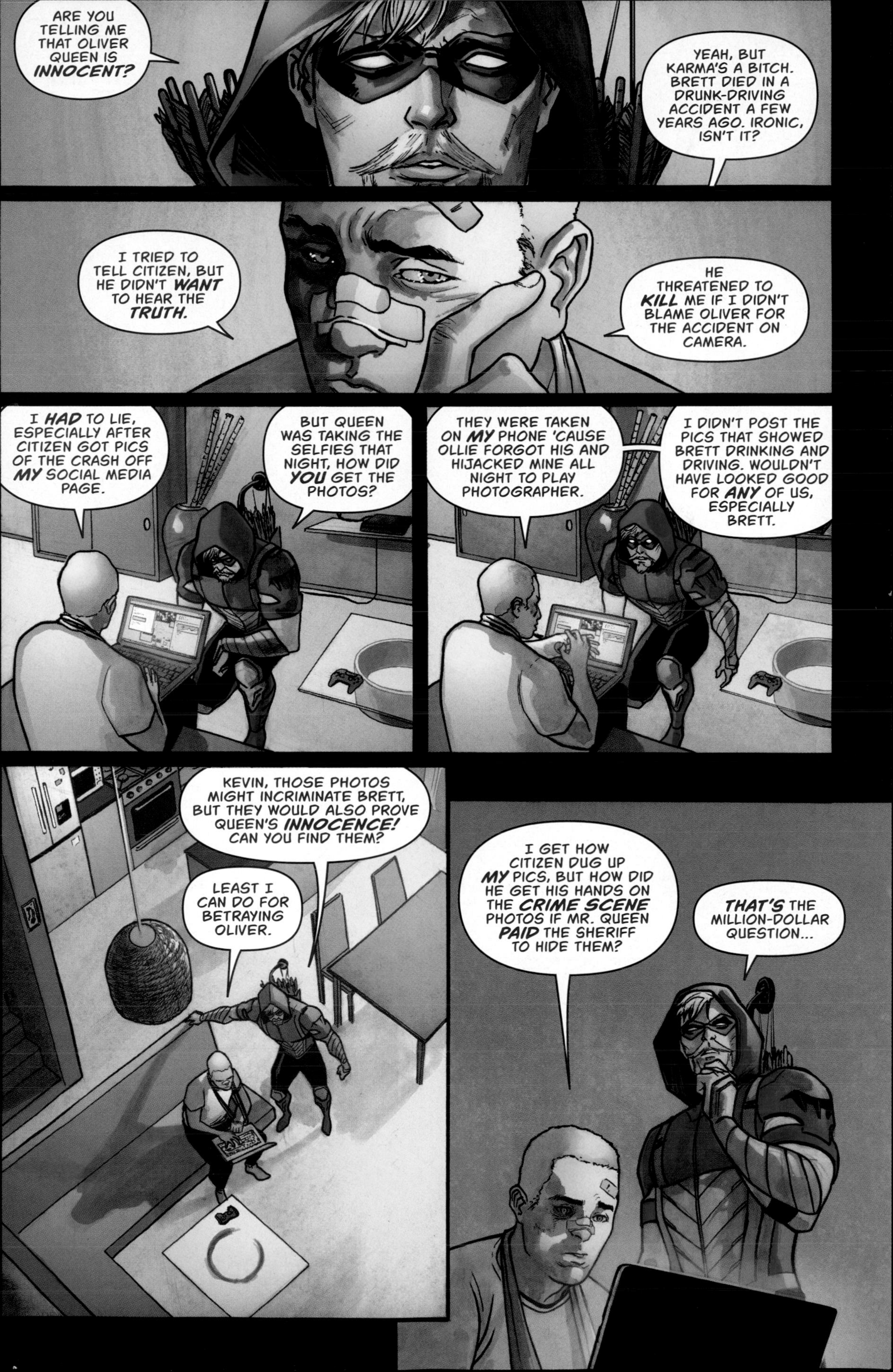

ARE YOU TELLING ME THAT OLIVER QUEEN IS INNOCENT?
YEAH, BUT KARMA'S A BITCH. BRETT DIED IN A DRUNK-DRIVING ACCIDENT A FEW YEARS AGO. IRONIC, ISN'T IT?
I TRIED TO TELL CITIZEN, BUT HE DIDN'T WANT TO HEAR THE TRUTH.
HE THREATENED TO KILL ME IF I DIDN'T BLAME OLIVER FOR THE ACCIDENT ON CAMERA.
I HAD TO LIE, ESPECIALLY AFTER CITIZEN GOT PICS OF THE CRASH OFF MY SOCIAL MEDIA PAGE.
BUT QUEEN WAS TAKING THE SELFIES THAT NIGHT, HOW DID YOU GET THE PHOTOS?
THEY WERE TAKEN ON MY PHONE 'CAUSE OLLIE FORGOT HIS AND HIJACKED MINE ALL NIGHT TO PLAY PHOTOGRAPHER.
I DIDN'T POST THE PICS THAT SHOWED BRETT DRINKING AND DRIVING. WOULDN'T HAVE LOOKED GOOD FOR ANY OF US, ESPECIALLY BRETT.
KEVIN, THOSE PHOTOS MIGHT INCRIMINATE BRETT, BUT THEY WOULD ALSO PROVE QUEEN'S INNOCENCE! CAN YOU FIND THEM?
LEAST I CAN DO FOR BETRAYING OLIVER.
I GET HOW CITIZEN DUG UP MY PICS, BUT HOW DID HE GET HIS HANDS ON THE CRIME SCENE PHOTOS IF MR. QUEEN PAID THE SHERIFF TO HIDE THEM?
THAT'S THE MILLION-DOLLAR QUESTION...

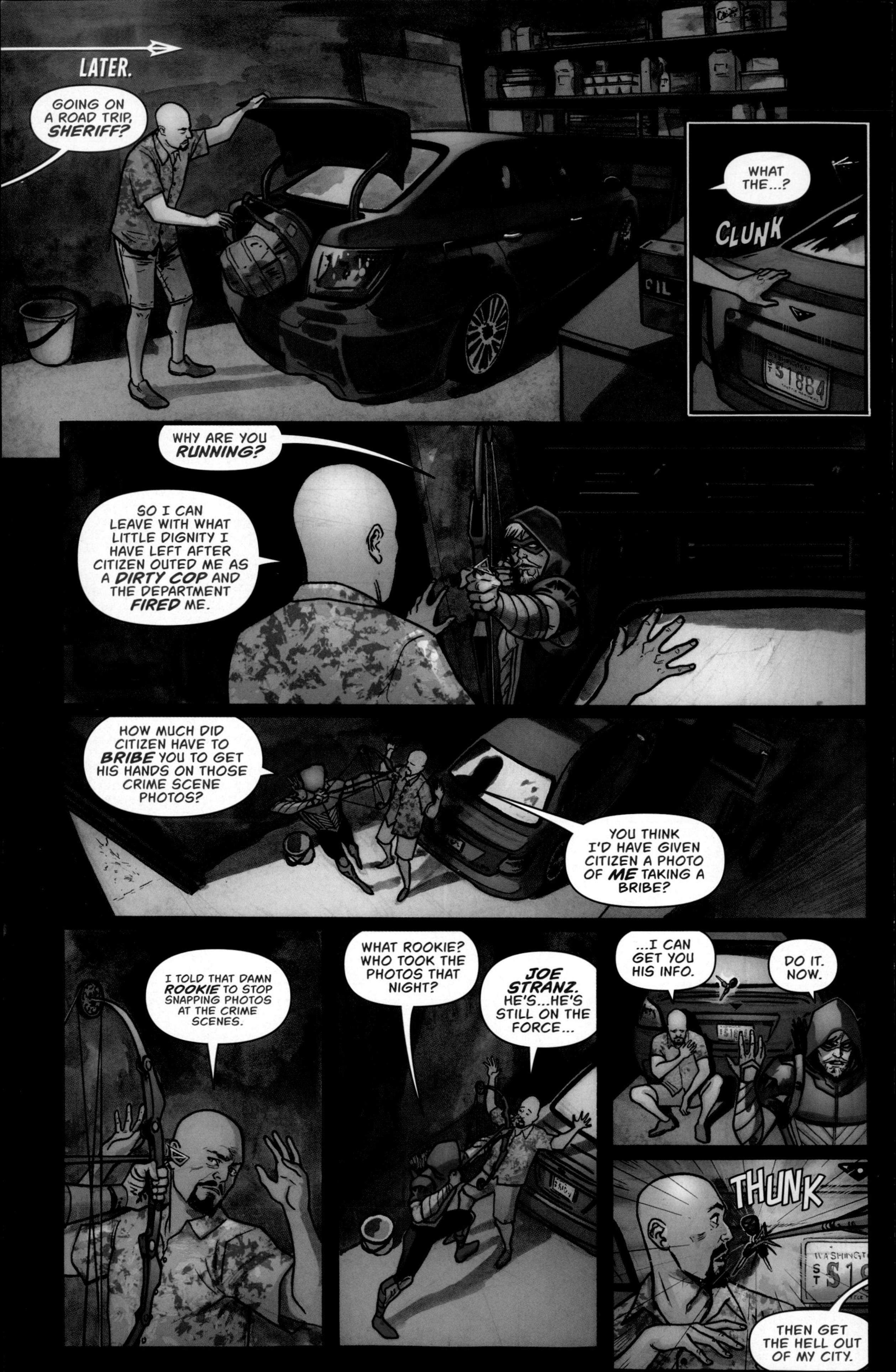
LATER.
GOING ON A ROAD TRIP, SHERIFF?
WHAT THE...?
CLUNK
WHY ARE YOU RUNNING?
SO I CAN LEAVE WITH WHAT LITTLE DIGNITY I HAVE LEFT AFTER CITIZEN OUTED ME AS A DIRTY COP AND THE DEPARTMENT FIRED ME.
HOW MUCH DID CITIZEN HAVE TO BRIBE YOU TO GET HIS HANDS ON THOSE CRIME SCENE PHOTOS?
YOU THINK I'D HAVE GIVEN CITIZEN A PHOTO OF ME TAKING A BRIBE?
I TOLD THAT DAMN ROOKIE TO STOP SNAPPING PHOTOS AT THE CRIME SCENES.
WHAT ROOKIE? WHO TOOK THE PHOTOS THAT NIGHT?
JOE STRANZ. HE'S...HE'S STILL ON THE FORCE...
...I CAN GET YOU HIS INFO.
DO IT. NOW.
THUNK
THEN GET THE HELL OUT OF MY CITY.

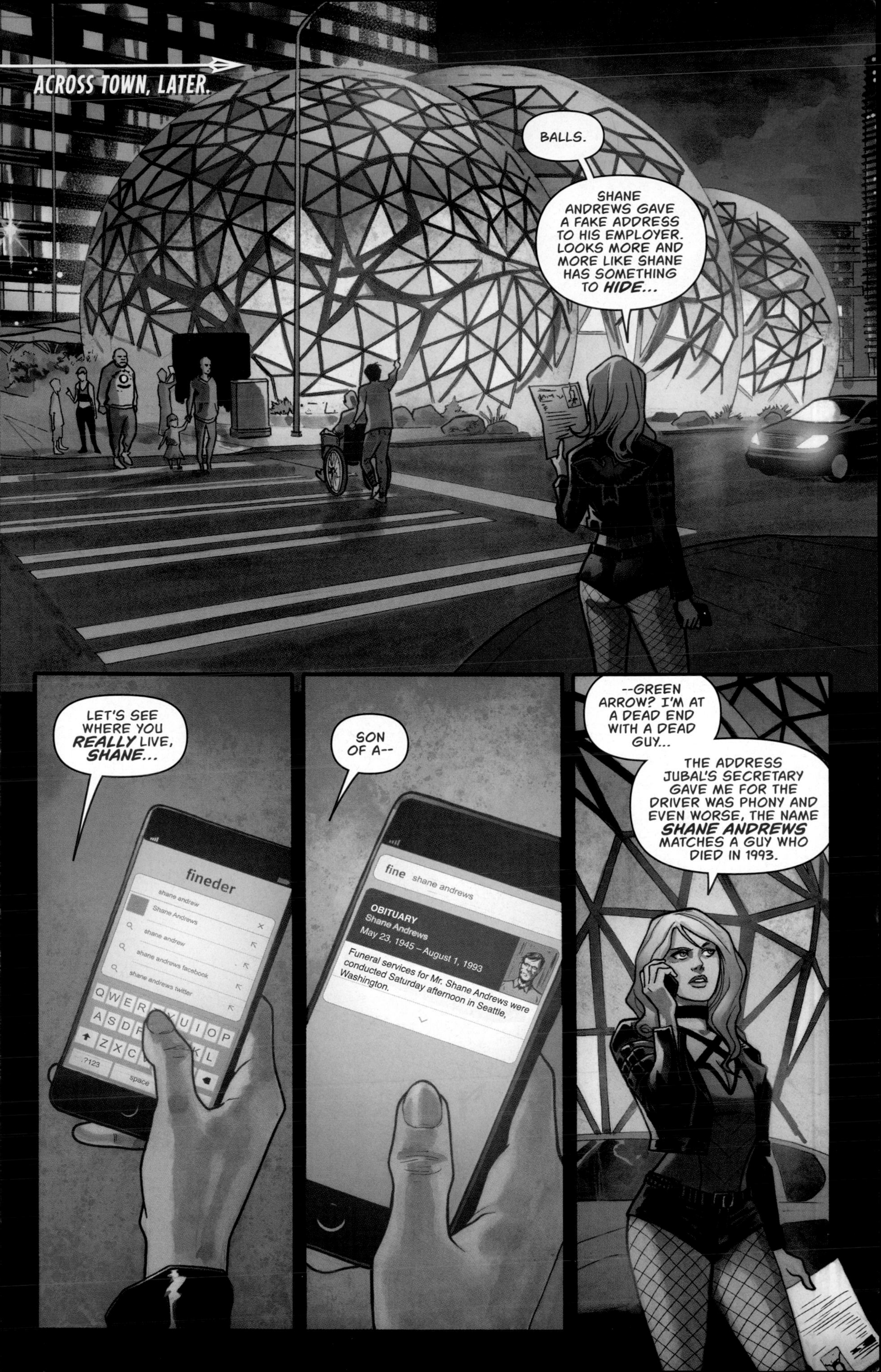
ACROSS TOWN, LATER.
BALLS.
SHANE ANDREWS GAVE A FAKE ADDRESS TO HIS EMPLOYER. LOOKS MORE AND MORE LIKE SHANE HAS SOMETHING TO *HIDE...*
LET'S SEE WHERE YOU *REALLY* LIVE, *SHANE...*
fineder
shane andrew
Shane Andrews
shane andrew
shane andrews facebook
shane andrews twitter
SON OF A--
fine
shane andrews
OBITUARY
Shane Andrews
May 23, 1945 – August 1, 1993
Funeral services for Mr. Shane Andrews were conducted Saturday afternoon in Seattle, Washington.
--GREEN ARROW? I'M AT A DEAD END WITH A DEAD GUY...
THE ADDRESS JUBAL'S SECRETARY GAVE ME FOR THE DRIVER WAS PHONY AND EVEN WORSE, THE NAME *SHANE ANDREWS* MATCHES A GUY WHO DIED IN 1993.

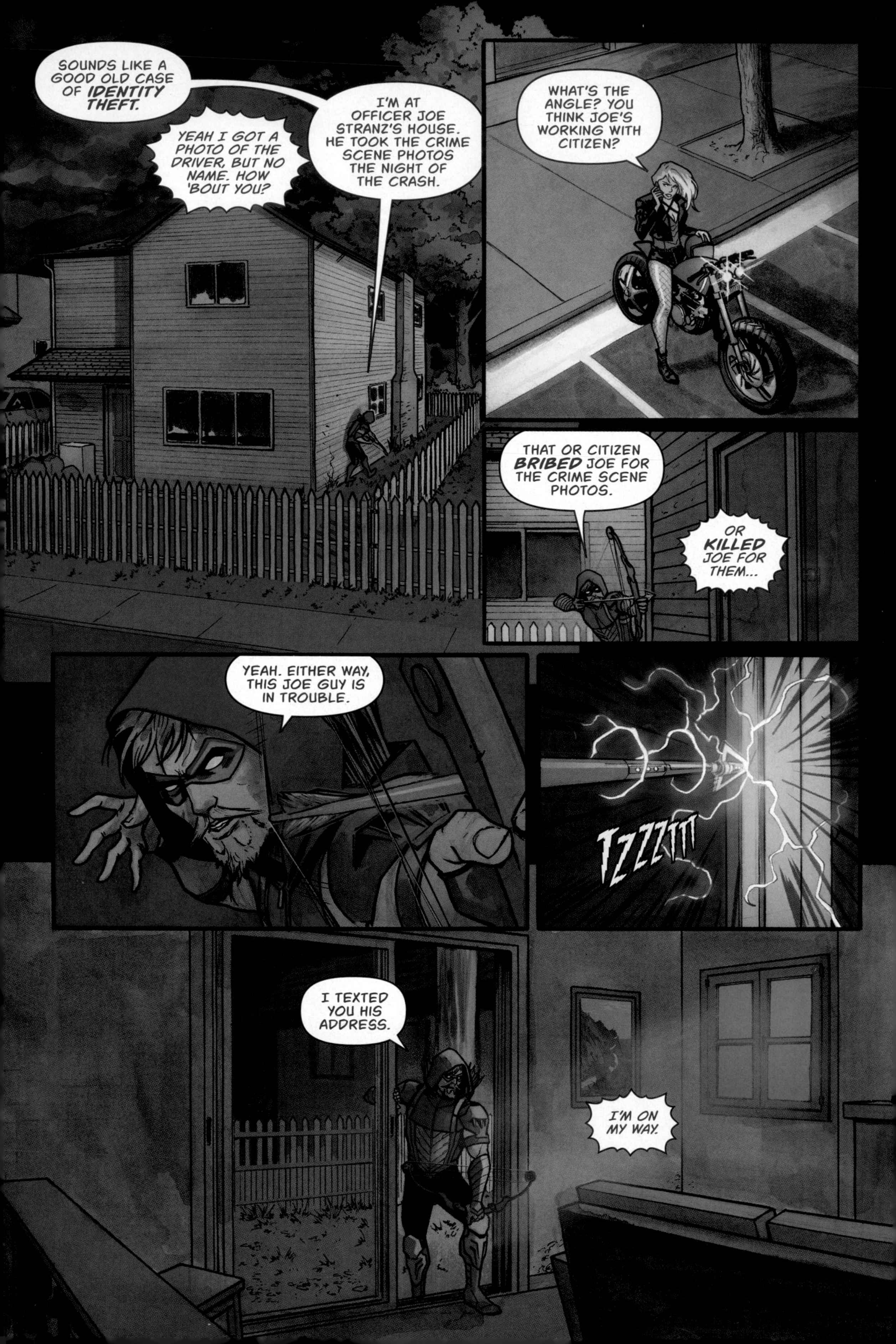
SOUNDS LIKE A GOOD OLD CASE OF IDENTITY THEFT.
YEAH I GOT A PHOTO OF THE DRIVER, BUT NO NAME. HOW 'BOUT YOU?
I'M AT OFFICER JOE STRANZ'S HOUSE. HE TOOK THE CRIME SCENE PHOTOS THE NIGHT OF THE CRASH.
WHAT'S THE ANGLE? YOU THINK JOE'S WORKING WITH CITIZEN?
THAT OR CITIZEN BRIBED JOE FOR THE CRIME SCENE PHOTOS.
OR KILLED JOE FOR THEM...
YEAH. EITHER WAY, THIS JOE GUY IS IN TROUBLE.
TZZZTT
I TEXTED YOU HIS ADDRESS.
I'M ON MY WAY.

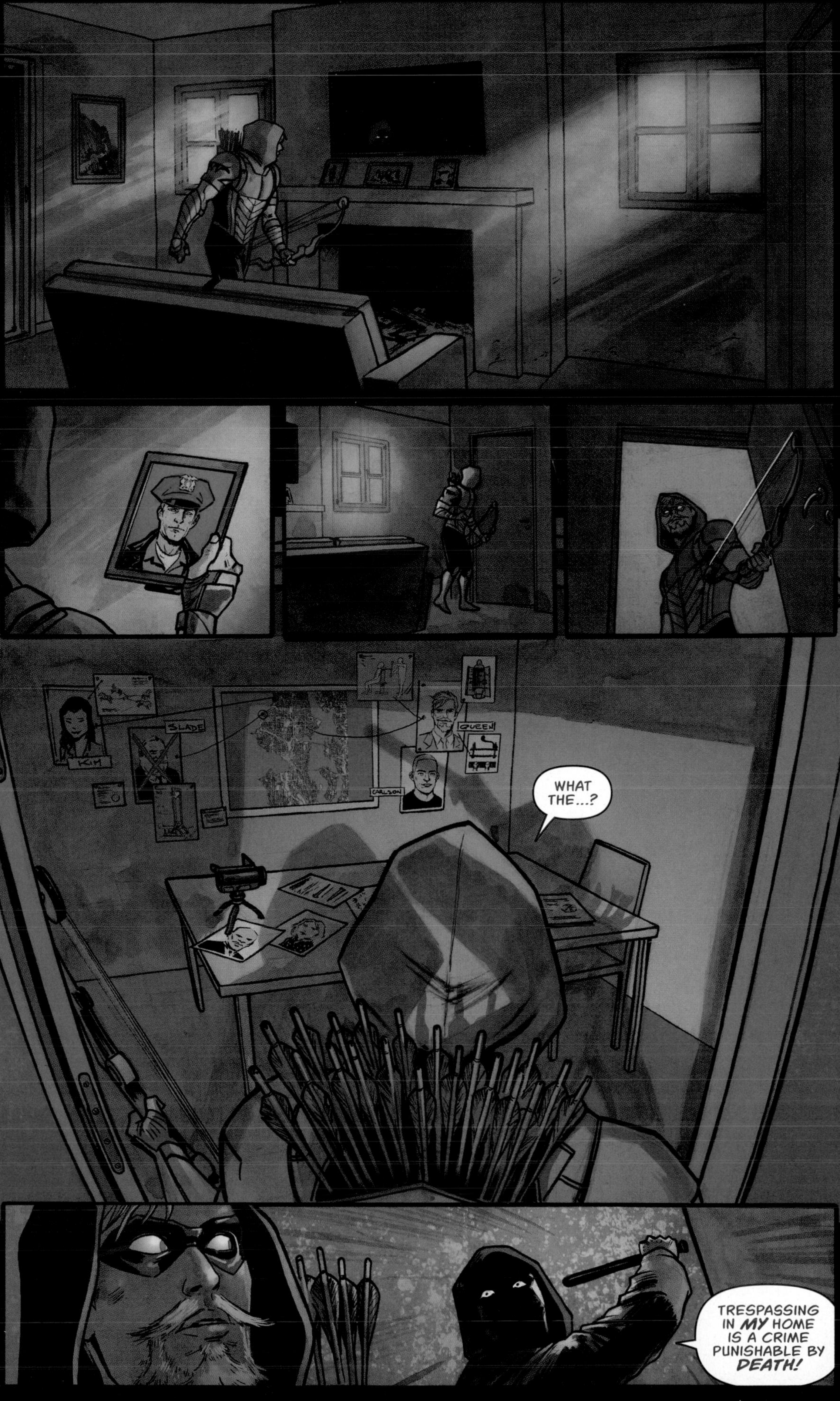
SLADE
KIM
QUEEN
CARLSON
WHAT THE...?
TRESPASSING IN *MY* HOME IS A CRIME PUNISHABLE BY ***DEATH!***

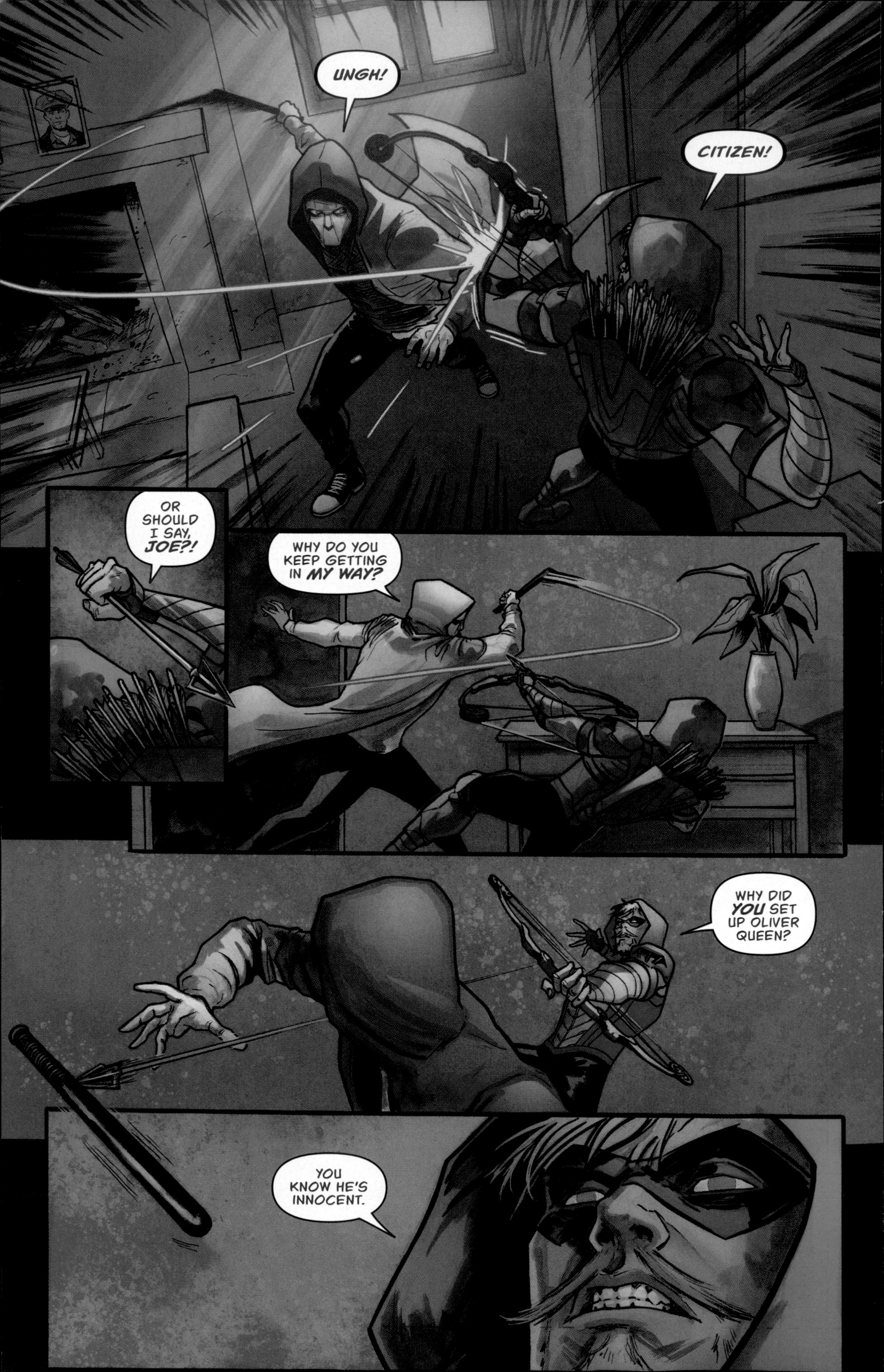
UNGH!
CITIZEN!
OR SHOULD I SAY, JOE?!
WHY DO YOU KEEP GETTING IN MY WAY?
WHY DID YOU SET UP OLIVER QUEEN?
YOU KNOW HE'S INNOCENT.

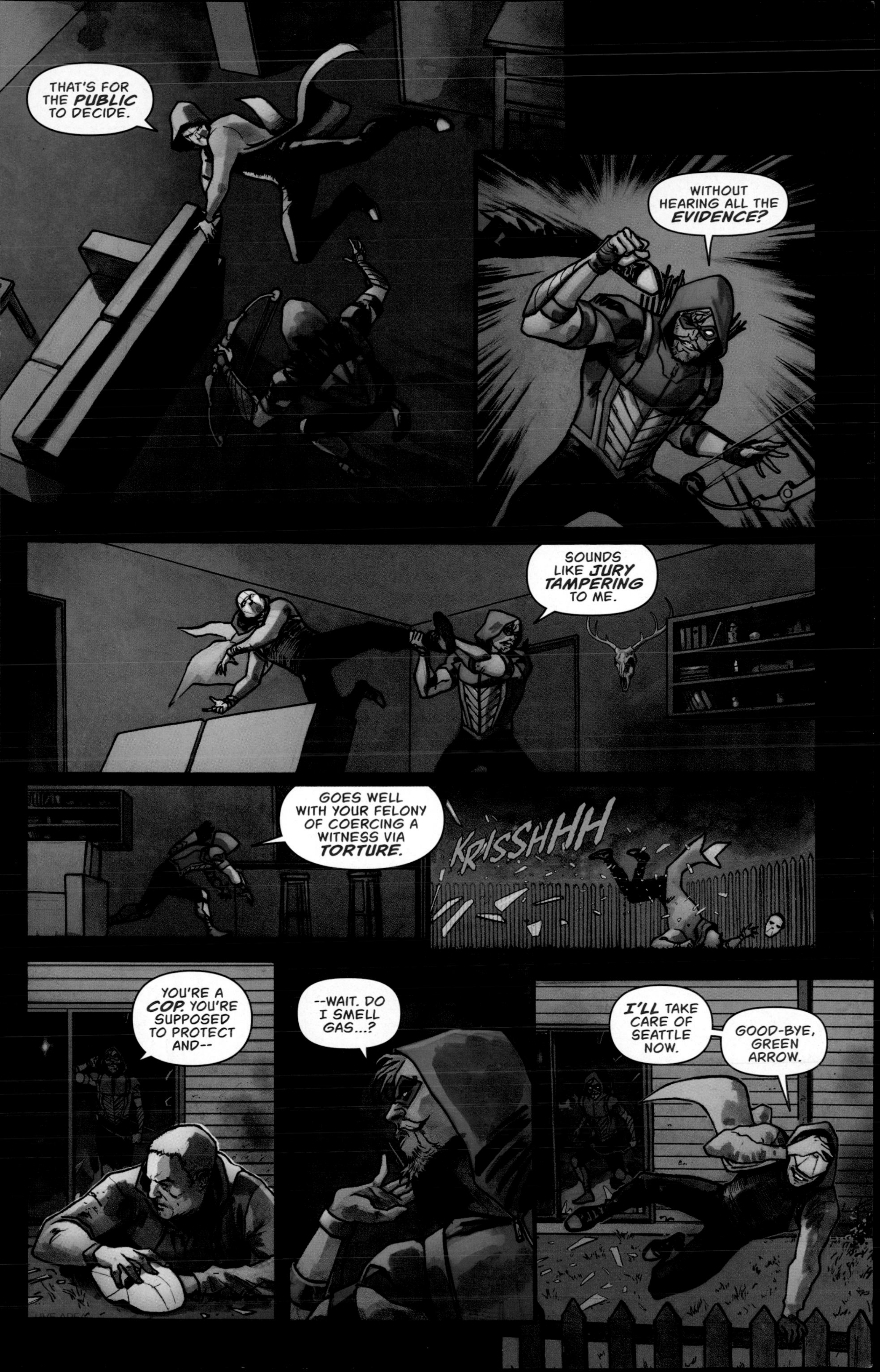
THAT'S FOR THE PUBLIC TO DECIDE.
WITHOUT HEARING ALL THE EVIDENCE?
SOUNDS LIKE JURY TAMPERING TO ME.
GOES WELL WITH YOUR FELONY OF COERCING A WITNESS VIA TORTURE.
KRISSHHH
YOU'RE A COP. YOU'RE SUPPOSED TO PROTECT AND--
--WAIT. DO I SMELL GAS...?
I'LL TAKE CARE OF SEATTLE NOW.
GOOD-BYE, GREEN ARROW.

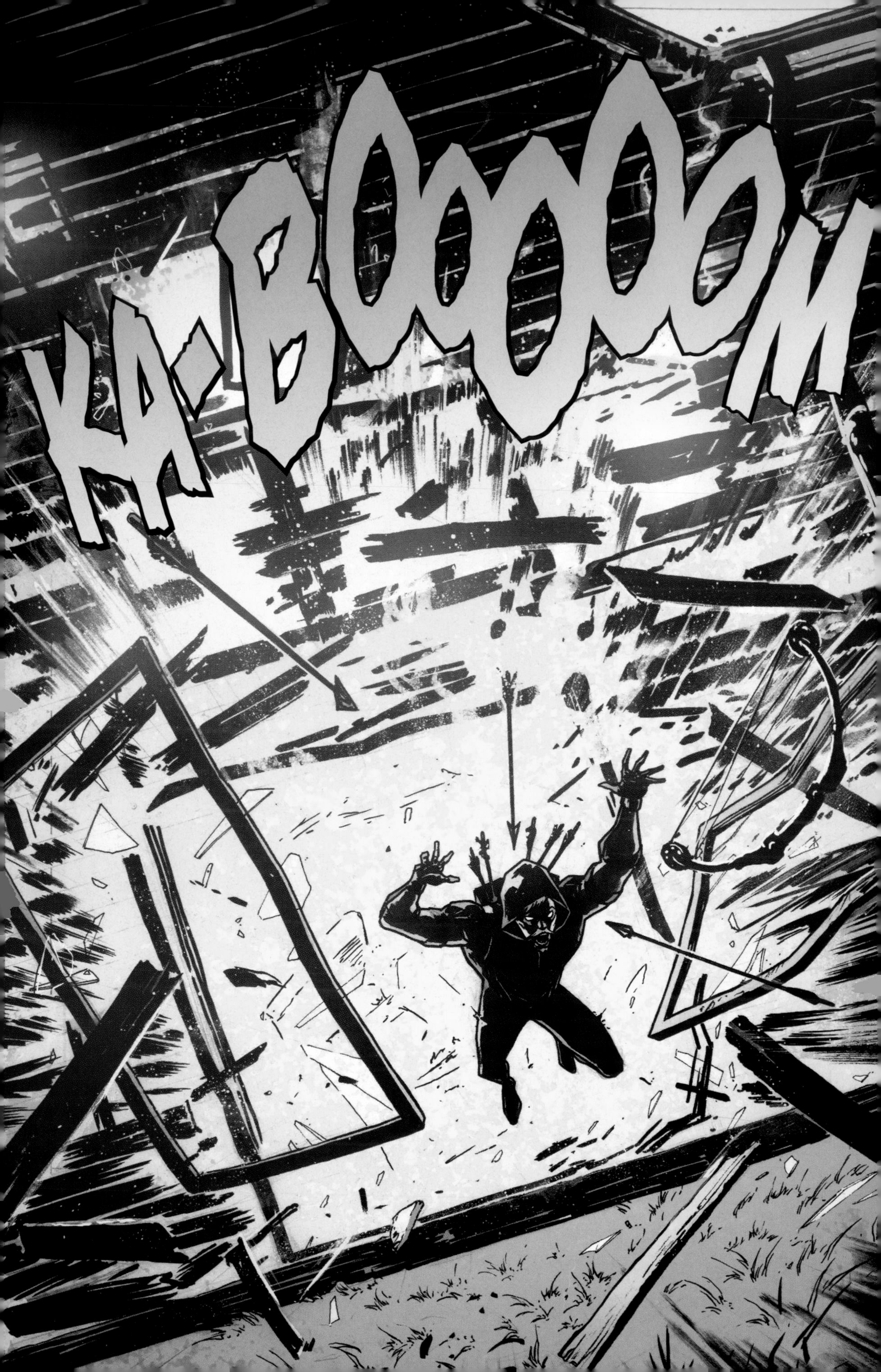
KA-BOOOOOM

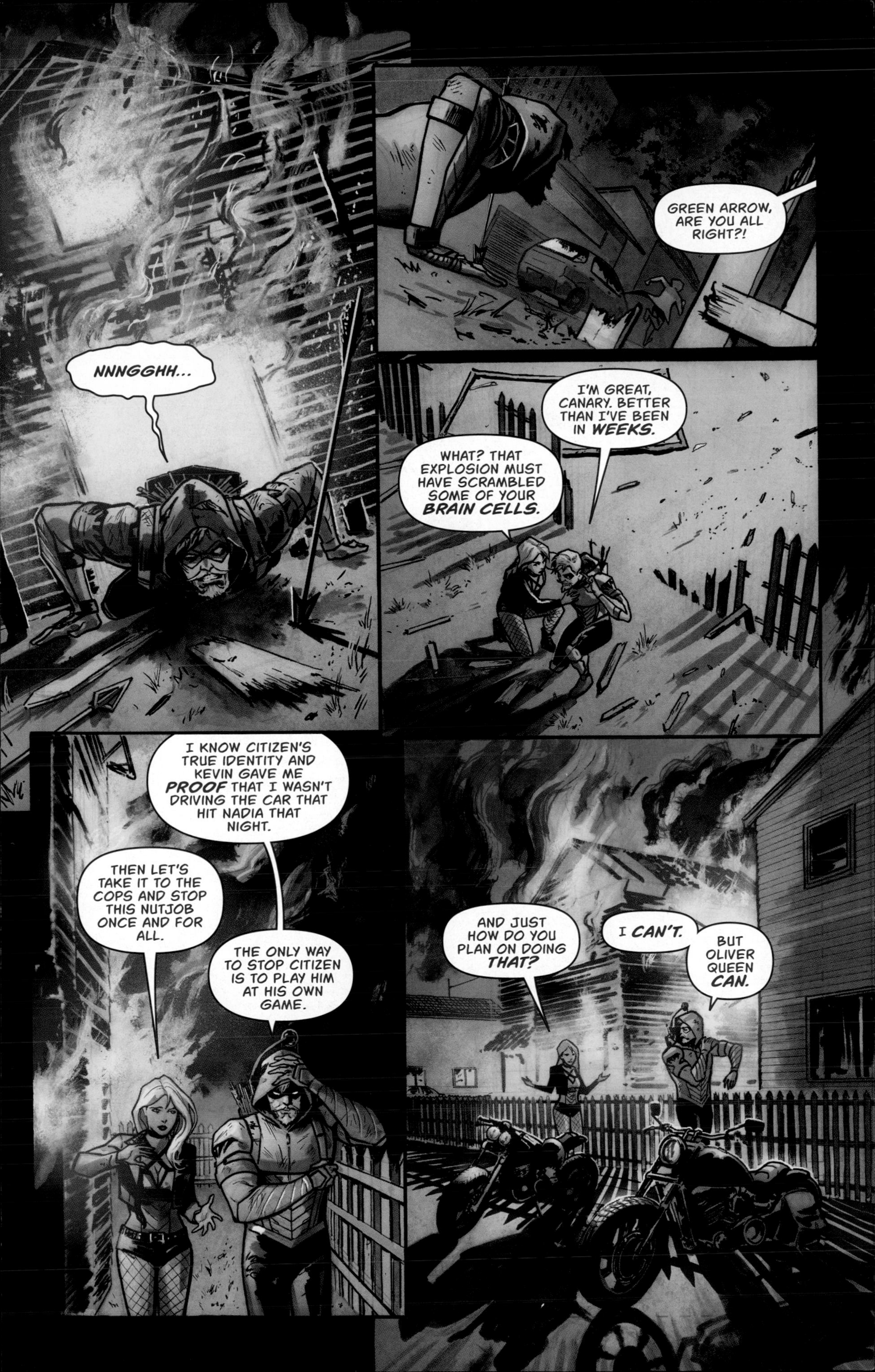
NNNGGHH...
GREEN ARROW, ARE YOU ALL RIGHT?!
WHAT? THAT EXPLOSION MUST HAVE SCRAMBLED SOME OF YOUR BRAIN CELLS.
I'M GREAT, CANARY. BETTER THAN I'VE BEEN IN WEEKS.
I KNOW CITIZEN'S TRUE IDENTITY AND KEVIN GAVE ME PROOF THAT I WASN'T DRIVING THE CAR THAT HIT NADIA THAT NIGHT.
THEN LET'S TAKE IT TO THE COPS AND STOP THIS NUTJOB ONCE AND FOR ALL.
THE ONLY WAY TO STOP CITIZEN IS TO PLAY HIM AT HIS OWN GAME.
AND JUST HOW DO YOU PLAN ON DOING THAT?
I CAN'T.
BUT OLIVER QUEEN CAN.

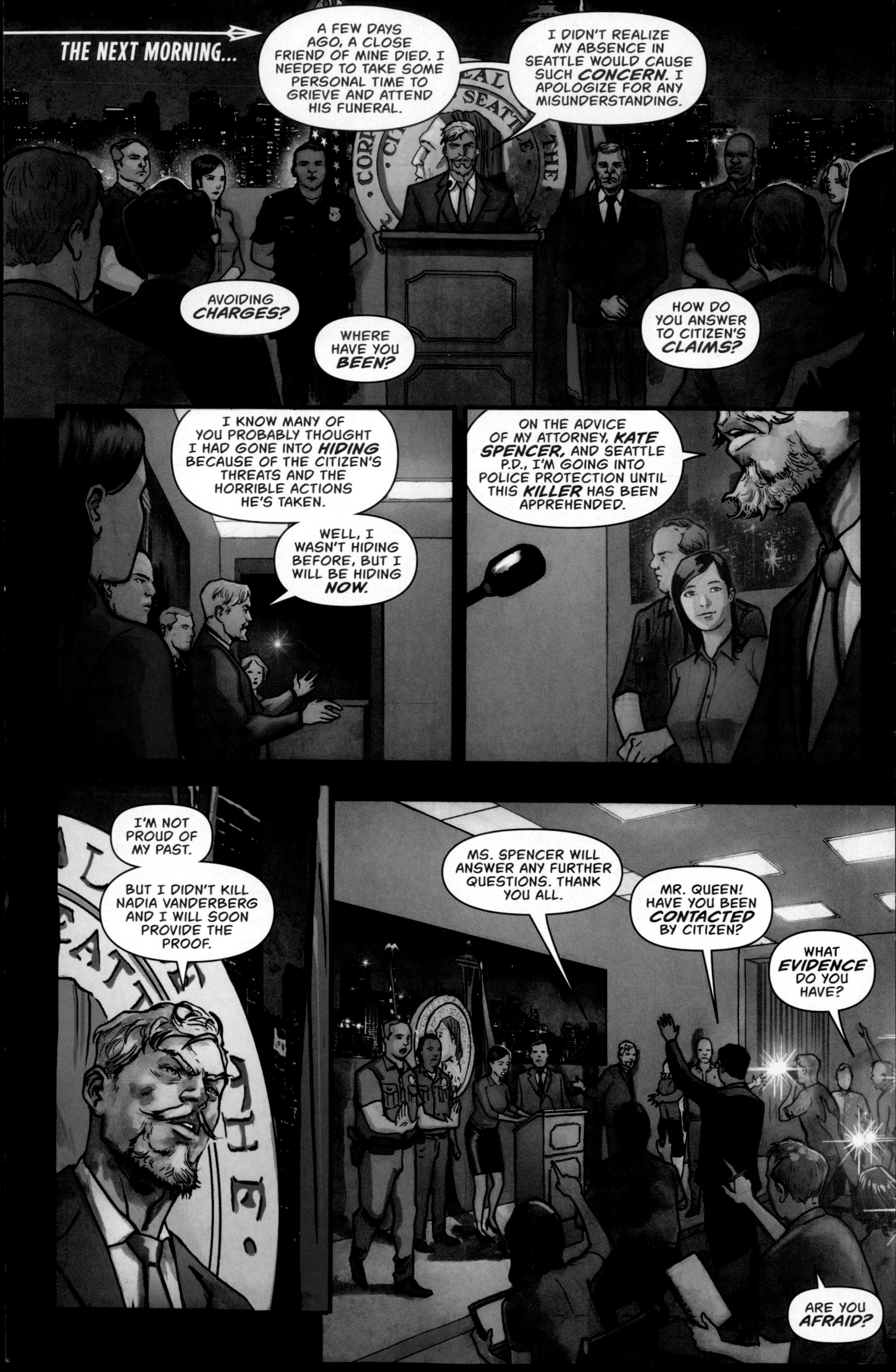
THE NEXT MORNING...
A FEW DAYS AGO, A CLOSE FRIEND OF MINE DIED. I NEEDED TO TAKE SOME PERSONAL TIME TO GRIEVE AND ATTEND HIS FUNERAL.
I DIDN'T REALIZE MY ABSENCE IN SEATTLE WOULD CAUSE SUCH CONCERN. I APOLOGIZE FOR ANY MISUNDERSTANDING.
AVOIDING CHARGES?
WHERE HAVE YOU BEEN?
HOW DO YOU ANSWER TO CITIZEN'S CLAIMS?
I KNOW MANY OF YOU PROBABLY THOUGHT I HAD GONE INTO HIDING BECAUSE OF THE CITIZEN'S THREATS AND THE HORRIBLE ACTIONS HE'S TAKEN.
WELL, I WASN'T HIDING BEFORE, BUT I WILL BE HIDING NOW.
ON THE ADVICE OF MY ATTORNEY, KATE SPENCER, AND SEATTLE P.D., I'M GOING INTO POLICE PROTECTION UNTIL THIS KILLER HAS BEEN APPREHENDED.
I'M NOT PROUD OF MY PAST.
BUT I DIDN'T KILL NADIA VANDERBERG AND I WILL SOON PROVIDE THE PROOF.
MS. SPENCER WILL ANSWER ANY FURTHER QUESTIONS. THANK YOU ALL.
MR. QUEEN! HAVE YOU BEEN CONTACTED BY CITIZEN?
WHAT EVIDENCE DO YOU HAVE?
ARE YOU AFRAID?

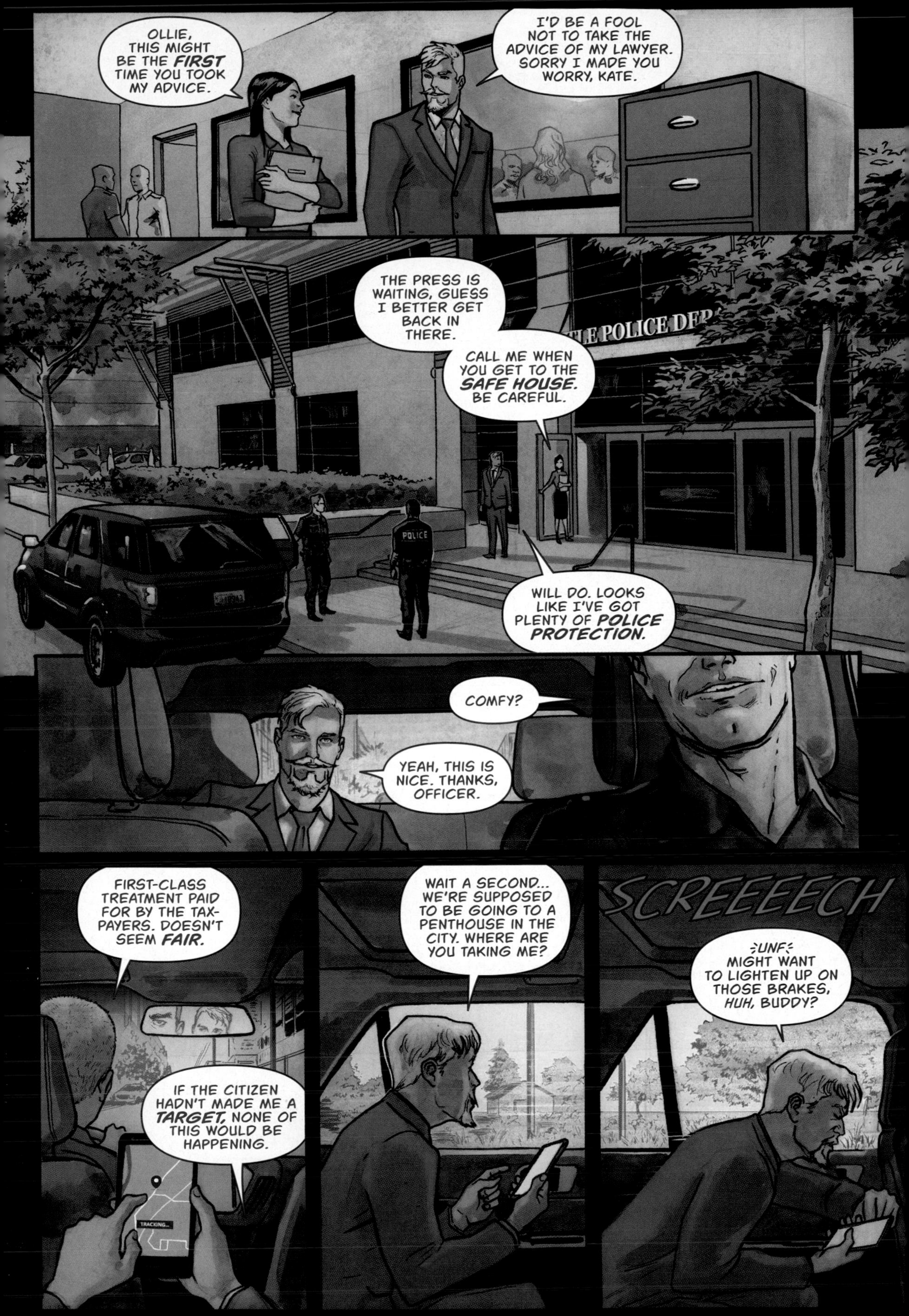
OLLIE, THIS MIGHT BE THE FIRST TIME YOU TOOK MY ADVICE.
I'D BE A FOOL NOT TO TAKE THE ADVICE OF MY LAWYER. SORRY I MADE YOU WORRY, KATE.
THE PRESS IS WAITING, GUESS I BETTER GET BACK IN THERE.
CALL ME WHEN YOU GET TO THE SAFE HOUSE. BE CAREFUL.
WILL DO. LOOKS LIKE I'VE GOT PLENTY OF POLICE PROTECTION.
POLICE
COMFY?
YEAH, THIS IS NICE. THANKS, OFFICER.
FIRST-CLASS TREATMENT PAID FOR BY THE TAX-PAYERS. DOESN'T SEEM FAIR.
IF THE CITIZEN HADN'T MADE ME A TARGET, NONE OF THIS WOULD BE HAPPENING.
TRACKING...
WAIT A SECOND... WE'RE SUPPOSED TO BE GOING TO A PENTHOUSE IN THE CITY. WHERE ARE YOU TAKING ME?
SCREEEECH
UNF
MIGHT WANT TO LIGHTEN UP ON THOSE BRAKES, HUH, BUDDY?

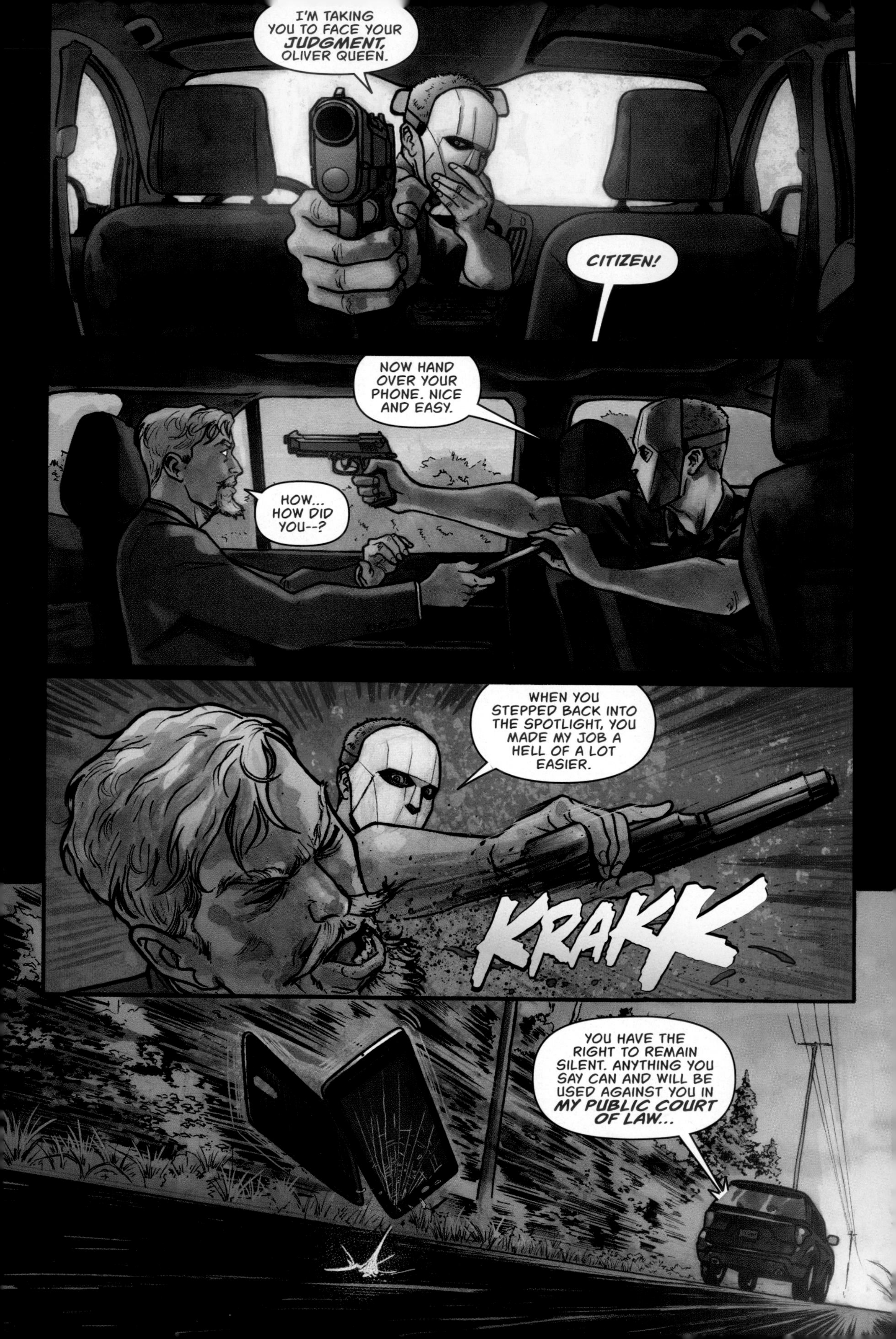
I'M TAKING YOU TO FACE YOUR JUDGMENT, OLIVER QUEEN.
CITIZEN!
NOW HAND OVER YOUR PHONE. NICE AND EASY.
HOW... HOW DID YOU--?
WHEN YOU STEPPED BACK INTO THE SPOTLIGHT, YOU MADE MY JOB A HELL OF A LOT EASIER.
KRAKK
YOU HAVE THE RIGHT TO REMAIN SILENT. ANYTHING YOU SAY CAN AND WILL BE USED AGAINST YOU IN MY PUBLIC COURT OF LAW...

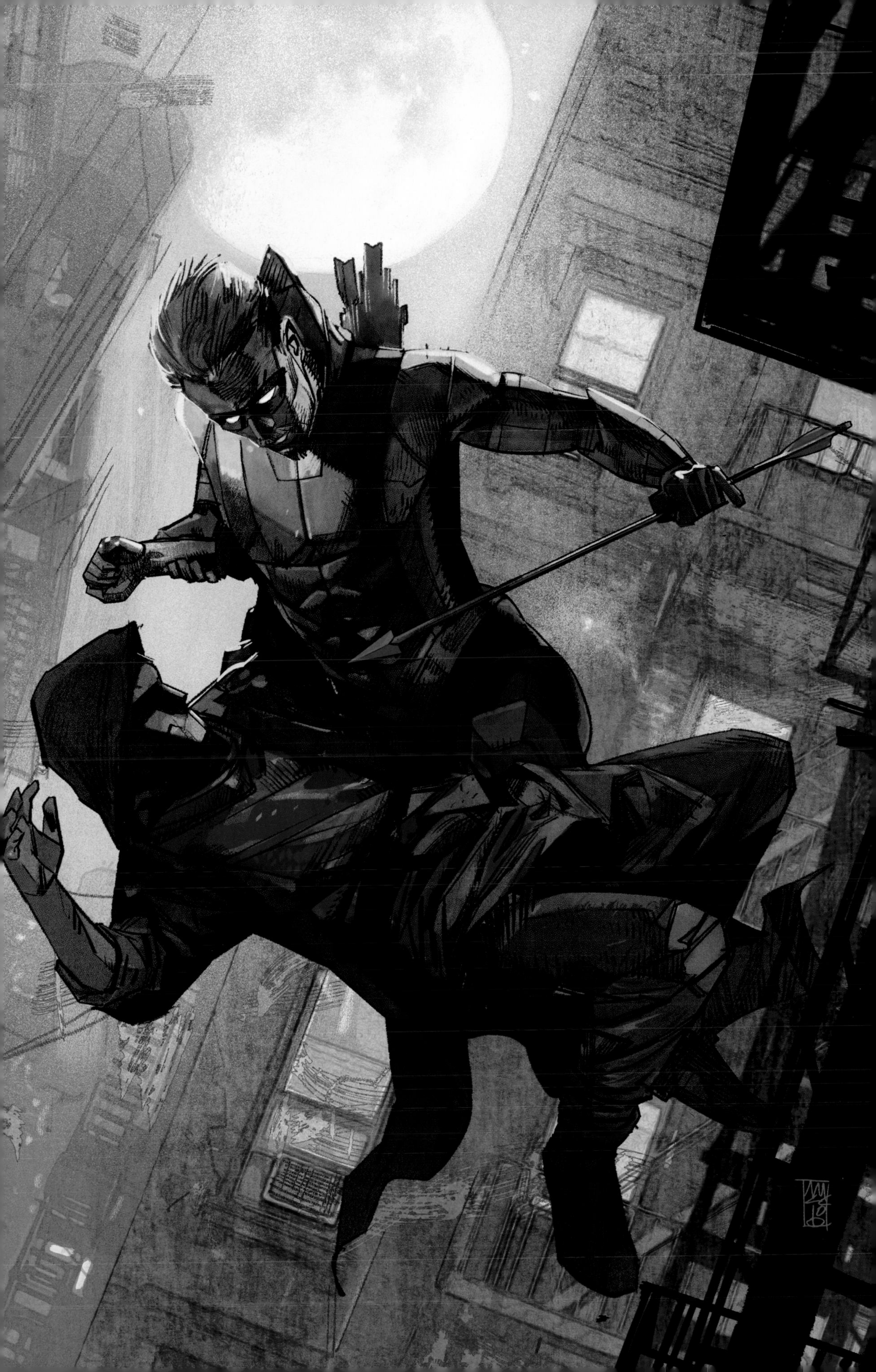

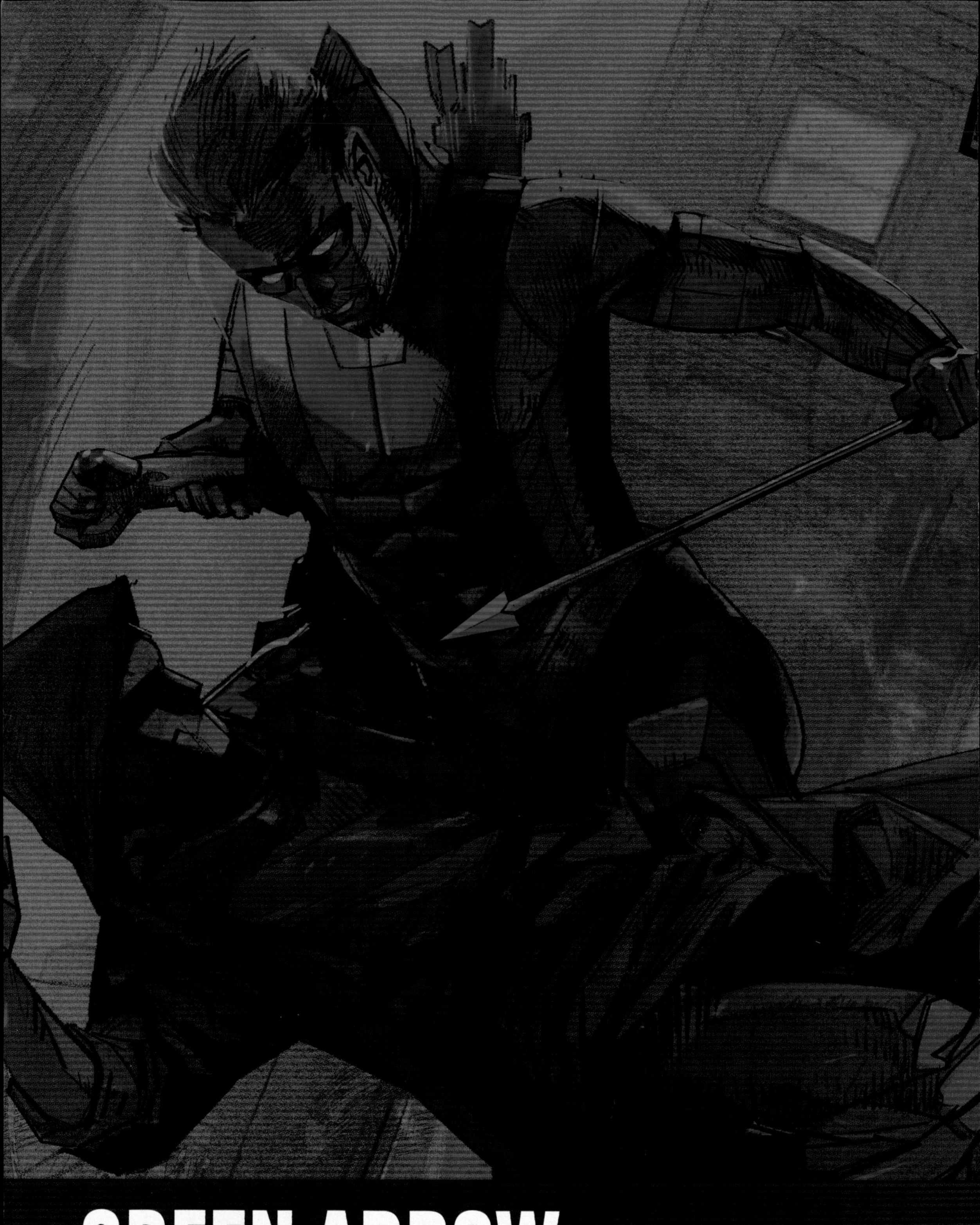

GREEN ARROW
#47

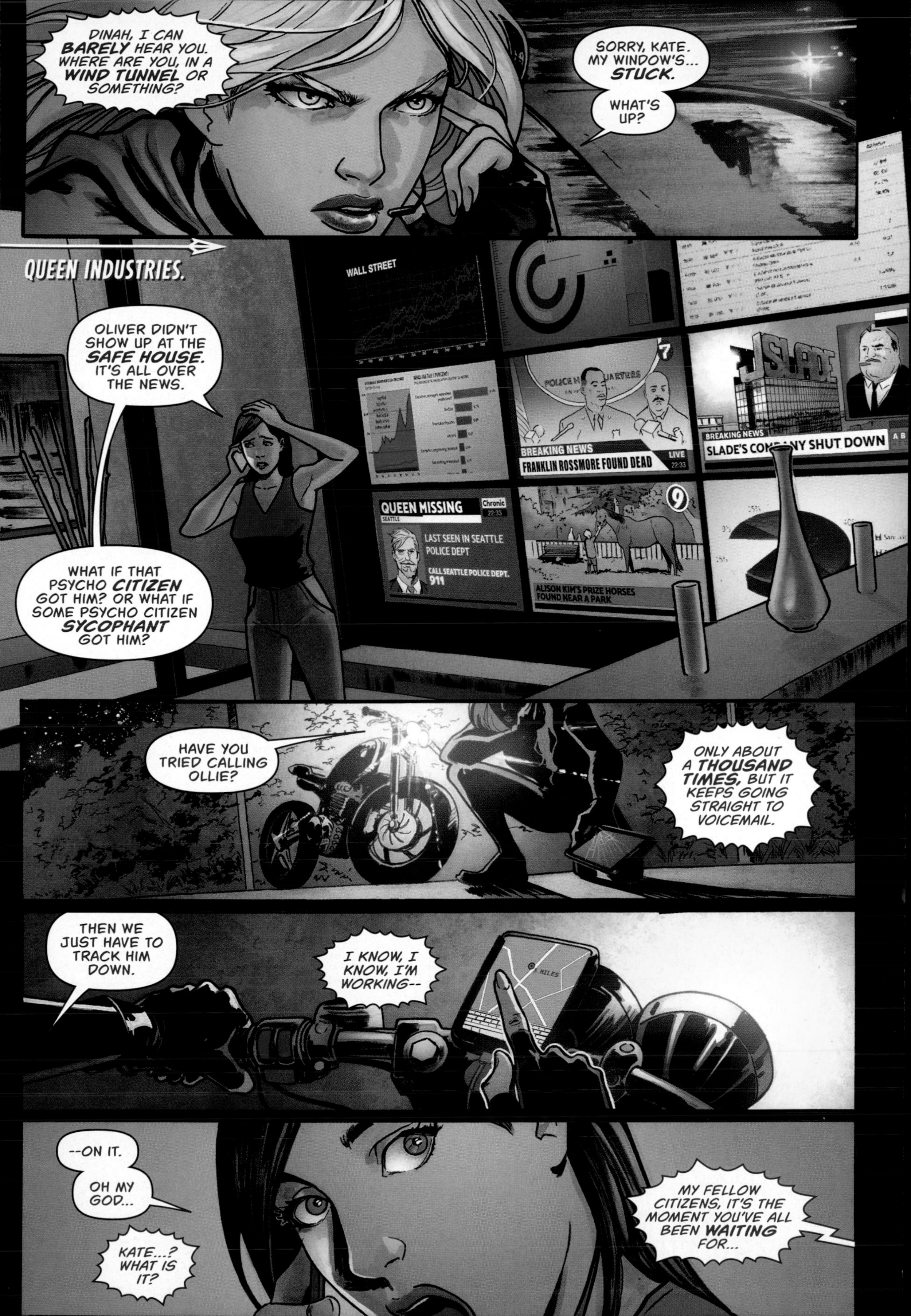

DINAH, I CAN BARELY HEAR YOU. WHERE ARE YOU, IN A WIND TUNNEL OR SOMETHING?
SORRY, KATE. MY WINDOW'S... STUCK.
WHAT'S UP?
QUEEN INDUSTRIES.
WALL STREET
OLIVER DIDN'T SHOW UP AT THE SAFE HOUSE. IT'S ALL OVER THE NEWS.
BREAKING NEWS
FRANKLIN ROSSMORE FOUND DEAD
LIVE
22:33
BREAKING NEWS
SLADE'S COMPANY SHUT DOWN
QUEEN MISSING
Chronic
22:33
SEATTLE
LAST SEEN IN SEATTLE POLICE DEPT
CALL SEATTLE POLICE DEPT. 911
ALISON KIM'S PRIZE HORSES FOUND NEAR A PARK
WHAT IF THAT PSYCHO CITIZEN GOT HIM? OR WHAT IF SOME PSYCHO CITIZEN SYCOPHANT GOT HIM?
HAVE YOU TRIED CALLING OLLIE?
ONLY ABOUT A THOUSAND TIMES, BUT IT KEEPS GOING STRAIGHT TO VOICEMAIL.
THEN WE JUST HAVE TO TRACK HIM DOWN.
I KNOW, I KNOW, I'M WORKING--
--ON IT.
OH MY GOD...
KATE...? WHAT IS IT?
MY FELLOW CITIZENS, IT'S THE MOMENT YOU'VE ALL BEEN WAITING FOR...

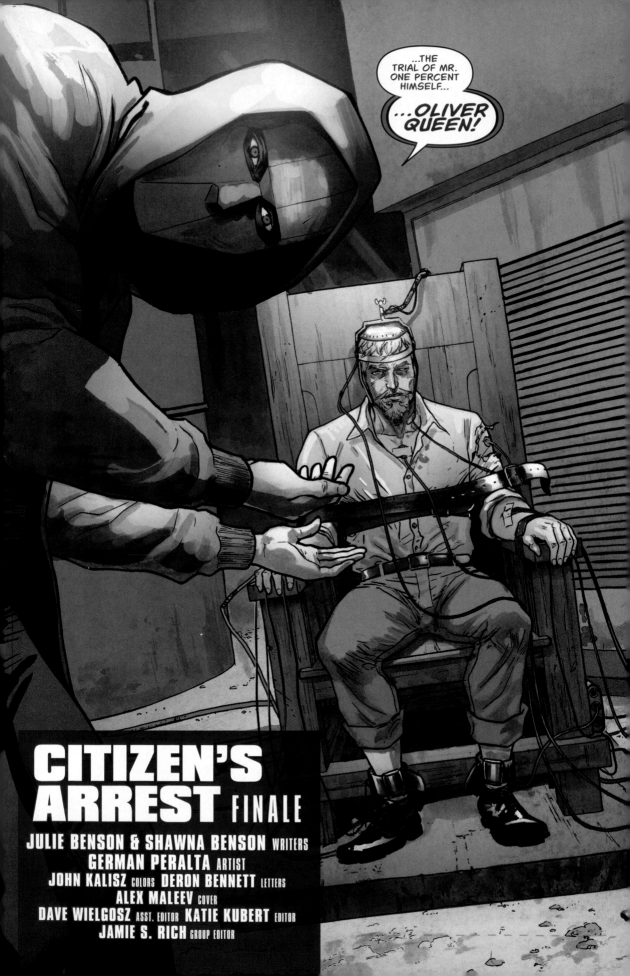

...THE TRIAL OF MR. ONE PERCENT HIMSELF...

...OLIVER QUEEN!

CITIZEN'S ARREST FINALE

JULIE BENSON & SHAWNA BENSON WRITERS

GERMAN PERALTA ARTIST

JOHN KALISZ COLORS DERON BENNETT LETTERS

ALEX MALEEV COVER

DAVE WIELGOSZ ASST. EDITOR KATIE KUBERT EDITOR

JAMIE S. RICH GROUP EDITOR

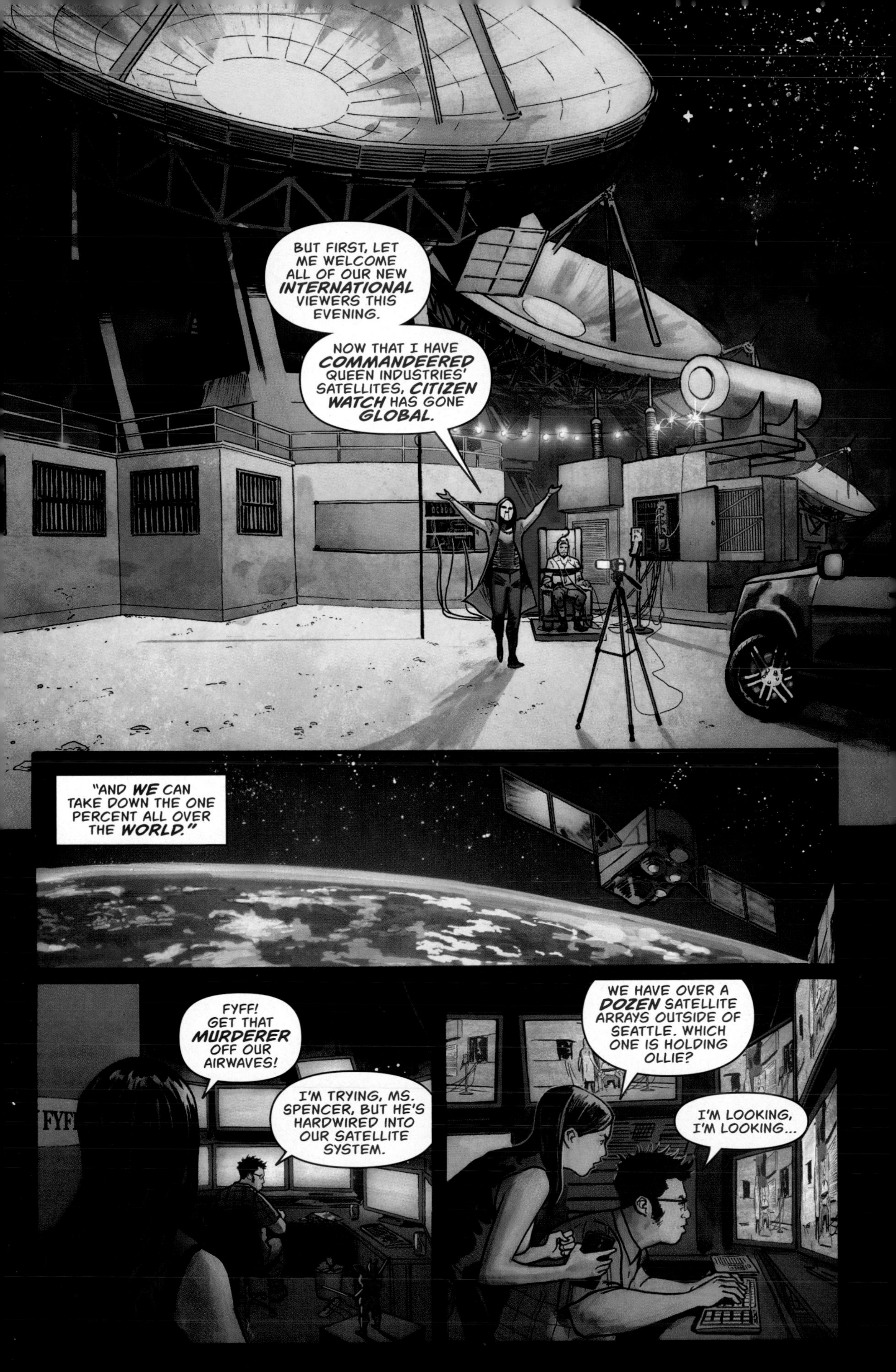
BUT FIRST, LET ME WELCOME ALL OF OUR NEW INTERNATIONAL VIEWERS THIS EVENING.
NOW THAT I HAVE COMMANDEERED QUEEN INDUSTRIES' SATELLITES, CITIZEN WATCH HAS GONE GLOBAL.
"AND WE CAN TAKE DOWN THE ONE PERCENT ALL OVER THE WORLD."
FYFF! GET THAT MURDERER OFF OUR AIRWAVES!
I'M TRYING, MS. SPENCER, BUT HE'S HARDWIRED INTO OUR SATELLITE SYSTEM.
WE HAVE OVER A DOZEN SATELLITE ARRAYS OUTSIDE OF SEATTLE. WHICH ONE IS HOLDING OLLIE?
I'M LOOKING, I'M LOOKING...

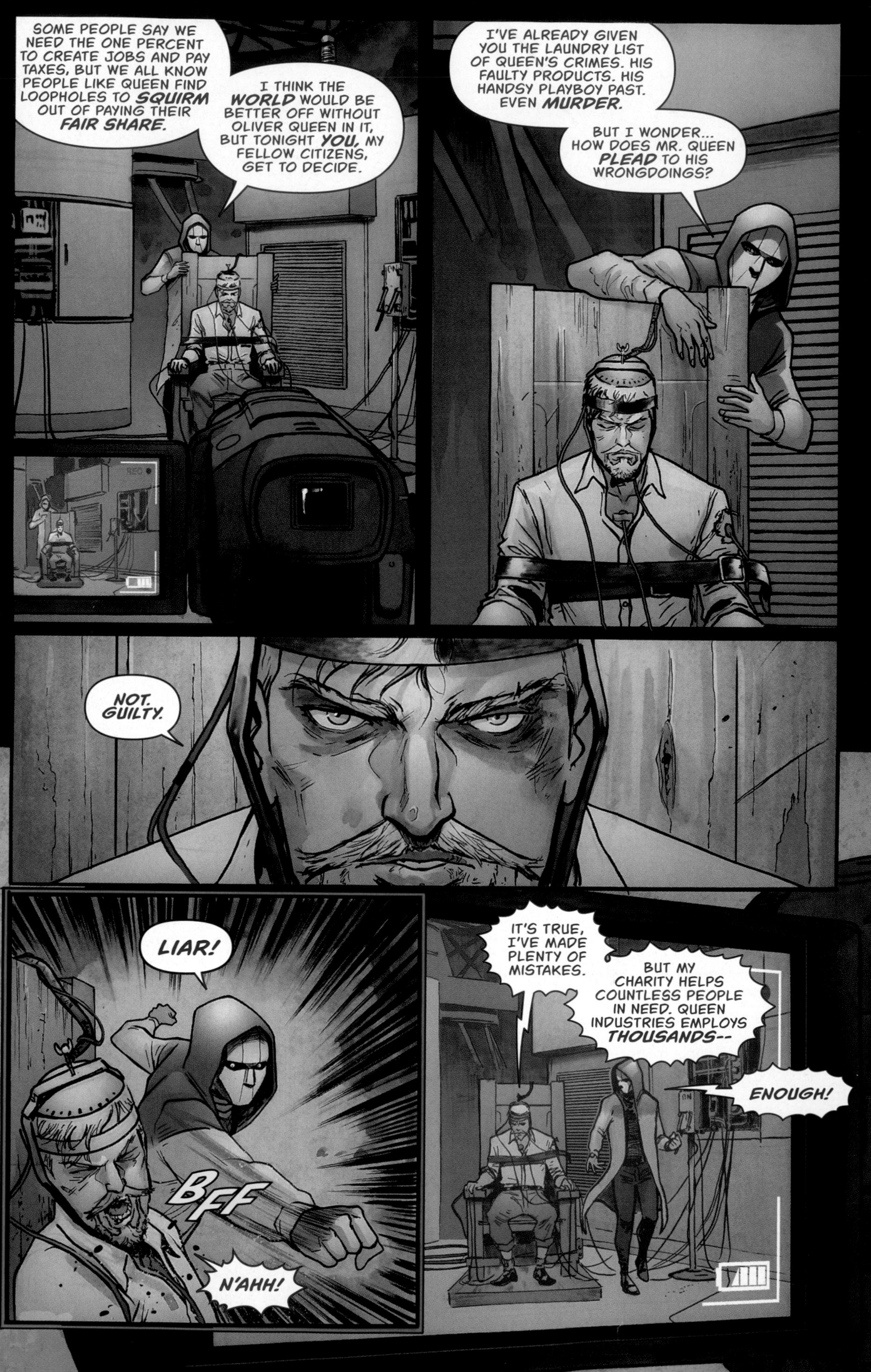
SOME PEOPLE SAY WE NEED THE ONE PERCENT TO CREATE JOBS AND PAY TAXES, BUT WE ALL KNOW PEOPLE LIKE QUEEN FIND LOOPHOLES TO SQUIRM OUT OF PAYING THEIR FAIR SHARE.
I THINK THE WORLD WOULD BE BETTER OFF WITHOUT OLIVER QUEEN IN IT, BUT TONIGHT YOU, MY FELLOW CITIZENS, GET TO DECIDE.
I'VE ALREADY GIVEN YOU THE LAUNDRY LIST OF QUEEN'S CRIMES. HIS FAULTY PRODUCTS. HIS HANDSY PLAYBOY PAST. EVEN MURDER.
BUT I WONDER... HOW DOES MR. QUEEN PLEAD TO HIS WRONGDOINGS?
NOT. GUILTY.
LIAR!
BFF
N'AHH!
IT'S TRUE, I'VE MADE PLENTY OF MISTAKES.
BUT MY CHARITY HELPS COUNTLESS PEOPLE IN NEED. QUEEN INDUSTRIES EMPLOYS THOUSANDS--
ENOUGH!

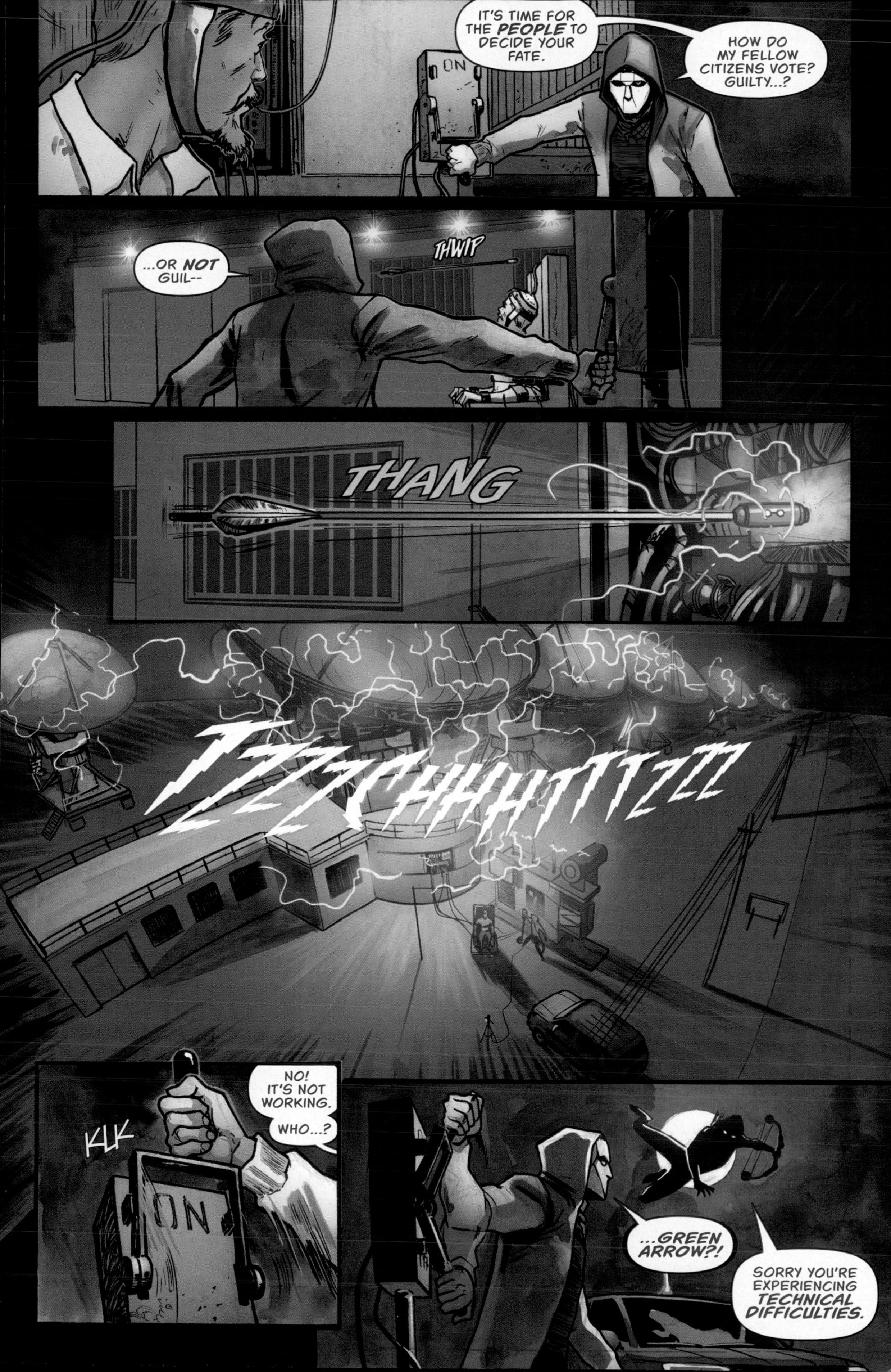

IT'S TIME FOR THE PEOPLE TO DECIDE YOUR FATE.
HOW DO MY FELLOW CITIZENS VOTE? GUILTY...?
ON
...OR NOT GUIL--
THWIP
THANG
ZZZZCHHHHTTTTZZZ
NO! IT'S NOT WORKING.
WHO...?
KLK
ON
...GREEN ARROW?!
SORRY YOU'RE EXPERIENCING TECHNICAL DIFFICULTIES.

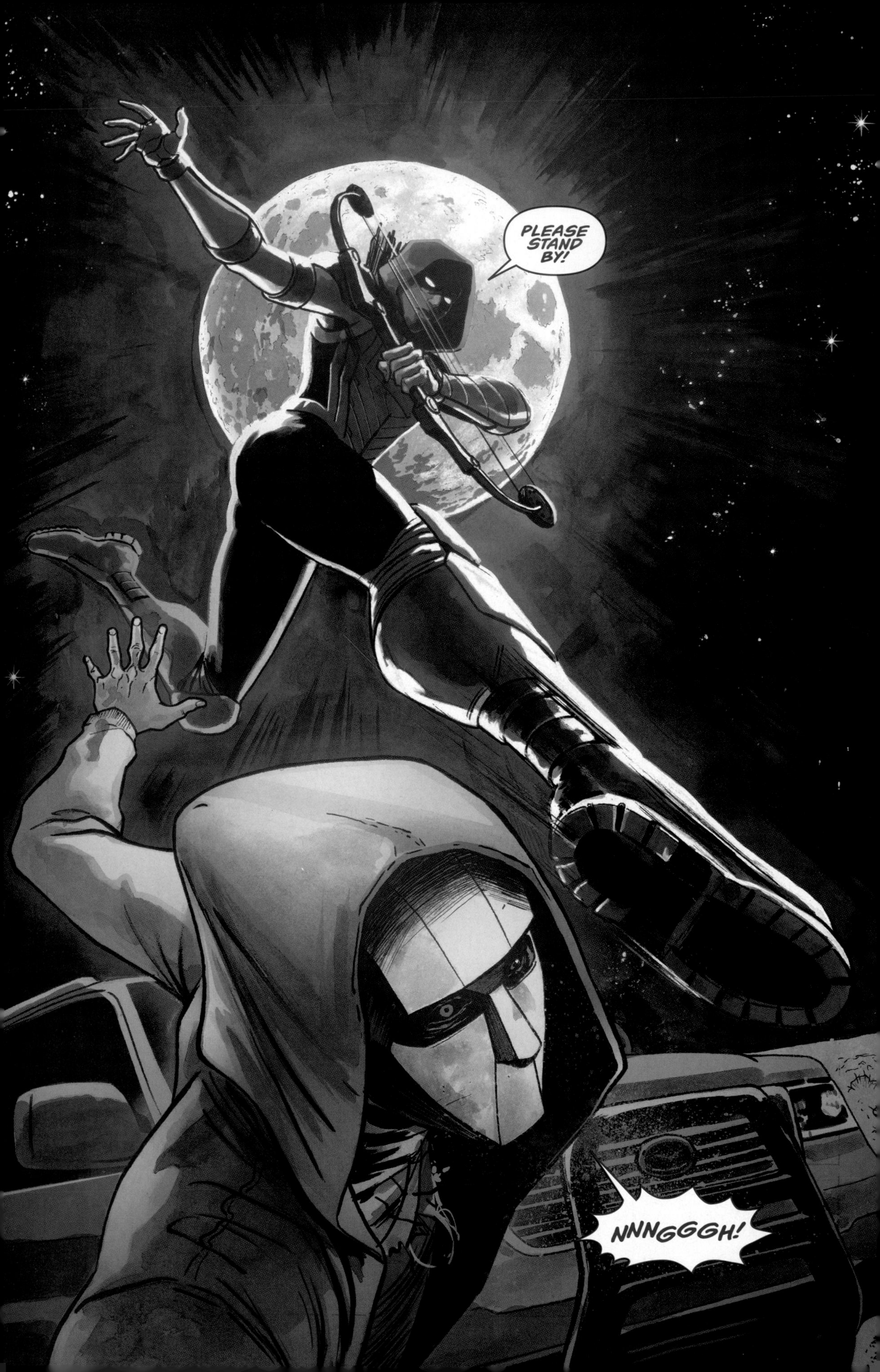
PLEASE STAND BY!
NNNGGGH!

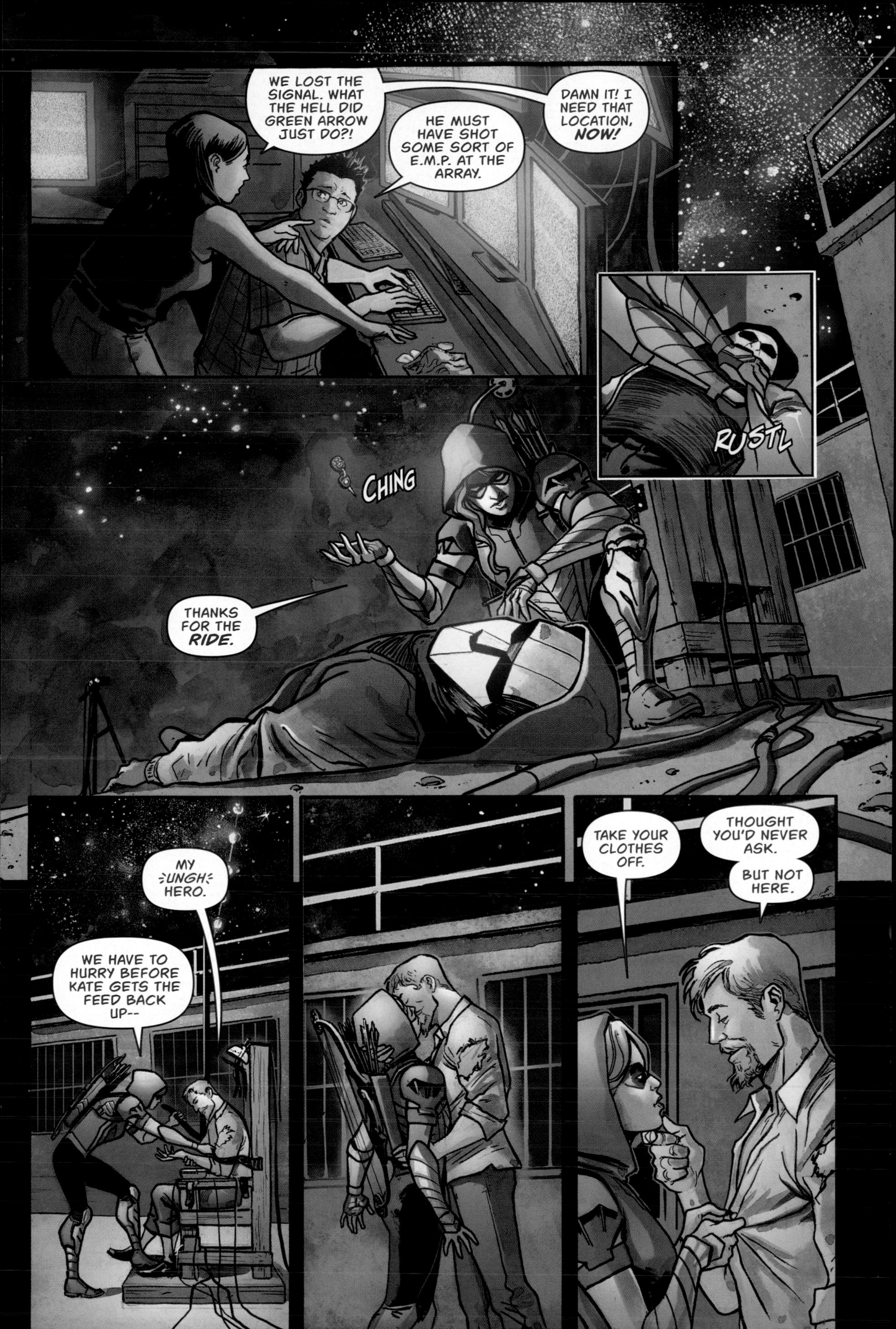
WE LOST THE SIGNAL. WHAT THE HELL DID GREEN ARROW JUST DO?!
HE MUST HAVE SHOT SOME SORT OF E.M.P. AT THE ARRAY.
DAMN IT! I NEED THAT LOCATION, NOW!
RUSTL
CHING
THANKS FOR THE RIDE.
MY UNGH HERO.
WE HAVE TO HURRY BEFORE KATE GETS THE FEED BACK UP--
TAKE YOUR CLOTHES OFF.
THOUGHT YOU'D NEVER ASK.
BUT NOT HERE.

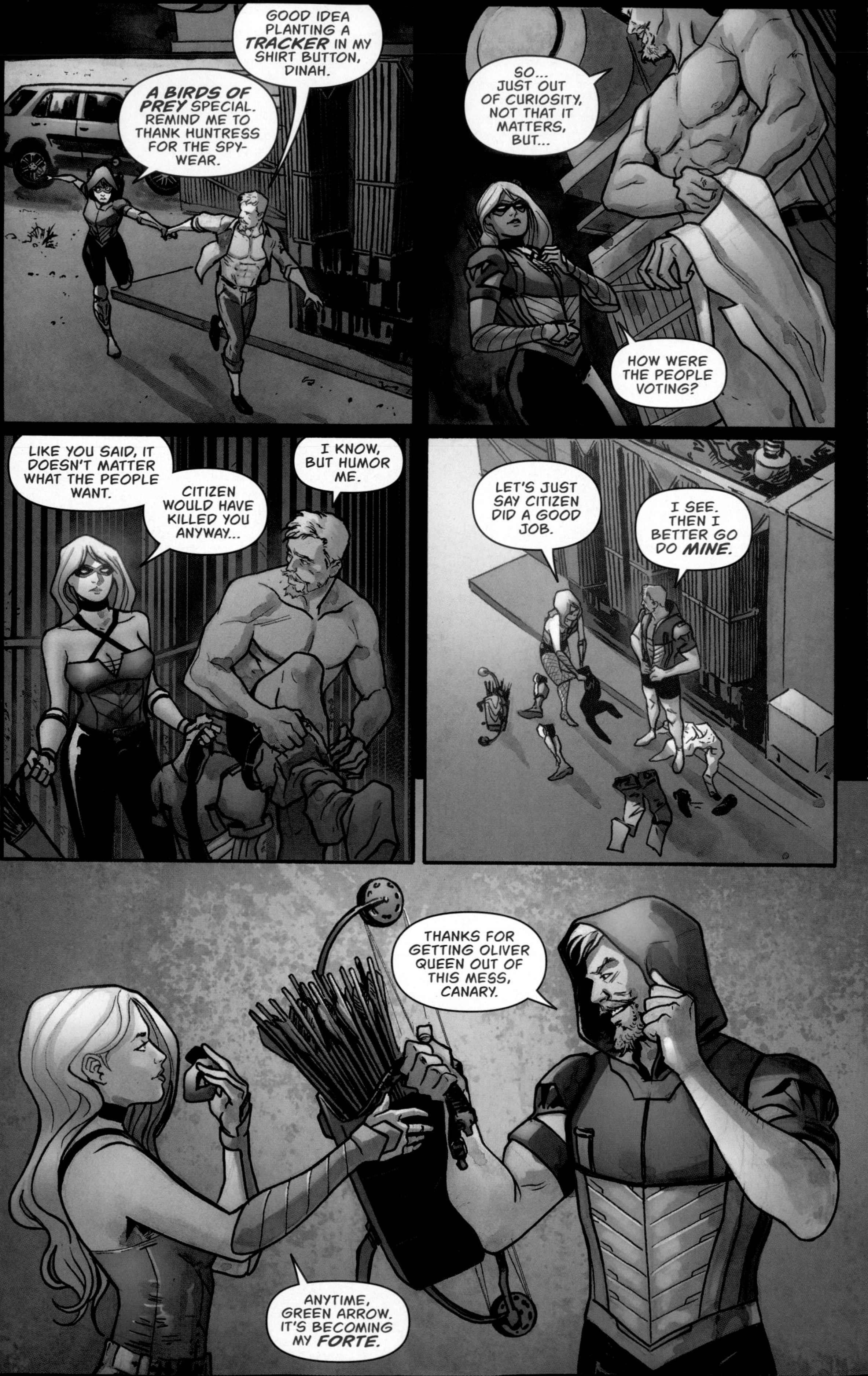

GOOD IDEA PLANTING A TRACKER IN MY SHIRT BUTTON, DINAH.
A BIRDS OF PREY SPECIAL. REMIND ME TO THANK HUNTRESS FOR THE SPY-WEAR.
SO... JUST OUT OF CURIOSITY, NOT THAT IT MATTERS, BUT...
HOW WERE THE PEOPLE VOTING?
LIKE YOU SAID, IT DOESN'T MATTER WHAT THE PEOPLE WANT.
CITIZEN WOULD HAVE KILLED YOU ANYWAY...
I KNOW, BUT HUMOR ME.
LET'S JUST SAY CITIZEN DID A GOOD JOB.
I SEE. THEN I BETTER GO DO MINE.
THANKS FOR GETTING OLIVER QUEEN OUT OF THIS MESS, CANARY.
ANYTIME, GREEN ARROW. IT'S BECOMING MY FORTE.

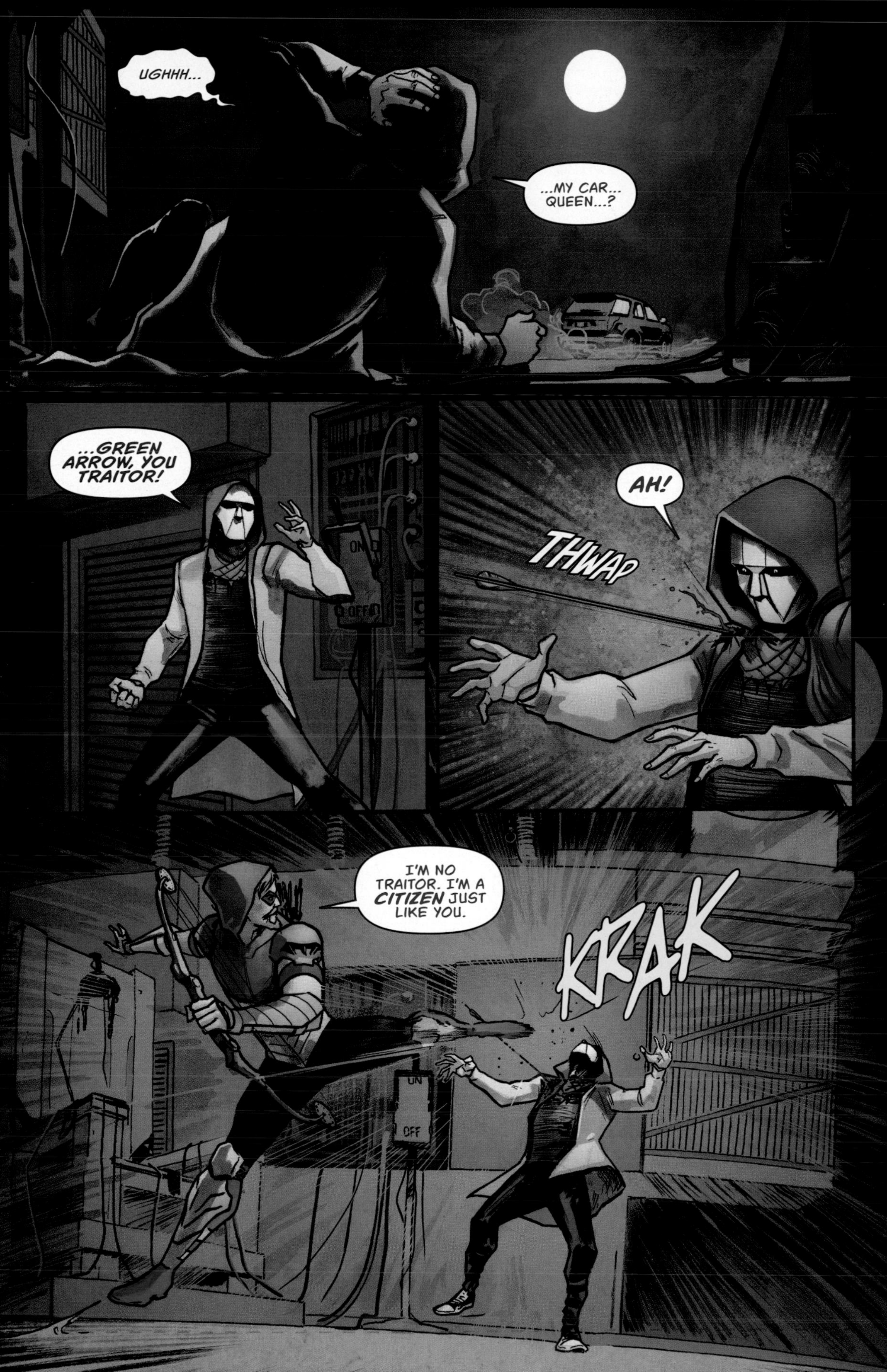
UGHHH...
...MY CAR... QUEEN...?
...GREEN ARROW, YOU TRAITOR!
AH!
THWAP
I'M NO TRAITOR. I'M A CITIZEN JUST LIKE YOU.
KRAK

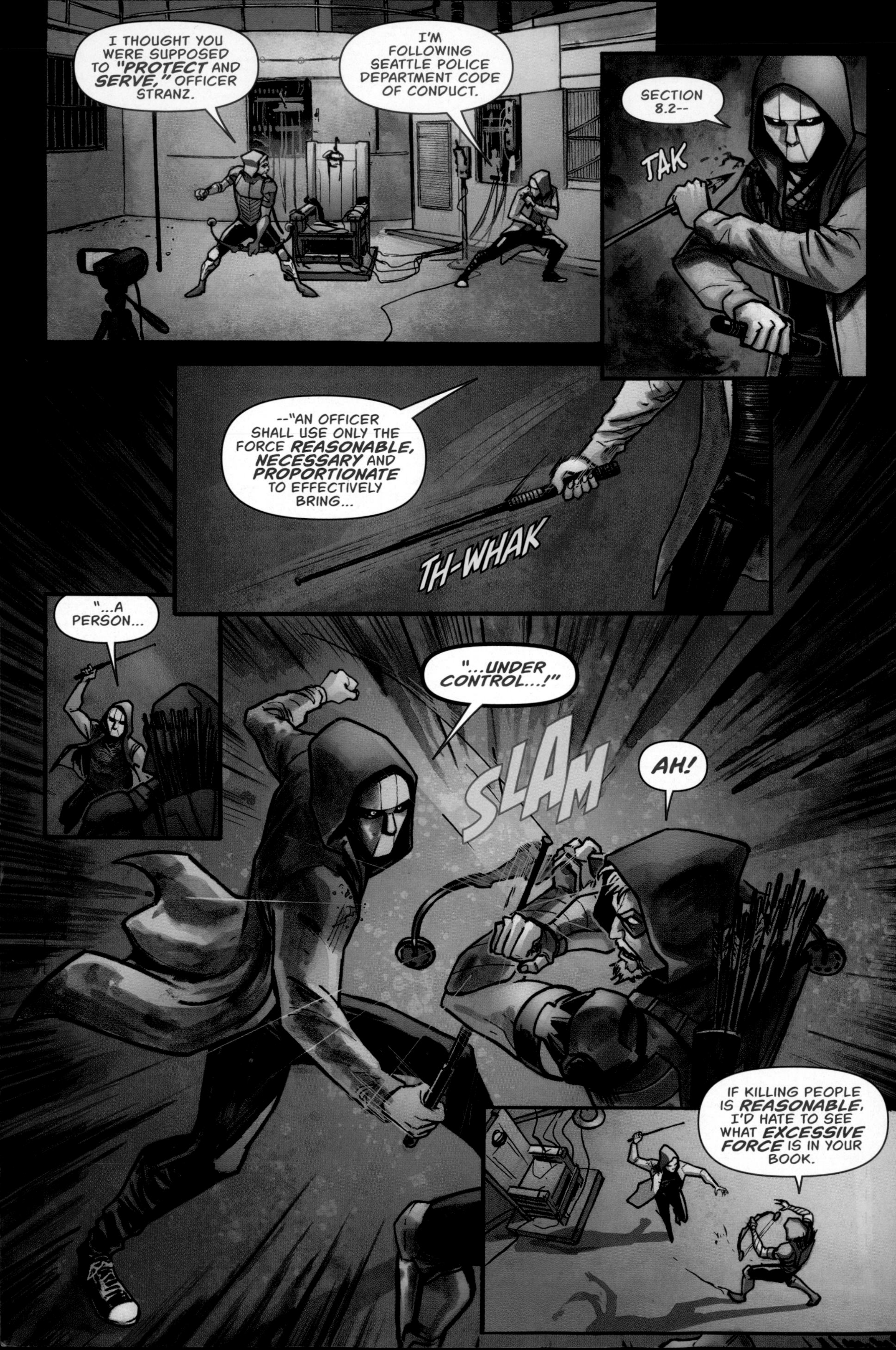
I THOUGHT YOU WERE SUPPOSED TO "PROTECT AND SERVE," OFFICER STRANZ.
I'M FOLLOWING SEATTLE POLICE DEPARTMENT CODE OF CONDUCT.
SECTION 8.2--
TAK
--"AN OFFICER SHALL USE ONLY THE FORCE REASONABLE, NECESSARY AND PROPORTIONATE TO EFFECTIVELY BRING...
TH-WHAK
"...A PERSON...
"...UNDER CONTROL...!"
SLAM
AH!
IF KILLING PEOPLE IS REASONABLE, I'D HATE TO SEE WHAT EXCESSIVE FORCE IS IN YOUR BOOK.

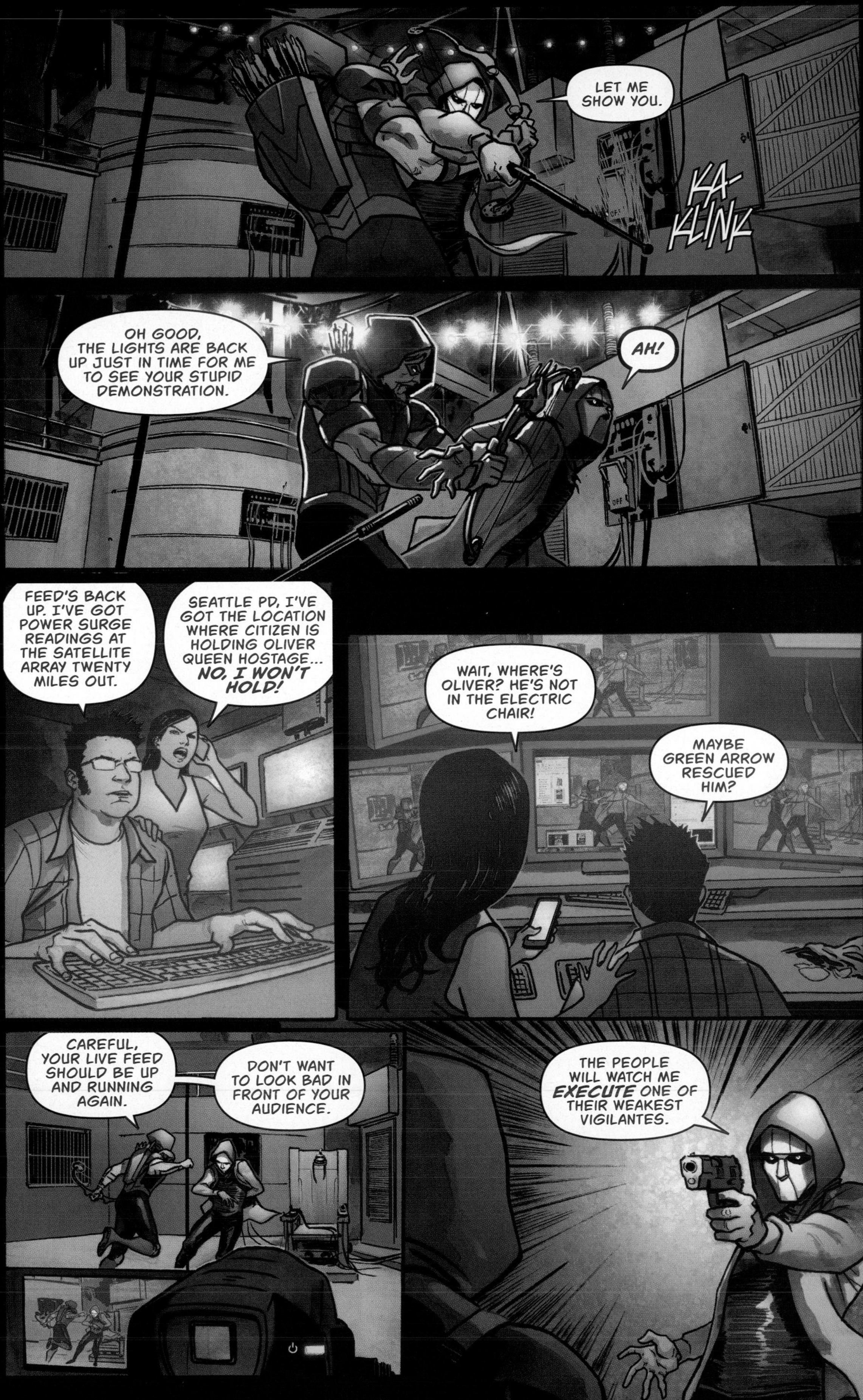
LET ME SHOW YOU.
KA-KLINK
OH GOOD, THE LIGHTS ARE BACK UP JUST IN TIME FOR ME TO SEE YOUR STUPID DEMONSTRATION.
AH!
FEED'S BACK UP. I'VE GOT POWER SURGE READINGS AT THE SATELLITE ARRAY TWENTY MILES OUT.
SEATTLE PD, I'VE GOT THE LOCATION WHERE CITIZEN IS HOLDING OLIVER QUEEN HOSTAGE... NO, I WON'T HOLD!
WAIT, WHERE'S OLIVER? HE'S NOT IN THE ELECTRIC CHAIR!
MAYBE GREEN ARROW RESCUED HIM?
CAREFUL, YOUR LIVE FEED SHOULD BE UP AND RUNNING AGAIN.
DON'T WANT TO LOOK BAD IN FRONT OF YOUR AUDIENCE.
THE PEOPLE WILL WATCH ME EXECUTE ONE OF THEIR WEAKEST VIGILANTES.

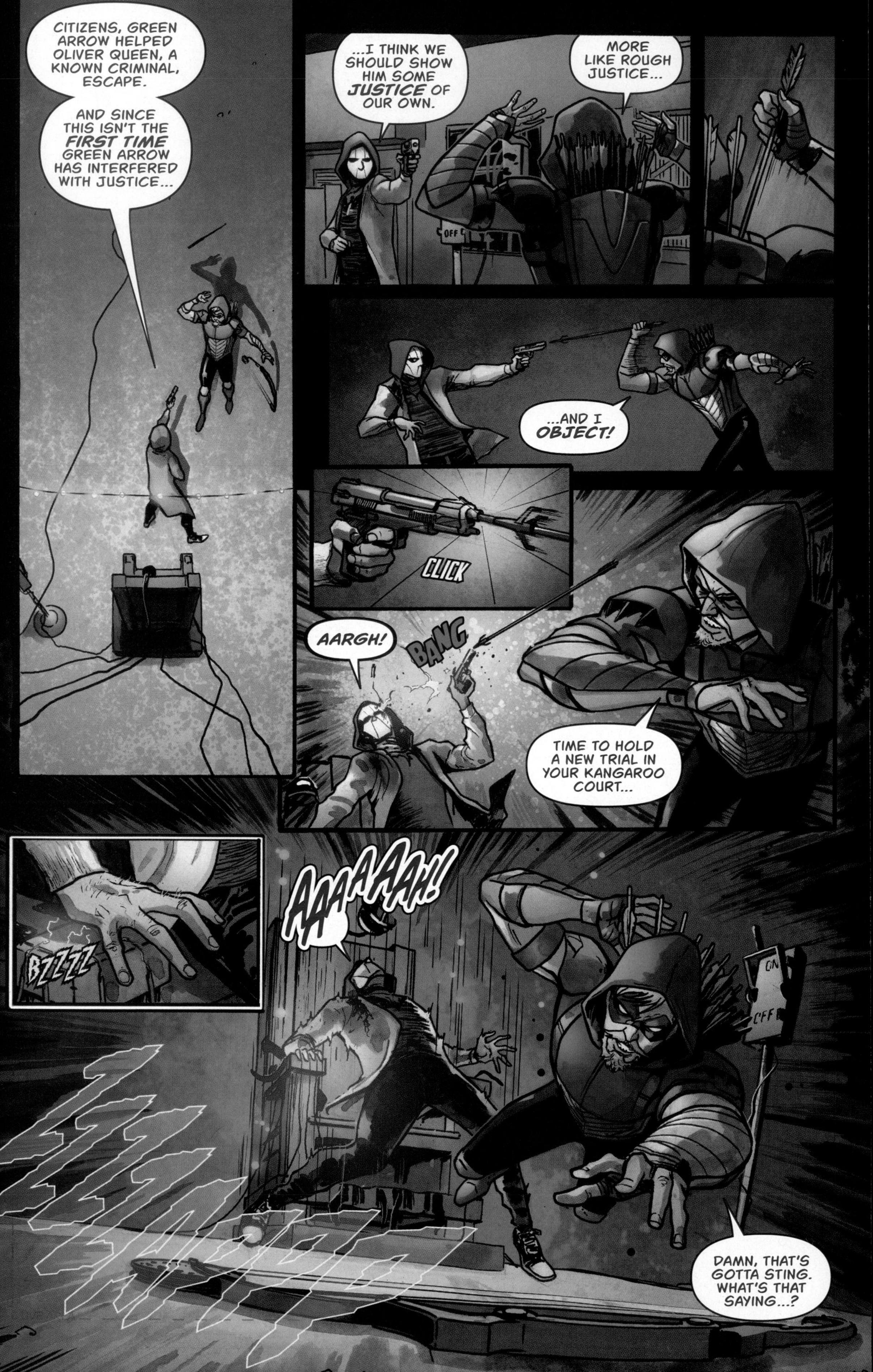
CITIZENS, GREEN ARROW HELPED OLIVER QUEEN, A KNOWN CRIMINAL, ESCAPE.
AND SINCE THIS ISN'T THE FIRST TIME GREEN ARROW HAS INTERFERED WITH JUSTICE...
...I THINK WE SHOULD SHOW HIM SOME JUSTICE OF OUR OWN.
MORE LIKE ROUGH JUSTICE...
OFF
...AND I OBJECT!
CLICK
AARGH!
BANG
TIME TO HOLD A NEW TRIAL IN YOUR KANGAROO COURT...
BZZZZ
AAAAAAH!
ON
OFF
DAMN, THAT'S GOTTA STING. WHAT'S THAT SAYING...?

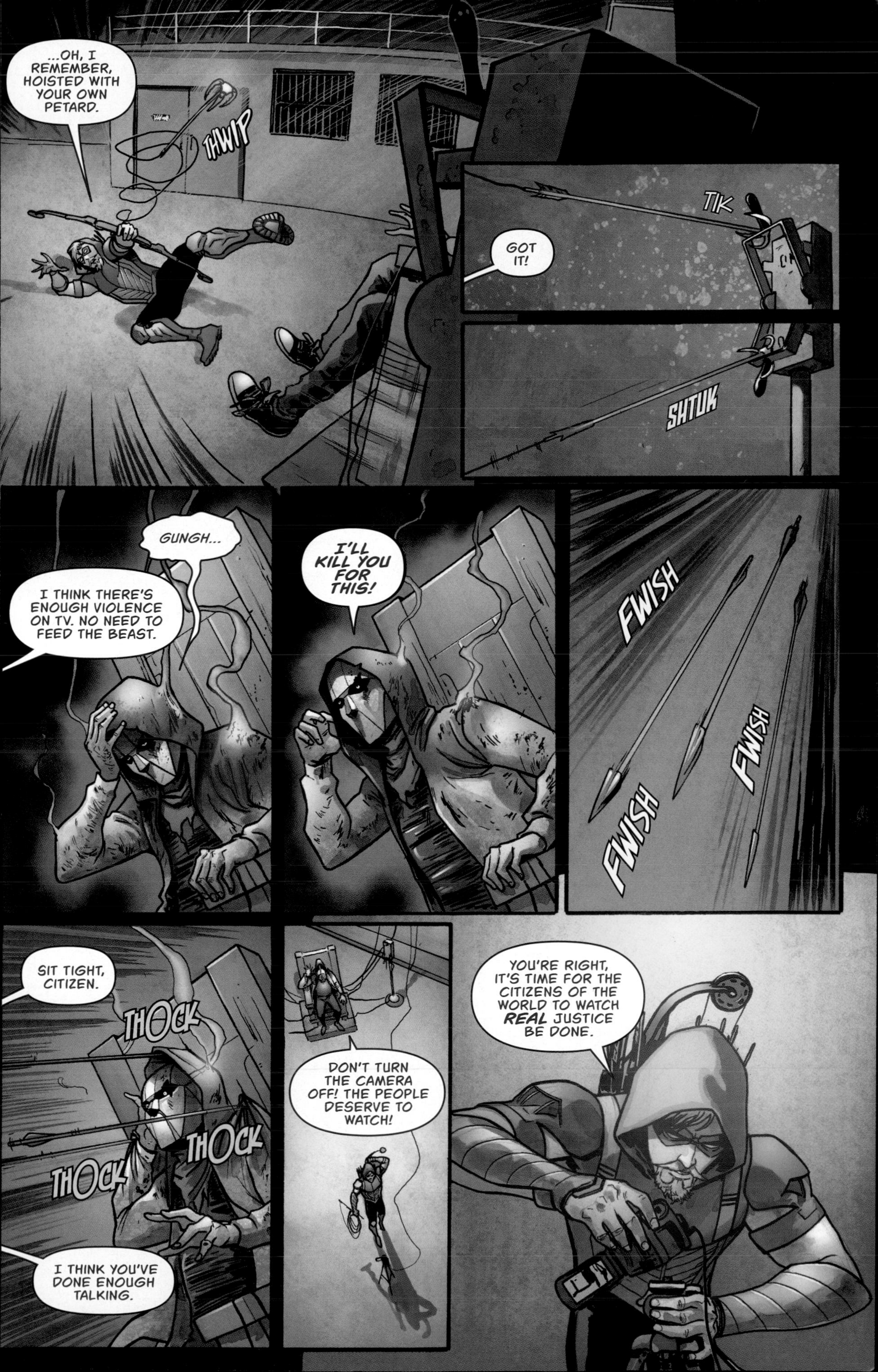
...OH, I REMEMBER, HOISTED WITH YOUR OWN PETARD.
THWIP
TIK
GOT IT!
SHTUK
GUNGH...
I THINK THERE'S ENOUGH VIOLENCE ON TV. NO NEED TO FEED THE BEAST.
I'LL KILL YOU FOR THIS!
FWISH
FWISH
FWISH
SIT TIGHT, CITIZEN.
THOCK
THOCK
THOCK
I THINK YOU'VE DONE ENOUGH TALKING.
DON'T TURN THE CAMERA OFF! THE PEOPLE DESERVE TO WATCH!
YOU'RE RIGHT, IT'S TIME FOR THE CITIZENS OF THE WORLD TO WATCH REAL JUSTICE BE DONE.

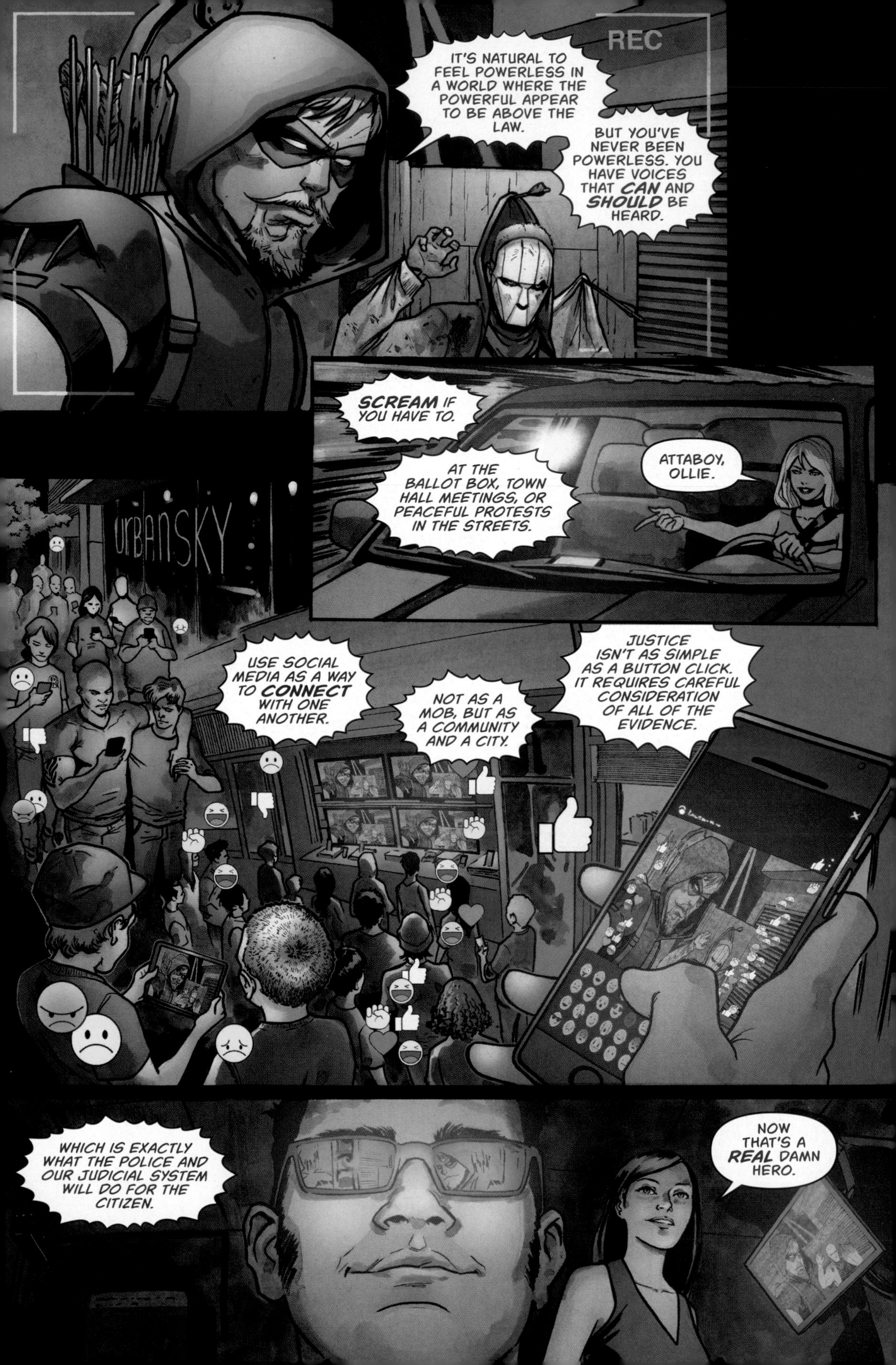
REC
IT'S NATURAL TO FEEL POWERLESS IN A WORLD WHERE THE POWERFUL APPEAR TO BE ABOVE THE LAW.
BUT YOU'VE NEVER BEEN POWERLESS. YOU HAVE VOICES THAT CAN AND SHOULD BE HEARD.
SCREAM IF YOU HAVE TO.
AT THE BALLOT BOX, TOWN HALL MEETINGS, OR PEACEFUL PROTESTS IN THE STREETS.
ATTABOY, OLLIE.
URBANSKY
USE SOCIAL MEDIA AS A WAY TO CONNECT WITH ONE ANOTHER.
NOT AS A MOB, BUT AS A COMMUNITY AND A CITY.
JUSTICE ISN'T AS SIMPLE AS A BUTTON CLICK. IT REQUIRES CAREFUL CONSIDERATION OF ALL OF THE EVIDENCE.
WHICH IS EXACTLY WHAT THE POLICE AND OUR JUDICIAL SYSTEM WILL DO FOR THE CITIZEN.
NOW THAT'S A REAL DAMN HERO.

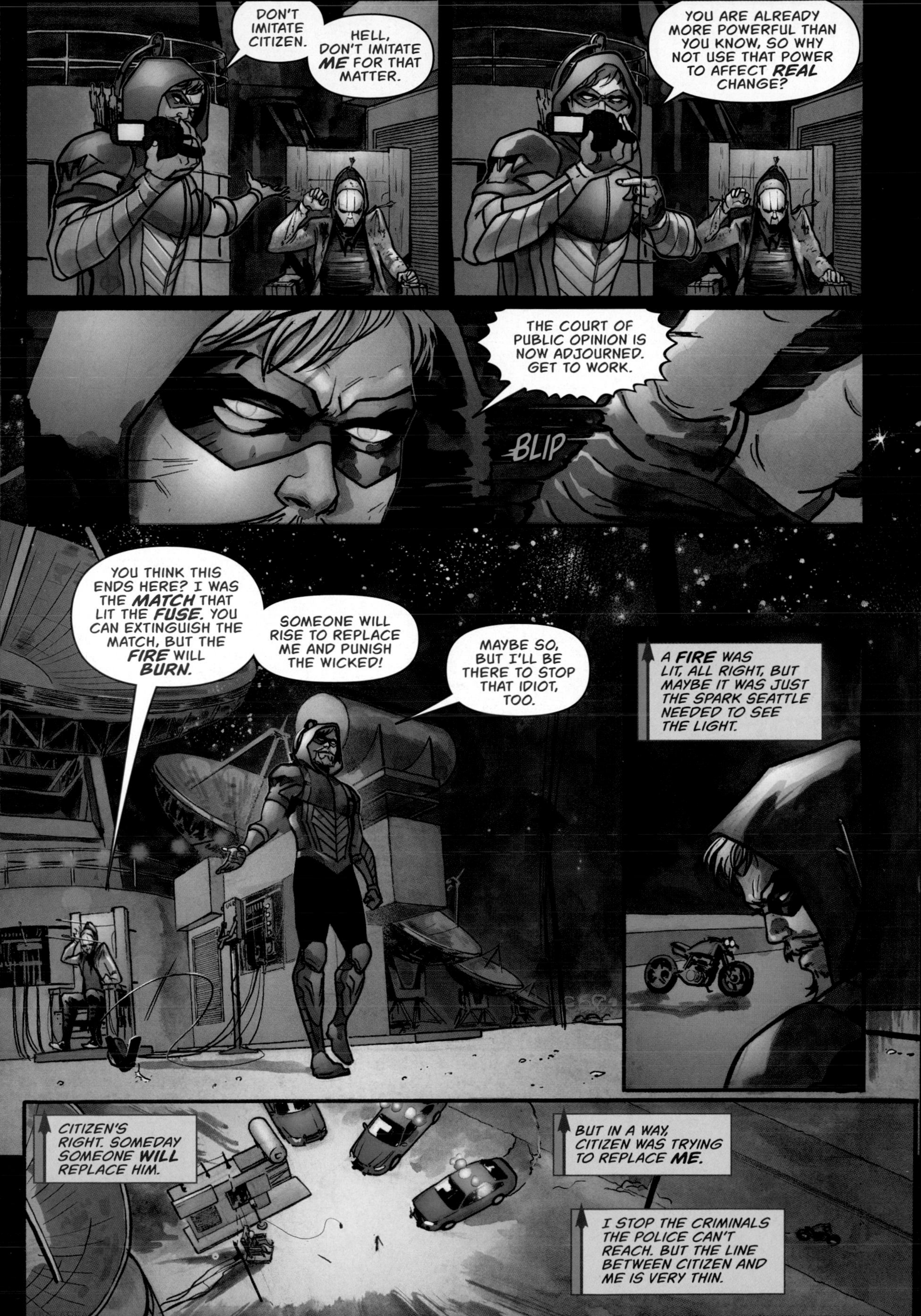
DON'T IMITATE CITIZEN.
HELL, DON'T IMITATE ME FOR THAT MATTER.
YOU ARE ALREADY MORE POWERFUL THAN YOU KNOW, SO WHY NOT USE THAT POWER TO AFFECT REAL CHANGE?
THE COURT OF PUBLIC OPINION IS NOW ADJOURNED. GET TO WORK.
BLIP
YOU THINK THIS ENDS HERE? I WAS THE MATCH THAT LIT THE FUSE. YOU CAN EXTINGUISH THE MATCH, BUT THE FIRE WILL BURN.
SOMEONE WILL RISE TO REPLACE ME AND PUNISH THE WICKED!
MAYBE SO, BUT I'LL BE THERE TO STOP THAT IDIOT, TOO.
A FIRE WAS LIT, ALL RIGHT, BUT MAYBE IT WAS JUST THE SPARK SEATTLE NEEDED TO SEE THE LIGHT.
CITIZEN'S RIGHT. SOMEDAY SOMEONE WILL REPLACE HIM.
BUT IN A WAY, CITIZEN WAS TRYING TO REPLACE ME.
I STOP THE CRIMINALS THE POLICE CAN'T REACH. BUT THE LINE BETWEEN CITIZEN AND ME IS VERY THIN.

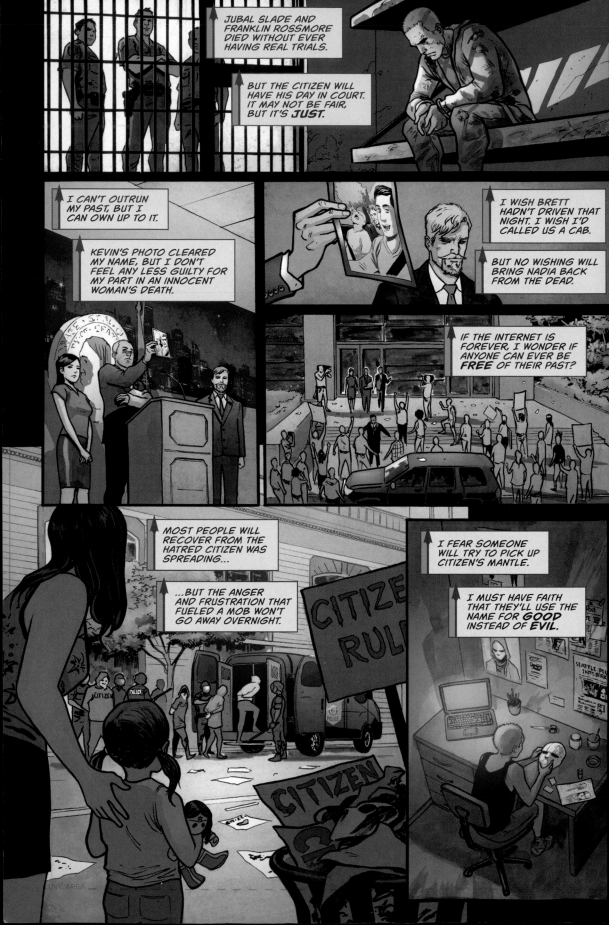

JUBAL SLADE AND FRANKLIN ROSSMORE DIED WITHOUT EVER HAVING REAL TRIALS.

BUT THE CITIZEN WILL HAVE HIS DAY IN COURT. IT MAY NOT BE FAIR, BUT IT'S *JUST*.

I CAN'T OUTRUN MY PAST, BUT I CAN OWN UP TO IT.

KEVIN'S PHOTO CLEARED MY NAME, BUT I DON'T FEEL ANY LESS GUILTY FOR MY PART IN AN INNOCENT WOMAN'S DEATH.

I WISH BRETT HADN'T DRIVEN THAT NIGHT. I WISH I'D CALLED US A CAB.

BUT NO WISHING WILL BRING NADIA BACK FROM THE DEAD.

IF THE INTERNET IS FOREVER, I WONDER IF ANYONE CAN EVER BE *FREE* OF THEIR PAST?

MOST PEOPLE WILL RECOVER FROM THE HATRED CITIZEN WAS SPREADING...

...BUT THE ANGER AND FRUSTRATION THAT FUELED A MOB WON'T GO AWAY OVERNIGHT.

I FEAR SOMEONE WILL TRY TO PICK UP CITIZEN'S MANTLE.

I MUST HAVE FAITH THAT THEY'LL USE THE NAME FOR *GOOD* INSTEAD OF *EVIL*.

CITIZEN RUL[E]

CITIZEN

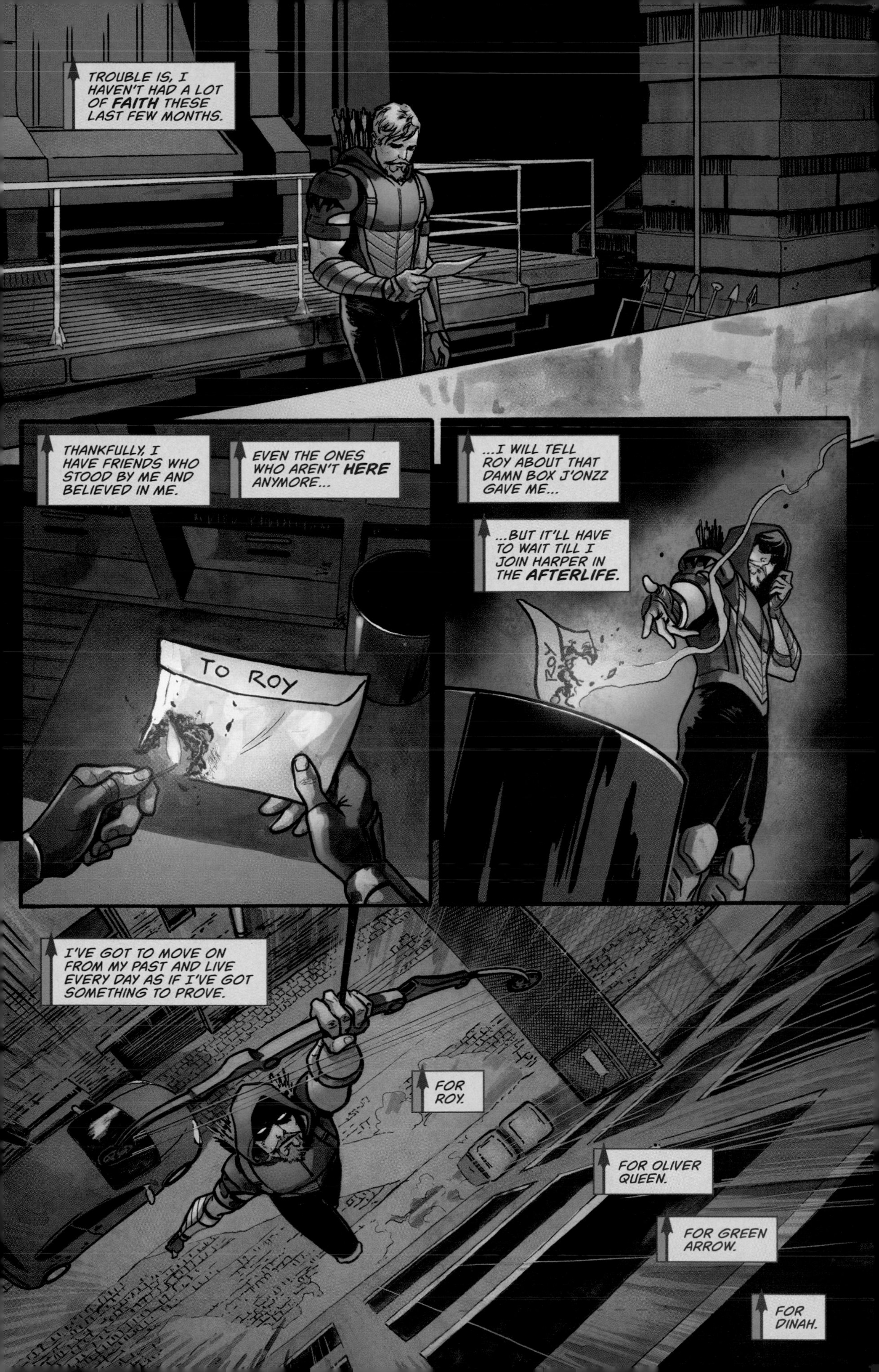
TROUBLE IS, I HAVEN'T HAD A LOT OF FAITH THESE LAST FEW MONTHS.
THANKFULLY, I HAVE FRIENDS WHO STOOD BY ME AND BELIEVED IN ME.
EVEN THE ONES WHO AREN'T HERE ANYMORE...
TO ROY
...I WILL TELL ROY ABOUT THAT DAMN BOX J'ONZZ GAVE ME...
...BUT IT'LL HAVE TO WAIT TILL I JOIN HARPER IN THE AFTERLIFE.
I'VE GOT TO MOVE ON FROM MY PAST AND LIVE EVERY DAY AS IF I'VE GOT SOMETHING TO PROVE.
FOR ROY.
FOR OLIVER QUEEN.
FOR GREEN ARROW.
FOR DINAH.

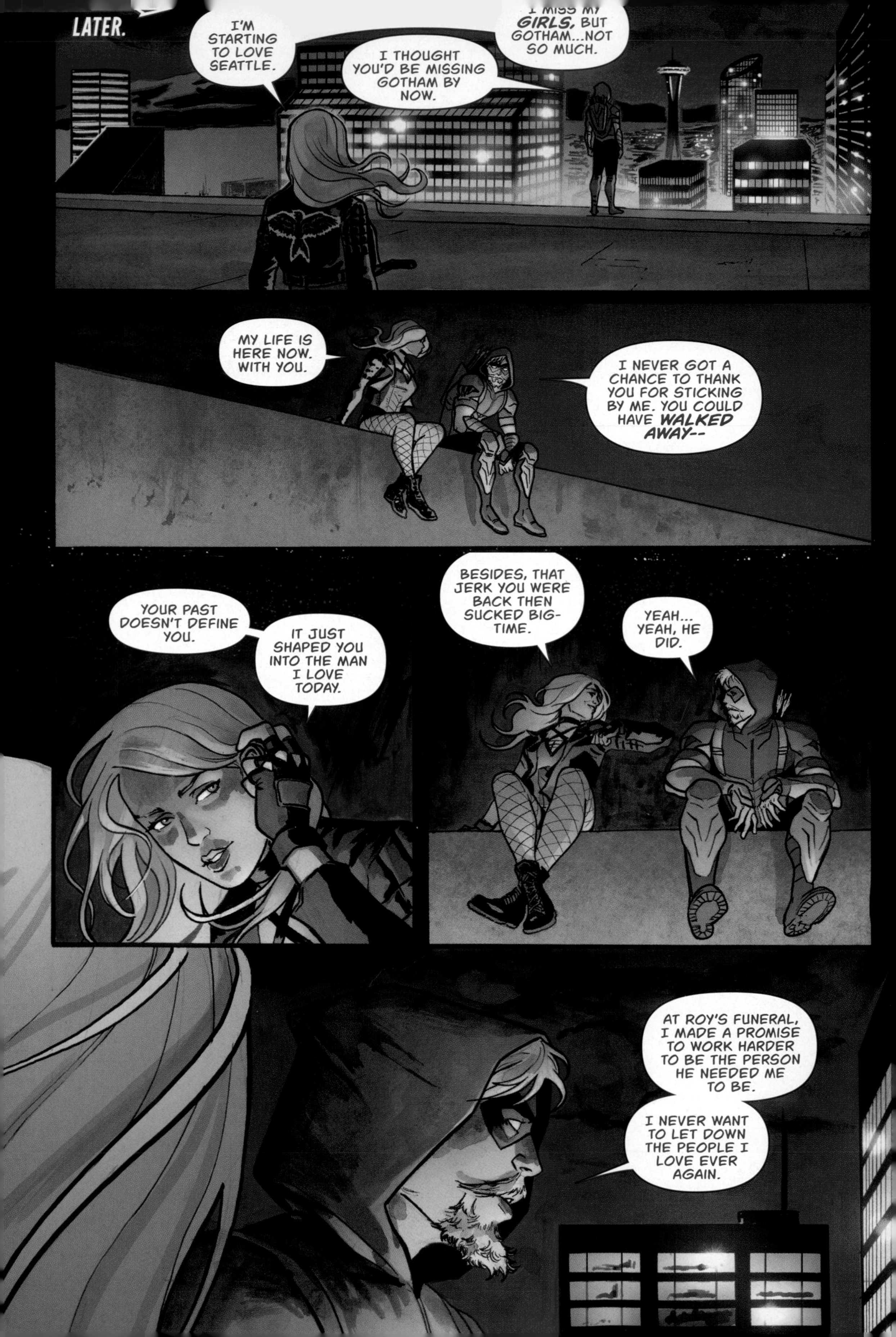
LATER.
I'M STARTING TO LOVE SEATTLE.
I THOUGHT YOU'D BE MISSING GOTHAM BY NOW.
I MISS MY GIRLS, BUT GOTHAM...NOT SO MUCH.
MY LIFE IS HERE NOW. WITH YOU.
I NEVER GOT A CHANCE TO THANK YOU FOR STICKING BY ME. YOU COULD HAVE WALKED AWAY--
YOUR PAST DOESN'T DEFINE YOU.
IT JUST SHAPED YOU INTO THE MAN I LOVE TODAY.
BESIDES, THAT JERK YOU WERE BACK THEN SUCKED BIG-TIME.
YEAH... YEAH, HE DID.
AT ROY'S FUNERAL, I MADE A PROMISE TO WORK HARDER TO BE THE PERSON HE NEEDED ME TO BE.
I NEVER WANT TO LET DOWN THE PEOPLE I LOVE EVER AGAIN.

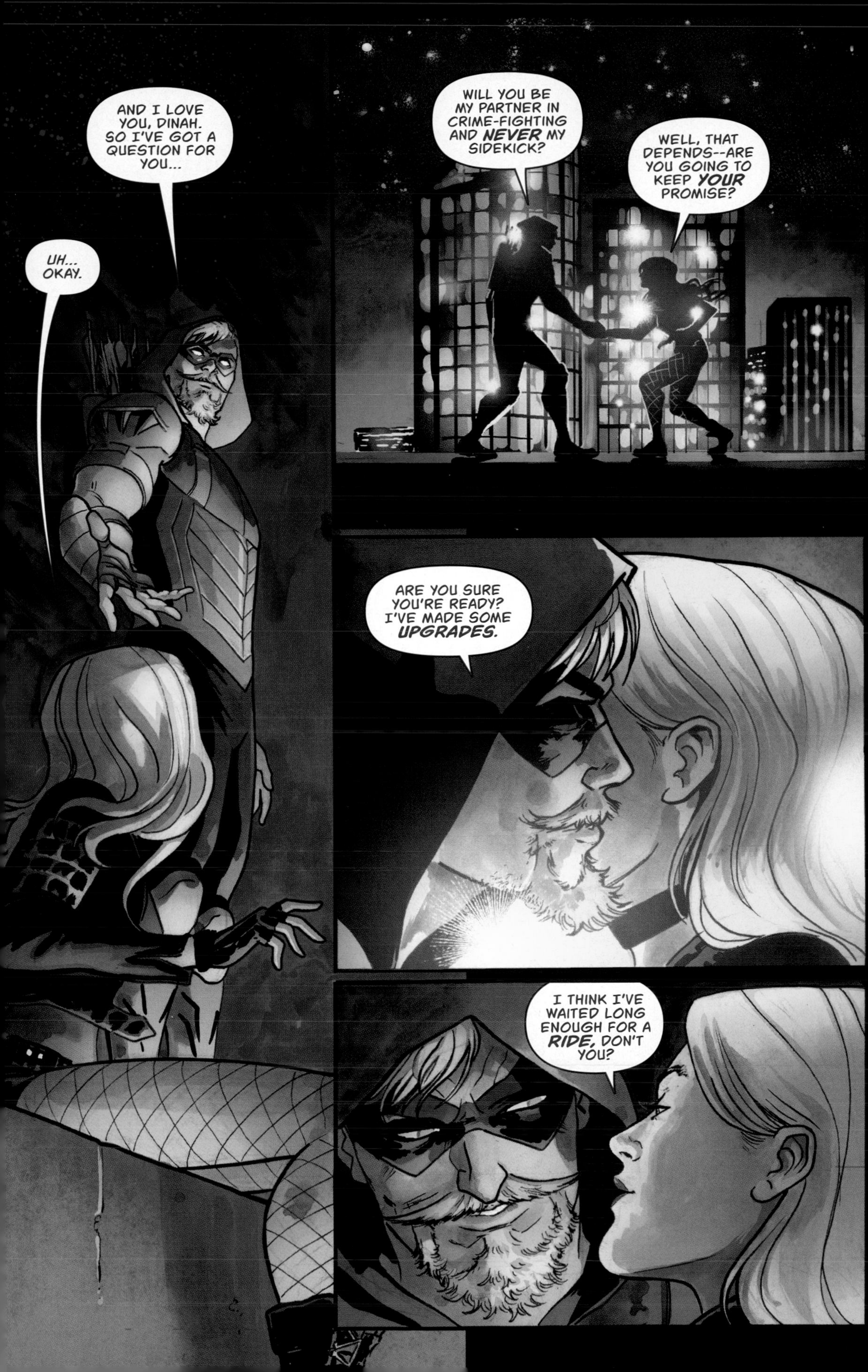
AND I LOVE YOU, DINAH. SO I'VE GOT A QUESTION FOR YOU...
UH... OKAY.
WILL YOU BE MY PARTNER IN CRIME-FIGHTING AND NEVER MY SIDEKICK?
WELL, THAT DEPENDS--ARE YOU GOING TO KEEP YOUR PROMISE?
ARE YOU SURE YOU'RE READY? I'VE MADE SOME UPGRADES.
I THINK I'VE WAITED LONG ENOUGH FOR A RIDE, DON'T YOU?

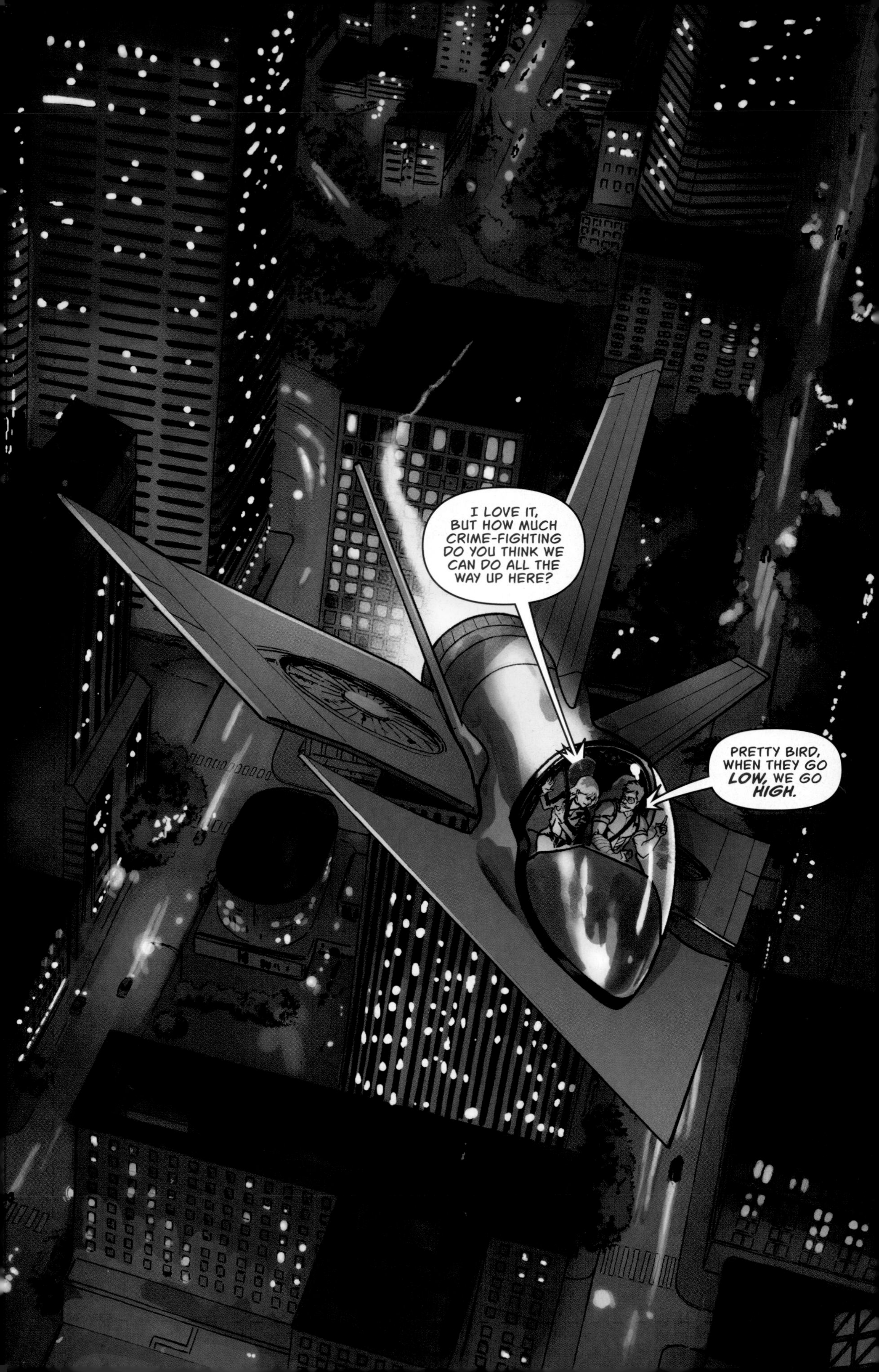
I LOVE IT, BUT HOW MUCH CRIME-FIGHTING DO YOU THINK WE CAN DO ALL THE WAY UP HERE?
PRETTY BIRD, WHEN THEY GO LOW, WE GO HIGH.

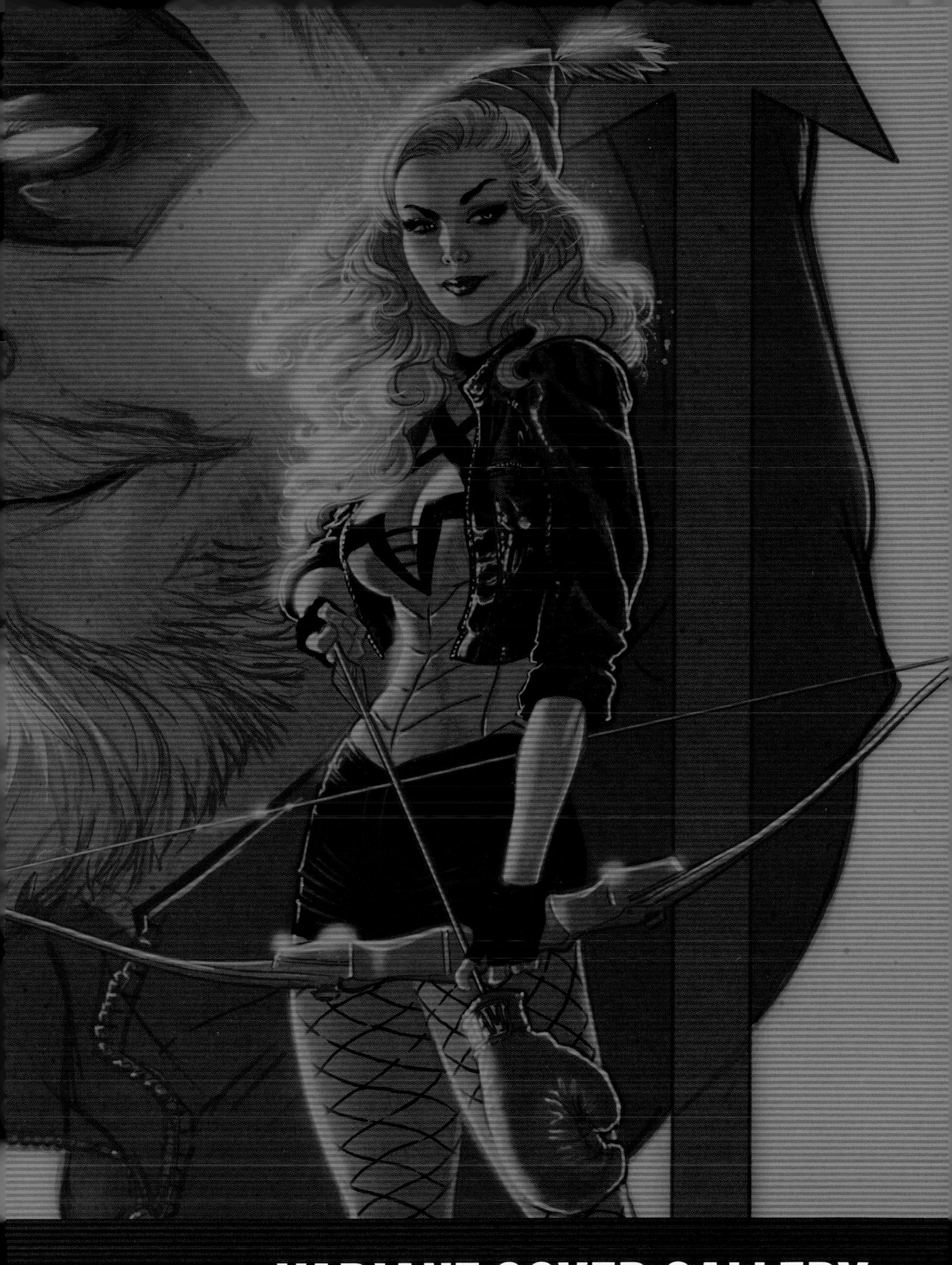

VARIANT COVER GALLERY

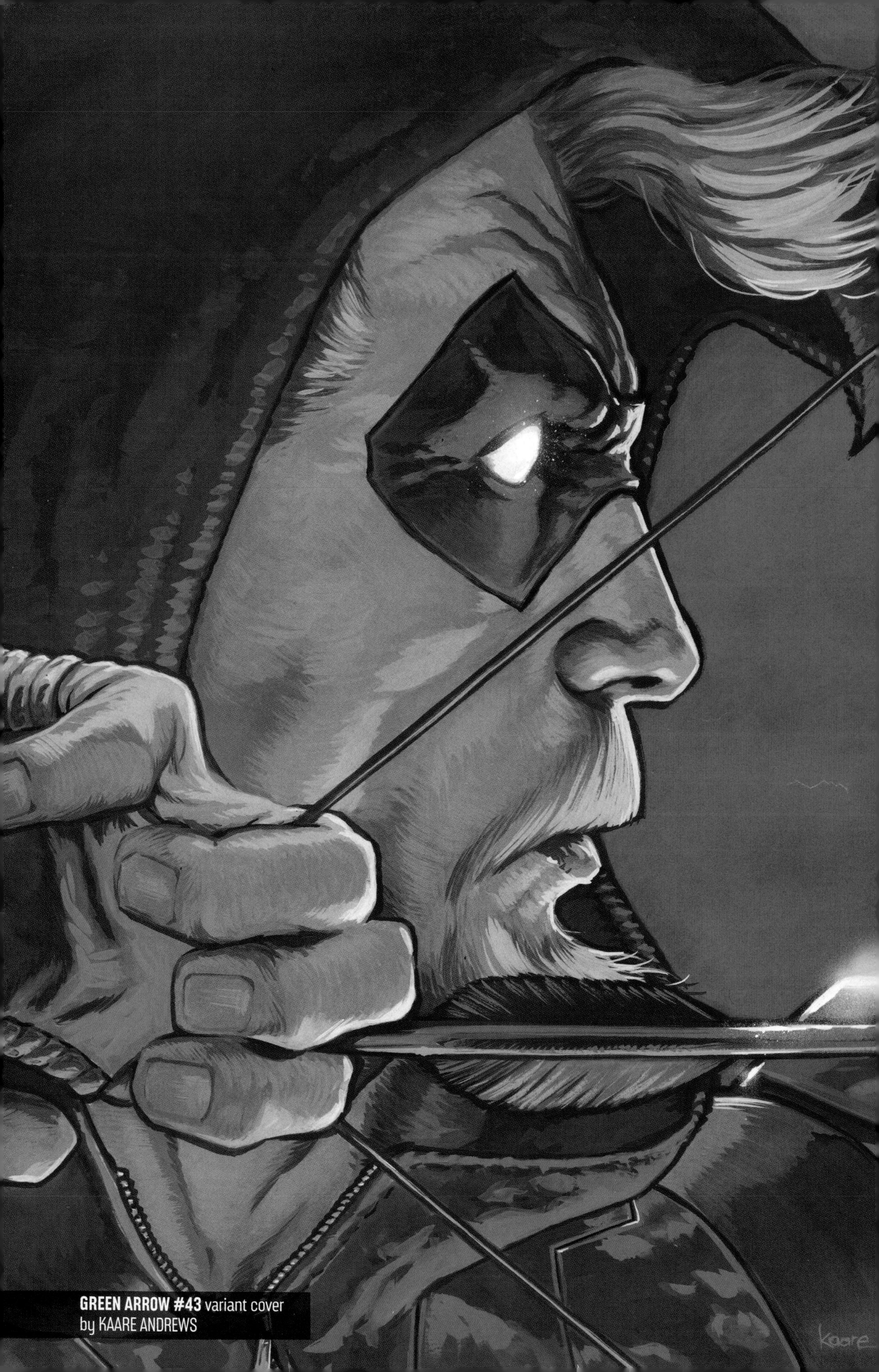
kaare

GREEN ARROW #43 variant cover
by KAARE ANDREWS

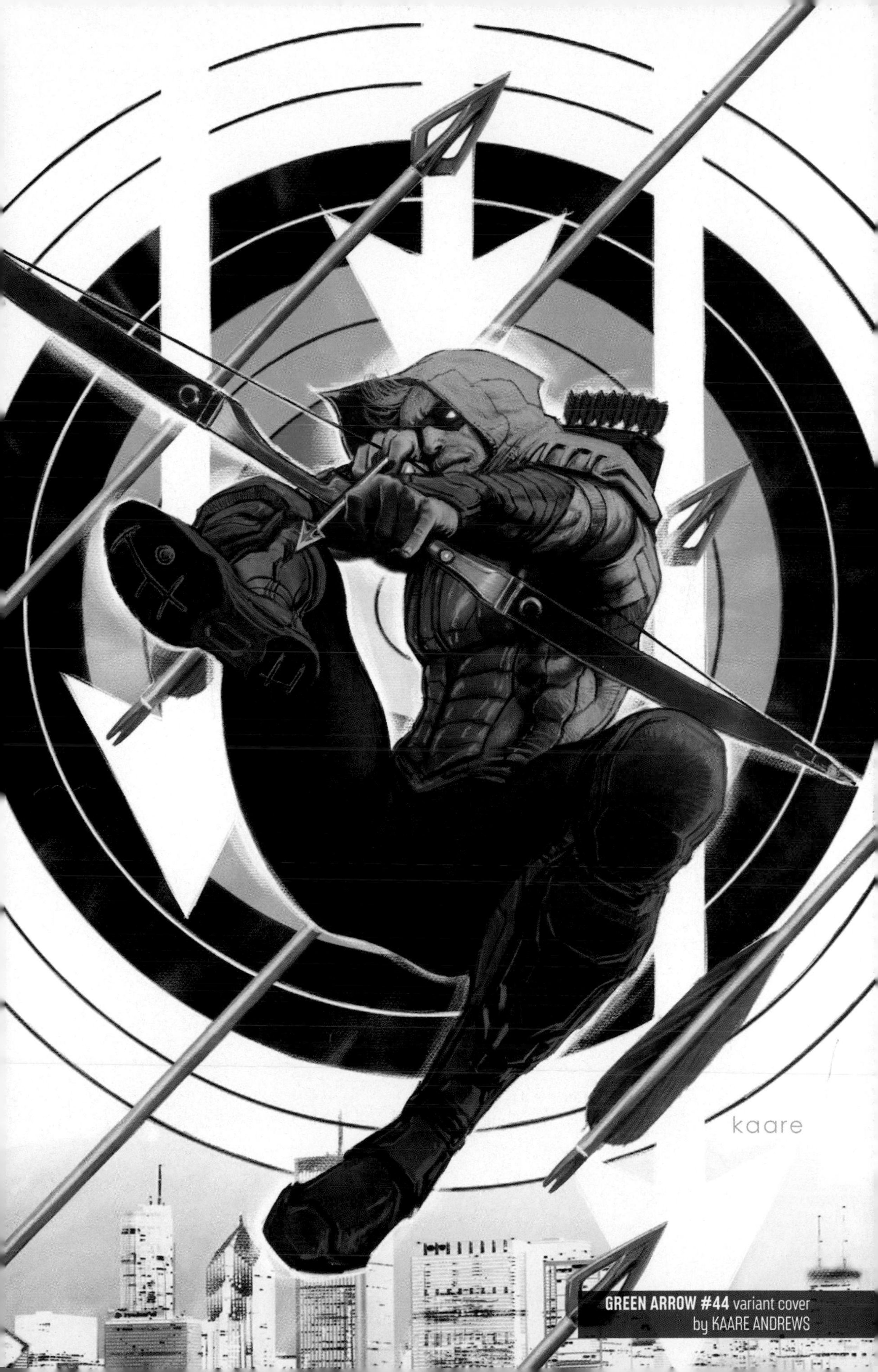
kaare
GREEN ARROW #44 variant cover
by KAARE ANDREWS

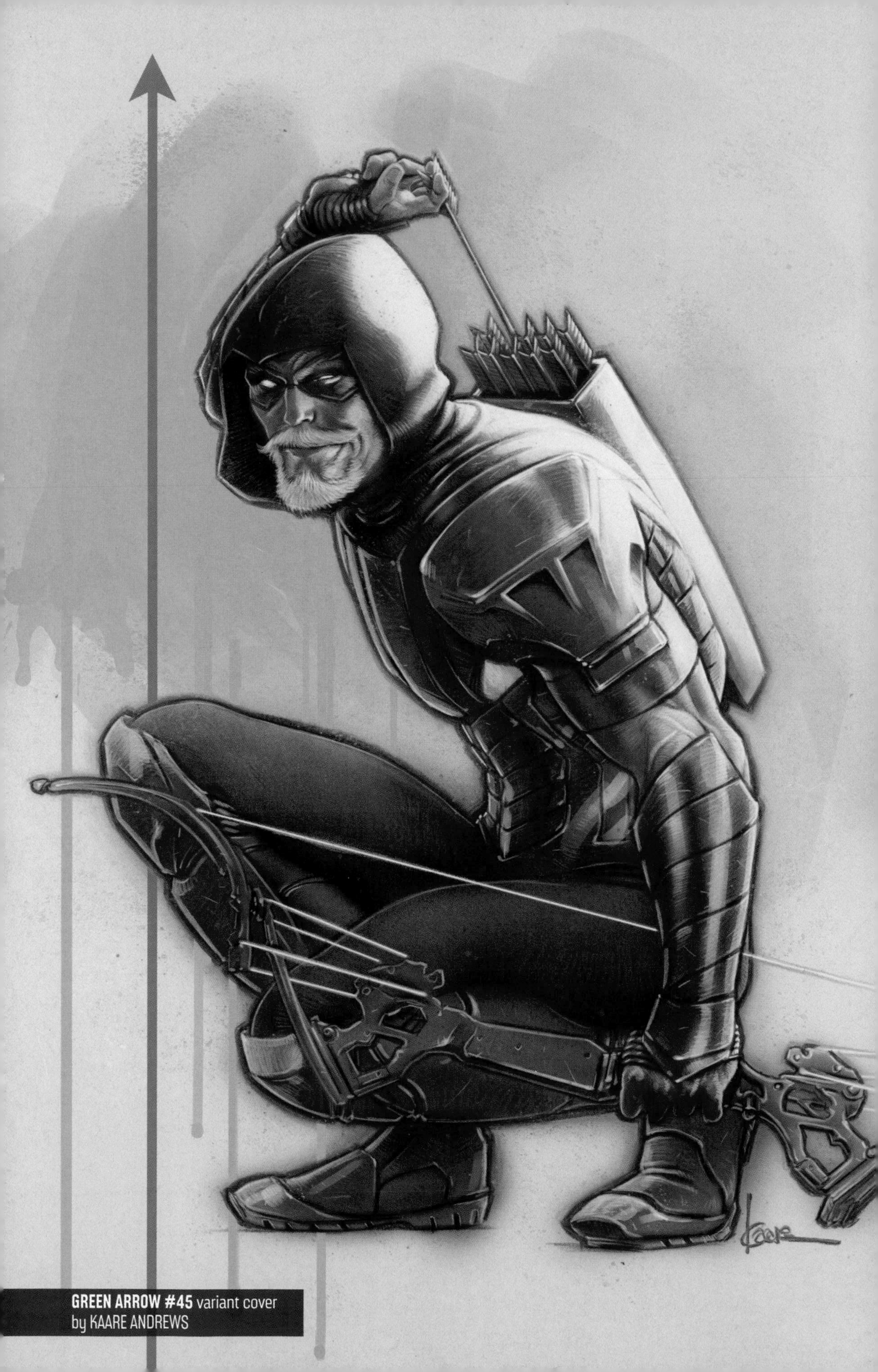

GREEN ARROW #45 variant cover
by KAARE ANDREWS

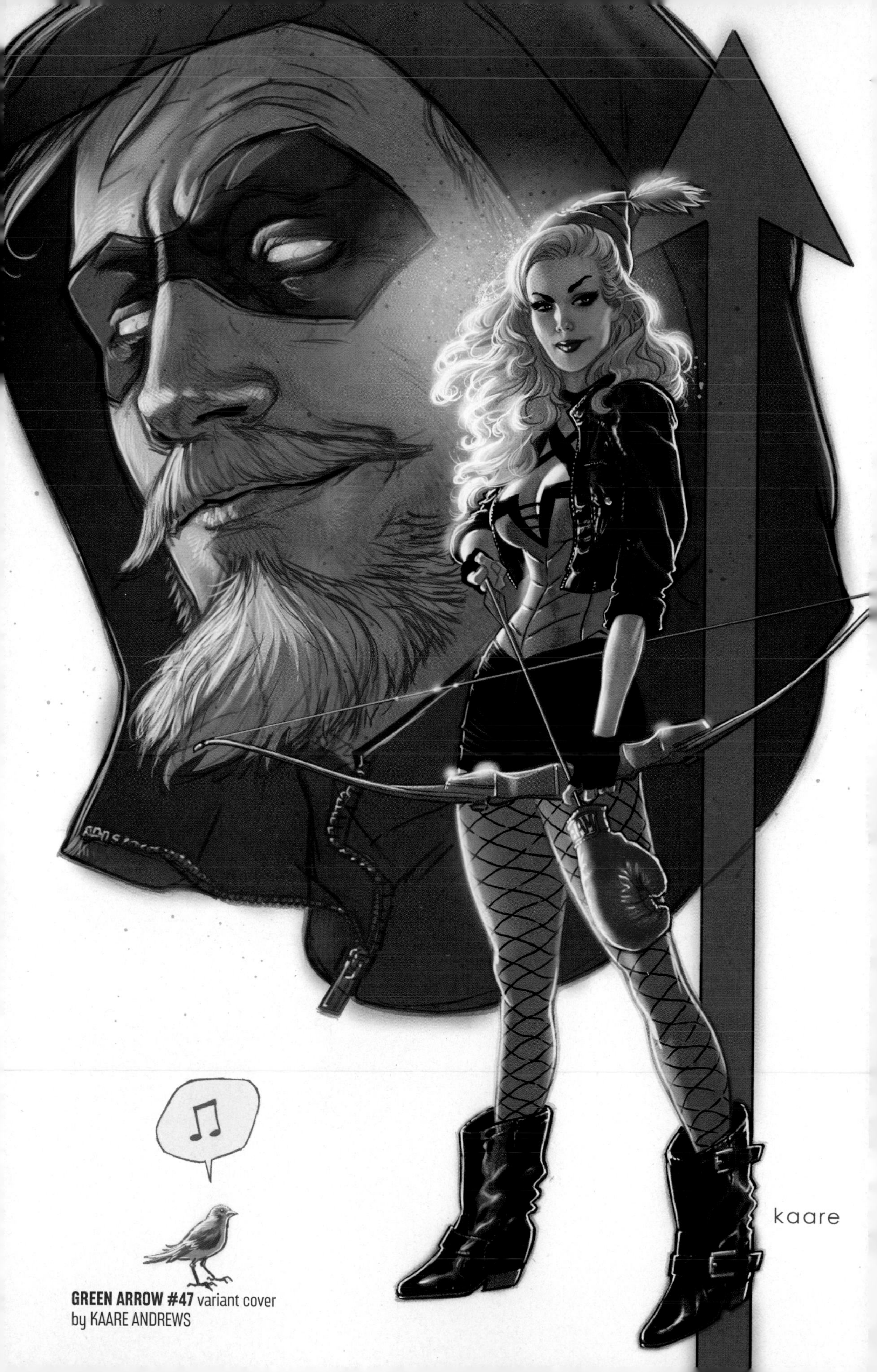

♫
kaare

GREEN ARROW #47 variant cover
by KAARE ANDREWS

GREEN ARROW #46 variant cover
by KAARE ANDREWS

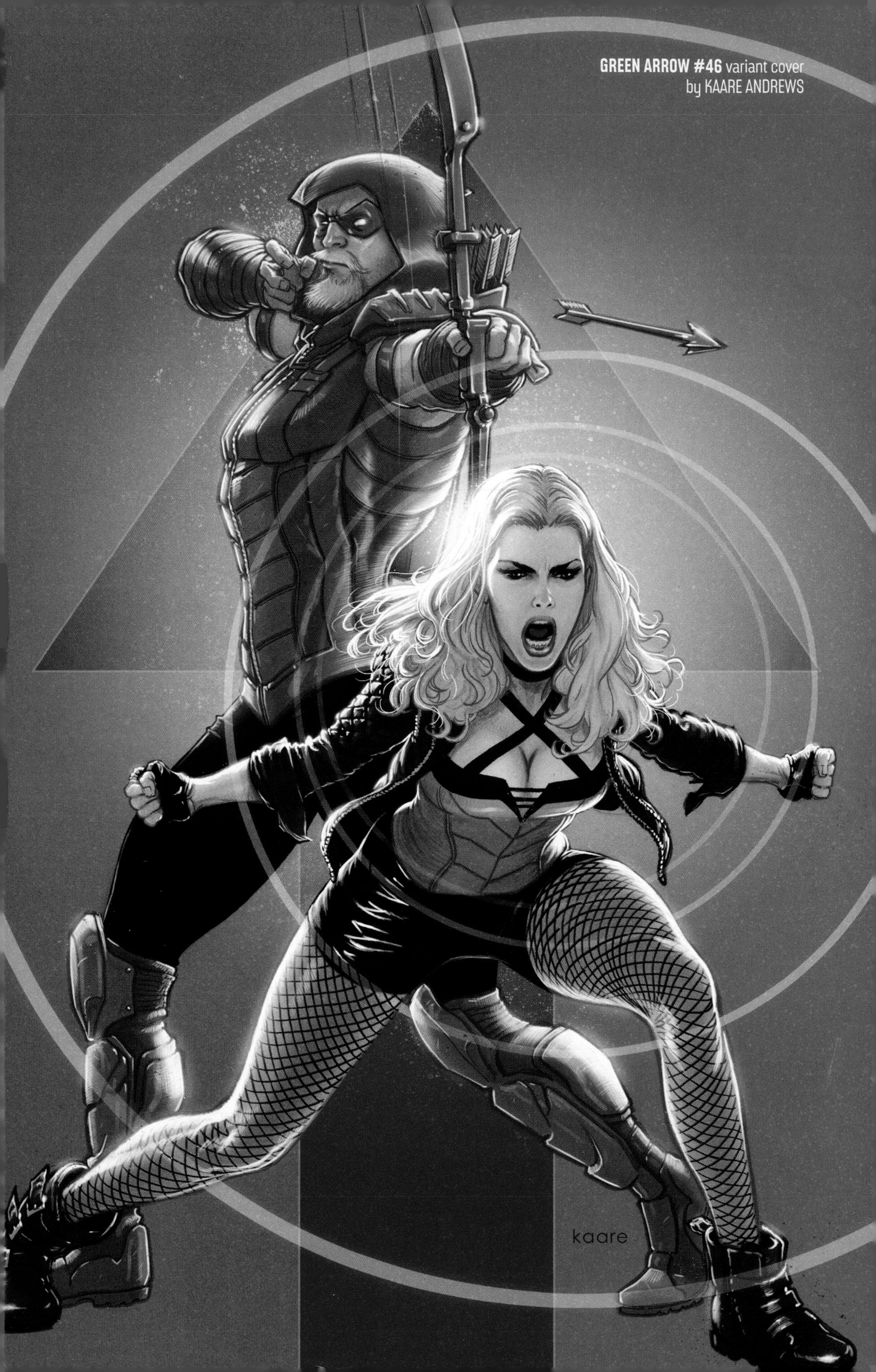
kaare